DATE DUE

JUN 3 0 1993	
NOV - 1 1993	
FEB 1 5 1994	
MAR 1 4 1994	
NOV - 2 1994	
DEC - 9 1994	
FEB 1 0 1995	
FEB 2 4 1995	
MAR 0 8 1995	
MAR 2 0 1995	
APR - 4 1995	
OCT 2 9 1995	
OUC-506	
JUL 1 4 1996	
FEB 2 5 1997	
APR 1 9 2002	

Child and Adolescent Therapy

Cognitive–Behavioral Procedures

Child and Adolescent Therapy

Cognitive–Behavioral Procedures

Edited by

PHILIP C. KENDALL
Temple University

FOREWORD BY DONALD MEICHENBAUM

THE GUILFORD PRESS
New York   London

© 1991 Philip C. Kendall and The Guilford Press
A Division of Guilford Publications, Inc.
72 Spring Street, New York, NY 10012

Printed in the United States of America

This book is printed on acid-free paper.

Last digit is print number: 9 8 7 6 5 4 3 2 1

Library of Congress Cataloging-in-Publication Data

Child and adolescent therapy: cognitive–behavioral procedures /
  edited by Philip C. Kendall.
    351p. cm.
    Includes bibliographical references.
    Includes index.
    ISBN 0-89862-448-7
    1. Cognitive therapy for children. 2. Cognitive therapy for
teenagers.   I. Kendall, Philip C.
    [DNLM: 1. Cognitive Therapy—in adolescence. 2. Cognitive
Therapy—in infancy & childhood. WS 350.6 C5355]
RJ505.C63C45 1990
618.92′89142—dc20
DNLM/DLC
for Library of Congress   90–13806
                                               CIP

To my sons

Contributors

Lauren Braswell, PhD, Child Guidance Clinic, North Memorial Medical Center, Robbinsdale, Minnesota

Tamar Ellsas Chansky, MS, Child and Adolescent Anxiety Disorders Clinic, Department of Psychology, Division of Clinical Psychology, Temple University, Philadelphia, Pennsylvania

Drew Erhardt, MA, Department of Psychology, University of California, Los Angeles, California

Eva L. Feindler, PhD, Psychology Department, Long Island University, Greenvale, New York

Michael Freidman, EdD, Philadelphia Public Schools, Philadelphia, Pennsylvania

Steven Graham, EdD, Department of Special Education, University of Maryland, College Park, Maryland

Karen R. Harris, EdD, Department of Special Education, University of Maryland, College Park, Maryland

Stephen P. Hinshaw, PhD, Department of Psychology, University of California, Los Angeles, California

Philip C. Kendall, PhD, ABBP, Department of Psychology and Director, Child and Adolescent Anxiety Disorders Clinic, Temple University, Philadelphia, Pennsylvania

Ray Kim, MS, Child and Adolescent Anxiety Disorders Clinic, Department of Psychology, Division of Clinical Psychology, Temple University, Philadelphia, Pennsylvania

Elizabeth Kortlander, MS, Child and Adolescent Anxiety Disorders Clinic, Department of Psychology, Division of Clinical Psychology, Temple University, Philadelphia, Pennsylvania

Ronald Livingston, BA, Department of Educational Psychology, University of Texas, Austin, Texas

John E. Lochman, PhD, Division of Medical Psychology, Duke University Medical Center, Durham, North Carolina

Donald Meichenbaum, PhD, Department of Psychology, University of Waterloo, Waterloo, Ontario

Lawrence W. Rouse, BA, Department of Educational Psychology, University of Texas, Austin, Texas

Mary F. Scherzinger, Department of Psychology, University of Notre Dame, Notre Dame, Indiana

Frances M. Sessa, MS, Department of Psychology, Temple University, Philadelphia, Pennsylvania

Lynne Siqueland, MS, Child and Adolescent Anxiety Disorders Clinic, Department of Psychology, Division of Clinical Psychology, Temple University, Philadelphia, Pennsylvania

Kristen S. Sommer, MA, Department of Psychology, University of Notre Dame, Notre Dame, Indiana

Kevin D. Stark, PhD, Department of Educational Psychology, University of Texas, Austin, Texas

James W. Varni, PhD, Departments of Psychology Pediatrics, and Psychiatry, University of Southern California, Los Angeles, California, and Orthopaedic Hospital, Los Angeles, California

Gary A. Walco, PhD, Schneider Children's Hospital of Long Island Jewish Medical Center, New Hyde Park, New York and Albert Einstein College of Medicine, Bronx, New York

Kathleen K. Wayland, PhD, Division of Medical Psychology, Duke University Medical Center, Durham, North Carolina

Karen J. White, PhD, Department of Psychology, University of Notre Dame, Notre Dame, Indiana

Thomas L. Whitman, PhD, Department of Psychology, University of Notre Dame, Notre Dame, Indiana

Bernice Y. L. Wong, PhD, Faculty of Education, Simon Fraser University, Barnaby, British Columbia

Foreword: Common Themes and Unresolved Challenges

This is a much welcomed volume by the leading clinical researchers of cognitive behavior modification (CBM) with children and adolescents. Each author has been intimately involved in the development, refinement, and evaluation of CBM procedures. The chapters are marked by a combination of a scholarly critical evaluation of the state of the art and by descriptive accounts of innovative cognitive–behavioral training programs. This book will be of great service to both practicing clinicians and researchers.

As I eagerly read this volume, four major issues or themes emerged. Hopefully, sensitizing the reader to these issues will encourage a collaborative set, whereby the reader will be encouraged to help search for possible solutions to the major challenges that therapists must address when working with children, adolescents, and their families.

First, I was struck by the repeated finding of comorbidity in children who experience affective disorders and behavioral problems. For example, Stark, Rouse, and Livingston (Chapter 6) note that anger problems were evident in 33% of clinically depressed children, often with accompanying inattention problems. Similarly, Hinshaw, and Erhardt (Chapter 4) observe that 50% of children with Attention-deficit Hyperactivitry Disorder (ADHD) evidence problems with aggression, while Kendall and his colleagues (Chapter 5) report the high co-occurrence of anxiety and depression in their clinical child population. Thus, there is an increasing demand to recognize the multiple behavioral and affective needs of the children we work with. Moreover, given the high incidence of psychopathology, marital distress, and stressful life events in the families of these troubled and troubling children and adolescents, as highlighted by Feindler (Chapter 3) and Braswell (Chapter 10), it is necessary that clinicians employ comprehensive multifaceted interventions. Simply focusing on teaching children various skills by means of either self-control training, relaxation, problem solving, social skills training, affective reeducation, or moral education, will likely prove inadequate.

A second issue emphasized by many of the contributors to this volume is the need for both diagnosticians and therapists to be sensitive to devel-

opmental changes. These developmental influences can express themselves in terms of: (1) changes in symptom patterns; (2) differential sensitivity of self-report measures versus parent or peer-report measures in
identifying children who have difficulties; (3) changes in the appropriateness of different interpersonal strategies in handling social situations; and
perhaps, most importantly, (4) changes in both the influence of the peer
group and the changing stability of the child's peer group status. For instance, the latter finding on peer influences has particular significance in
conducting treatment and preventative interventions with children, especially with identified "high risk" children. As children become older, their
peer reputations become more stable. Thus, it will become more and more
difficult to successfully change both children's social reputation and status
in their peer groups as they progress through school grades. Even if interventions are successful in improving a child's self-control and social skills,
it is highly likely that the child's peer group, as well as his or her teacher,
will be more responsive to the child's *former* social reputation, rather than
to the child's *newly learned* posttraining behavioral repertoire. This fact un-
derscores the need for a therapist's intervention to go beyond the treated
child in trying to also influence the child's social status in his or her peer
group and in the classroom. A corollary is the need to intervene early in
the developmental cycle (perhaps by grades 3 and 4), before the child's
social reputation becomes too "ossified". But once again, such interventions have to be sensitive to the chld's cognitive capacity (à la Piagetian
stages of cognitive development or à la development changes in social skills).
The nature and form of the intervention needs to be both developmentally
sensitive and individually tailored.

A third central theme that emerges in this volume is the promise of
both a social learning and information processing perspective in understanding the nature of children's emotional, social, academic and familial
difficulties (Kendall, Chapter 1). The authors each underscore the interdependence of thoughts, feelings, behavior, and resultant consequences.
Constructs like cognitive deficits, cognitive distortions, schemas, or scripts
are each viewed as being reciprocally determined and influenced by the
child's as well as the family's feelings, beliefs, behaviors, and interpersonal
contexts. Those who have embraced a cognitive–behavioral perspective have
gone well beyond any simplistic notion that cognitions cause emotional disturbance or maladaptive behaviors. Embracing a more multifaceted model
of child and adolescent psychopathology has highlighted the adantages of
combining different modes of interventions. Sometimes, as in the case of
hyperactive (ADHD) children, treatment will entail combinations of stimulant medication, self-control, social skills, metacognitively oriented academic strategy instruction, and parent training. In the instance of conduct
disordered children where marital discord is often such a predominant concomitant, marital or family intervention may be necessary. But once again,

a cognitive–behavioral treatment approach, whether it is in the form of coping modeling films, problem solving, cognitive restructuring, stress inoculation training, or relapse prevention holds much promise in addressing these complex familial problems as illustrated in Robin and Foster's (1989) work on negotiating parent–adolescent conflict.

Finally, a central theme that cuts across each of the chapters is the authors' preoccupation with the issues of generalization and maintenance of treatment effects. The bottom line in the area of interventions with children and adolescents is that "nothing generalizes" unless one explicitly trains for generalization. As Stokes and Baer (1977) observe, we should not lament the absence of generalization, rather we should train for generalization explicitly. The authors of the present volume also highlight the need to explicitly build generalization into the training program from the outset. Specific illustrative examples of how generalization can be nurtured are offered in the chapters by Lochman, White, and Wayland on aggressive children (Chapter 2); Walco and Varni on children with chronic illnesses (Chapter 7); Wong, Harris, and Graham on learning disabled students (Chapter 8); and Whitman, Scherzinger, and Sommer on children with developmental disabilities (Chapter 9). Additional suggestions of how the generalization and maintenance of treatment effects can be increased are offered by Brown and Palincsar (1989) and Hughes and Hall (1989).

In 1980, I reviewed the research on cognitive behavior modification with children and concluded that it reflected a promise yet unfulfilled. As we enter the 1990s, this volume illustrates that we are coming much closer to fulfilling that promise.

Donald Meichenbaum, PhD

REFERENCES

Brown, A. L., & Palincsar, A. S. (1989). Guided, cooperative learning and individual knowledge acquisition. In L. B. Resnick (Ed.), *Knowing, learning and instruction*. Hillsdale, N. J.: Erlbaum Associates Publishers.

Hughes, J. N., & Hall, R. J. (Eds). (1989). *Cognitive behavioral psychology in the schools*. New York: Guilford Press.

Meichenbaum, D. (1980). Cognitive behavior modification with exceptional children: A promise yet unfulfilled. *Exceptional Education Quarterly*, *1*, 83–88.

Robin, A. L., & Foster, S. L. (1989). *Negotiating parent adolescent conflict: A behavioral-family systems approach*. New York: Guilford Press.

Stokes, T. & Baer, D. (1977). An implicit technology of generalization. *Journal of Applied Behavior Analysis*, *10*, 349–367.

Preface

Early reports of applications of cognitive–behavioral interventions with children and adolescents were exciting, and the results sparked many and varied research and clinical endeavors. Indeed, in the present decade of growth for cognitive–behavioral thearpy there have been advances in treatment procedures, theoretical perspectives, and empirical foundations.

Several factors influenced me to undertake the editing of the present volume. First, I have been impressed with the "specificity" of the treatment programs that have been developed. That is, cognitive–behavioral therapy is not a monolithic treatment to be applied wholesale to various disorders; It is a set of strategies that, when applied, are linked to the nature of the underlying psychopathology. For example, teaching coping strategies is a consistent theme throughout the book, but the actual applications for youth differ, depending on the different behavioral and emotional problems. I sought to produce a volume that would offer descriptions of procedures applicable to specific types of maladaptive behavior.

Second, there has been major progress in the integration of cognitive strategies, behavioral procedures, and emotional processing. This integrative stance has moved the field forward, as has the maintenance of a strong commitment to its empirical foundation. The result is an eclectic approach to therapy that is squarely rooted in the empirical literature. Contemporary applications of cognitive–behavioral procedures reflect this integrationism.

Third, interventions for children and adolescents are becoming increasingly sensitive to developmental issues. It is no longer the case that youth are lumped together as if they are uniform along cognitive, emotional, or social lines, and it is equally true that children and adolescents no longer receive watered-down versions of adult therapies. Cognitive–behavioral interventions, perhaps more than any other systematic approach, deserve praise for their sensitivity to developmental issues as well as empirical soundness.

Lastly, I wanted to produce this volume to serve the many professionals who have asked me for resources for providing cognitive–behavioral interventions for their youthful clients. I can't tell you how many times I referred this caller or that letter writer to one or the other of the authors of the various chapters in this book. At times I sent notes with references;

other times I copied chapters and reprints, or provided phone numbers. Now, I can save many hours by simply referring all inquirers to this book.

One theme that is laced throughout the present book is the focus on developing and evaluating the best program for working with the child or adolescent. These programs are typically provided in either a one-to-one or small group setting. This is not to downplay the role of families or schools in the ability to produce and maintain behavior change, but rather to state upfront that the clear focus of cognitive–behavioral strategies seems to be on building the individual's cognitive and behavioral coping skills. However, as you will see in the pages that follow, there are cases where family interventions are described and where teachers are tied into the treatment process. These familial and school links are an emerging trend to be encouraged within cognitive–behavioral therapy for children and adolescents.

The opening chapter provides guiding theory for the educational and mental health professionals working with youth. Consideration is given to a model for conceptualizing the development and treatment of the various disorders, a description of the posture taken by the cognitive–behavioral therapist, and the goals that are sought. The chapters that follow represent major contributions by the leading clinicians/investigators. Each chapter describes a summary of related research and a description of the actual intervention procedures. There are chapters dealing with externalizing disorders (aggression; anger; Attention-deficit Hyperactivity Disorder), internalizing disorders (anxiety, depression), applications with special populations (learning disabled, mentally retarded, medically ill), as well as approaches for increasing parental involvement. My intent from the outset has been to direct the work toward the practitioner and the researcher. Therefore, a sizable part of the work includes how-to material that is geared to facilitate applications, as well as an integration of the relevant literature that provides the foundation for the program and the stimulus for continued inquiry.

I wish to thank each of the contributors for their participation in the present volume. Also, I wish to thank Gloria Basmajian of the word processing service of the College of Arts and Sciences, Temple University, for her secretarial support of my research. Ms. Beatrice Smith deserves mention for her energy and cooperativeness during the hectic times. To my graduate-student colleagues, the many children who have been a part of the research and clinical programs described in this book, and to the universities, medical schools, and educational settings that have cooperated over the years I offer a collective thank you. Lastly, for their support, enthusiasm, and intellectual curiosity, I thank my spouse, Sue, and my children, Mark and Reed.

Contents

Child and Adolescent Therapy

Cognitive–Behavioral Procedures

PART I
GUIDING THEORY

Guiding Theory for Therapy with Children and Adolescents

PHILIP C. KENDALL
Temple University

Descriptions of the various psychological therapies are related, in large measure, to a form of theory. In some, the theory is built on clinical experiences, in others the applied theory is adapted from complementary theories in more basic areas of psychology, and in still others, the theory is extrapolated from empirical observations. It is difficult, if not unwanted, to be totally atheoretical when implementing treatment programs.

The most direct and useful theories for clinical work are those that propose to explain the *processes of change*. Given our special attention to children and adolescents, we can benefit greatly from consideration of theories that deal with psychological change in youth and that address aspects of development. What may be alarming, especially to those well versed in either theories of behavior change or those of development, is that there is precious little connection in applied work between these two arenas.

In this chapter, along with consideration of other related themes, I outline a cognitive–behavioral theory in which behavioral events, associated anticipatory expectations and postevent attributions, ongoing cognitive information processing, and emotional states combine to influence behavior change. Relatedly, the theory adapts to the different challenges facing different levels of development. The theory is problem-solving oriented, deals largely with cognitive information processing, incorporates social/interpersonal domains, and emphasizes performance-based interventions.

Why problem solving? Problems occur, and problem solving is an essential ingredient to adequate adjustment in childhood, and across the lifespan. Different developmental challenges face youth, and they differ in their ability to recognize a problem in need of a solution. Further, their ability to generate alternatives and competently evaluate each option will form the quality of their psychological health.

Why cognitive information processing? Solutions to problems do not materialize from thin air, nor are they handed to someone carte blanche. Rather, successful solutions emerge from use of and involvement with cognitive strategies. These strategies are not transmitted through genetic codes, but are learned through observations and through interactions with others, and can be maximized through planned intervention. Styles of information processing have profound effects on how one makes sense of the world and one's experiences in it, and dysfunctional information processing requires attention and modification.

Why social/interpersonal domains? As mental health professionals we are interested in effective coping in social situations. Stated differently, the problems in need of solutions are social/interpersonal ones, not impersonal problems. Also, developmental theory has underscored the importance of social relationships (peers) to psychologically healthy adjustment (Hartup, 1984). It is the social domain in which the individual interacts reciprocally.

Why performance-based interventions? Interventions are intended to teach skills and/or remediate skill deficits and it is through performance-based procedures that such goals are best reached. Practice of new skills, with encouragement and feedback, leads to further use and refinement of those skills. Proper contingencies are implemented to shape involvement, to firm up intrinsic interest, or to promote motivation in otherwise disinterested participants. Workbooks for the child-client to use in learning new skills allow for structured practice. For example, the *Stop and Think Workbook* (Kendall, 1989a) provides training materials for use of cognitive strategies to control impulsivity, whereas the *Coping Cat Workbook* (Kendall, 1990) teaches skills for managing unwanted anxious arousal. As will become evident, the guiding cognitive-behavioral theory places greatest emphasis on integrating the modification of cognitive information processing of social contexts with behavioral practice-oriented strategies, while concurrently paying attention to the affective tone and involvement of the participant youth.

TOWARD A DEFINITION

There are numerous forms of intervention designed to facilitate child and adolescent adjustment and, at times, it is easy for one to wonder and speculate about the similarities and differences that actually exist among the different treatment philosophies. Until empirical studies of specific therapies are undertaken, we can only judge the distinct and overlapping features of different therapies from their written descriptions. For the cognitive–behavioral approaches, they can be described as a rational amalgam: a purposeful attempt to preserve the demonstrated positive effects of behavioral therapy within a less doctrinaire context and to incorporate the cognitive activities of the client into the efforts to produce therapeutic change (Kendall & Hollon, 1979). Accordingly, *cognitive–behavioral strategies use enactive performance-based procedures as well as cognitive interventions to produce changes in thinking, feeling, and behavior.*

The cognitive–behavioral analyses of child and adolescent disorders and adjustment problems, as well as related analyses of treatment-produced gains, include considerations of the child's internal and external environment and represent an integrationist perspective (Meichenbaum, 1977). The model places greatest emphasis on the learning process and the influence of the contingencies and models in the environment while underscoring the centrality of the individual's mediating/information-processing style in the development and remediation of psychological distress. The term *cognitive–behavioral* is not a direct insult to the role of affect and the social context. Rather, it is a hybrid representing an integration of cognitive, behavioral, affective, and social strategies for change. Abandoning an adherence to a singularly behavioral model, the cognitive–behavioral model includes the relationships of cognition and behavior to the affective state of the organism and the functioning of the organism in the larger social context.

Affect has been assigned to both primary and ancillary roles in childhood psychopathology. Bernard and Joyce (1984) ascribed primary responsibility to affect; child psychopathology is said to be caused by emotional problems. Santostefano and Reider (1984) viewed cognition and affect as "one and the same" (p. 56) and thereby assigned a comparable etiological contribution to each. I argue that while cognition and affect are interrelated, the variance in the etiology of some disorders may be best accounted for by cognitive assessments and analyses, whereas some other disorders may be best understood by a more direct appraisal of affect. Still other disorders are best viewed as largely behavioral.

Social/interpersonal factors play a crucial role. Because behavioral patterns in the external world and cognitive interpretations in the internal world pertain to social/interpersonal contexts, the cognitive–behavioral perspective must consider the importance of the social context. For children and adolescents the centrality of the social context must be underscored. Indeed, satisfactory relations with peers is a crucial component of a child's successful adjustment, and an understanding of peer relationships is required for meaningful assessment and intervention. The role of the family need not be contested, for this social microcosm sets many of the rules and roles for later social interaction. Acknowledgments of peer and family contributions to psychopathology, however, far outweigh the research data base that is currently available, and the need for further inquiry in these areas cannot be overemphasized. Indeed, parents are presently involved in the programs designed for children despite the lack of empirical data on the nature of their influence. For example, parents serve as consultants when they provide input into the determination of the nature of the problem and when they assist in the implementation of program requirements. Parents are also involved in their child's treatment to the extent that their cognitive and behavioral functioning is maladaptive and/or contributing to the child's distress. Changes in the family system should be used in conjunction with the skill building that is provided for the child. Cognitive–behavioral interventions should assess, consider, and incorporate social/interpersonal matters into their programs.

THE POSTURE OF THE THERAPIST

Using the term *posture* to refer to one's mental attitude, we can describe the posture of the cognitive–behavioral therapist working with children and adolescents. I choose to describe the three characteristics of the therapist's posture using the terms *consultant, diagnostician,* and *educator.*

By *consultant* I am referring to the therapist as a person who does not have all the answers, but one who has some ideas worthy of trying out and some ways to examine whether or not the ideas have value for the individual client. Telling a child and/or adolescent exactly what to do is not the idea; giving the client an opportunity to try something and helping him or her to make sense of the experience is the idea. The therapist as consultant strives to develop skills in the client that include thinking on his or her own and moving toward independent, mature problem solving. The consultant (therapist) is a problem-solving model working with the client. When the client asks "Well, what am I supposed to do?" the therapist might reply "Let's see, what do you want to accomplish here?," and then "What are our options?" or "What's another way we could look at this problem?" The exchange is geared toward facilitating the process of problem solving, but without giving a specific solution. The youngster and therapist interact in a collaborative problem-solving manner.

The term *diagnostician* might suggest labeling with a diagnostic system (e.g., DSM-III-R) but, while this is not criticized, it is also not the thrust of the meaning of the term when used here to describe the therapist's posture. The mental attitude associated with "diagnostician" is one of going beyond the verbal report and/or behavior of the client and his or her significant others. The diagnostician integrates data and, judging against a background of knowledge of psychopathology, normal development, and psychologically healthy environments, makes meaningful decisions. Consider the following example: Suppose that you win a brand new Mercedes Benz automobile. You're driving it around for 2 days and you notice a "clug-clug" sound in the front when you make a right-hand turn. There is no noise when you go straight or when you turn left. You contact a mechanic and tell him about the noise and that the front tie-rod ends need repair. The next day you leave the car for repair and pick it up at the end of the day. Your tie-rod ends are repaired. Would you be satisfied? My answer is a definite "no." What do I know about tie-rod ends? I just won the car, I am not a mechanic, and I should not be diagnosing the problem. The auto mechanic is the expert who should be making the determinations—he should look under the hood! He should not fix what I say is wrong since I am not the expert. He can use my ideas as helpful information, but should nevertheless make his own determination.

Similarly, we (mental health professionals/educators) cannot let others tell us what is wrong and what needs to be fixed when we are working with children and adolescents with psychological problems. That a parent or teacher says that a child is hyperactive is not sufficient to initiate a medication regime and/or a cognitive–behavioral therapy. The fact that a parent or teacher suspects hyperactivity in a child is a piece of useful information, but there are rival hypotheses that must be considered. For example, the child's behavior may be within normal limits but appearing as troubled when judged against inappropriate parental (teacher) expectations about child behavior. There is also the possibility of alternative disorders; hyperactivity may be the term used by the referring adults, but aggressive noncompliance may be a better description in terms of mental health professionals' communications. Also, the child's identified problem may be a reflection of a dysfunctional family interaction pattern, with the parenting styles needing the greatest attention, not the child per se. In a nutshell, the cognitive–behavioral therapist serves as a diagnostician by taking into account the various sources of information and, judging against a background of knowledge, determines the nature of the problem and the optimal strategy for its treatment.

The third term used to describe the therapeutic posture of cognitive–behavior therapists is *educator*. The use of educator here is intended to communicate that we are talking about interventions for learning behavior control, cognitive skills, and emotional developmental, and we are talking about optimal ways to communicate to help someone to learn. A good educator stimulates the students to think—to think for themselves. An active and involved coach is a good educator.

Let's consider the following sports story. You are off to a tennis camp for adults. You arrive and learn that for your $1,200 fee you will lie on the couch and tell your instructor how you feel about tennis, about the racket, about hitting the ball, and about your early experiences at tennis. Your answer might be "Excuse me, but I'd like to improve my tennis game, my serve is terrible." The instructor then replies "What is it about serving that you don't like? Does it make you feel that you are being subservient?" "No-no" you reply, "my serve is weak and my backhand is slow." "Aha," he mumbles, "backhand, is there any meaning to that—are you nervous about your backside, perhaps?"

In contrast, what does a good educator or coach do? He or she gets you out on the court and watches you play, observing how you hit the ball and determining for himself or herself (diagnostician) if your serve is weak or if your backhand is slow. The observations would take place on different occasions, against different partners, and under easy and difficult conditions. Then there would be some feedback about strengths and weaknesses and some discussion of alternative solutions (consultant). For example, the coach might inform you that your serve is inconsistent, and that you might want to do serve drills, tossing the ball in the air over and over until you toss it to the right height almost automatically. Videotaping might be used, along with modeling of service styles, and group lessons could be integrated as well.

Importantly, a good educator/coach does not make all players play the game the same way. A good coach observes how the student is playing and helps to maximize strengths while reducing hindrances. If a player uses two hands for a backhand, there is no reason to force the player to hit with one hand, or in a way that is the same as everybody else. Individualized attention means that individuals can and should do things differently. A good educator/coach also pays attention to what the learner is saying to himself or herself, as this internal dialogue can be interfering with performance. An effective therapist, just as an effective teacher or coach, is involved in the process.

The posture, or mental attitude, of the cognitive–behavioral therapist working with children and adolescents is one that has a collaborative quality (therapist as consultant), integrates and decodes information (therapist as diagnostician), and teaches through experiences with involvement (therapist as educator). A high-quality intervention, be it provided by a psychologist, psychiatrist, school counselor, special educator, classroom teacher, or parent, is one that alters how the client makes sense of experiences and the way the client will behave in the future. Such correction in thought and action places the client on track toward improved adjustment.

CONSIDERING COGNITION

Many psychologists, educators, and mental health professionals have viewed cognition as inaccessible. True, cognition refers to a complex system, but the system can be subdivided for increased understanding. For instance, it has been suggested (Ingram & Kendall, 1986, 1987; Kendall & Ingram, 1987, 1989) that cognitive content (events), processes, products, and structures can be distinguished. The idea being that cognition is not a singular or unitary concept. Cognitive structures can be defined as memory, and the manner in which information is internally represented in memory. Cognitive content refers to the information that is actually represented: the contents of the cognitive structures. Cognitive processes are the procedures by which the cognitive system operates: how we go about perceiving and interpreting experiences. Cognitive products (e.g., attributions) are the cognitions that result from the interaction of information, cognitive structures, content, and processes. Psychopathology may be related to problems in any or all of these areas and effective therapy includes consideration of each of these factors for each individual client.

Consider the experience of stepping in something a dog left on the lawn. The first reaction ("Oh, sh——") is probably a self-statement that reflects dismay. Individuals then proceed to process the experience. Some might begin to analyze the potential for social embarrassment, some might become self-denigrating, while others might be inattentive to processing environmental cues and may simply keep walking. The manner of processing the event contributes to the behavioral and emotional consequences. After the unwanted experience (i.e., stepping in it) conclusions are reached regarding the causes of the misstep—cognitive products, such as causal attributions, which may vary across individuals. Some may attribute the misstep to their inability to do anything right; such a global internal, and stable attribution often characterizes depression (Abramson, Seligman, & Teasdale, 1979). An angry individual, in contrast, might see the experience as the result of someone else's provocation ("Whose dog left this here—I bet the guy knew someone would step in it!"); attributing the mess to someone else's intentional provocation is linked to aggressive retaliatory behavior. Cognitive content, processes, and products are involved in each individual's making sense of environmental events.

Cognitive structures, or templates, are an accumulation of experiences in memory and serve to filter or screen new experiences. The anxious child, for instance, brings a history to new events; the memory of this past, also referred to as a schema, influences current information processing. A dominant schema or structure for anxious children/adolescents is threat—threat of loss, criticism, or harm (see Kendall et al., Chapter 5, this volume). An individual who brings an anxiety-prone structure to the misstep experience noted earlier would see the threat of embarrassment and the risk of germs, and process the experiences accordingly. Anxious cognitive processing of the experience might include self-talk such as "What if somebody notices the bad smell; they'll think I'm dirty." "What if germs get into my shoes and then to my socks, and my feet? Should I throw these shoes away?"

Cognitive structures serve to trigger automatic cognitive content and information processing about behavioral events. Attributions about the event reflect the influence of the pre-existing structure as well as contribute to the schema that is brought to the next behavioral event. Therapeutically, cognitive–behavioral interventions seek to provide experiences that attend to cognitive content, process, and product so that the child/adolescent builds a structure that will have a positive influence on future experiences. Cognitive–behavioral interventions also provide an arena to challenge the existing structures. Knowing that we all, figuratively, step in it at times, what is needed is a *structure for coping* with these unwanted events when they occur. Role-playing experiences are opportunities for learning and the focus on cognitive activities during the experience bolsters the impression made on the client's current and future information processing.

Not all dysfunctional cognition is the same. Understanding the nature of the cognitive dysfunction has important implications for treatment. One central issue for children and adolescents concerns the differentiation between *cognitive deficiency* and *cognitive distortion*. Deficiencies refer to an absence of thinking (lacking careful information processing where it would be beneficial), whereas distortions refer to dysfunctional thinking processes. I have elsewhere (Kendall, 1981) made this distinction to highlight the differences between the forerunners of cognitive–behavioral therapy with adults that focused on modifying distorted thinking (e.g., Beck, 1976; Ellis, 1971) and early cognitive–behavioral training with children that dealt mostly with teaching to remediate deficiencies in thinking (e.g., self-instructions; Kendall, 1977; Meichenbaum & Goodman, 1971). The distinction can be furthered when other childhood and adolescent disorders are considered. Anxiety and depression, for example, are typically linked to misconstruals or misperceptions of the social/interpersonal environment. There is active information processing, but it is distorted (illogical, irrational, crooked). In a series of studies of depressed children, for example, depressed youngsters viewed themselves as less capable than did nondepressed children when, in fact, teachers (the source of an objective outsiders' judgment) saw the two groups of children as nondistinct (Kendall, Stark, & Adam, 1990). In the teachers' eyes, the depressed children were not less competent across several dimensions. It was the depressed children who evidenced distortion through their misperception of their actual competencies.

Hyperactive and impulsive children, in contrast to the anxious and depressed youngsters, are often found to act without thinking and perform poorly due to the lack of forethought and planning. Here, cognitive deficiencies are implicated. These children are not engaging in careful information processing and their performance suffers as a result. Consider the case of a small group of youngsters playing soccer. Twelve players are on the field; some are kicking at the ball, others looking around and talking, while others are standing still. A nonparticipating child sits on the sidelines and, when asked why he isn't playing, replies "I can't play, I'm not good at soccer." In reality, the child can stand, talk, kick at a ball, and so on, and could easily participate at a modest skill level. His comment on the demands of the situation, however, indicate that he thinks he couldn't play as well as the others—that they are good players, but he isn't. In reality, these are distorted perceptions and such thinking is tied to his feeling inadequate, isolated, and withdrawn. Contrast the overly self-critical and isolating style of the withdrawn child to the impulsive child who runs directly onto the soccer field and starts after the ball. He is kicking and running, but does not yet know what team he is on, who is on his team, or which goal he is going for. His difficulties emerge more as a result of failing to stop and think (cognitive deficiency) than from active but distorted processing of information.

The terms *deficiency* and *distortion* have been used in the extant literature to describe features of cognitive dysfunction. In the many instances where the terms have been employed their use has been, even if unwittingly, consistent with my distinction. For instance, Prior (1984; often citing Hermalin & O'Connor, 1970) described the considerable evidence concerning "the nature of the cognitive deficits in autism" (p. 8) (e.g., suggested inability to use meaning to aid recall). The dominant role assigned to distortions (errors) by rational–emotive theory is evident in DiGiuseppe and Bernard's (1983) comment that "emotional disturbance develops because of one of two types of cognitive errors: empirical distortions of reality that occur . . . (inferences) and exaggerated and distorted appraisals of inferences" (p. 48). In contrast, Spivack and Shure (1982) contend that deficits in interpersonal cognitive problem-solving skills carry etiological clout, and Meichenbaum (1977) and Kendall (1977) have described impulsivity as a disorder resulting from mediational deficits.

To further illustrate the differences between *distortions* and *deficiencies*, consider the role of cognition in overcontrolled and undercontrolled childhood disorders. Anorexia, most often observed in adolescent females, is related to setting perfectionistic goals and demands, carrying an inaccurate view of the self (e.g., self-perception of body), and being "too good" behaviorally. These features of an overcontrolled problem reflect cognitive distortions. Anxiety and depression are also considered internalizing problems and they, too, evidence cognitive distortions that are dysfunctional. Impulsive acting-out and aggressive behaviors, more characteristic of young boys, are related to a lack of self-control, a failure to employ verbal mediational skills, and a lack of perspective taking. The undercontrolled problem child seems to evidence a deficiency in activating and following careful and planful cognitive processing.

In aggression, there is evidence of both cognitive deficiency and cognitive distortion (Kendall, Ronan, & Epps, 1990). There are data to suggest that aggressive youth have deficiencies in interpersonal problem solving (Deluty, 1981) and data to document that they also show distortions in their processing of information. Limited ability to generate alternative, nonaggressive solutions to interpersonal problems is an example of their deficiencies, while misattribution of the intentionality of others' behavior (Dodge, 1985) demonstrates a tendency for distorted processing. My argument is that (1) Undercontrol versus overcontrol (or externalizing versus internalizing; see Achenbach, 1966) is an important behavioral differentiation; (2) Distortions versus deficiencies is an important cognitive differentiation; and (3) There are meaningful relationships between the two. Internalized problems are linked more to maladaptive distorted processing, whereas externalizing problems reflect, in part, deficiencies in processing.

TEMPORAL MODEL

Research continues to document the role of cognitive concepts such as expectations, attributions, self-statements, beliefs, and schemata in the development of both adaptive and maladaptive behavior patterns and in the process of behavior change. However, the interrelationships of these and other cognitive factors themselves has yet to be clarified. How are the functional effects of self-statements similar to or different from those of attributions? How does an individual's maladaptive schema relate to his or her level of irrational beliefs? Do inconsistent or anxious self-statements reduce interpersonal cognitive processing and problem solving? Quite simply, we know only a modest amount about the organization and interrelations of the cognitive concepts receiving clinical and research attention.

A model with some potential utility is one built along a temporal dimension. The model must take into account and be able to reflect the cognitions associated with behavior across time (e.g., cognitions that occur before, during, and after events). Because events do not occur in a vacuum and because behavior is determined by multiple causes, the model must allow for the feedback that results from multiple, sequential behavioral events. That is, cognitions before an event vary, depending on the outcomes of previous events. The model must also allow for fluctuations in pre-event cognitions associated with the different outcomes (e.g., successful, unsuccessful) of prior events. Moreover, because repetitions of cognitive–event sequences result in some consistency in cognition, the model must highlight the development of more regularized cognitive processing (e.g., cognitive structures, cognitive styles).

The proposed model is presented in Figure 1-1. The figure illustrates the flow of cognition across behavioral events of different emotional intensity. The starting point is the initial behavioral event (BE), and our discussion will move from the BE point on Figure 1-1 (at the left) to the cognitive consistency that results (at the right). Attributions are the cognitive concepts often studied at the culmination of a behavioral event. How do children disambiguate the causes of their behavior once it has already taken place? Stated differently, of all possible explanations for behavior that can be proposed, how do youth explain their own and others' behavior to themselves? Attributions are temporally short-lived in that their occurrence is at the termination of an event. One could, however, assess an attribution long after an event, although numerous factors (e.g., recall from memory) may

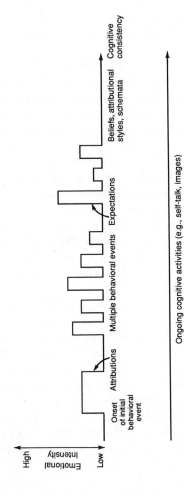

FIGURE 1-1. A temporal model of the flow of cognition across behavioral events of different emotional intensity. Self-statements and images occur at any point and can be studied at various points in the temporal flow. Problem-solving processes also occur at various points, especially where conflicts arise.

13

interfere with accurate recall. Typically, attributions are assessed recently after the behavioral event has taken place.

Repetition of behavioral events (multiple BEs in Figure 1-1) and the related cognitive processing will result in some degree of consistency in both behavior and cognition. The figure illustrates that cognitive consistency (i.e., beliefs, an attributional style, or a cognitive structure) results from multiple events. These cognitive variables (consistencies over time) are more stable than a single attribution. More stable cognitive style variables may be more predictive in a general sense, but are less predictive in specific situations than the actual cognitions at the time of the specific behavioral event.

Upon the accumulation of a history of behavioral events and event outcomes, the child or adolescent entertains more precise anticipatory cognition (i.e., expectancies). Expectancies have been described, for example, as outcome expectancies and self-efficacy expectancies (Bandura, 1977). Other anticipatory cognitions include intentions, plans, and commitments. These latter variables may be more stable and consistent over time than situationally specific expectancies. The generalized expectancy (i.e., locus of control), by its very general, transsituational nature, can also be seen as an attributional style. For instance, the generalized expectancy of an external locus of control could be present both before (expectancy) and after (attribution) an event. Before the event, the person's externality leads to an anticipation of having a minimal effect: "Why bother to speak up, no one listens to me." After the event, when a decision has been reached without the individual's input, the event is attributed to powerful others. "See, the big mouths always get their way."

In addition to the cognitions mentioned thus far, other cognitive variables have been demonstrated to be important in a cognitive–behavioral analysis—imagery, self-statements, and cognitive problem-solving skills. These factors occur at all points along the temporal flow depicted in the figure and assessments of these factors (e.g., self-talk) can prove valuable in understanding and treating children and adolescents.

Emotional intensity is represented vertically in Figure 1-1. The higher the bar indicating a behavioral event the more emotionally intense the the behavioral event. Emotional intensity contributes because the more intense the experience, the greater the impact on the development of a cognitive structure (schema). Thus, minor events, in terms of emotional involvement, may have a limited influence of attributions, future expectations, and memory, whereas an emotionally significant event has greater impact on the development of a schema and on future thinking. Early negative experiences can result in future dysfunctional thinking. One would want therapy to be an emotionally positive and involving experience, leading to coping and adaptive cognitive processing. As will be discussed later in this chapter, therapy can help to reduce the support for dysfunctional schemas

and to help to construct a new schema through which the client can identify and solve problems.

Regarding therapy for children and adolescents, an effective program
is one that capitalizes on creating behavioral experiences with intense emotional involvement while paying attention to the cognitive activities of the
participant. The therapist guides both the youngsters' attributions about
prior behavior and his or her expectations for future behavior. Thus, the
youngster can acquire a cognitive structure for future events that includes
the adaptive skills and accurate cognition associated with adaptive functioning.

GOALS

To what end does the cognitive–behavioral therapist aspire? What goals are
set before us as worthy of conscientious effort? To answer these questions
we will consider (1) the trajectory of normal development, (2) rational therapist expectations about behavior change, and (3) theoretical models that
detail the nature of our goals.

Normal Developmental Trajectory

The organism, from birth, is set on a course of development that, in general, moves toward the acquisition of coping skills, self-direction, autonomy, and satisfaction in life. That is, when developmental trajectories are
not deflected, an organism moves toward a satisfying self-determined role.
Assuming such a trajectory, what place do cognitive–behavioral interventions serve?

Interventions for children and adolescents can be therapeutic, preventative, or enhancement-focused. Ameliorative interventions (therapy) are
designed to help youth overcome problems that already exist, whereas prevention attempts to forestall problems before they emerge. Enhancements
are aimed at the improvement of the quality of life for individuals not currently or necessarily at risk for maladaption. The clear majority of cognitive–behavioral interventions are therapeutic, with a substantial number being
currently or potentially preventative. It is considered beneficial to help currently suffering individuals as well to prevent future suffering by intervening to help build self-determined persons.

Children and adolescents, as clients, require that the therapist give
special consideration to treatment goals. To what extent does the therapist
want to help the client make a better adjustment to the present life situation? To what extent does the therapist want to help the client to alter his
or her life situation? When family members, schools, and other adult au-
thorities are involved the matter becomes even more complicated. Adjust-

ing to a life situation that is psychologically unhealthy would not be advised, yet one cannot always alter a life situation as dramatically as might be construed when thinking of optimal adjustment for the client. The resolution offered by the cognitive–behavioral approach is one that focuses on individual problem solving. The client is given skills that can be used to make self-determinations. Skills that are in natural agreement with the move toward autonomy. Problem-solving skills allow for individual choices, unique to the client, that are optimal for the individual at the time. A child or adolescent client is supported through the thinking processes, encouraged to consider alternative solutions, rewarded and encouraged for effort, and helped to practice the skills needed for future challenges to adjustment. In this manner, the child or adolescent is guided through the process of becoming an active participant in a problem-solving process that, while it does not dictate which answers to choose, does allow for choice and self-determination. Helping to identify options, think through options in a careful manner, and guide the testing and evaluation of options is a goal of cognitive–behavioral therapy.

To return to the notion of a natural trajectory, psychologically healthy adjustment, as it unfolds in nature, builds on resolutions to prior challenges. When one is on a fault-free course of adjustment, interventions may be unnecessary. However, when prior challenges have not been met successfully, new skills are needed and, to the extent possible, generic skills that can be applied to a multitude of new challenges are promising. By demonstrating, teaching, and honing problem-solving skills, the cognitive–behavioral therapist's efforts coincide with changes in normal development to provide skills for use in later challenges to adjustment. The goal is a better prepared individual—prepared for the inevitable difficulties of life with a set of skills that can facilitate problem resolution.

Rational Therapist Expectations

The best hitter in major league baseball hits approximately .340, professional bowlers do not bowl 300 routinely, and not every play in football leads to a touchdown, yet we, as mental health professionals, often carry expectations that we (and our therapies by implication) are expected to help almost all of our clients. To expect such a success rate is irrational.

Rational therapist expectations include the belief that interventions will be helpful in the movement toward successful adjustment and the belief that individuals who acquire the skills communicated in therapy will at some time experience the benefit of those skills. What is irrational is to expect that any child, with any problem, can be "fixed" using psychotherapy, cognitive–behavioral or otherwise. The notion that therapy provides a "cure" is a troublesome and misleading belief (see Kendall, 1989b).

Children and adolescents do not, automatically, evidence benefit from psychotherapy. And, even in cases where some success is obvious, the chance of relapse remains ever present. If relapse does occur, was the therapy ineffective? Should therapy be expected to prevent all relapse as a part of the "cure" of psychopathology? A rational expectation for therapists to hold is that psychotherapy does not cure maladaption. Therapy does provide help, but the help is more of the form of a strategy for the *management* of psychopathology. The anxiety-disordered adolescent will not receive a treatment that will totally remove all perceptions of situations as anxiety provoking, but he or she will be able to employ newly acquired strategies in the management of anxious arousal when it does occur. The attention-deficit child may not erase all impulses for immediate action, but will have available skills that can be implemented when more cautious, thoughtful action is needed. To expect cures is irrational; to expect to impart the wisdom that, through experience, will facilitate adjustment is sage.

Relapse, or the task of dealing with relapse temptations, is a part of life. Even our most successful clients will be challenged by the many opportunities for decisions that are less than optimal. Our goal is not to "have all go well forever," but to improve upon the trajectory that was evident before treatment began. To *alter* a nonadaptive trajectory is to produce therapeutic gains, and such an expectation is rational.

Many therapists working with children and adolescents deal with problems of detrimental anxiety and unwanted depression. Youth with these emotional problems have, as part of their distress, a maladaptive manner of processing their world that requires intervention. As is true with adult clients suffering from these same disorders, cognitive–behavioral interventions strive to rectify the distorted information processing that is linked to the emotional distress. Unfortunately, the popular press has overpromoted the "power of positive thinking." Do we want our clients to become big-time positive thinkers? Is such a goal a rational and desired outcome of treatment? As it turns out, theory suggests and some research evidence supports the notion that it is not so much the power of positive thinking that is related to emotional adjustment or improvement in treatment as it is the reduction in negative thinking. I have elsewhere referred to this as "the power of non-negative thinking" (Kendall, 1984).

Individuals who think or talk to themselves in only positive terms are not psychologically healthy. We all experience life events that have negative features and a rational individual accepts these inevitables. One would not want to be thinking only positive thoughts when in a difficult situation. For example, one would not want to be on an intercontinental airplane trip, during excessive air turbulence, sitting next to someone who sees everything positively. There are times when a negative thought or two is quite reasonable. Purely positive information processing is distorted. What then should therapists hold as a rational expectation for the outcome of interventions designed to reduce the negative self-critical styles of thinking of the anxious and depressed client?

The ratio of positive to negative thinking that has been found to be associated with adjustment is .62:.38 (see Kendall, Howard, & Hays, 1989; Schwartz & Garamoni, 1989). These findings are reported for college-age samples, but the concept likely holds true for younger persons as well. Generally speaking, this 2:1 ratio suggests that positive thinking occupies two-thirds of the thinking whereas negative thinking occupies one-third of the thinking in individuals who are not maladjusted. Depressed cases, identified psychometrically and clinically, show a 1:1 ratio: the 50–50 split indicating an equal frequency of positive and negative thinking. How does this affect the expectations to be held by therapists? I suggest that knowing that an optimal ratio of positive to negative thinking is 2:1 serves as a guide for the therapist. Overly optimistic thinking is not necessarily healthy, and shifting too much toward a 1:1 ratio is unhealthy as well. It is healthy to acknowledge certain unwanted situations have a negative thought or two, and then proceed to counter the negative aspects with some positive thinking. Positive thinking helps overrule negative thinking, but negative thinking should not be totally eliminated.

Is it the case that children and adolescents want to display their newly acquired skills and thank the therapist for the help? Sometimes, as the many fortunate therapists can attest, clients do offer a warm and genuine thanks. However, it is possible that children and adolescents learn from our therapeutic interactions but, for a variety of reasons, do not want to let us know—they act as if they were right all along and didn't need nor benefit from the therapy. It is irrational to expect that all clients will demonstrate that they have benefited from our interventions.

It is possible that there will be beneficial effects, but that these effects will not be readily evident at the end of treatment. I refer to these effects as "sleeper effects." For example, completion of a therapy that provides an opportunity for learning social-problem solving skills might not produce immediate use of these skills. It may be that after the passage of time, the percolation of the ideas at various times, and the successful use of parts of the problem-solving process the child/adolescent client comes to employ and recognize the benefits of a problem-solving approach. It has been my experience, for instance, that interpersonal skills learned by a child during early childhood take a temporary backseat to the social pressure of peers. After further developmental changes, the skills acquired earlier can emerge without conflict and better serve the individual's current adjustment.

Theoretical Models Regarding Goals

Children and adolescents with behavioral and emotional difficulties have associated maladaptive qualities in cognitive information processing. For the depressed adolescent who is misattributing negative outcomes to internal/global/stable features, as well as for the impulsive/hyperactive child who is active in behavior but deficient in planful forethought, modifications of the cognitive processing are in order. Theoretically speaking, how might we conceptualize the needed changes? How best to describe the nature of the cognitive changes that are a part of the goals of treatment?

As noted in the earlier discussion, some cognitive distortions require modification. New experiences, with guided processing of the experiences, will help to straighten out crooked thinking. What is being suggested is that the existing cognitive structure is not erased, but that new skills and means of construing the world are built and these new constructions come to serve as new templates for making sense of future experiences. Therapy does not provide a surgical removal of unwanted cognitive structures, but offers to help to build new schemata with new strategies that can be employed in place of the earlier dysfunctional ones.

Returning to the discussion of Figure 1-1, therapy offers exposure to multiple behavioral events with concurrent cognitive processing such that new schemata can be built over time. Positive emotional tones can increase the potency of the experience and add to its impact on the new schema. As these new schemata are incorporated into the child's view of the world and his or her place in it, future experiences are construed differently (less maladaptively). Using the newly constructed schemata the individual moves forward to confront new challenges with the skills needed to manage former maladaptive tendencies.

CLOSING

Children and adolescents do not, typically, call or refer themselves for services from a mental health professional. Quite the contrary, individuals other than the child or adolescent, such as parents, teachers, or guardians, are often the initiators of psychological interventions. In contrast, adults, who themselves are in personal suffering, seek their own mental health services—they are suffering and they seek help for themselves. The fact that children are sent for treatment, whereas adults often seek it, is an important distinction that has clinical implications. Children and adolescents must, on their own, come to see the potential benefits of therapy. Accordingly, efforts to create a pleasant affective environment and a motivation for further participation are essential.

One of the main challenges facing the developing organism is the movement toward autonomy and independence. Central to this movement is the family, specifically the parents, and their supportive or constraining styles. Child and adolescent clients are not fully capable, as yet, to be entirely independent and family, school and other contextual influences must be considered. Indeed, while the thrust of the present theory is on individual change, multiple influences have been considered and incorporated.

Little discussion has been assigned to factors such as trust, respect, and relationship as part of the therapeutic process. It is not because these matters are unimportant, but rather because they are essential to all forms of therapeutic intervention, they need not be given special reconsideration here. Suffice it to say factors that contribute to a strong relationship are to be encouraged, as are behavioral patterns that clearly communicate mutual respect and trust. The cognitive–behavioral theory outlined herein is one that complements and contributes to basic clinical wisdom about positive adult–child interactions and building an open and trusting relationship.

ACKNOWLEDGMENTS

The author expresses gratitude to the graduate students and faculty of the clinical psychology doctoral training program, Temple University, for their helpful input. The input of Frances M. Sessa is especially appreciated.

REFERENCES

Abramson, L. Y., Seligman, M. E. P., & Teasdale, J. D. (1978). Learned helplessness in humans: Critique and reformulation. *Journal of Abnormal Psychology, 87,* 49–74.

Achenbach, T. M. (1966). The classification of children's psychiatric symptoms: A factor analytic study. *Psychological Monographs,* 80 (Whole No. 615).

Bandura, A. (1977). Self-efficacy: Toward a unifying theory of behavior change. *Psychological Review, 84,* 191–215.

Beck, A. T. (1976). *Cognitive therapy and the emotional disorders.* New York: International Universities Press.

Bernard, M. E., & Joyce, M. R. (1984). *Rational emotive therapy with children and adolescents: Theory, treatment strategies, preventive motives.* New York: Wiley.

Deluty, R. H. (1981). Alternative-thinking ability of aggressive, assertive and submissive children. *Cognitive Therapy and Research, 5,* 309–312.

DiGiuseppe, R., & Bernard, M. E. (1983). Principles of assessment and methods of treatment with children: Special consideration. In A. Ellis & M. E. Bernard (Eds.), *Rational-emotive approaches to the problems of childhood* (pp. 45–88). New York: Plenum Press.

Dodge, K. (1985). Attributional bias in aggressive children. In P. C. Kendall (Ed.), *Advances in cognitive–behavioral research and therapy* (Vol. 4). New York: Academic Press.

Ellis, A. (1971). *Growth through reason.* Hollywood, CA: Wilshire Books.

Hartup, W. W. (1984). Peer relations. In P. Mussen (Ed.), *Handbook of child psychology.* New York: Wiley.

Hermalin, B., & O'Connor, W. (1970). *Psychological experiments with autistic children.* Oxford, England: Pergamon Press.

Ingram, R. E., & Kendall, P. C. (1986). Cognitive clinical psychology: Implications of an information processing perspective. In R. E. Ingram (Ed.), *Information processing approaches to clinical psychology* (pp. 3–21). New York: Academic Press.

Ingram, R. E., & Kendall, P. C. (1987). The cognitive side of anxiety. *Cognitive Therapy and Research, 11,* 523–537.

Kendall, P. C. (1977). On the efficacious use of verbal self-instructional procedures with children. *Cognitive Therapy and Research, 1,* 331–341.

Kendall, P. C. (1981). Assessment and cognitive–behavioral interventions: Purposes, proposals and problems. In P. C. Kendall & S. D. Hollon (Eds.), *Assessment strategies for cognitive–behavioral interventions.* New York: Academic Press.

Kendall, P. C. (1984). Behavioral assessment and methodology. In G. T. Wilson, C. M. Franks, K. D. Brownell, & P. C. Kendall, *Annual review of behavior therapy: Theory and practice* (Vol. 9). New York: Guilford Press.

Kendall, P. C. (1989a). *Stop and think workbook.* Available from the author, 238 Meeting House Lane, Merion Station, PA 19066.

Kendall, P. C. (1989b). The generalization and maintenance of behavior change: Comments, considerations, and the "no-cure" criticism. *Behavior Therapy, 20,* 357–364.

Kendall, P. C. (1990). *Coping cat workbook.* Available from the author, 238 Meeting House Lane, Merion Station, PA 19066.

Kendall, P. C., & Braswell, L. (1985). *Cognitive–behavioral therapy for impulsive children.* New York: Guilford Press.

Kendall, P. C., & Hollon, S. D. (1979). Cognitive–behavioral interventions: Overview and current status. In P. C. Kendall & S. D. Hollon (Eds.), *Cognitive–behavioral interventions: Theory, research and procedures* (pp. 1–13). New York: Academic Press.

Kendall, P. C., Howard, B. L., & Hays, R. C. (1989). Self-referent speech and psychopathology: The balance of positive and negative thinking. *Cognitive Therapy and Research, 13,* 583–598.

Kendall, P. C. & Ingram, R. E. (1987). The future for cognitive assessment of anxiety: Let's get specific. In L. Michelson & M. Ascher (Eds.), *Anxiety and stress disorders: Cognitive–behavioral assessment and treatment.* New York: Guilford Press.

Kendall, P. C. & Ingram, R. E. (1989). Cognitive–behavioral perspectives: Theory and research on depression and anxiety. In P. C. Kendall & D. Watson (Eds.), *Anxiety and depression: Distinctive and overlapping features.* New York: Academic

Kendall, P. C., Ronan, K., & Epps, J. (1990). Aggression in children/adolescents: Cognitive–behavioral treatment perspectives. In D. Pepler & K. Rubin (Eds.), *Development and treatment of childhood aggression.* Hillsdale, NJ: Erlbaum.

Kendall, P. C., Stark, K., & Adam, T. (1990). Cognitive deficit or cognitive distortion in childhood depression. *Journal of Abnormal Child Psychology, 18,* 267–283.

Meichenbaum, D. (1977). *Cognitive–behavior modification: An integrative approach.* New York: Plenum Press.

Meichenbaum, D., & Goodman, J. (1971). Training impulsive children to talk to themselves: A means of developing self-control. *Journal of Abnormal Psychology,* 77, 115–126.

Prior, M. (1984). Developing concepts of childhood autism: The influence of experimental cognitive research. *Journal of Consulting and Clinical Psychology, 52,* 4–16.

Santostefano, S., & Reider, C. (1984). Cognitive controls and aggression in children: The concept of cognitive–affective balance. *Journal of Consulting and Clinical Psychology, 52,* 46–56.

Schwartz, R. M., & Garamoni, G. L. (1989). Cognitive balance and psychopathology: Evaluation of an information processing model of positive and negative states of mind. *Clinical Psychology Review, 9,* 271–294.

Spivack, G., & Shure, M. B. (1982). The cognition of social adjustment: Interpersonal cognitive problem-solving thinking. In B. B. Lahey & A. E. Kazdin (Eds.), *Advances in clinical child psychology* (Vol. 5, pp. 323–372). New York: Plenum Press.

PART II

EXTERNALIZING DISORDERS

CHAPTER 2

Cognitive–Behavioral Assessment and Treatment with Aggressive Children

JOHN E. LOCHMAN
Duke University Medical Center

KAREN J. WHITE
University of Notre Dame

KATHLEEN K. WAYLAND
Duke University Medical Center

Aggression is a set of primarily interpersonal actions that consist of verbal or physical behaviors that are destructive or injurious to others or to objects (Bandura, 1973; Lochman, 1984). While almost all children display some aggressive behavior, it is only when aggression is exceptionally severe, frequent and/or chronic that it becomes indicative of psychopathology. Children with high levels of aggressive behavior are most often diagnosed as having Conduct Disorders or Oppositional Defiant Disorders, but aggressive behavior can be comorbid with other diagnostic categories as well (Lochman, White, Curry, & Rumer, in press). Longitudinal research has indicated that aggressive behavior is quite stable during childhood and adolescence, and that aggression is more consistent over time than most other behavioral patterns (Gesten, Langer, Eisenberg, Simcha–Fagan, & McCarthy, 1976; Olweus, 1979). Children who display a wide range of different kinds of aggressive, antisocial behavior, and who are highly antisocial in multiple settings (e.g., home, school, community) are at greatest risk for continued disorder (Loeber & Dishion, 1983; Loeber & Schmaling, 1985). Aggressive children are not only at risk for continuing to be aggressive, but they also are at risk for a wide range of negative outcomes, including criminality, personality disorder, and substance abuse (Coie, Christopoulous, Terry, Dodge, & Lochman, in press; Huesmann, Eron, Lefkowitz, &

Walder, 1984; Kandel, 1982; Lochman, 1990; Robins, 1978). Since aggression is a broad risk factor, it has become an important focus for intervention.

In this chapter, we will present a social–cognitive model for aggression, and discuss the cognitive–behavioral assessment techniques and intervention strategies associated with this model. An anger coping program will be described. We will review only cognitive–behavior therapy results and procedures with aggressive children and will not cover adolescence or impulsive, hyperactive behaviors. Other chapters in this volume address adolescent aggression (Feindler) and Attention-deficit Hyperactive Disorder (Hinshaw), which frequently accompany childhood aggression.

CONCEPTUAL FRAMEWORK FOR COGNITIVE–BEHAVIORAL THERAPY

Cognitive–behavioral therapy focuses upon the perceptions and thoughts of aggressive children, as they encounter perceived threats and frustrations. The techniques and goals of cognitive–behavior therapy are directed at children's deficiencies and distortions in their cognitive processing of events. Refinements in CBT techniques have arisen largely because of new research and models of these deficits in children's processing of social conflicts. Before examining cognitive–behavioral therapy with aggressive children, we will first review two of the major areas of conceptual roots for CBT, and then examine the social–cognitive model used as a foundation for our anger coping program.

Historical Roots of CBT

While a number of factors have influenced the sharp increase in interest and development of CBT procedures with children, (Hughes, 1988; Kendall & Braswell, 1985; Meyers & Craighead, 1984) two factors that have important implications for this chapter are social learning theories and research on self-regulation.

Social Learning Theories

The social learning theories (SLT) developed by Rotter and by Bandura represent early precursors of current CBT approaches with children. In Rotter's SLT (Rotter, Chance, & Phares, 1972), the potential, or likelihood, of a specific behavior being emitted by an individual was the result of situationally specific reinforcement values and of expectancies that the reinforcement could be attained with the specific behavior. While external consequences were assumed to be important determinants of an individual's behavior, the behavior was seen as the direct product of the individual's cognitive evaluations of how valuable the available reinforcements were, and of how successful it was expected that they could be in attaining the reinforcement. If the value of a reinforcement was high (e.g., a portable stereo) but the expectation for attaining the reinforcement with a socially approved behavior was low (e.g., getting a job and saving for the stereo), then the individual would logically use other behaviors for which the individual had higher expectations for successful reinforcement acquisition (e.g., breaking into an apartment to steal a stereo). Each decision about a behavior would be influenced by expectations for an array of positive and negative consequences. Rotter's SLT emphasized the situational specificity of these cognitive processes, but it recognized that cross-situational cognition also developed in the form of generalized expectancies (e.g., loss of control) and reinforcement values (needs or goals).

Bandura's (1977) SLT added an emphasis on other cognitive factors, such as an individual's expectations about competently enacting a given behavior (efficacy expectations), self-reinforcement, and the tendency to attend selectively to certain observed models (Hughes, 1988). The constructs evident in these SLTs foreshadow many of our current concepts in CBT.

Research on Self-regulation

Another primary empirical influence on CBT has been the investigation of self-regulation. With adults, this has included research on self-monitoring, self-evaluation, and self-reinforcement (Kanfer, 1970). To understand acquisition of self-regulation in childhood, a developmental perspective has been required. While children's level of cognitive development is often ignored in the day-to-day implementation of CBT, two strands of developmental research played a key role in Meichenbaum's early application of CBT to children. (Meichenbaum & Goodman 1971) Meichenbaum was influenced by the research of Luria and of Vygotsky, and by Mischel's work on delay of gratification. These approaches suggested that children's acquisition of behavioral self-control was due to their use of language and of cognitive controls. Children are seen as learning to regulate their behavior through their experiences with significant others, as they "learn-by-doing" (Brown, 1987; Vygotsky 1978).

In Vygotsky's theory, internal psychological processes have a social basis. Thoughts mirror interpersonal transactions that are observed and experienced, and the transactions become internal communication when they have been transformed through experience into an intrapersonal process (Brown, 1987). Thus, the development of cognitive control can be regarded as a social process rooted originally in adult–child communication. As the caregiver (parent, older relative, teacher) structures the child's activities and solves problems concerning the child and others in the presence of the child, the child acquires these idiographic ways of perceiving the world and ways of attempting to control events and feelings and solve problems (Kopp, 1987). Caregivers who are most adept at promoting internalization operate in the "zone of proximal development" (Kopp, 1987), in which caregivers adjust their verbal and nonverbal behavior to assist children resolve partially mastered tasks.

According to Vygotsky, (1978), the child's internalization of control on these tasks is a gradual step-wise process, in which the caregiver first controls and guides the child's activity, then the adult and child begin to share in the initiation of problem solving, although the adult still guides when the child fails, and finally the caregiver supportively permits the child to exercise control (Brown, 1987). As internalization progresses, the child's ability to self-monitor and self-evaluate becomes more apparent. Mischel's research has exemplified the importance of cognitive mechanisms such as attention and strategy production in the developmental change in ability to delay gratification (Kopp, 1987), which is a central aspect of self-regulation.

Implication of These Historical Roots

The theoretical and empirical work on social learning theories and on self-regulation has had clear, but often indirect, impacts on all forms of CBT with children, (Hughes, 1988; Kendall & Braswell, 1985). Perhaps more importantly, these conceptual roots also can guide our thinking about the future evolution of CBT with children. Five implications for CBT that arise from this brief review include: (1) Examination of additional, and ideally theoretically interrelated, cognitive processes such as outcome expectations and reinforcement values; (2) Exploration of cognitive processes that are situational, as well as those that are cross-situational; (3) Emphasis on developmental changes in cognition in CBT; (4) Integrating our understanding of basic cognitive processes such as attention, retrieval, and organization of information in memory into social information-processing models and into CBT, and (5) Consideration of the importance of early caregivers on the evolution of children's cognitive controls. The latter point is an essential one, since collateral intervention with parents and teachers is nearly nonexistent in the literature on CBT with children. We will return to these implications as we propose a social information-processing model for aggressive children, and again after we examine current CBT approaches with these children.

Social–Cognitive Model of Anger and Aggression

The anger coping program we use with aggressive children is based on an evolving social–cognitive model (Lochman, 1984; Lochman, Meyer, Rabiner, & White, in press; Lochman, Nelson, & Sims, 1981) of how anger develops in children and results in aggressive responses. In these types of processing models, Kendall (1985; see also Chapter 1, this volume) differentiated cognitive deficiencies, which involve an insufficient amount of cognitive activity, from cognitive distortions, which involve misperceptions. Both types of cognitive dysfunctions can be seen in aggressive children's social–cognitive dysfunctions. The model presented here originally derived in large part from Novaco's (1978) conceptualization of anger arousal in adults, and has been substantially affected by Dodge's (1986) social information-processing model. In the social–cognitive model depicted in Figure 2-1, the child encounters a potentially anger-arousing stimulus event, but the emotional and physiological reaction is due to the child's perception and appraisal of the event, rather than due to the event itself. These perceptions and appraisals can be accurate or inaccurate, and are derived from prior expectations that filter the event, and from the child's selective attention to specific aspects, or cues, in the stimulus event. If the child has interpreted the event to be threatening, provocative or frustrating, he or she

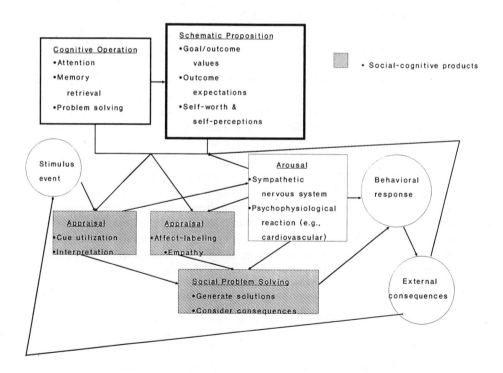

FIGURE 2-1. Social–cognitive model.

can then experience physiological arousal, and also will become engaged in another set of cognitive activities directed at deciding upon an appropriate behavioral response to the event. The internal arousal has a reciprocal interaction with the individual's appraisal processes, since the child has to interpret and label the emotional connotations of the arousal. Children determine, for example, if they are afraid or angry. These three sets of internal activities, (1) perception and appraisal, (2) arousal, and (3) social problem solving contribute to the child's behavioral response and to the resulting consequences the child receives from peers and adults and experiences internally as self-consequences. These consequent reactions from others can then become stimulus events, which feed back into the model, becoming recurrent, connected behavioral units.

We will provide an overview of the social–cognitive deficiencies and distortions which have been found in research with aggressive children, and will propose how other cognitive, physiological, and familial factors could affect these social–cognitive products. While the social–cognitive processes we have described account for sequential activation of situational, moment-by-moment processes, they do not specify the structural relationship of more basic cognitive activities to social cognitions. Social information-processing models often fail to indicate how enduring, cross-situational cognitive schemata affect immediate, momentary processing. Similarly, the effects of psychophysiological processes and family influences are generally unspecified.

We use an adaptation of the Cognitive Taxonomic System (Ingram & Kendall, 1986; Kendall & Ingram, 1989) to organize the relevant sets of cognitive activities into three clusters, which will then be integrated into our model (see Figure 2-1). *Schematic propositions* are the stored information in cognitive structures in memory. *Cognitive operations* are various procedures that process stored and incoming information (e.g., attention, encoding, retrieval), and, in our case, can be separated from the content of *social–cognitive products*. Social–cognitive products are the results of interaction between stored schematic proportions, cognitive operations, and incoming sensory data about stimulus events. Social–cognitive products include social–cognitive appraisals, social problem-solving and cognitive–emotional linkages. Finally, the role of key social influences, and especially parents, will be noted.

Social–Cognitive Products

Social–Cognitive Appraisals

These social–cognitive products consist of the first two stages in Dodge's (1986) social information-processing model: cue utilization, and attributions about others' intentions. Aggressive children have been found to perceive and encode cues in the environment around them in a different manner than do nonaggressive children. Dodge and his colleagues have had children listen to series of audiotaped and videotaped segments in which child actors describe and portray hostile, benevolent, and neutral situations. After listening to, or viewing, the segments, the children were asked to remember as many cues as they could. In comparison with nonaggressive children, aggressive children remember more of the last statements they heard, indicating that they had a developmental lag in their cue utilization (Milich & Dodge, 1984).

Another developmental lag has been evident in aggressive boys' tendencies to decide to attend to few cues while attempting to interpret the meaning of other's behavior (Dodge & Newman, 1981). When given an opportunity to listen to as many taped statements about a child's intentions as they wished, nonaggressive boys listened to 40% more cues before making a decision than did aggressive boys. In addition, aggressive children have been found to encode and retrieve significantly more cues that convey hostile connotations than do nonaggressive children (Dodge, Pettit, Mc-Claskey, & Brown, 1986; Lochman, 1989; Milich & Dodge, 1984).

These findings indicate that aggressive children are hypervigilant in scanning their social environment, attending to more immediate cues, especially hostile cues, than do nonaggressive children. Aggressive children do not appear to use sustained search strategies in examining the environment, and thus do not planfully consider more complex inferences about others' behavior.

In the milliseconds after cues are perceived, aggressive children form inferences about others' intentions, and these efforts to decipher the meaning of others' behavior have been found to be significantly influenced by their higher rate of detection of hostile cues and by their prior expectations that others would be hostile toward them (Dodge & Frame, 1982). As a result, aggressive boys have been found to be 50% more likely than nonaggressive boys to infer that antagonists in hypothetical provocations acted with hostile rather than neutral or benign intent (Dodge, 1980). This attributional bias about others' intentions has been replicated in a series of studies with both aggressive children and adolescents, using experimental stimuli consisting of written or videotaped hypothetical vignettes, and in live observation of another child knocking down a block building that the aggressive children had made (Dodge et al., 1986; Milich & Dodge, 1984; Nasby, Hayden, & DePaulo, 1980; Steinberg & Dodge, 1983).

In actual competitive dyadic discussions with nonaggressive peers, aggressive boys not only tend to overperceive the peer's aggressiveness, but they also substantially underestimate their own aggressiveness (Lochman, 1987). Due to their distorted perceptions of the peer and of themselves, aggressive boys implicitly attribute responsibility for the conflict to the peer. This pattern of distorted perceptions and interpretation of others in early stages of a conflict sequence can contribute to the boy's subsequently feeling quite justified in responding in an intensely aggressive manner.

Social Problem Solving

While cognitive distortions are evident in aggressive children's appraisal processes, cognitive deficiencies are more evident in their social problem-solving difficulties (Lochman, Meyer et al., in press). Social problem solving refers to the last three of Dodge's (1986) stages, and includes generation of alternative solution, consideration of consequences of solutions, and behavioral implementation of solutions (Allen, Chinsky, Larcen, Lochman, & Selinger, 1976). Solution generation and consideration of consequences are social–cognitive products in our model (see Figure 2-1). Mixed findings exist as to whether aggressive children in general actually generate a smaller quantity of solution than nonaggressive children (Deluty, 1981; Dodge et al., 1986; Kendall & Fischler, 1984; Lochman & Lampron, 1986; Richard & Dodge, 1982), but evidence does indicate that boys with the very highest level of aggressive behavior, in comparison with moderately aggressive boys, have a marked paucity in the range of problem solution they consider (Lochman, Lampron, Burch, & Curry, 1985). In contrast to these qualified findings about the quantitative aspect of the social problem-solving process, aggressive children have displayed consistent and characteristic deficiencies in the content or quality of the solution they generate.

Aggressive children have been found to generate fewer verbal assertion solutions and more nonverbal, direct action solutions than did nonaggressive children (Asarnow & Callan, 1985; Deluty, 1981; Lochman & Lampron, 1986), on hypothetical open-middle and open-ended vignettes. Aggressive children have been found to consider more of the aggressive responses in their second or third solution to a problem, indicating they have more aggressive, ineffective backup solutions to social problems (Richard & Dodge, 1982). The findings about verbal assertion are particularly important, since nonaggressive children, by verbally labeling what they want in a simple, direct manner, are better able to indicate their intentions to those around them. Aggressive children's nonverbal direct actions, in contrast, can easily lead their peers to assume that the aggressive children's intentions may have been hostile, and can lead to progressive escalations of aggression.

Aggressive children and adolescents also appear to have deficiencies in their anticipation of consequences, and in their planning of how to enact solutions, although considerably less research has been conducted on this topic (Dodge et al., 1986; Platt, Spivack, Altman, Altman, & Peizer (1974). When assessing individual children, as we will soon discuss, it is important to identify the specific pattern of social problem-solving deficiencies for each aggressive child.

Appraisal of Internal Arousal and Emotional Reactions

The manner in which aggressive children perceive, or label, the arousal they begin to experience during conflicts constrains the kinds of behavioral responses they consider using. Aggressive children have distortions in this affect-labeling process, as they are more apt to label affect-arousing situations as producing anger, rather than other emotions such as sadness (Garrison & Stolberg, 1983). It is likely that certain responses children deem appropriate for responding to sadness-evoking situations would not be considered appropriate for anger-evoking situations, thus serving to narrow the range of solutions that aggressive children would consider.

The relationship between aggression and affective factors such as empathy has also received attention. This body of research explores the hypothesis that empathic responding inhibits one's tendency to engage in aggressive or antisocial interpersonal acts. In Feshbach and Feshbach's (1982) three-component model of empathy, empathy consists of (1) the capacity to discriminate another's emotional state (affect identification); (2) the ability to assume the perspective and role of another (cognitive perspective taking); and (3) the ability to respond emotionally (affective responsivity). This model thus suggests that empathy is a complex intrapsychic and interpersonal phenomenon which involves several cognitive and affective skills.

In two extensive reviews of the literature on the relationship between empathy and antisocial and prosocial behaviors (Eisenberg & Miller, 1987; Miller & Eisenberg, 1988), the authors concluded that empathy is positively correlated to prosocial behaviors, and negatively correlated with antisocial behaviors. Empathy is defined by these authors as a form of "emotional matching" in which a vicarious emotional response is consistent with, or identical to, to another's emotional state. The relationship between empathy and pro- or antisocial behavior appears to be influenced by such factors as age, the method of assessing behavior, and the means of assessing empathy (Eisenberg & Miller, 1987; Miller & Eisenberg, 1988). These authors conclude that there is stronger evidence for the relationship between empathy and pro- and antisocial behaviors among school-aged children and adolescents than preschool children, and in studies which use questionnaire methods to assess empathy. Questionnaires provide "trait" or dispositional measures of empathy, which typically assess one's general understanding of others' emotions and degree of emotional responsiveness across a range of situations. Evidence for the relationship between empathy and behavior is weakest or nonexistent when empathy is measured by asking children to indicate their emotional responses to hypothetical vignettes presented as brief pictures or stories. Picture story methods provide "state" measures of empathy, which assess children's immediate response to stimuli designed to elicit emotional reactions. As Eisenberg and Miller note, inconsistent results may be due to different methods of assessing empathy for different-aged children, or to actual developmental differences in children's capacity for empathic responding. The moderating effect of age on the relationship between behavior and empathic responsivity is unknown.

Cognitive Operations

The operations used to manipulate information that individuals encounter externally and internally include attention, retrieval processes from short- and long-term memory, and concept formation and problem-solving processing. External information is evident in cues from the environment around the individual, and internal information is present in physiological cues and in images, thoughts, or beliefs accessed from memory. Attention can be conceived as an operation that assists other cognitive operations such as encoding and retrieval (Cohen & Schleser, 1984); thus, the efficiency and quality of the attentional operations can have major effects on the quality of other cognitive operations and products.

There is suggestive evidence that links deficiencies in sustaining and focusing attention to aggression in children. Mirsky (1989) administered a variety of attentional measures, including the Continuous Performance Task (CPT), to adolescents involved in a ten-year follow-up of a population sample. Aggressive adolescents had difficulty concentrating and sustaining attention on the CPT, in comparison to other adolescents. These attentional deficits produce impairments in encoding of information so that individuals did not perceive relevant bits of information (omission errors), and they perceived information that was not present (commission errors, or intrusions). Similar impairments on attention tasks have been found with aggressive children (Agrawal & Kaushal, 1988), and with ADHD children who are comorbid for Conduct Disorder or Oppositional Disorder (Werry, Elkind, & Reeves, 1987).

These attentional impairments may also be related to a distinct pattern of deficiencies in retrieval from short-term memory for aggressive children. Lochman (1989) examined group differences in basic recall and attention (using Santostefano and Roder's [1984] Leveling-Sharpening House Test) and a parallel social–cognitive measure of utilization of social cues (audiotape recall measure from Milich & Dodge, 1984). In comparison with non-aggressive boys, the aggressive boys had higher rates of intrusive commission errors on the recall tasks. Since a similar pattern was evident for both social and nonsocial stimuli, the cue perception deficits appear to be partly due to operational defects.

In addition to deficient retrieval from short-term memory, which has an impact on distortion in appraisal processes, aggressive children have characteristic styles of retrieving known strategies from long-term memory, which contribute to social-problem solving deficiencies. Lochman, Lampron, and Rabiner (1989) found children responding to the PSM-C in the usual open-middle format, which simulates automatic retrieval processes, had different patterns of responses than children responding to the PSM-C with a multiple-choice format. The multiple-choice format simulated more deliberate, comparative retrieval processes, similar to a process of carefully sifting through stored solutions in "memory bins." In the open-middle condition, aggressive elementary school boys produced significantly more direct action solutions and tended to produce fewer verbal assertion solutions than nonaggressive children, replicating the Lochman and Lampron (1986) results. In the multiple-choice condition, both aggressive and nonaggressive boys had higher rates of verbal assertion solutions and lower rates of direct action solutions than occurred in the open-middle condition; however, aggressive boys still had lower rates of verbal assertion and higher rates of help-seeking solutions than did nonaggressive boys. Thus, aggressive boys' solutions to social problems seemed to be affected by salience effects during retrieval from long-term memory, as well as by learned patterns stored in memory. In a subsequent study, Rabiner, Lenhart and Lochman (in press) replicated these findings while using a more direct paradigm in which automatic retrieval processes were forced by requiring children to provide responses immediately, while deliberate processing was facilitated by having children wait 20 seconds after hearing the problem vignette before responding.

Schematic Propositions

In Ingram and Kendall's (1986) Cognitive Taxonomic System, cognitive propositions are defined as the content of cognitive structures, and essentially are personal information or general knowledge stored in memory (e.g, beliefs, expectations). Cognitive structure is the architecture of functional psychological mechanisms such as short-term memory, long-term memory, cognitive networks, and memory nodes. Propositions and structure are classified as categories of schema, but only the schematic propositions are relevant for our discussion here. Schematic propositions are also similar to the "cognitive structures" identified by Meichenbaum (1985) and others. Schematic propositions are ideas and thoughts stored in memory which have a direct influence on how new information, or cognitive products, is processed moment by moment. Classes of schematic proposition which have been found to be related to children's aggressive behavior, and which, therefore, may influence social–cognitive products, are goal values, generalized outcome expectations, beliefs, and perceived competence and self-worth.

In a study of the direct effect of adolescents' social goals on their solutions to social problems, Lochman and White (1989) used a social learning theory framework (Rotter et al., 1972) to examine boys' ratings of (1) the value of four social goals in a conflict situation (avoidance, dominance, revenge, affiliation), (2) the solution they would use to accomplish each goal, and (3) their level of expectations that they could attain the goals with their selected responses. Aggressive boys had significantly higher value ratings for the dominance and revenge goals and lower ratings for an affiliation goal, in comparison to nonaggressive boys. Although aggressive and non-aggressive boys endorsed similar patterns of behavioral solutions to attain each of the goals, aggressive boys had substantial differences from nonaggressive boys in solutions they would use to gain their main goal. This suggests the direct effect of goals (schematic proposition) on problem solutions (cognitive products). Due to their overvaluing of dominance and revenge goals, aggressive boys had more aggressive and verbal assertion solutions and fewer bargaining solutions than did nonaggressive boys. These results also are consistent with Brion–Meisels and Selman's (1984) view that developmental changes take place in children's interpersonal negotiation tactics. While simple verbal assertion strategies are competent and adaptive means of resolving social conflicts in the preadolescent years, by midadolescence complex mutual bargaining strategies appear to be more normative for nonaggressive boys.

In a conceptually related study of goals, Rabiner (in Lochman, Meyer et al., in press) found that aggressive-rejected children were less able to integrate self-oriented and other-oriented concerns than average and popular boys. In another study documenting aggressive children's self-oriented goals for dominance, Boldizar, Perry, and Perry (1989), used the Rotter el al. (1972) social learning framework to examine outcome values. In their goal-oriented outcome values, aggressive children were found to place more value on achieving control of the victim, and less value on suffering by the victim, retaliation from the victim, peer rejection, or negative self-evaluation. These sets of findings about goals and outcome values are also consistent with moral reasoning research in which children consider the consequences of their hypothetical actions. Aggressive children and adolescents have lower level of moral reasoning (Edelman & Goldstein, 1981; Jurkovic & Prentice, 1977; Nucci & Herman, 1982), generally at a preconventional level. That is, they primarily attempt to avoid punishment of authority figures, and do not act cooperatively to bolster the positive consequences for themselves and others.

In addition to their stored schematic representation of their goal and outcome values, aggressive children have certain patterns of expectations of achieving the outcomes/goals. Perry, Perry, and Rasmussen (1986) found aggressive children to be more confident that aggressive behavior would produce tangible rewards and would reduce aversive treatment from others, in comparison with nonaggressive children. In Slaby and Guerra's (1988) study of beliefs, antisocial aggressive youth similarly believed that aggressive behavior would increase self-esteem, would avoid a negative image, would not cause victims to suffer, and was a legitimate response. This set of beliefs could certainly inhibit the formation of cognitive products involving accurate empathy.

In addition to the goals and expectations identified already, it is likely that other generalized expectations (e.g., locus of control) and other types of schematic propositions, such as self-esteem, would have effects on social–cognitive products. Lochman and Lampron (1986) have found that aggressive children have lower levels of self-worth than nonaggressive boys, and aggressive children's self-esteem and perception of competence have been found to be responsive to CBT (e.g., Lochman, Burch, Curry, & Lampron, 1984). Self-esteem weaknesses appear to be most pronounced in certain types of aggressive children. Lochman and Lampron (1985) found that highly aggressive preadolescent boys who also had low levels of social status with their peers had the most pronounced impairment in self-esteem. Since this same category of boys has been noted subsequently to have higher levels of depressive and anxiety symptoms (Lochman, Wayland, & Cohen, 1990) it appears that children's conceptions of their worth and esteem have strong associations with affective states as well as serving as cognitive schemata. The complex network of associations between stored cognitive representations, physiological arousal, and affective states is not well understood at this time.

Noncognitive Influences

Psychophysiology and Arousal

In speculation about parameters which can influence social–cognitive products, the role of children's arousal state has been increasingly noted (Dodge, 1985; Lochman, 1984). It has been hypothesized that children's initial appraisals of an event can produce immediate increases in arousal, possibly due to a classically conditioned reaction in which a stimulus has become capable of automatically eliciting an aroused psychophysiological state in an individual. Once aroused, preemptive cognitive processing becomes likely, as the individual responds quickly and automatically. In this way, it is anticipated that arousal would produce marked influences on social–cognitive products, as well as being influenced by social–cognitive appraisals.

Aggressive children's cognitive processing has been noticeably affected by arousal. Dodge and Somberg (1987) found that threat-induced arousal affected children's attribution. After overhearing an audiotaped confederate threatening to fight them, aggressive boys made more hostile attributions of others' intentions in hypothetical vignettes, and they tended to be less accurate in detecting cues that indicated provocation may have been accidental. Similarly, Gordon, Lochman, and Ribordy (1986) found that

aggressive boys provided significantly more direct action and aggressive problem solutions after experimentally induced peer rejection than did nonaggressive boys.

While these studies supported the assumption that aggressive children's pre-emptive cognitive operations can further impair their social–cognitive products, they have not examined the direct effect of biological arousal
on cognition. Arousal has been conceptualized as an end-product of the
activational properties of the neuroendocrine and sympathetic nervous systems (Brain, 1984). In this regard, aggressive adolescents have been found
to have higher levels of serum and salivary testosterone than nonaggressive
adolescents (Christiansen & Knussmann, 1987; Dabbs, Jurkovic, & Frady,
1988; Olweus, Mattsson, Schalling, & Low, 1980). Testosterone levels have
been found to fluctuate in response to provocations, and the testosterone
has effects on brain areas such as the hypothalamus associated with the
production of aggressive behavior. Olweus (1984) has suggested that testosterone may have a direct effect on frustration tolerance, which in turn influences adolescents' aggressive behavior. Research on the integrated assessment of biological, psychophsiological, and social–cognitive processes would
be valuable in the years ahead.

Parental and Other Social Influences

We assume that parents and other adult caregivers, and subsequently children's peers, have a formative influence on children's schematic propositions and social–cognitive products. Research on families of aggressive children indicate that parents and siblings display high levels of aversive behavior,
as well as other maladaptive parental processes, such as vague "beta" commands, inaccurate monitoring of children's behavior, low cohesion, and rigid
or chaotic control efforts (Forehand & Long, 1988; Patterson, 1986; Rodick, Henggeler, & Hanson, 1986). Lochman and Dodge (1990) have found
that, in comparison with nonaggressive boys' parents, aggressive boys' parents report that they and other adult caregivers provide high levels of verbally aggressive and physically aggressive behavior to the target children,
and they also report high levels of verbally aggressive behavior in adults'
relationships in the household. These results imply that children's social–
cognitive products may be affected through modeling of their parents' ways
of perceiving and responding to conflicts with spouses and children.

A more direct test of the transmission of social–cognitive products from
parents to children involves assessing the attributional processes of parents.
Following findings of attributional biases in child-abusing parents (e.g.,
Larrance & Twentyman, 1983; Dix and Lochman, in press) found that in
contrast to a nonaggressive groups, mothers of aggressive boys attributed
the cause of children's misdeeds more to the child rather than to the external circumstances. Similar investigations can begin to examine the relation-

ship between the social–cognitive products of additional significant others in children's lives (teachers, peers, other relatives) and the aggressive children's appraisal and problem-solving processes. Table 2-1 summarizes the cognitive distortions and deficiencies that we have reviewed.

ASSESSMENT OF AGGRESSION IN CHILDREN

Conducting a thorough assessment of the factors related to a child's aggressive tendencies is an extremely important part of designing a comprehensive treatment plan. In this section, a rationale will be provided for evaluating children on a number of behavioral and social–cognitive variables. Implications for assessment from empirical research will be noted, followed by a proposed model for an indepth evaluation procedure.

We have used a battery of all these types of assessment tools in clinical research with our school-based anger coping program. In our clinic-based Conduct Disorders program we have used selected subsets of the measures, and have often informally assessed for aspects of the social–cognitive defi-

TABLE 2-1. Cognitive Characteristics of Aggressive Children

Social–Cognitive Products
Social–cognitive appraisals
  Overly sensitive to hostile cues
  Bias in attributing hostile intention to others
  Underestimate own aggressiveness
Social problem solving
  Limited repertoire of solutions for the most aggressive
  For preadolescent aggressive children: few verbal assertion solution and excess direct action solutions
  Aggressive backup solutions
Appraisal of internal arousal
  Overlabeling of affective arousal as anger
  Low levels of empathy

Cognitive Operations
  Difficulty in sustaining attention
  Commission errors in short-term memory
  Retrieval of salient solutions when automatically retrieving solutions from long-term memory

Schematic Propositions
  Higher value on social goals of dominance and revenge rather than affiliation
  Less value placed on outcomes such as victim suffering, victim retaliation, or peer rejection
  Expectation that aggressive behavior will produce tangible rewards and reduce aversive reactions
  Low self-esteem

ciencies and distortions during comprehensive structured and unstructured interviews. It is anticipated that the breadth of the assessment battery will be affected by practical factors.

Behavioral Presentation of the Child

It is important to look at aggression within the context of all other observable behavior problems, interaction styles, and environmental factors. Often these patterns of behavior problems will vary with respect to the environmental context (e.g., location, home vs. school; person involved, peer vs. teacher). Therefore it is important to obtain information from as many sources as possible.

Behavioral Rating Scales

Probably the best way to easily obtain a "reading" of the breadth and severity of the problem is through the use of behavioral checklists (McMahon & Forehand, 1988). A checklist allows assessment of a broad range of behaviors, including low-frequency behaviors (e.g., aggression, stealing), requires little time to administer, and incorporates the perceptions of significant others (e.g., parents, teachers) in the child's life.

Probably the most commonly used and best validated behavioral rating scale is the Child Behavior Checklist (CBCL; Achenbach & Edelbrock, 1983). Several features make this measure particularly useful: extensive normative data, access to perceptions from multiple informants (parents, teachers, and children), provision of both broad-band (e.g., externalizing–internalizing) and narrow-band (e.g., aggression) syndromes, and evaluation of prosocial behavior (a relatively rare quality among child behavior checklists). Other useful rating scales include the revised Behavior Problem Checklist (RBPC; Quay & Peterson, 1983), the Eyberg Child Behavior Inventory (ECBI; Eyberg, 1980), and the Missouri Child Behavior Checklist (Sines, Pauker, Sines, & Owen, 1969).

Interviews

Interviews with aggressive children, their parents, and teachers can be extremely helpful in identifying situational variables related to the occurrence of aggressive behavior. Several structured interview formats (e.g., for parents, Forehand & McMahon, 1981; teachers, McMahon & Forehand, 1988; and children, Patterson & Bank, 1986) may be used to access information from a specific informant. Perhaps more helpful are interview formats with parallel forms for parent and child, thereby allowing for comparisons of different perceptions and convergence of reported problem areas. For these purposes, interviews such as the Child Assessment Schedule (CAS; Hodges,

1987) and the Diagnostic Interview Schedule for Children (DISC; Costello, Edelbrock, Dulcan, & Kalas, 1984) may be most useful, as they allow for important distinctions regarding the setting and objects of aggression (e.g., toward peers and siblings, cruelty to animals). The CAS and DISC and other similar diagnostic interviews provide information about both externalizing (e.g., overactivity) and internalizing (e.g., depression, anxiety) symptoms, the presence of which may provide critical information in developing a comprehensive understanding of the context in which the aggressive behavior occurs. The interview of antisocial behavior of Kazdin and Esveldt–Dawson (1986) may be particularly useful in determining patterns of covert–overt symptomatology. We have found that with children with fairly serious problems with aggression, the use of a less-structured clinical interview may also be helpful, especially in uncovering a child's attributions and reasoning about a particular incident. For instance, some children and young adolescents attribute their poor reasoning in aggressive interactions to the use of drugs or associating with a particular set of peers. Their descriptions of relatively extreme acts of violence (e.g., muggings) may provide important clinical "hunches" about their capacity for empathy, their assessment of their own self-control, and sense of remorse.

Behavioral Observation

As McMahon and Forehand (1988) explain, behavioral observations may yield some of the most useful information about aggressive children. The aforementioned measures may be subject to perceptual biases or motivation to deny specific behavior problems. Comparing data obtained from direct observation, checklists, and interviews will most likely indicate focuses for treatment (e.g., schoolbased intervention with peers, or parent–child interaction).

Peer Evaluation

Not surprisingly, many aggressive children have problematical peer relations. They are judged as being less socially competent by parents (e.g., Achenbach & Edelbrock, 1983) and teachers (e.g., Dodge & Frame, 1982) and lower in social acceptance by peers (e.g., Coie, Dodge, & Coppotelli, 1982). Use of peer evaluations may be particularly helpful in identifying a subgroup of aggressive socially rejected children who exhibit a combination of risk factors (e.g., attentional and learning problems, low self-esteem, peer rejected status) that point to possible situational factors related to their experience of frustration and aggressive outbursts. (Dodge, Coie, & Brakke, 1982; Lakey, Green, & Forehand, 1980; Lochman & Lampron, 1985). Lochman and Lampron found that another group of highly aggressive children who were more socially accepted reported higher general and school-related self-esteem, even in comparison to socially accepted boys who were less aggressive. Since these children enjoy greater social acceptance and self-esteem they may be less motivated to cooperate with treatment efforts to reduce their aggressive behavior.

Evaluation of Social–Cognitive/Affective Characteristics

As presented in the social–cognitive model of aggression, the current literature on aggressive children clearly indicates that there are particular characteristics of their social–cognitive style that differ in a meaningful way from nonaggressive children. Based upon empirical findings, measures will be proposed for use in a "battery" of assessment techniques for clinical evaluation. It is important to caution that while meaningful group differences exits on these measures, the psychometric properties are yet to be determined. Therefore, the following procedures are offered for consideration as a means by which to obtain relevant clinical information to be collected along with other measures (e.g., IQ and achievement tests, behavioral checklists) with well-established psychometric properties.

Most researchers and clinicians with any experience with highly aggressive children readily agree that these children seem to perceive the social world in a very different manner than nonaggressive children. In delineating these differences in a specific child one might pose the question: What does this child attend to and encode when presented with information in a social situation?

As discussed, Dodge (1980) and his colleagues (Dodge & Frame, 1982; Dodge & Newman, 1981; Dodge et al., 1986; Milich & Dodge, 1984) have developed a number of interesting measures to test a series of related hypotheses about aggressive children's skills for encoding different types of social cues. Dodge and Frame (1982) have presented videotaped "hypothetical situations" to children in which a child experiences hostile, benign, or neutral outcomes in a peer interaction. Children's responses to this measure can be used to evaluate their (1) ability to recall cues freely from the interaction, (2) recognition of events that actually occurred, (3) "mistaken" accounts of the event (commission errors, intrusions), and (4) attributions and expectations about a hypothetical peer's intentions or future behavior. Generally, aggressive children tend to attend to and remember hostile cues selectively in interaction with peers, particularly when they are asked to imagine being a participant in the interaction.

A second general question about aggressive children's way of thinking is: What kinds of ideas do they have about how to interact and "solve" social situation? How does this aforementioned style of information processing influence their strategies (or lack therefore) in social problem solving? In evaluating the actual content of social problem-solving solutions a number of factors need to be considered: (1) the type of social task (e.g., peer group entry, initiating friendships, resolving conflict situations); (2) the persons involved in the hypothetical situation (peers, teachers, parents); (3) the apparent intentions (hostile, benevolent, ambiguous).

Lochman and Lampron (1986) evaluated aggressive children's social problem-solving strategies to two types of situational variables while holding constant a third variable, type of social task. The Problem Solving Measures for Conflict (PSM-C) presents hypothetical stories involving only interpersonal conflict and systematically varies the type of antagonist (peer, teacher, parent) and the expressed intent of the antagonist (hostile or ambiguous frustration of the protagonist's wishes). On this measure aggressive boys, compared to nonaggressive boys, had lower rates of "verbal assertion" solutions for conflicts with peers and those involving a hostile antagonist (of any type; peer, parent, teacher). They had higher rates of direct action solutions for conflicts with teachers and hostile antagonists, and a higher rate of physically aggressive solutions in peer conflicts.

The following examples illustrate deficits in appraisal and problem-solving strategies exhibited by two aggressive boys. These boys' responses to the same stimuli from the PSM-C (Lochman) and Dodge's recall test will be provided. M. is a 15-year-old highly aggressive and sociopathic youth referred for evaluation and treatment following adjudication for property offenses and assault charges.

J. is a 12-year-old male referred for treatment to address chronic oppositional behavior in school. J. is particularly prone to respond passive aggressively in response to adult authority, and to have trouble labeling emotions. In response to the following story on the PSM-C:

> Some of Ed's friends borrowed his soccer ball during lunch period but did not return it. When Ed came out of school at the end of the day, the other boys had already started playing with it again. Ed was supposed to go right home after school, and he wanted to have his soccer ball back. The story ends with Ed walking home with his soccer ball. What happens in between Ed not having his soccer ball, and later when he walked home with it?

M.'s immediate response represents an attempt to seek help from an authority figure:

> "They wouldn't let Ed have the ball, right? So Ed went to the principal and told him the situation, he went back to the kids and told them to give Ed the soccer ball back and if they messed with Ed they would be expelled from school. Because Ed is the kind of person who doesn't like violence or to fight— he has values and stuff."

M's initial backup solution:

"He could have gone up there, say for instance if he had a knife or something, he could have cut one of them up."

M's final solution:

"He could have come over to the school with is mother, his mother could have got the ball back."

Thus, after paying lip service to prosocial thinking, M. generated an extremely antisocial response, and then resorted to immature help seeking. J's initial response represents a direct action solution:

"Ed went up and act like he was fixing to play with the soccer ball, but took the ball and walked away with it."

J's backup solutions:

"He could have just took the soccer ball without playing with them."
"He could have went home and next morning seen them playing with and gone up to them and taken it without asking."
"Next morning if it's in the locker he could have went in the locker and took it out."

J. is clearly fixated on direct action solutions, which characterize each of the four problem-solving strategies he provided. Together, these boys demonstrate aggressive boys' tendency to rely on physically aggressive or direct action solutions, and to be deficient in their use of verbal assertion.

In response to a series of audiotaped five hostile, benevolent, and neutral statements on one segment of Milich and Dodge's (1984) Recall Test (this segment contains two positive, five hostile, and two neutral statements):

M: "He stole somebody's money. He hit this boy so hard that his nose started bleeding. He hates this boy named Kenny so much that he wishes his arms would fall off."
J: "There was this boy who made him so mad that he punched him in the nose. There was this other boy who was crippled, the boy helped him get his lunch. One day he told this boy to beat up this other boy."

Both boys exhibited a tendency to overrecall hostile cues, and to include hostile commission errors or intrusions, as they remembered some items in hostile terms, rather than in their original positive or neutral form.

Clearly, aggressive children not only perceive social situations in a different light, but tend to generate solutions to problematical situations that are maladaptive. This pattern leads to the question of "Why"? Are there particular beliefs or expectations or goals that aggressive children hold that are related to, or perhaps lead them to, their unskilled handling of social situations? In addition to assessing for the answers to these questions during interview, several experimental measures can also be useful. The Outcome-Expectation Questionnaire and Self-Efficacy Questionnaire (Perry, Perry, & Rasmussen, 1986), measures of beliefs and expectations (Slaby & Guerra, 1988), and a measure of social goals (Lochman & White, 1989) have all been used to distinguish aggressive children and adolescents from less aggressive peers. Assessment of such schematic propositions permit a more detailed and coherent understanding of aggressive children's maladaptive behavior and approaches for intervention with them.

Other Domains of Functioning in the Aggressive Child

A thorough assessment of familial/parental functioning is necessary so that a complete picture of the behavioral contingencies and influences can be outlined. Again, McMahon and Forehand's (1988) chapter on assessment of conduct disorders is an excellent resource. Parental and marital adjustment need to be thoroughly investigated to determine what types of social problem-solving styles are being modeled and to evaluate the degree to which parents are able to be receptive to intervention efforts. Commonly used instruments for which there is adequate psychometric validation, include the following: (1) for parental depression, Beck Depression Inventory (BDI; Beck, Rush, Shaw, & Emery, 1980), the Depression Adjective Check Lists (DACL; Lubin, 1967); (2) for parental stress, the Parenting Stress Index (PSI; Abidin, 1983); (3) for marital adjustment, the Locke's Marital Adjustment Test (MAT; Locke & Wallace, 1959) and the Dyadic Adjustment Scale (DAS; Spanier, 1976). Measures that can yield an assessment of the child's exposure to marital hostility and experience of direct or indirect use of force include the O'Leary–Porter Scale (Porter & O'Leary, 1980) and the Conflict Tactics Scale (CTS; Straus, 1979). The Child Perceptions of Marital Discord (CPMD; Emery & O'Leary, 1982) has been found to be a useful index of child distress, and a correlate of parent report of aggression (Wayland, Schoenwald, & Lochman 1989).

In addition to assessing familial and parental functioning, it is well known that children with aggressive behavior disorders often have other cognitive/academic deficits (see McMahon & Forehand, 1988, for a brief overview). A thorough evaluation of intellectual and academic strengths and weaknesses should be conducted. An accurate assessment of the types of obstacles and frustrations experienced in the learning environment (e.g., specific learning disabilities, especially reading) may shed some light on the reasons why children may be perceived as defensive, defiant, or argumentative by teacher and peers.

Measures of the aggressive child's subjective experience are also important and have implications for response to treatment (e.g., Lochman et al., 1985). The Coopersmith Self-Esteem Inventory (CSI; Coopersmith, 1967) and the Self-Perception Profile for Children (Harter, 1985) yield self-ratings of competence in a number of areas (e.g., home vs. school, cognitive vs. social). Given the aggressive child's high likelihood of difficulties in multiple areas (e.g., academic achievement, peer relations) it would be important to be aware of areas of functioning about which a child may feel particularly sensitive as well as those for which a sense of pride and accomplishment is present.

COGNITIVE–BEHAVIOR THERAPY WITH AGGRESSIVE CHILDREN

Cognitive–Behavioral Therapy (CBT) addresses the deficient and distorted social–cognitive processes in aggressive children, including distortions in their perceptions of others' and their own behavior, biases in their attribution of the hostile intention of others, and overreliance on nonverbal direct action solutions, and underreliance on verbal assertion solutions. CBT programs can include training in self-instruction, social problem-solving, perspective taking, affect labeling, or relaxation, and most programs include a combination of several of these techniques. All of these programs have a common focus on children's social cognitions during frustrating or provocative situations.

Anger Coping Program

To provide a flavor for the kinds of cognitive–behavioral techniques that can be used with aggressive children, we will describe our anger coping program. We will address the major content and process issues which constitute the focuses of CBT interventions (see Lochman, Lampron, Gemmer, & Harris [1987] for a session-by-session description of the program). The school-based anger coping program has been developed and refined over a period of several years, and consists of eighteen 45- to 60-minute sessions. Sessions are highly structured, with specific goals, objectives, and structured exercises outlined for each session. This model was designed for use with elementary school-aged children, and has been used primarily with 4th- and 5th-grade boys. Thus, groups are typically homogeneous with respect to age, gender, and presenting problem/psychiatric symptomatology (aggressive and disruptive behavior). While our model has most often been implemented in schools, it can easily be adapted for use in clinic settings.

We believe there are several advantages to use of group therapy as the modal form of treatment. Peer and group reinforcement is frequently more effective with children than reinforcement provided in a dyadic context, or by adults (Rose & Edleson, 1987). This may be especially true for children with disruptive behavior disorders, who research suggests are relatively resistant to social reinforcement. Additionally, the group context provides *in vivo* opportunities for interpersonal learning and development of social skills.

The anger coping program addresses both cognitive and affective processes, and is designed to remediate skill deficits in conflictual situations involving affective arousal. Specific goals are to increase children's awareness of internal cognitive, affective, and physiological phenomena related to anger arousal; enhance self-reflection and self-management skills; facilitate alternative, consequential and means–end thinking in approaching social problems; and increase children's behavioral repertoire when faced with social conflict. To do so, sessions are organized around the teaching of specific social–cognitive skills. The major components of the program, which consist of self-management/monitoring skills, perspective-taking skills and social problem-solving skills, will be presented in this section, along with process variables such as the behavioral management system, goal setting, and interpersonal group process.

Self-management/monitoring Skills

First, children are taught to become more competent observers of internal states related to affective arousal. As is true of other skills taught, this process occurs throughout the entire course of treatment. Through modeling, observation, structured exercises and group discussion, children are taught to identify physiological and affective cues of anger arousal. For example, they are asked to define the concept of anger in terms of its affective and behavioral concomitants (e.g., "anger is the feeling you have when you think you cannot get something you want, or do something you want to do, or when you feel provoked" (Lochman et al., 1987, p. 347). Children are asked to identify environmental cues and precipitants by generating examples of anger-arousing stimuli (e.g., situations at home and at school that make them angry with peers and authority figures. Next, physiological aspects of anger arousal are addressed. A videotaped instruction is used to introduce the topic, showing a boy displaying several overt symptoms of anger arousal. The signal function of these cues is emphasized, and group brainstorming/discussion is used to identify a variety of physiological cues of anger (blood rushing to one's face, quickening pulse, increased muscle tension, affective flooding). Children are asked to identify the specific ways in which they and others experience anger arousal (facial and gestural expression, tone of voice, body posture, thoughts, statements, actions). This implicitly communicates that people differ in their internal experience of, and behavioral response to anger and is intended to help children become better observers of a wide range of cues regarding their own and others' anger. Children may be encouraged to differentiate their affective experience of anger on the dimension of intensity (e.g., to generate situations which make them angry "on a scale of one to ten," to label affective state of different intensity such as "simmering," "steaming," "boiling"). The phenomenological experience of anger can thus be conceptualized as occurring on a continuum, and children can be taught to identify affective and physiological symptoms at lower and more manageable levels of affective arousal. Children can also be taught to link affective states of different intensity to specific environmental events or cues. One such method of helping children concretize their understanding of these issues is use of role plays. Children can be asked to provide "Academy Award portrayals" of anger arousal and anger coping, including nonverbal and verbal cues.

In addition to self-monitoring strategies designed to increase awareness of environmental triggers, and of affective and physiological states related to anger, cognitive self-control strategies are also taught. Instruction in this area attempts to address deficiencies in verbal mediation strategies which help to regulate behavior. Children are helped to appreciate the impact of cognition on subsequent affective arousal and behavior, and are instructed on the role of internal dialogue in enhancing or decreasing the experience of anger arousal. This concept is taught through the construct of "self-talk." Through repeated instruction, children are helped to identify anger-enhancing and anger-reducing cognitions, and to understand the impact of private speech on emotions and behavior. A series of verbal taunting games is particularly useful in concretizing this concept. In this application, children receive insults or taunts from other group members, and discuss their thoughts and feelings in response to this structured provocation. Stimuli are presented in a hierarchical format, progressing from relatively distanced stimuli (e.g., taunting of puppets) to increasingly more threatening stimuli (direct taunting of group members). Instruction on self-talk is combined with exercises designed to increase awareness of individual perceptual processes. For example, group members may be asked to identify the kinds of assumptions they are most likely to make in situations of social conflict, the kinds of anger-reducing statements that are most likely to facilitate adaptive coping. In this way, children are encouraged to develop a repertoire of coping statements that will work specifically for them. Through discussion of self-monitoring techniques, children are implicitly taught that the triggers for anger arousal vary from individual to individual, and from event to event.

One activity in this section includes verbal taunting during a domino-building task. One group member builds a tower for 30 seconds, using one hand, while the others taunt him. Each member receives a turn building a tower, and the highest tower wins. The discussion after the task centered on how hard it was to concentrate on the domino building, how group members kept their attention focused, if they started to feel angry, if the anger hurt their concentration, if the players used self-talk to help them do well, and how anger-management was critical for winning.

In summary, through hierarchical exposure to stimuli of increasing threat, behavioral rehearsal, and group discussion, children are encouraged to develop cognitive and affective self-reflection/self-monitoring strategies for situations involving interpersonal conflict. Children are provided opportunities to write "scripts" including the set of skills and coping strategies they have been developing, and practice these skills through the use of videotapes.

Social Perspective-taking Skills

Research suggests that children with externalizing disorders exhibit egocentric and distorted perceptions of social situations (Chandler, 1973; Dodge, 1980; Lochman, 1987). As noted earlier, these social cognitive deficiencies involve difficulty integrating self- and other-oriented concerns (Lochman et al., in press), overattribution of hostile intent on the part of others (Dodge, 1980), and deficient perspective-taking skills (Kendall, Zupan, & Braswell, 1981). Such maladaptive interpersonal processing places aggressive children at high-risk for dysfunctional social relationships (for example, a child who quickly assumes hostile intent on the part of others may respond to social conflict based on inaccurately perceived threat; a child who has difficulty adopting others' perspectives may quickly disregard others' views or needs, and respond entirely from his or her own vantage point). A series of perspective-taking exercises is presented to address these issues, employing a variety of techniques (structured exercises, role plays, modeling, and group discussion). Perspective-taking instruction attempts to improve children's ability to infer accurately other's thoughts and intentions (cognitive perspective taking), and to enhance their understanding of others' feelings and internal emotional states (affective perspective taking). Children are asked to differentiate individual cognitive and affective processes by identifying similarities and differences between people; by delineating alternative interpretations of social cues; and by generating inferences of what others may be thinking or feeling. For example, a prototypical exercise presents children with an ambiguous picture, asks them to generate independently "stories" about the picture, and engages them in a discussion about differences in their perceptions to the same stimulus. Perspective-taking instruction is routinely provided when children present examples of conflict with peers, teachers, and family members, and is used to address interpersonal conflict as it arises in the group. Thus, this component of the intervention continues throughout the course of the group.

Social Problem-solving Skills

Aggressive children exhibit deficiencies in their ability to resolve interpersonal problems successfully. The anger coping program addresses the deficient problem-solving strategies exhibited by aggressive boys by helping them to identify conflictual situations as problematical, and by encouraging them to increase their repertoire for responding to these situations. A sequential, step-wise model of handling social conflict is presented, including the following three components: problem identification; generation of multiple-response alternatives; and evaluation and prediction of consequences for their actions. A variety of techniques are used to help children learn and implement this model, including modeling, instruction in divergent and consequential thinking, practice generating and elaborating solutions, and behavioral rehearsal. The latter is accomplished through role playing and the use of videotaping, in which children develop scripts for handling conflictual situations and enact them on videotape. Children are encouraged to incorporate into these scripts the personalized menu of anger coping strategies (self-talk, conflict resolution strategies) they have developed over the course of the group. A critical aspect of this instruction involves helping children to identify a potentially problematical situation early on, before it escalates to a point where they are unable to respond adaptively. Children's use of direct action solutions is discouraged and their use of verbal expression, discussion, and negotiation solutions is reinforced. Attention is also placed on identifying how solutions are affected by social goals, how solutions can be competently enacted, and how there is a need to have backup solutions when initial solutions fail or when obstacles arise in the implementation of a solution. In summary, the social problem-solving component provides children with a model for responding to social conflicts, and encourages qualitative and quantitative improvements in their range of coping solutions.

In addition to structured exercises, children also use social problem-solving with the real-life problems they bring into the group. In a recent group session, Bob began talking about an incident that had led to a 5-day suspension from school the prior week. Rather than continue with the scheduled group activity, the bulk of the session was spent in group problem solving about this situation. Bob described how the incident began when he and another boy disagreed over who could sit on a cushion in the library. After a brief exchange of insults took place, the two boys were quiet for the remainder of the library period. However, as the class left the library, Bob got up in the other boy's face and reinitiated the verbal assaults in a more provocative way. When the boy responded with verbal insults, Bob knocked him down and kept hitting him until he was pulled away by the assistant principal. The group discussion included a focus on perspective taking with regard to the other boy's intentions, which did not initially appear to be as purposefully malevolent as Bob had perceived, and with regard to the assistant principal's intentions. In a spirited discussion, the group noted the assistant principal may have been either mean or trying to protect the combatants when he grabbed Bob and swung him around (most group members eventually decided he was trying to be protective). After several other ways of handling the initial "cushion" problem were suggested to Bob, Bob asked each of the group members how they would have handled it. When the group member with the most street-wise demeanor suggested a nonconfrontational solution, Bob tentatively decided to try that strategy in the next conflict. Notable aspects of this discussion included how assaultive incidents often escalate from trivial initial problems, how Bob had great difficulty letting his anger dissipate after the initial provocation, how Bob's anger disrupted his ordinarily adequate social cognitions through pre-emptive processing, and how the group members were instrumental in providing training in social perspective taking and social problem solving.

Process Variables in Anger Coping Program

Three process variables are of central therapeutic importance in the anger coping model: a behavior management system, in which the social microcosm of the group is used to encourage prosocial behavior and to facilitate group cohesiveness; goal-setting activities, which provide a structured vehicle to encourage generalization of treatment effects; and use of the interpersonal "here and now" of the group to encourage development of the context of the group.

Behavior Management System

The primary mechanism for encouraging a "positive peer culture" is early development of group rules and specification of a behavior management system. Children are involved in the process of instituting rules, which allows them to assume psychological ownership of group norms and sensitizes them to aspects of behavior that would interfere with group process. Their participation in developing this shared social contract facilitates group cohesion, and helps to minimize the power struggle that can evolve between adults and conduct-disordered children. Contingency management techniques such as response cost or reward systems (Sulzer & Mayer, 1972) are essential to enable group leaders to shape, maintain, and reinforce desired behavior (participation, prosocial behavior). It is helpful to display group rules at each session, and to provide children with frequent feedback about their behavior (e.g., review number of points earned at the end of each session or periodically during the session). By seeing their peers receive corrective feedback on a regular basis, group members can come to feel less concern about "saving face" when they also are corrected. As children accumulate points to be exchanged for individual and group rewards, they are provided opportunities to delay immediate gratification, often a problem area for disruptive-behavior disordered children. Additionally, group contingencies provide a useful vehicle for further developing group cohesion. With respect to successful implementation of the behavior management system, it is useful to provide children with corrective feedback early on and to provide such feedback in a neutral, matter of fact manner. This early "detoxification" of corrective feedback helps to defuse aggressive children's tendencies to overpersonalize adult feedback and to respond with oppositional or challenging behavior.

Goal Setting

Each week children are encouraged to target a problematical behavior, to set a goal regarding behavior change, and to monitor their ability to meet their goal. Weekly goal sheets are used to help children concretize this process. Goals are selected with input from group leaders, teachers and parents, and individualized treatment goals are developed for each child based on the particular social–cognitive deficits or distortions exhibited by that child. Children are helped to set realistic expectations regarding change in problematical behaviors, and teachers may be contacted to provide external monitoring of children's progress. Goal setting thus provides a structured vehicle to enhance generalization of treatment effects, encourage children to assume responsibility for changing problematical aspects of their behavior, and facilitates the development of self-monitoring skills.

Interpersonal Group Process

The spontaneous interaction that occurs among group members throughout the course of treatment provides an excellent opportunity to assess children's interpersonal styles and deficits, and to identify peer relationship difficulties. Through modeling, coaching, and shaping of their behavior, children can be helped to develop listening skills; interact in a prosocial manner; increase their ability to respond in a verbally assertive manner; and better understand the perspective of their peers. The inevitable tensions that arise among group members, and children's negative reactions to corrective feedback from leaders provide *in vivo* opportunities to work with children on issues of anger control. Thus, in addition to the "cold" processing which occurs in structured exercises and role plays, "hot" processing provides an excellent opportunity to guide children in the use of newly acquired skills, that is, to label anger arousal as it occurs, and to practice the use of anger management techniques. In summary, through the social microcosm of "here and now" group process there is much opportunity for

interpersonal learning through modeling, processing of interpersonal con-
fict, in vivo social skills instruction, and opportunities to practice more
adaptive means of interacting with peers.

Overview of CBT Outcome

In this section, we will briefly overview the results of outcome research
using CBT with aggressive children and of studies examining child and
treatment characteristics which are predictive of treatment outcomes. More
detailed reviews of CBT outcome research with aggressive children and
adolescents are available elsewhere (Kazdin, 1987; Lochman, 1990; Lochman, White, et al., in press; McMahon & Wells, 1989).

Outcome Effects

Early, simple pre- and poststudies indicated that children's aggressive and
disruptive behavior changed following CBT. After studies had indicated
that CBT could help children behave less impulsively on impersonal problem-solving tasks (e.g., Meichenbaum & Goodman, 1971), Goodwin and
Mahoney (1975) developed a similar procedure to modify children's covert
self-statements during a verbal taunting game. The three treated boys had
marked increases in coping responses and improved levels of nondisruptive
classroom behavior. Robin, Schneider, and Dolnick (1976) trained 11 emotionally disturbed children in the turtle technique, which involved imagery
training and social problem solving, and found reductions in aggressive
classroom behavior. Lochman et al., (1981) developed the initial form of
the anger coping program for 12 second- and third-grade aggressive children. The children improved in teachers' daily ratings of on-task behavior,
and ratings of aggressive behavior.

Based on promising findings from pre- and poststudies, more controlled research was begun. These studies can be grouped into those that
had negative, mixed, or generally positive treatment effects. Three studies
have not found changes in aggressive behavior following CBT, although
two of these did produce improvements in the cognitive processes that were
hypothesized to mediate the behavior (Camp, Blom, Herbert, & van Doornick, 1977; Coats, 1979; Dubow, Huesmann, & Eron, 1987). In comparison to a control condition, Camp et al. (1977) found that aggressive second-
grade boys had become less cognitively impulsive and less inattentive and
generated more problem solutions after their involvement in the 6-week
Think Aloud Program. However, teacher-rated aggression did not improve.
Similarly, Coats (1979) found that boys treated in a 2-week intervention
demonstrated better delay of gratification and less verbal aggression, but
they made no gains relative to an attention control group in off-task classroom behavior or in teacher-rated aggression. Dubow et al. (1987) found

that not only did the 5-week cognitive training not produce relative reduction in teacher-rated aggressive behavior, but these treated children were actually rated as more aggressive than an attention-play condition at a 6-month follow-up.

Four studies with mixed findings have found improvements on some, but not all, behavioral measures. Forman's (1980) cognitive restructuring treatment produced reductions in inappropriate classroom behavior, although a response cost procedure was more effective in reducing teachers' ratings of aggressive behavior and classroom disturbance. In a CBT intervention with day-camp children, Kettlewell and Kausch (1983) found that treated children had less self-reported anger, fewer time-out restrictions and improvements in coping self-statements and generation of problem solutions. However, relative to a control condition, these children did not have improvements in counselor or peer-rated aggression. Using brief affective imagery training, Garrison and Stolberg (1983) found that aggressive children became more capable of accurately identifying which situations evoke compound anger, and teacher-observed aggression tended to decrease, but the changes were modest. Finally, in a recent broad-based intervention for black, lower-class, socially rejected children, Coie, Underwood, and Lochman (1990) used a combination of CBT and social-skills training with three annual cohorts. While the first two cohorts of treated children displayed little improvement in comparison to a control condition, the third cohort evidenced more optimistic results. Treated aggressive-rejected children had significantly higher peer ratings for social preference and prosocial behavior by posttreatment, and they tended to have reductions in teachers' ratings of aggression. This year-long, school-based intervention was progressively revised over the 3 cohort years, with the last and most successful intervention year emphasizing more contingency contracting and reframing of who wins in interpersonal conflicts.

Stronger treatment effects have been documented in three programmatic research efforts. Kendall, Ronan, and Epps (in press) adapted their CBT program for use with impulsive children to treat day-hospitalized CD children. Comparing 20 sessions of CBT with a "current conditions' treatment" in a cross-over design, CBT-treated children had improvements in teachers' ratings of children's self-control and prosocial behavior and in children's perceived social competence. However, reductions in cognitive impulsivity were not noted, and the treatment gains that were present at posttreatment did not persist to a 6-month follow-up. In the second programmatic research effort, Kazdin, Esveldt–Dawson, French, and Unis (1987b) used a 20-session problem-solving skills training (PSST) program with psychiatric inpatient children, and did find follow-up effects. Relative to two control conditions, PSST produced significant reductions in parents' and teachers' ratings of aggressive behavior at posttesting and at a 1-year follow-up. These results were replicated in a study which combined PSST with parent behavioral management training (Kazdin, Esveldt–Dawson, French, & Unis, 1987a) and in another recent study using PSST with antisocial children treated in outpatient and inpatient settings (Kazdin, Bass, Siegel, & Thomas, 1989). Treated children in the latter study were behaviorally improved in home and school settings.

The third programmatic series of studies has involved controlled studies of the anger coping program. In comparison with a minimal treatment and untreated control condition, Lochman et al. (1984) found that treated aggressive elementary schoolboys had reductions in independently observed disruptive-aggressive off-task classroom behavior, reduction in parents' ratings of aggression, and improvements in self-esteem. Other ratings by teachers and peers did not show improvement. The posttreatment behavioral improvements in this study have been replicated in subsequent studies (e.g., Lochman & Curry, 1986; Lochman, Lampron, Gemmer, Harris, & Wyckoff, 1989), and gains in classroom on-task behavior have been found in a 7-month follow-up (Lochman & Lampron, 1988). While some maintenance of treatment effects was evident in a 3-year follow-up, these results were mixed (Lochman, in press). In comparison to an untreated condition of aggressive boys, anger coping boys maintained their gains in self-esteem and had significantly lower levels of substance use. On these measures, the treated boys were in the same range as nonaggressive boys at follow-up. However, continued reduction in passive off-task behavior and in parents' ratings of aggression were only evident for anger-coping boys who had received a six-session booster treatment for themselves and their parents during the next schoolyear. Without the booster treatment, the reductions in aggressive behavior were not maintained.

Client and Treatment Characteristics as Predictors of Outcome

While efforts to find which aspects of CBT are most effective with which types of aggressive children are still in rudimentary stages, some initial findings have emerged. Kendall et al. (in press) have found that CBT with conduct-disordered children has been most effective in reducing conduct problems with children who had initially lower perceived levels of hostility and a more internalized attributional style. Lochman et al. (1985) found that boys in the anger coping program who had greatest reductions in aggressive behavior, relative to the control condition, were boys who initially were the poorest social problem solvers. In addition, better outcomes tended to occur for boys with more initial somatization and anxiety behaviors and lower social acceptance from peers, suggesting that these boys may have been more motivated for treatment because of a desire to alleviate distress and decrease peer rejection. Interestingly, those boys in the untreated condition who improved the most spontaneously had better problem-solving skills and higher self-esteem. The differential correlates of improvement for the treated and untreated conditions suggest that the anger coping program was most successful with those boys who were the poorest problem solvers and most in need of intervention.

In studies of treatment characteristics which could augment the effects of the anger coping program, Lochman et al. (1984) have found that inclusion of a behavioral goal-setting component tended to lead to lower aggression and disruptiveness. In this component, boys set weekly goals for themselves in their group meetings, these goals were monitored daily by teachers, and contingent reinforcement occurred for successful goal attainment. Similar evidence for the effectiveness of homework assignments in CBT has been obtained by Kazdin et al (1989). In addition, more widespread improvements in classroom behavior have been noted when the anger coping program was offered in an 18-session format instead of the original 12-session format (Lochman, 1985). We have not found that inclusion of 6 hours of structured teacher consultation (Lochman et al., 1989) or additional training in self-instruction training on nonsocial, academic tasks (Lochman, & Curry, 1986) augments the basic anger coping program's effects.

Implication for CBT Outcome Research

As Kazdin (1987) has noted, these research results present a generally positive and promising view of the effects of CBT with aggressive children. However, because of the mixed posttreatment and follow-up findings, further program development and outcome research is clearly needed. Future outcome research should address the following issues (see also Lochman, 1990): (1) Follow-up assessments in designs that include control conditions and direct behavioral observation measures; (2) Further explore child and treatment characteristics which predict outcome; and (3) More intensive CBT programs for childhood aggression, since research in treatment of chronic behavioral problems should focus on creating clinically meaningful improvement (Kazdin, 1987). More intensive CBT programs can include behavior modification components, longer treatment periods, and behavioral parent training, since all of these treatment components and characteristics have had documented effects on childhood aggression.

Future Direction for CBT: Broader and Earlier Intervention

Based on our review of the literature on cognitive–behavioral assessment and treatment, the following issues appear to be emerging "schematic propositions" that will be evident in the thinking of CBT clinicians and researchers. While we have already proposed a series of specific implications for the development of social–cognitive assessment and CBT research, the three most compelling emerging themes are (1) the inclusion of cognitive–

behavioral parent assessment and therapy, (2) intensification and broadening of CBT program, and (3) increasing focus on primary and secondary prevention.

The most striking deficiency in CBT programs and research with aggressive children up to this point has been the neglect of children's caregivers, especially parents. Intervening with these caregivers can be critical in strengthening treatment effects and in maintaining generalization of treatment effects over time. The best-documented effective treatment for childhood aggression is behavioral parent therapy (Kazdin, 1987; Lochman, 1990; McMahon & Wells, 1989). Behavioral parent training can focus on altering the deficient parenting skills and parental aggressiveness that are so often evident in families of aggressive children, thereby reinforcing the behavioral changes children begin to make in CBT. Behavioral training for teachers could be similarly useful. Perhaps more critically, parent treatment can, over time, promote changes in parents' appraisal distortions and social problem-solving deficiencies. As parents change these pathological patterns in thinking, which are shared by their children, the children can begin responding to the parents and teachers modeling of more adaptive and competent cognitive processes.

A cognitive–behavior therapy program can be broadened by including an emphasis on cognitive schemata and operations, and cognitive appraisal and coping with arousal, as well as social–cognitive products. By focusing on children's social goals, expectations of achieving goals, labeling and coping with affective states and concomitant arousal, we can be impacting key processes which are critical in successful use of self-instruction or social problem solving. To intensify CBT programs, intervention periods can be lengthened to reinforce the changes that are made in social–cognition and behavior. Lengthier treatment also permits the development of closer therapeutic relationships, and it is in the context of these relationships in individual or group therapy that children can begin to examine, trust, and try out others' perceptions of interpersonal events. These perceptual changes are slow in coming, since they involve revisions in internalized styles of attending to and interpreting events. In contrast, social problem-solving skills can be presented as more conscious, deliberate processes, and these skills can alter through role playing and discussion more rapidly. The intensification of treatment can involve use of booster treatment periods, and of more intensely "bunched" treatment, as in day-camp or day treatment settings.

Cognitive–behavior therapy can be easily and effectively adapted for primary and secondary prevention programs (Allen et al., 1976; Coie, Rabiner, & Lochman, 1989; Durlak, 1983; Lochman et al., 1987). To facilitate development of these programs, risk markers (e.g., temperament, parenting skills) for childhood aggression will have to be identified during the preschool and early elementary-school period. With a preventive orientation, CBT-based services can be provided in settings providing a broad access to children (e.g., schools, pediatric clinics, day care, community athletic facilities). Through early identification, and by not having to rely on caregivers' compliance with referrals to clinics, cognitive–behavior therapy can be provided to children and their caregivers at a time when children's self-regulation processes are being internalized.

REFERENCES

Abidin, R. R. (1983). *Parenting Stress Index–Manual*. Charlotteville, VA: Pediatric Psychology Press.

Achenbach, T. M. & Edelbrock, C. S. (1983). *Manual for the Child Behavior Checklist and Revised Child Behavior Profile*. Burlington: University of Vermont, Department of Psychiatry.

Agrawal, R., & Kaushal, K. (1988). Attention and short-term memory in normal children, aggressive children, and nonaggressive children with attention-deficit disorder. *Journal of General Psychology, 114*, 335–343.

Allen, G. J., Chinsky, J. M., Larcen, S. W., Lochman, J. E., & Selinger H. V. (1976). *Community psychology and the schools: A behaviorally oriented multilevel preventative approach*. Hillsdale, NJ: Erlbaum.

Asarnow, J. R., & Callan, J. W. (1985). Boys with peer adjustment problems: Social cognitive processes. *Journal of Consulting and Clinical Psychology, 53*, 80–87.

Bandura, A. (1973) *Aggression: A social learning analysis*. Englewood Cliffs, NJ: Prentice–Hall.

Bandura, A. (1977). *Social learning theory*. Englewood Cliffs, NJ: Prentice–Hall.

Beck, A. T., Rush, A. J., Shaw, B. F., & Emery, G. (1980). *Cognitive therapy of depression*. New York: Guilford Press.

Boldizar, J. P., Perry, D. G., & Perry, L. C. (1989). Outcome values and aggression. *Child Development, 60*, 571–579.

Brain, P. F., (1984). Biological explanations of human aggression and the resulting therapies offered by such approaches. An initial evaluation. In R. J. Blanchard & D. C. Blanchard, (Eds.), *Advances in the study of aggression*. Orlando: Academic Press.

Brion–Meisels, S., & Selman, R. L. (1984). Early adolescent development of new interpersonal strategies: Understanding and intervention, *School Psychology Review, 13*, 278–291.

Brown, A. (1987). Metacognition, executive control, self-regulation and other more mysterious mechanisms. In F. E. Weinert & R. H. Kluve (Eds.), *Metacognition, motivation and understanding*. Hillsdale, NJ: Erlbaum, pp. 65–116.

Camp, B. W., Blom, G. F., Herbert, F., & van Doornick, W. J. (1977). "Think Aloud": A program for developing self-control in young aggressive boys. *Journal of Abnormal Child Psychology, 5*, 157–169.

Chandler, M. J. (1973). Egocentrism and antisocial behavior: The assessment and training of social perspective-taking skills. *Developmental Psychology, 9*, 326–332.

Christiansen, K., & Knussmann, R. (1987). Androgen levels and components of aggressive behavior in men. *Hormones and behavior, 21*, 170–180.

Coats, K. I. (1979). Cognitive self-instructional training approach for reducing disruptive behavior of young children. *Psychological Reports, 44*, 127–134.

Cohen, R., & Schleser, R. (1984). Cognitive development and clinical implications. In A. W. Meyers & W. E. Craighead (Eds.), *Cognitive behavior therapy with children*. New York: Plenum Press, pp. 45–68).

Coie, J. D., Dodge, K. A., & Coppotelli, H. (1982). Dimensions and types of status: A cross-age perspective. *Developmental Psychology, 18*, 557–570.

Coie, J. D. Rabiner, D. L., & Lochman, J. E. (1989). Promoting peer relations in school settings. In L. A. Bond, B. E. Compas, & C. Swift (Eds.), *Prevention in the schools*. Newburg Park, CA: Sage.

Coie, J. D. Underwood, M., & Lochman, J. E. (1990). Preventing intervention with aggressive children in the school setting. In D. J. Pepler & K. H. Rubin (Eds.), *Development and treatment of childhood aggression*. Toronto: L. Erlbuam.

Cole, J. D., Christopoulous, C., Terry, R., Dodge, K. A., & Lochman, J. E. (in press). Types of aggressive relationships, peer rejection and developmental consequences. In B. H. Schneider, C. Attili, J. Nodel, & R. Weissberg (Eds), *Social competence in developmental perspective*. Hingham, MA: Kluwer Press.

Connors, C. K. (1973). Rating scales for use in drug studies with children. *Psychopharmacology Bulletin, 9*, 24–84.

Coopersmith, S. (1967). *Antecedents of self-esteem*. San Francisco: Freeman.

Costello, A. J. Edelbrock, C. S., Dulcan, M. K., & Kalas, R. (1984). *Testing of the NIMH Diagnostic Interview Schedule for Children (DISC) in a clinical population* (Contract No. DB–81–0027, final report to the Center for Epidemiological Studies, National Institute for Mental Health). Pittsburgh: University of Pittsburgh.

Dabbs, J. M., Jr., Jurkovic,v G. L., & Frady, R. L. (1988). *Saliva testosterone and cortisol among young male prison inmates*. Unpublished manuscript, Georgia State University.

Deluty, R. H. (1981). Alternative-thinking ability of aggressive, assertive, and submissive children. *Cognitive Therapy and Research, 5*, 309–312.

Dix, T., & Lochman, J. E. (in press). Social cognition and negative reactions to children: A comparison of mothers of aggressive and nonaggressive boys. *Journal of Social and Clinical Psychology*.

Dodge, K. A. (1980). Social cognition and children's aggressive behavior. *Child Development, 51*, 162–170.

Dodge, K. A. (1985). Attributional bias in aggressive children. In P. C. Kendall (Ed.), *Advances in cognitive–behavioral research and therapy* (Vol. 4). New York: Academic Press.

Dodge, K. A. (1986). A social information processing model of social competence in children. In M. Perlmutter (Ed.), *The Minnesota Symposia on Child Psychology: Vol. 18. Cognitive perspectives on children's social and behavioral development* (pp. 77–125). Hillsdale, NJ: Erlbaum.

Dodge, K. A., Coie, J. D., & Brakke, N. P. (1982). Behavior patterns of socially rejected and neglected preadolescents: The roles of social approach and aggression. *Journal of Abnormal Child Psychology, 10*, 389–410.

Dodge, K. A., & Frame, C. L. (1982), Social cognitive biases and deficits in aggressive boys. *Child Development, 53*, 620–635.

Dodge, K. A., & Newman, J. P. (1981). Biased decision-making processes in aggressive boys. *Journal of Abnormal Psychology, 90,* 375–379.

Dodge, K. A. Pettit, G. S., McClaskey, C. L., & Brown, M. M. (1986). Social competence in children. *Monographs of the Society for Research in Child Development, 51* (2, Serial No. 213).

Dodge, K. A., & Somberg, D. R. (1987). Hostile attributional biases among aggressive boys are exacerbated under conditions of threat to the self. *Child Development, 58,* 213–224.

Dubow, E. F., Huesmann, L. R., & Eron, L. D. (1987). Mitigating aggression promoting pro-social behavior in aggressive elementary schoolboys. *Behavior Research and Therapy, 25,* 527–531.

Durlak, J. A. (1983). Social problem-solving as a primary prevention strategy. In R. D. Felner, L. A. Jason, J. N. Moritsugu, & S. S. Farber (Eds.), *Prevention psychology: Theory research and practice* (pp. 31–48). New York: Pergamon Press.

Edelman, E. M., & Goldstein, A. P. (1981). Moral education. In A. P. Goldstein, E. G., Carr, W. S. Davidson III, & P. Mohr (Eds.), *In response to aggression: Methods of control and prosocial alternatives.* New York: Pergamon Press, pp. 253–315.

Eisenberg, N., & Miller, P. A. (1987). The relation of empathy to prosocial and related behaviors. *Psychological Bulletin, 101,* 91–119.

Emery, R., & O'Leary, D. (1982). Children's perceptions of marital discord and behavior of boys and girls. *Journal of Abnormal Child Psychology, 10,* 11–24.

Eyberg, S. M. (1980). Eyberg Child Behavior Inventory, *Journal of Clinical Child Psychology, 9,* 29.

Feshbach, N. D., & Feshbach, S. (1982). Empathy training and the relation of aggression: Potentialities and limitations. *Academic Psychology Bulletin, 4,* 399–413.

Forehand, R., & Long, N. (1988). Outpatient treatment of the acting out child: Procedures, long term follow-up data, land clinical problems. *Advances in Behaviour Research and Therapy, 10,* 129–177.

Forehand, R. L., & McMahon, R. J. (1981). *Helping the noncompliant child: A clinician's guide to parent training.* New York: Guilford Press.

Forman, S. G. (1980). A comparison of cognitive training and response cost procedures in modifying aggressive behavior of elementary school children. *Behavior Therapy, 11,* 94–600.

Garrison, S. R., & Stolberg, A. L. (1983). Modification of anger in children by affective imagery training. *Journal of Abnormal Child Psychology, 11,* 115–130.

Gesten, J. C., Langer, T. S., Eisenberg, J. G., Simcha–Fagan, D., & McCarthy, E. D. (1976). Stability and change in types of behavioral disturbance of children and adolescents. *Journal of Abnormal Child Psychology 4,* 111–127.

Goodwin, S. F., & Mahoney, J. J. (1975). Modification of aggression through modeling: An experimental probe. *Journal of Behavior Therapy and Experimental Psychiatry, 6,* 200–202.

Gordon, S. E., Lochman, J. E., & Ribordy, S. C. (1986). *A comparative study of cognitive impulsivity, attribution, and problem-solving in aggressive and nonaggressive latency-aged boys.* Unpublished manuscript, Georgetown University, Washington, D.C.

Harter, S. (1985). *The Self-Perception Profile for Children: Revision of the Perceived Competence Scale for Children* (manual), University of Denver.

Hodges, V. K. (1987). Assessing children with a clinical research interview: The Child Assessment Schedule. In R. J. Priz (Ed.), *Advances in Behavioral Assessment of Children and Families.* Greenwich, CT: JAI Press.

Huesmann, L. R., Eron, L. D., Lefkowitz, M. M., & Walder, L. O. (1984). Stability of aggression over time and generations. *Developmental Psychology, 20,* 1120–1134.

Hughes, J. N. (1988). *Cognitive behavior therapy with children in schools.* New York: Pergamon Press.

Ingram, R. E., & Kendall, P. C., (1986). Cognitive clinical psychology: Implications of an informational processing perspective. In R. E. Ingram (Ed.), *Information processing approaches to clinical psychology.* New York: Academic, pp. 3–21.

Jurkovic, G., & Prentice, N. M. (1977). Relation of moral and cognitive development to dimensions of juvenile delinquency. *Journal of Abnormal Psychology, 86,* 414–420.

Kandel, D. B. (1982). Epidemiological and psychosocial perspectives in adolescent drug abuse. *Journal of the American Academy of Child Psychiatry, 21,* 328–347.

Kanfer, F. H. (1970). Self-regulation: Research, issues and speculations. In C. Neuringer & J. L. Michael (Eds.), *Behavior modification in clinical psychology.* New York: Appleton–Century–Crofts.

Kazdin, A. E. (1987). Treatment of antisocial behavior in children: Current status and future directions. *Psychological Bulletin, 102,* 187–203.

Kazdin, A. E., Bass, D., Siegel, T., & Thomas, C. (1989). Cognitive–behavioral therapy and relationship therapy in the treatment of children referred for antisocial behavior. *Journal of Consulting and Clinical Psychology. 57,* 522–535.

Kazdin, A. E., & Esveldt–Dawson, K. (1986). The Interview for Antisocial Behavior: Psychometric characteristics and concurrent validity with child psychiatric inpatients. *Journal of Psychopathology and Behavioral Assessment, 8,* 289–303.

Kazdin, A. E., Esveldt–Dawson, K., French, N. H., & Unis, A. S. (1987a). Effects of parent management training and problem-solving skills training combined in the treatment of antisocial child behavior. *Journal of the American Academy of Child and Adolescent Psychiatry, 26,* 416–424.

Kazdin, A. E., Esveldt–Dawson, K., French, N. H., & Unis, A. S. (1987b). Problem-solving skills training and relationship therapy in the treatment of antisocial child behavior. *Journal of Consulting and Clinical Psychology, 55,* 76–85.

Kendall, P. C. (1985). Toward a cognitive–behavioral model of child psychopathology and a critique of related interventions. *Journal of Abnormal Child Psychology, 13,* 357–372.

Kendall, P. C., & Braswell, L. (1985). *Cognitive–behavioral therapy for impulsive children.* New York: Guilford Press.

Kendall, P. C., & Fischler, G. L. (1984). Behavioral and adjustment correlates of problem-solving: Validational analyses of interpersonal cognitive problem-solving measures. *Child Development, 55,* 879–892.

Kendall, P. C., & Ingram, R. E. (1989). Cognitive behavioral perspective: Theory and research. In P. C. Kendall & D. Watson (Eds.), *Anxiety & depression: Distinctive and overlapping features.* New York: Academic Press.

Kendall, P. C., Ronan, K. R., & Epps, J. (in press). Aggression in children-adolescents: Cognitive–behavioral treatment perspectives. In D. Popler & K. Rubin (Eds.), *Development and treatment of childhood aggression.* Toronto: Erlbaum.

Kendall, P. C., Zupan, B. A., & Braswell, L. (1981). Self-control in children: Further analyses of the Self Control Rating Scale. *Behavior Therapy, 12,* 667–681.

Kettlewell, P. W., & Kausch, D. F. (1983). The generalization of the effects of a cognitive–behavioral treatment program for aggressive children. *Journal of Abnormal Child Psychology, 11,* 101–114.

Kopp, C. B. (1987). The growth of self-regulation: Caregivers and children. In N. Eisenberg (Ed.), *Contemporary topics in developmental psychology.* New York: Wiley.

Laney, B. B., Green, K. E., & Forehand, R. (1980). On the independence of ratings of hyperactivity, conduct problems, and attention deficits in children: A multiple regression analysis. *Journal of Consulting and Clinical Psychology, 48,* 566–574.

Larrance, D. T., & Twentyman, C. T. (1983). Maternal attributions and child abuse. *Journal of Abnormal Psychology, 92,* 449–457.

Lochman, J. E. (1984). Psychological characteristics and assessment of aggressive adolescents. In C. R. Keith, (Ed.), *The aggressive adolescent: Clinical perspectives* (pp. 17–62). New York: Free Press.

Lochman, J. E. (1985). Effects of different treatment lengths in cognitive behavioral interventions with aggressive boys. *Child Psychiatry and Human Development, 16,* 45–56.

Lochman, J. E. (1987). Self and peer perceptions and attributional biases of aggressive and nonaggressive boys in dyadic interactions. *Journal of Consulting and Clinical Psychology, 55,* 404–410.

Lochman, J. E. (1988, September). *Long-term efficacy of cognitive behavioral interventions with aggressive boys.* Paper presented to the World Congress on Behavior Therapy, Edinburgh, Scotland.

Lochman, J. E. (1989, February) *Hardware versus software: Land of deficiency in social-cognitive processes of aggressive boys.* Paper presented at the first annual meeting of the Society for Research in Child and Adolescent Psychopathology, Miami.

Lochman, J. E. (1990). Modification of childhood aggression. In M. Hersen, R. Eisler, & P. M. Miller (Eds.), *Progress in behavior modification* (Vol. 25). Newbury Park, CA: Sage.

Lochman, J. E., Burch, P. R., Curry, J. F., & Lampron, L. B. (1984). Treatment and generalization effects of cognitive–behavioral and goal-setting interventions with aggressive boys. *Journal of Consulting and Clinical Psychology, 52,* 915–916.

Lochman, J. E., & Curry, J. F. (1986). Effects of social problem-solving training and self-instruction training with aggressive boys, *Journal of Clinical Child Psychology, 15,* 159–164.

Lochman, J. E., & Dodge, K. A. (1990, January). *Dysfunctional family and social-cognitive process with aggressive boys.* Paper presented at the annual meeting of the Society for Research in Child and Adolescent Psychopathology, Costa Mesa, CA.

Lochman, J. E., & Lampron, L. B. (1985). The usefulness of peer ratings of aggressive and social acceptance in the identification of behavioral and subjective difficulties in aggressive boys. *Journal of Applied Developmental Psychology, 6,* 187–198.

Lochman, J. E., & Lampron, L. B. (1986). Situational social problem-solving skills and self-esteem of aggressive and nonaggressive boys. *Journal of Abnormal Child Psychology, 14*, 605–617.

Lochman, J. E., & Lampron, L. B. (1988). Cognitive behavioral interventions for aggressive boys: Seven months follow-up effects. *Journal of Child and Adolescent Psychotherapy, 5*, 15–23.

Lochman, J. E., Lampron, L. B., Burch, P. R., & Curry, J. F. (1985). Client characteristics associated with behavior change for treated and untreated boys. *Journal of Abnormal Child Psychology, 13*, 527–538.

Lochman, J. E., Lampron, L. B., Gemmer, T. V., & Harris, R. (1987). In P. A. Keller & S. R. Heyman (Eds.), *Innovations in clinical practice: A source book* (Vol. 6). Sarasota FL: Professional Resource Exchange.

Lochman, J. E., Lampron, L. B., Gemmer, T. C., Harris, R., & Wyckoff, G. M. (1989). Teacher consultation and cognitive–behavioral interventions with aggressive boys. *Psychology in the Schools, 26*, 179–188.

Lochman, J. E., Lampron, L. B., & Rabiner, D. L. (1989). Format and salience effects in the social problem-solving of aggressive and nonaggressive boys. *Journal of Clinical Child Psychology, 18*, 230–236.

Lochman, J. E., Meyer, B. L., Rabiner, D. L., & White, K. J. (in press). Parameters influencing social problem-solving of aggressive children. In R. Prinz (Ed.), *Advances in behavioral assessment of children and families* (Vol. 5). Greenwich, CT: JAI Press.

Lochman, J. E., Nelson, W. M., III, & Sims, J. P. (1981). A cognitive behavioral program for use with aggressive children. *Journal of Clinical Child Psychology, 13*, 527–538.

Lochman, J. E., Wayland, K., & Cohen, C. (1990, August). *Prediction of adolescent behavioral problems for subtypes of aggressive boys.* Paper presented at the American Psychological Association Annual Convention, Boston.

Lochman, J. E., & White, K. J. (1989, March). *Social problem-solving deficits of aggressive boys.* Paper presented at the annual meeting of the American Association of Psychiatric Service for Children, Durham, NC.

Lochman, J. E., White, K. J., Curry, J. F., & Rumer, R. (in press). Antisocial behavior. In V. B. Van Hasselt & D. J. Kolko (Eds.), *Inpatient behavior therapy for children and adolescents:* New York: Plenum Press.

Locke, H. J., & Wallace, K. M. (1959). Short marital adjustment and prediction tests: Their reliability and validity. *Marriage and Family Living, 21*, 251–255.

Loeber, R., & Dishion, T. J. (1983). Early predictors of male delinquency: A review. *Psychological Bulletin, 94*, 68–99.

Loeber, R., & Schmaling, K. B. (1985). Empirical evidence for overt and covert patterns of antisocial conduct problems: A meta-analysis. *Journal of Abnormal Child Psychology, 13*, 337–352.

Lubin, B. (1967). *Manual for the Depression Adjective Check List.* San Diego: Educational and Industrial Testing Service.

McMahon, R. J., & Forehand, R. (1988). Conduct disorder. In E. J. Mash & L. G. Terdal (Eds.), *Behavioral assessment of childhood disorders* (2nd ed.). New York. Guilford Press, pp. 105–153.

McMahon, R. J., & Wells, K. C. (1989). Conduct disorders. In E. J. Mash &

R. A. Barkley (Eds.), *Treatment of childhood disorders*. New York: Guilford Press, pp. 73–134.

Meichenbaum, D. (1985), *Stress inoculation training*. New York: Pergamon Press.

Meichenbaum, D. H., & Goodman, J. (1971). Training impulsive children to talk to themselves: A means of developing self control. *Journal of Abnormal Psychology, 77*, 115–126.

Meyers, A. W., & Craighead, W. E. (1984). Cognitive behavior therapy with children: A historical, conceptual, and organizational overview. In A. W. Meyers & W. E. Craighead (Eds.), *Cognitive behavior therapy with children*. New York: Plenum Press, pp. 1–18.

Milich, R., & Dodge, K. A. (1984). Social information processing in child psychiatric populations. *Journal of Abnormal Child Psychology, 12*, 471–490.

Miller, P. A., & Eisenberg, N. (1988). The relation of empathy to aggressive and externalizing/antisocial behavior. *Psychological Bulletin, 103*, 324–344.

Mirsky, A. F. (August, 1989). *The neuropsychology of attention: Developmental neuropsychiatric implications*. Paper presented at the 97th annual convention of the American Psychological Association, New Orleans.

Nasby, W., Hayden, B., & DePaulo, B. M. (1980). Attributional bias among aggressive boys to interpret unambiguous social stimuli as displays of hostility. *Journal of Abnormal Psychology, 11*, 257–272.

Novaco, R. W. (1978). Anger and coping with stress: Cognitive–behavioral intervention. In J. P. Foreyet & D. P. Rathjen (Eds.), *Cognitive behavioral therapy: Research and application*. New York: Plenum Press.

Nucci, L. P., & Herman, S. (1982). Behavior disordered children's conceptions of moral, conventional, and personal issues. *Journal of Abnormal Child Psychology, 10*, 411–426.

Olweus, D. (1979). Stability of aggressive behavior patterns in males: A review. *Psychological Bulletin, 86*, 852–875.

Olweus, D. (1984). Development of stable aggressive reaction patterns in males. In R. J. Blanchard & D. C. Blanchard (Eds.), *Advances in the study of aggression*. New York: Academic Press.

Olweus, D., Mattsson, A., Schalling, D., & Low, H. (1980). Testosterone, aggression, physical and personality dimensions in normal adolescent males. *Psychosomatic Medicine, 42*, 253–269.

Patterson, G. R. (1986). Performance models for antisocial boys. *American Psychologist, 41*, 432–444.

Patterson, G. R., & Bank, L. (1986). Bootstrapping your way in the nomological thicket. *Behavioral Assessment, 8*, 49–73.

Perry, D. G., Perry, L. C., & Rasmussen, P. (1986). Cognitive social learning medicators of aggression. *Child Development, 57*, 700–711.

Platt, J. J., Spivack, G., Altman, N., Altman, D., & Peizer, S. B. (1974). Adolescent problem solving thinking. *Journal of Consulting and Clinical Psychology, 42*, 787–793.

Porter, B., & O'Leary, K. D. (1980). Marital discord and child behavior problems. *Journal of Abnormal Child Psychology, 8*, 287–295.

Quay, H. C., & Peterson, D. R. (1983). *Interim manual for the Revised Behavior Problem Checklist*. Unpublished manuscript, University of Miami.

Rabiner, D., Lenhart, L., & Lochman, J. E. (in press). Automatic versus reflective social problem-solving in popular, average, and rejected children. *Developmental Psychology*.

Richard, B. A., & Dodge, K. A. (1982). Social maladjustment and problem-solving in school-aged children. *Journal of Consulting and Clinical Psychology, 50,* 226–233.

Robin, A. L., Schneider, M., & Dolnick, M. (1976). The turtle technique: an extended case study of self-control in the classroom. *Psychology in the Schools, 73,* 449–453.

Robins, L. N. (1978). Sturdy childhood predictors of adult antisocial behavior: Replications from longitudinal studies. *Psychological Medicine, 8,* 611–622.

Rodick, J. D., Henggeler, S. W., & Hanson, C. L. (1986). An evaluation of family adaptability and cohesion evaluation scales and the circumplex model. *Journal of Abnormal Child Psychology, 14,* 77–87.

Rose, S. D., & Edleson, J. L. (1987). *Working with Children and Adolescent in Groups*. San Francisco/London: Jossey–Bass.

Rotter, J. B., Chance, J. E., & Phares, E. J. (1972). *Applications of a social learning theory of personality*. New York: Holt, Rinehart, & Winston.

Santostefano, S., & Roder. C. (1984). Cognitive controls and aggression in children: The concept of cognitive–affective balance. *Journal of Consulting and Clinical Psychology, 52,* 46–56.

Sines, J. O., Pauker, J. D., Sines, L. K., & Owen, D. R. (1969). Identification of clinically relevant dimensions of children's behavior. *Journal of Consulting and Clinical Psychology, 33,* 728–734.

Slaby, R. G., & Guerra, N. G. (1988). Cognitive mediators of aggression in adolescent offenders: 1. Assessment. *Developmental Psychology, 24*(4), 580–588.

Spanier, G. B. (1976). Measuring dyadic adjustment: New scales for assessing the quality of marriage and similar dyads. *Journal of Marriage and the Family, 38,* 15–28.

Steinberg, M. D., & Dodge, K. A. (1983). Attributional bias in aggressive adolescent boys and girls. *Journal of Social and Clinical Psychology, 1,* 312–321.

Straus, M. A. (1979). Measuring intrafamily conflict and violence: The Conflict Tactics (CT) Scales. *Journal of Marriages and the Family, 41,* 79–88.

Sulzer, B., & Mayer, G. R. (1972). *Behavior modification procedures for school personnel*. Hinsdale, IL: Dryden.

Vygotsky, L. S. (1978). *Mind in society: The development of higher psychological processes.* (M. Cole, V. John–Steiner, S. Scribner, & E. Souberman, Eds. and Trans.). Cambridge, MA: Harvard University Press.

Wayland, K. K., Schoenwald, S. K., & Lochman, J. E. (1989, August). *Marital adjustment, family conflict and children's perceptions of marital discord*. Paper presented at the American Psychological Association Annual Convention, New Orleans, LA.

Werry, J. S., Elkind, G. S., & Reeves, J. C. (1987). Attention Deficit, Conduct, Oppositional, and Anxiety Disorders in Children: III. Laboratory differences. *Journal of Abnormal Child Psychology, 15,* 409–428.

CHAPTER 3

Cognitive Strategies in Anger Control Interventions for Children and Adolescents

EVA L. FEINDLER
Long Island University

The antisocial behavior of children and adolescents presents a significant challenge to the clinical community. Prevalence rates of aggressive behaviors and criminal acts are high, and conduct disorders in childhood and adolescence portend problems in adulthood (Kazdin, 1987). Further, aggression in children, if untreated, appears stable over time (Olweus, 1979) and results in significant social adjustment difficulties. Since cognitive processes, such as attributions, self-statements, and problem-solving skills, play a major role in the development of anger and the sometimes resultant aggressive response to provocation (Novaco, 1986), and since the correlated social and problem-solving skills deficiencies of antisocial children and adolescents have been documented, cognitive–behavioral anger control training programs for such children and adolescents have been developed.

Novaco's (1975) cognitive–behavioral conceptualization of anger and anger control problems functions as the basis for the anger control procedures described by Feindler and her colleagues (1984, 1986). Based on Meichenbaum's (1975) stress inoculation model, Novaco (1985) identifies anger as a stress reaction with three response components: cognitive, physiological, and behavioral. The cognitive component is characterized by one's perception of social stimuli and provocation cues in the social context, interpretation of these stimuli, attributions concerning causality and/or responsibility, and by one's evaluation of oneself and the situation. This component represents the most significant area for intervention with aggressive adolescents as their perceptions and attitudes serve to prompt most behavioral responses to provocation. In addition to cognitive deficits and distortions, aggressive adolescents display high states of emotional and physiological arousal, as well as other social and self-control skill deficits.

Recent reformulations of the frustration–aggression hypothesis indicate that the cognitive aspects of the hypothesis need further emphasis (Berkowitz, 1989). Indeed, Dodge (1985) has indicated that this hypothesis would benefit from the incorporation of key social information-processing concepts. His studies of attributional bias have demonstrated that the individual's perception of whether one's goals have been thwarted and how they have been thwarted are critical to the prediction of an aggressive reaction. Further, Dodge (1985) has postulated specific cognitive deficiencies and distortions (Kendall, Chapter 1, this volume; Kendall, Ronan, & Epps, 1990) that characterize aggressive children and adolescents and are targeted for remediation in current anger control programs.

Finally, recent evidence from developmental psychology points to cognitive schemata as a key ingredient in the development of stable behavior patterns. As Olweus (1984) and others (Huesmann, Eron, Lefkowitz, & Walder, 1984) have indicated, children who display angry and aggressive behavior patterns are quite likely as adults to display aggression more frequently and more intensely. In a follow-up study of 600 subjects Huesmann et al. (1984) found early aggressiveness in school to be predictive of later, serious antisocial behavior, including criminal behavior, spouse abuse, traffic violations, and self-reported physical aggression. Slaby and Guerra (1988) suggest that these aggressive behavior patterns might be changed by addressing those cognitive factors (i.e., beliefs, attributions, and moral judgments) they may play a central organizing role in social–emotional development.

This chapter will review the recent research on the faulty perceptions, biases, and beliefs of aggressive children and adolescents, and current anger control interventions as they apply to adolescents and their families. Particular attention will be paid to cognitive deficits and distortions that have been identified and treatment strategies that directly target misattributions, misperceptions, and poor problem solving. Anger control strategies designed to effect change in the physiological and behavioral components will be briefly described in a detailed case study (see also Feindler, in press, for a detailed discussion). Recommendations for future research and clinical intervention in the areas of generalization enhancement, diagnostic decision making, and cultural diversity will also be made.

COGNITIVE INTERVENTIONS

According to Novaco's (1975) original conceptualization, anger arousal is meditated by the individual's expectations and appraisals of a provoking event and surrounding context. Others have noted that the key cognitive processes of memory and attribution are instrumental in anger arousal and the elicitation of aggression (Baron, 1983). Therefore, an understanding of the cognitive processing deficiencies and distortions of aggressive youth will help identify appropriate and effective treatment strategies (Kendall et al., 1990). Although there has been little research documenting cognitive processing difficulties in adolescents, a review of the literature suggests specific deficits and biases that influence anger and aggressive behavior. Indeed, to account for the stability of aggressive behavior patterns, Eron (1987) has hypothesized that as children mature, their patterns of aggression are governed to an increasing extent by internalized and habitual patterns of cognition. It would seem that self-instruction training and cognitive restructuring forms could be used to target each cognitive deficit and distortion outlined below.

Deficits in Social Information Processing

One factor influencing the aggressive responses of angry adolescents may be the absence of inhibitory or self-control statements. Typically, these youth respond impulsively in social situations with little reflection about the context or possible alternate response. In hypothetical problem-solving situations, aggressive youths have generated fewer effective solutions and fewer potential consequences (Asarnow & Callan, 1985). Clearly, the remediation of these deficits would include discrete problem-solving training similar to that developed by Kendall (*Stop and Think Workbook*, 1989) and Camp (*Think Aloud*, 1977), and to that conceptualized by D'Zurilla and Goldfried (1971). The stages of problem solving that Feindler and Ecton (1986) have incorporated into their anger control training program include:

1. Problem definition: "What is a problem?"—Youths are prompted to identify the antecedent stimuli, including provoking stimulus, situational variables, and internal anger cues.
2. Generation of alternative solutions: "What can I do?"—This phase requires individuals to brainstorm all of the possible responses to the problem situation. This process precludes the evaluation or critique of any response generated to a later time.
3. Consequence evaluation: "What will happen if. . . ?"—Youths are prompted to identify the most probable consequences occurring subsequent to each of the responses generated in Phase 2. Both positive and negative consequences and both long- and short-term ones are delineated.
4. Choosing a problem solution: "What will I do?"—Youths are asked to rank all solutions according to the desirability–undesirability or severity of the consequences described above. The ideal choice is

the solution that optimizes positive consequences, minimizes negative consequences, and solves the problem.

5. Feedback: "How did it work?"—The final step is this problem-solving procedure involving the evaluation of the solution based on its effectiveness in solving the problem. If the selected solution has not been effective, the second choice solution is then implemented.

Distortions in Social Information Processing

In addition to deficits in appropriate cognitions, aggressive children and adolescents display active information processing that is irrational, illogical, or distorted in some manner (Kendall et al., 1989). These distortions seem directly related to anger arousal and aggressive responding and require direct intervention.

Hostility Bias

Dodge (1985) hypothesized that the persistently aggressive child is biased toward interpreting events in his or her world as evidence that peers (and others) are hostile and that any provocation cue will be a conditioned stimulus to respond with retaliatory aggression. This perceptual distortion may prompt the aggressive youth to view neutral events as provoking and to interpret those events as direct attacks. Additional aspects of this hostility bias include the incomplete utilization of environmental cues, selective attention to aggressive cues, and overattribution of hostile intent (Kendall et al., 1990). If adolescents seek less information that might aid them in appropriate attributions and problem solving, then self-instructions that prompt information seeking or attention to other cues could be taught. These might include:

"Is there anything else I could consider?"
"What might be another reason for his behavior?"

If aggressive adolescents attend more to aggressive environmental cues than nonaggressive cues, then self-instructions to discount aggressive cues and to enhance nonaggressive cues could be taught:

"They don't mean to criticize, they just don't understand the situation."

Finally, if the adolescent's hostile attribution bias reflects a tendency to "assume the worst" regarding the intentions of peers (or others) in neutral situations, self-instructions could emphasize positive or neutral intentions.

In fact, adolescents could be taught to make a "forgiving" or "accidental" interpretation as in the following example.

"He probably didn't mean it, but was just trying to get my attention."
"He couldn't have meant to start with me—he must be joking!"

A change in the adolescent's attributions that may be related to anger arousal could be achieved by drawing attention to informational cues that have not been considered previously and are not inconsistent with their current inferences (Hayes & Hesketh, 1989).

Beliefs about the Legitimacy of Aggression and Retaliation

In their work with adolescent offenders, Slaby and Guerra (1988) have emphasized cognitive content in the form of generalized beliefs that represent adopted standards of conduct supporting the use of aggression. In order to assess these beliefs, Slaby and Guerra (1988) administered a hypothetical, social problem-solving measure and a beliefs measure to three groups of adolescents. One group of antisocial adolescents were incarcerated at a state correctional facility, while the other groups were comprised of high school students rated as either high aggressive or low aggressive by their teachers. The Beliefs Measure consisted of 18 statements that assessed the following: the legitimacy of aggression, and the notions that aggression increase self-esteem, that aggression helps to avoid a negative image, that victims deserve aggression, and that victims don't suffer.

In general, results indicated that high levels of aggression were associated with poor problem-solving skills and high endorsement of beliefs-supporting aggression. An interesting result, however, was that violent juvenile offenders differed from both groups of high school students on the belief that victims deserve aggression, but the findings were in the unexpected direction. In fact, violent juvenile offenders were *least* likely to hold this belief. Perhaps this can be explained by the likelihood that incarcerated, antisocial youth, in addition to being perpetuators of violence, have also frequently been victims themselves (Fagan, 1988).

In terms of sex differences, Slaby and Guerra (1988) report that males were more inclined than were females to hold beliefs supporting aggression, were more likely to base problem definitions and goal selection on the perception that the other was a hostility-motivated adversary, and were less likely to seek information that would disconfirm this perception. Interestingly, females were more likely than were males to hold beliefs that victims deserve to be victimized. The data from this assessment study raise the possibility that cognitive factors representing habitual patterns of cognitive mediation that underlie aggression may serve to differentiate and stabilize an individual's use of aggression in particular situations (Slaby & Guerra, 1988). However, before the connection between these beliefs and actual aggressive responding could be defined, this investigation would need replication with measurement of actual rates of aggressive responding. It is still unclear how these biases and beliefs influence the natural occurrence of aggressive behavior.

As a follow-up, Guerra and Slaby (in press) designed a 12-session, cognitive-mediation program for incarcerated adolescent offenders in order to effect change in these underlying beliefs hypothesized to be related to aggression. In small groups, 20 males and 20 females received social problem-solving and self-control training. The control of impulsive responding was presented as a precursor to searching for relevant information, setting goals, and searching for alternative solutions. In order to modify the beliefs supporting aggression, attitude change techniques (whereby youth were asked to develop arguments reflecting particular social beliefs and to present those arguments orally) were used. For example, an adolescent might be asked to refute a specific statement endorsing the use of aggression (e.g., "If a small child is screaming and won't stop, it's a good idea to slap him or her hard.") Pre- and postintervention results indicated that, compared with offenders in the control groups, treatment subjects showed improved social problem solving, a reduction in their endorsement of beliefs supporting aggression, and decreases in staff ratings of problem behaviors within the institution. These results are quite positive; however, there were no significant group differences in subsequent parole violations, which raises questions about the generalization and maintenance of the treatment gains. Since the data indicate that an endorsement of general beliefs supporting the use of aggression influences and aggressive responding, it is necessary to address these beliefs in any comprehensive anger control training program and perhaps incorporate attitude change procedures.

Legitimacy of Retaliation

Related to the cognitive distortions already outlined is the belief that victims have the right to strike back. Ferguson and Rule (1983) have hypothesized that the degree of anger and subsequent hostile retaliation in response to perceived insult, attack, or frustration depend on attributions related to the initial provocation cues. Anger is greater than the provocation is seen as intentional, foreseeable, and perpetuated for socially unacceptable reasons. In an investigation of children's evaluations of retaliatory aggression, Ferguson and Rule (1988) presented four types of provocation stories to 72 elementary-school children. These types were: (1) *accidental:* in which initial harm was neither intended or avoidable; (2) *foreseeable:* harm that was unintended but avoidable; (3) *justifiably intended:* harm that was intended but acceptably motivated; (4) *unjustifiably intended:* harm that was intended and unacceptably motivated. Children were asked to rate the aggressor's intentionality, the avoidability of the event, and the acceptability of motives, the victim's reaction, and to decide if the initial provocation was fair and deserved. The results indicated that the legitimacy of retaliation is not an inverse function of the initial aggressor's causal responsibility, but rather, retaliation, in response to provocation that is perceived as unjustifiably intended, is judged as the *most* legitimate. In contrast, retaliation against a provocation that is seen as justifiably intended is judged by children as the *least* legitimate. Finally, accidental aggression was seen as less intentional and less avoidable than foreseeable aggression which was, in turn, seen as less intentional and less avoidable than justifiably intended or unjustifiably intended aggression (Ferguson & Rule, 1988). Clearly, the initial perceptions of a provocation and the attributions one makes concerning intentionality and motivation contribute to an internal justification for aggressive responding.

In another study, Lochman (1987) assessed differences in self-perceptions, peer perceptions, and attributions of relative responsibility for 20 aggressive and 18 nonaggressive elementary-school boys during a competitive dyadic discussion. The results indicated that aggressive boys displayed different attributional processes about perceived aggression than did nonaggressive boys in actual social situations. Lochman (1987) hypothesized that during the initial behavior exchange, aggressive boys may begin to place the responsibility for any conflict or disagreement on a peer (other blame), thus justifying subsequent aggression toward the blamed peer if the conflict escalates. In contrast, nonaggressive boys tend to assume greater responsibility for aggression in the early stages of conflict and this attribution of greater self-blame may motivate their efforts to modulate their expression of hostility.

Each of these perceptions of the initial aggressor's causal responsibility would seem to be further enhanced by a hostility bias, leading the aggressive youth to perceive many more events as provocative, intentional, and the other's fault. If these cognitive distortions or misattributions lead to verbal and physical aggression, specific cognitive restructuring techniques must be emphasized to realign these attributions more appropriately. Since anger is greatest when the adolescent views the provocation as intentional, foreseeable, and initiated for unacceptable reasons, coping states could directly target these misperceptions.

"It's not anyone's fault."

"He can't help himself."

"He didn't mean to do it."

"Accidents can happen."

"He doesn't have the brains to plan something like this out."

Or perhaps, the adolescent can be taught to make attributions about causation by viewing the characteristics of the situation, rather than personal characteristics of the provoker.

"He must be as fed up with this place as I am."
"The pressure must be getting to him."
"Everyone who is in this place seems uptight."
"He's just trying to get the teacher's attention."

Further, Baron (1983) suggests that cognitive interventions designed to lessen the recall of anger-inducing events or situations, to shift attributions toward external causes, and to provide explanations stressing mitigating circumstances may prove effective in the reduction of anger and aggression. There is promising evidence from laboratory research indicating that if provocative actions by another person stem from circumstances beyond that person's control, rather than from his or her traits, intentions, or motives (e.g., Zillman & Cantor, 1976), aggressive arousal is reduced; however, investigation with clinical populations is required.

Finally, although perhaps difficult to achieve, it would be beneficial if the adolescent could reinterpret the onset of the initial provocation event. An adolescent who assumes some self-responsibility may use this reinterpretation to mediate anger arousal. In fact, children who evidence an internal locus of control seem to have a better response to cognitive–behavioral interventions for aggression reduction (Kendall et al., 1990). In an investigation of anger, perceived control, and school problems among adolescents with learning problems, Smith, Adelman, Nelson, and Taylor's (1988) results indicated that perceived control accounted for the greatest variance in anger scores. The authors' definition of perceived control as "the degree of freedom one expects to have other processes one believes must be pursued to accomplish particular aims" (p. 518), seems related to attributions of self-responsibility and self-efficacy (Bandura, 1977).

Outcome Expectancies

In his reformulation of the original Frustration–Aggression Hypothesis, Berkowitz (1989) suggests that people are "apt to become aggressive on not attaining their desired objective only to the extent that they have been anticipating the pleasure this outcome would bring them" (p. 65). Further, the reason why some frustrated people inhibit their aggressive responding is because they anticipate that such behavior may bring punishment (Berkowitz, 1989). It would seem then that another cognitive variable influencing the arousal of anger and the occurrence of aggression would be response–outcome expectancies. Perry, Perry, and Rasmussen (1986) measured the perception of self-efficacy and the response–outcome expectancies of aggressive and nonaggressive preadolescents. Male and female students, fourth- through seventh-grade, were classified via peer nominations as either aggressive or nonaggressive, and they then responded to questionnaire items about their abilities to perform aggressive and prosocial behaviors and their beliefs about the reinforcing and punishing consequences of aggression. Results indicated that aggressive children reported that it is easier to perform aggression, more difficult to inhibit aggressive impulses, and that they are more confident that aggression would produce tangible rewards, and reduce future aversive treatment by others.

Although conclusions of these self-report data are limited because actual aggressive behavior was not assessed, the authors suggest the influence of negative reinforcement in maintaining aggressive responding. Aggressive children may favor aggression, not because it brings them social or material rewards, but rather because it brings them a desired material reinforces or it removes an annoying or aversive event (Perry et al., 1986). A final interpretation of age correlates indicated that as children get older, they report that aggression leads to positive self-evaluations and may function to restore self-esteem (Perry et al., 1986).

In a follow-up investigation of sex differences in the consequences that fourth through seventh graders anticipate for aggression, Perry, Perry, and Weiss (1989) found variations according to sex and two situational variables (the degree of provocation and the target child's sex). Boys expected less negative self-evaluation and less parental disapproval for behaving aggressively toward boys than toward girls. Perhaps in support of the legitimacy of retaliation bias, when provoked, children expected more tangible rewards, less negative self-evaluation, and less parental disapproval for aggression than when unprovoked. Other sex differences were evident vis-à-vis the victims. When using aggression against girls, children expected more tangible rewards, less negative self-evaluation, more victim suffering, more disapproval from the female peer group, but not from the male peer group (Perry et al., 1989). The results certainly raise issues relating to early sex role bias and outcome expectancies that may affect not only the perception and interpretation of the initial provocation but decision making regarding an aggressive response. This study is also noteworthy as a first investigation into the sex differences of children's cognitive mediation of aggressive behavior.

Clearly, cognitive responses or self-statements reflecting outcome expectancies must be explored with adolescents who are aggressive in the natural environment. More can be learned about response–outcome expectancies and their influence on aggression from the work by Guerra (in press; Guerra & Slaby, 1989) on consequential thinking. In addition to evaluating problem-solving skills, Guerra and Slaby (1989) examined the number of consequences generated, the percentage of consequences focused on others, and the anticipated affective reaction to the consequences generated to hypothetical problems. Forty-eight elementary-school children, rated on aggressiveness by their teachers, completed a problem-solving measure. Results indicated that high aggressive boys generated fewer consequences to a hypothetical aggressive response and evidenced a general lack of concern (i.e., "wouldn't care") about possible negative consequences.

In a study with black, inner city, high school students, Guerra (in press) further examined beliefs about potentially inhibitory consequences for deviant behavior. Using a consequential thinking measure designed to evaluate the importance, the probability, and the severity of legal, moral, and social consequences, students were asked to imagine committing a transgression and estimate the consequences. In general, students labeled as delinquents, based on a self-report measure of frequency of antisocial behavior, held beliefs that minimized the importance, probability, and severity of consequences of deviant behavior. However, these general beliefs seemed to be mediated by the particular situational context. Specifically, the differences between adolescents categorized as either delinquents or nondelinquents were significant only in regard to the rule-breaking transgression and not to the potentially violent transgression (Guerra, in press).

Taken together, these results on response–outcome expectancies indicate that the anticipation of consequences of aggressive responding plays an instrumental role in both the performance of aggression and in the potential inhibition of aggression. These response–outcome expectancies should be assessed and targeted for possible remediation in any anger control program. Feindler and Ecton (1986) have employed a *Think Ahead* procedure to assist the aggressive adolescent in controlling impulsive responding. The procedure requires that the adolescent estimate the probability of future negative consequences of the aggressive response he or she wishes to display and then use this estimation as an avoidance self-statement.

"If I punch this guy out now, I'll probably get placed on restriction because he'll report me. And I don't want to miss rec program. So, maybe it's not worth it to me."

Clinically, it has often been observed that antisocial adolescents express immunity to potential legal, moral, and social consequences ("It will never happen to me," or "I won't get caught.") or a lack of concern over possible consequences. Because of this, it is important to stay focused on short-term, practical, and highly probable consequences that will have immediate and direct impact on the adolescent. Although the *Think Ahead* procedure has not yet been evaluated as a separate component of the anger control program, it seems clinically viable. Not only does this cognitive strategy delay responding, which may reduce the likelihood of the adolescent's selecting an aggressive solution to a problem (Dodge & Newman, 1981), but it also helps realign their response–outcome expectancies so as to inhibit aggressive responding.

Of further interest in understanding how the anticipation consequences might help cause actual aggressive behavior is the empirical evidence reviewed by Baron (1983). According to his summary, the impact of threats of punishment upon aggression is strongly mediated by several different factors. He suggests that punishment procedures will usually succeed only when: (1) potential aggressors area *not* very angry; (2) they have relatively little to gain from aggressive behavior; (3) the magnitude of punishment anticipated is great; and (4) the probability that such unpleasant treatment will be delivered is high. Not only do these conclusions have direct indications for the cognitive strategies incorporated into anger control, but they may explain why contingency management strategies alone are minimally effective with aggressive youth (Feindler & Ecton, 1986).

Other Norms/Expectations

Cairns, Cairns, Neckerman, Ferguson, and Gariepy (1989), following fourth graders for 6 years, assessing changes in patterns of aggression from childhood to adolescence. Results indicated emergent sex differences in themes for conflict that may have direct implication for anger control interventions. In male–male conflicts, there was a developmental persistence of direct confrontation and physical attacks which may support the aggression-begets-aggression norm. Further, there seemed to be a norm regarding the prohibition of physical assaults by boys toward girls, but not toward other boys. In contrast, for female–female conflicts, social manipulation and ostracism (i.e., alienation, rumors, and social rejection) are major aspects of aggressive behaviors (Cairns et al., 1989). These conclusions require replication with clinical populations and must be supported by comparison with rates of actual aggressive behavior; the findings emphasize previously disregarded sex differences with regard to conflict negotiation in adolescence. Future anger control interventions must include problem-solving and emotional strategies specific to the sex of the client and must examine underlying norms and expectations for aggressive responding.

Summary

This review of research on cognitive deficits and distortions in aggressive children has highlighted key biases, outcome expectancies, and misattributions that directly affect anger arousal and aggressive behavior. Since these distortions probably interact in any given provocation event, cognitive interventions must focus on: (1) the perception of the initial provocation,

(2) the interpretation of the valence and the responsibility of that provocation, (3) the legitimacy and the type of the retaliatory response selected, (4) the estimation of consequences of the selected response, and (5) the evaluation of one's response to the provocation event.

Cognitive restructuring strategies, such as identification of self-statements, cessation of automatic, negative thoughts, substitution of rational coping statements, and disputing irrational ideas, are easily applied to interventions with aggressive youth. These strategies can be used at each step first to identify the adolescent's misperceptions and misattributions and then to replace them with appropriate self-statements. Hayes and Hesketh (1989) suggest that shifting the emphasis from attributions to the processing of antecedent information will help direct the intervention at the individual and his or her interactions with the environment rather than at cognitions in isolation. Although the specific content of self-statements must be tailored to the individual, in general, aggression reducing self-statements must: (1) prompt attention to nonhostile cues, (2) increase probability of nonaggressive interpretations of events, (3) emphasize alternate explanations for the provoker's behavior, (4) assist in acceptance of self-responsibility for the event, (5) focus on predictable negative consequences, (6) prompt self-reinforcement for the control of anger and the inhibition of aggressive responding.

Only future research can determine the exact causal influence of each of these cognitions during a provocation event. Clinicians and researchers are encouraged to examine not only the relationship of cognitive mediation in the performance of actual aggressive behavior but also the process whereby an aroused or frustrated adolescent inhibits responding.

CASE STUDY: ANDREW

This case study describes the cognitive–behavioral treatment of a highly aggressive adolescent who evidenced disruptive behavior at school and at home. At intake, 15-year-old Andrew was argumentative and overtly hostile toward the therapist and his parents. Andrew's mother had initiated therapy because of his highly explosive behavior. The aggressive behavior had escalated over the months as Andrew's mother who, although asserting that she desired a divorce, refused to move out of the home.

Background Information

Andrew's family had moved to the current school district during the summer and he had not adjusted well to the ninth grade. His parents indicated that this school was much larger and had a "faster" crowd than his previous school and Andrew had experienced much stress. He was extremely angry about the move and frequently became quite verbally aggressive toward his family. Andrew had a history of learning difficulties and attention problems; as a child his diagnosis was Attention Deficit Disorder with Hyperactivity. Further, his behavior patterns were described as highly oppositional and impulsive with a strongly defiant attitude toward adults, especially women, in authority positions.

At the time of the referral, Andrew had been suspended from the tenth grade after he came to school drunk, got into an argument with the custodian, and attacked him. School reports indicated that Andrew was an extreme discipline problem with frequent absences, foul language, and combativeness toward all adults with particular disrespect toward women. Further, he was often seen drinking and smoking on campus.

Andrew had not responded to traditional school consequences, expressed no remorse, had no respect for rules, and had extremely low academic motivation. Testing records indicated an average IQ with potential for academic success; however, there were some visual motor processing deficits.

Recent incidents at home included extreme abusiveness toward his mother (both verbal and physical), incorrigibility, unresponsiveness to curfew rules, and suspected drug sales and involvement, and he had "taken" a car and was involved in a minor accident.

Upon intake, the parents presented with extreme marital dysfunction. They were openly hostile toward each other and were unable to concentrate on information gathering related to their son. After his mother indicated divorce intentions, Andrew expressed a desire to live with his father and cut all contact with is mother. The decision was made at that point to work with father–son dyad.

Treatment Formulation

The following cognitive–behavioral treatment formulation was developed:

The current distress over the breakup of the family was manifested in Andrew's (and his father's) anger directed toward his mother or toward anyone attempting to place limits on his out-of-control behavior. Andrew used this marital crisis to justify his extremely aggressive behavior. He believed that aggression was a legitimate response.

Andrew probably had a long-standing history of poor impulse control and frustration tolerance and had developed an aggressive style in peer relationships to intimidate those who were more successful academically. He viewed others' behavior as provoking even when it was neutral.

Andrew's verbal style was either argumentative, littered with foul language and very provocative, or withdrawn, indicating that he didn't care what he did or did not do. This verbal pattern was hypothesized to be an aversive control strategy maintained by negative reinforcement. Either Andrew's hostile response would result in removal of a demand or control contingency or it would result in an escalating counterresponse, thereby legitimatizing further aggression.

His hostile style may actually have been a compensation for depression. Although Andrew boasted about himself and his apparent immunity to consequences for his anger and aggressive behavior, he could not help but feel like a failure. He was unsuccessful in the school environment and his family life was deteriorating; the aggression and suspected substance abuse were means for Andrew to avoid the realities of his situation.

Andrew's cognitive style indicated extreme impulsivity. He had virtually no capacity to reflect on actions, take another's perspective, plan ahead, or generate alternative solutions to conflicts. Further, he had an extremely egocentric view, blamed others for everything, saw others' actions as provocations and his own as retaliatory, believed in aggression as a legitimate solution, and believed that "victims" deserved aggression.

> "The janitor at school shouldn't have tried to get in my way—then, I wouldn't have had to punch him out."
>
> "My mother deserved it every time I spit in her face because she ruined everything. Get her out of my face and I won't have to threaten her."

Andrew placed responsibility for family conflict on his mother, which helped justify subsequent aggression toward her when the conflicts escalated.

These core cognitive dysfunctions and the deficits (lack of problem-solving abilities) continued to support Andrew's explosive style. Further, his egocentric views (e.g., that he could overcome anything with aggression, that the law would never get him, and that he could manipulate anything to his advantage) were reinforced by a failure of family, school, and community systems to discipline him effectively.

According to DSM-III-R, Andrew received the following clinical diagnosis:

Axis I: 312.00, Conduct Disorder, solitary aggressive type
Axis II: V61.20 Parent–Child Problem, no diagnosis on Axis II
Axis III: None
Axis IV: Psychological stressor, change of school, marital conflict
   Severity: 4-Severe
Axis V: Current GAF: 45
   Highest GAF past year: 65

Treatment Strategies

Initial stages of resistance and extreme hostility kept early stages of treatment at a standstill. Andrew did not want to learn to control his anger toward his mother, so he did not accept any intervention. The clinical breakthrough began as his father learned to manage the contingencies surrounding his behavior, such as response–cost contingencies.

In order to control some of Andrew's acting-out behaviors, highly desired personal items were confiscated at each curfew and/or drinking infraction and could be earned back by following the rules. Andrew lost his leather jacket, parts of his sound system, his dirt bike, and so on. Andrew's response to contingency management was to begin to abuse his father with the same angry methods that he used with his mother; admittedly, he was banking on the fact that, "Dad wouldn't want to lose me and give Mom the satisfaction of seeing him fail." However, after 10 sessions, with much therapist support and contingency management training, his father did begin to control contingencies and Andrew reduced his opposition to a few basic rules. Although his anger remained and he lost his temper frequently, behavior at home began to improve.

However, school behavior continued to decline and eventually Andrew was referred for a special education evaluation. The evaluation team decided that residential placement was in order and until one could be obtained, Andrew was to receive homebound instruction. This contingency, although supporting his view that you can always get out of a bad situation by being aggressive, isolated Andrew from much of his peer group throughout the day. His mother also moved out at this time, so Andrew was at home alone. After several weeks of seemingly complete satisfaction that he had "beaten the system," Andrew began to express boredom and frustration with his "exile" from school. Further, he saw the limitations in the job world as he struggled to make some money parking cars. Facing these realities, he eventually became motivated to earn back his home privileges and re-entrance into high school, which was contingent upon improved self-control.

Work with Andrew focused on the following anger control strategies, which were presented across 20 sessions in the following sequence:

Arousal management (five sessions): Andrew benefited most from skills training in deep breathing and backward counting (see Feindler & Ecton, 1986). Following two sessions of physiological discrimination training, Andrew was able to recognize his particular arousal signals, such as getting flushed and clenching of jaw and fists. He was then taught a sequence of interventions: (1) recognize body warning signals, (2) stop and pull it from provoking situation, (3) divert eye gaze from provoker, (4) take two slow deep breaths, and (5) count backwards from 25 to zero. Although initially resistant to this "baby stuff," Andrew practiced this sequence during three consecutive sessions with his father in which hot topics, such as curfew and alcohol use, were discussed. Anecdotal reports from Andrew indicated that he successfully used this strategy with his home tutor, his brother, a police officer who pulled his car over, and his boss. Clinical implications indicated that the most important steps were the initial recognition of the physiological arousal, the diverted eye gaze and the required pause.

Cognitive restructuring (15 sessions): Andrew's distorted thinking style was targeted first. He presented with the following: hostile misattributions wherein he perceived most neutral commentary by adults (therapist, father, tutor, and boss) as being provocative and critical, strong beliefs in retaliation and legitimacy of aggression, extremely strong beliefs in his immunity from negative consequences. Although initial attempts were made to dispute these irrational beliefs via rationale dialogue, Andrew was often too agitated to profit from this approach. Thus, specific self-statements designed to target each of these areas were developed. Some of these are included in Table 3-1. Although these statements are just examples and are highly specific to the situations confronting Andrew, he began to generate spontaneously generalized coping strategies himself. He began to ask himself when he got angry, "What is really important here?" and as Andrew became focused on his future and some longer-term goals for himself and his family, the immediate anger response of "retaliate" became less important. These self-statements were generated over three sessions and then two sessions were spent on the cognitive restructuring procedure. In

TABLE 3-1. Self-Statements Designed to Reduce Cognitive Distortions

---

Hostile Attributions Bias
  "I'll try to stay calm and *listen* to what they say."
  "Are these good intentions behind what they are saying."
  "Not all adults are out to nail me."
  "Some people (i.e., father, therapist, teachers, tutor) do care about what happens to me."

Legitimization of Aggression and Retaliation
  "He or she may have started with me, but I don't have to respond in kind."
  "Is there another way to respond/solve the problem."
  "It doesn't have to be an eye for an eye; I'm better than that."
  "Ignoring them takes their power away and may be the best retaliation."

Immunity from Consequences
  "Getting kicked out of school means I can't control whether I graduate."
  "I have lost privileged and possessions as a result of my behavior."
  "If there is a possibility of negative consequence, I don't want to take a chance."
  "Maybe there are consequences I haven't considered."

---

role playing, first with the therapist and then later with his father, he was taught to implement the following sequence: (1) recognize arousal, (2) *stop*, (3) think about what to do (insert anger-reducing self-statement appropriate to situation). It took many practice trials to teach Andrew to inhibit his usually hostile attributions and replace them, even momentarily, with the coping statements. During the following three sessions, Andrew and his father engaged in discussions about his household responsibilities and the possible purchase of a car while the therapist prompted anger control strategies.

Next, the cognitive deficiencies were remediated via direct problem-solving training, with the steps described earlier in mind. Andrew was taught problem-solving skills, using at first hypothetical situations of other boys his age and then via a recall of past problem situations across these sessions. We reconstructed a number of critical and anger-producing events in Andrew's recent past (i.e., the attack on the janitor, a confrontation with the school vice-principal, which resulted in his expulsion, and intense altercations with his mother) and worked through each stage of problem solving. Andrew began to see that he had options in terms of his reactions to conflict and this increased perception of control reduced his anger in response to the recall of these events. Each of these problem-solving "reframings" also included appropriate self-statement training as described above. The remaining four sessions focused on problem situations either at home or with peers that surfaced during the week or situations requiring negotiations between father and son. Although in each of Andrew's proposals of solutions, there was always an aggressive response or two, he was also able to generate nonaggressive solutions. Anecdotal reports from his father and tutor indicated much less impulsivity in response to conflicts and problems and actual implementation of nonaggressive solutions. Finally, much problem solving focused on future planning in regard to: (1) car purchase and maintenance, (2) a return to and possible graduation from high school, (3) employment opportunities, and (4) the divorce process and relationship with his mother.

His self-concept, cognitions, and actions began to change, once Andrew discovered he could succeed at: (1) improving his relationship with is father, (2) following rules and shedding the "bad egg" role, (3) keeping a job and earning money toward a car loan, (4) passing home-tutored courses and two final examinations. Andrew displayed his achievements in a recent Child Study Evaluation meeting, where he appeared on his own behalf, holding his temper, actively deep breathing when past transgressions and "delinquent mentality" were emphasized by school personnel.

Once Andrew learned to control his affective reaction with several self-control strategies, his biases and hostile attributions were reduced and he was more receptive to problem solving related to his school and home situations.

A CRITICAL REVIEW OF ANGER CONTROL
INTERVENTIONS

The results of clinical research on the effectiveness of structured anger control training needs to be regarded relative to maintenance and generalization issues. Schlichter and Horan (1981) conducted one of the first anger control training programs for institutionalized delinquents. They reported changes on self-report measures of anger and aggression for 38 males; however, no effects were noted in institutional behavior ratings. Kettlewell and Kausch (1983) provided a 4-week coping skills program for 41 children aged 7 to 12 years in a summer camp setting. Although results indicate improved interpersonal problem-solving skills and decreased discipline for fighting, there were no changes in verbal aggression or peer rating of aggression. In their 7-month follow-up of 31 aggressive boys (mean age 11.7 yrs) who had received an anger control coping program, Lochman and Lampron (1988) noted that although the program increased on-task and reduced off-task passive behavior in the classroom, there were no differential effects for disruptive and aggressive off-task behavior. Their results also indicated that subjects who received an additional weekly behavioral goal-setting component for improved classroom behavior had the strongest follow-up improvements. This additional self-control training strategy, which required students to choose weekly behavioral goals for themselves and to present them to their teachers for daily monitoring and weekly reinforcement, may be necessary to enhance generalization.

In the Feindler et al. studies (1984, 1986), data from staff ratings of groups of adolescents receiving anger control training were collected to determine behavior change in extratherapeutic environments. As the treated adolescents showed reduced or maintained levels of disruptive classroom and ward behavior, some generalization was evident. What is of most interest in these studies, however, are the results from control groups of adolescents over the 16 and 20 weeks of these studies, respectively. Control subjects' rates of disruptive and aggressive behaviors actually increased across time. It may be that our intervention programs hold rates of aggressive behavior on a residential unit study while other adolescents deteriorate without intervention.

Saylor, Benson, and Einhaus (1985) conducted a controlled evaluation of an anger coping program with 14 inpatient psychiatric children (mean age of 11 years, 9 months). Although their multimethod and 10-week follow-up assessment approach is quite commendable, there were no differences between the treatment and control group at posttreatment on unit ratings for aggression, teacher ratings scales, or behavioral observations of aggression during gym class or unstructured unit activities. Further, there were predicted changes on the Children's Anger Inventory (Finch & Nelson, 1978) self-report scale; however, these were not maintained at follow-up. The authors suggest that although the cognitive anger control techniques might be successful in the reduction of mild to moderate levels of aggression, they may not be sufficient to impact on other aggressive behaviors of an inpatient population. Further, the extensive measures used may not have reflected changes resulting from increased anger control; namely, increased inhibition of aggressive responses or calming strategies that are covert.

Finally, a recent study by Tisdelle and St. Lawrence (1988) supports these mixed generalization results for a problem-solving skills program for eight conduct-disordered adolescents. Their results indicate that although subjects had learned the cognitive strategies for more effective problem resolution, they failed to employ these strategies when they encountered real-life or *in vivo* confrontation situations. Further, there seems to be no relationship between self-reported changes in problem-solving abilities and overall adjustment in the natural setting.

General Issues

A general conclusion concerning anger control training is that self-report data usually indicate positive outcome. Adolescents report less anger, fewer conflicts or hassles with others, and increased problem-solving ability. However, these changes in verbal behavior do not seem to impact significantly on the rates of aggression in the natural environment; if there is some effect, it is one of maintaining or slightly reducing levels of disruptive or aggressive behavior. It would seem critical to look at the correspondence between saying and doing as adolescents may have the skills but are not performing them. A one-to-one relationship between saying and "doing" may not be obtainable, particularly for an antisocial adolescent population in which there is a wide topography of possible aggressive behaviors ranging from overt or confrontational antisocial behaviors, such as fighting, arguing, and tantrums, to covert or concealed antisocial behaviors, such as stealing, lying, and setting fires (Kazdin, 1987).

It is important to consider that the contingencies available in the natural environment may not elicit or reinforce anger control skills. Certainly, institutional contingencies and policy may work against the maintenance and generalization of anger control skills. For example, Saylor et al. (1985) reported on the uncontrollability of institutional policy. All of the subjects in that study were receiving other forms of treatment. In fact, one subject was being encouraged in individual therapy to act out his rage. Similarly, Schlichter and Horan (1981) discussed the staff's uncooperativeness with completing ratings; they indicated they had no time to notice specific behaviors on the scale and instead tended to make arbitrary global judgments. Further, other staff workers served to undermine the effectiveness of the anger control program as they modeled their own aggressive behavior in response to anger provocation. Another problem may be that the behavior or interest in anger control training is the *inhibition* of aggressive responding. Such inhibitory behaviors are not overt and, therefore, are less likely to elicit reinforcement from others. This also poses difficulties in assessment of anger control competency. Finally, competing contingencies also pose a problem. There certainly appears to be peer reinforcement for continued aggressive responding to provocation. Conflict is reinforced especially in environments and in families in which aversive control is a *modus operandi.*

Another generalization obstacle may be that adolescents are not discriminating where and when to implement anger control skills to maximize the outcome of a particular situation. Perhaps, self-observation and self-reinforcement skills have not been acquired or have not been of sufficient strength to control responding. There may be no motivation to perform an anger-controlled response as there may be no interest reinforcer available. Finally, it may be that antisocial youths are just too complicated and problematical to show much change with a simple cognitive–behavioral skills training program and a multimodal approach may be necessary (Kazdin, 1987).

Unfortunately, the oft-cited argument for the inclusion of cognitive training in behavioral intervention was that generalization beyond treatment situations would be enhanced because cognitive changes are trans-situational. What we are finding, however, is that we are not achieving behavioral changes in extratherapeutic environments except in the self-reported cognitive domain. Perhaps, the issue of social validity is also pertinent here. If anger control training only produces change in verbal responses to structured inventories and does not impact naturalistic aggressive behavior or global behavioral adjustment, is it even relevant? Indeed, we may have to look at alternative treatment methods and design.

Enhancing Maintenance and Generalization

There are numerous clinical strategies that can be implemented at the beginning, throughout, and following an anger control training program that will enhance with maintenance and generalization and behavioral gains. First, there is group training. Feindler and her colleagues (Feindler, Marriott, Iwata, 1984; Feindler, Ecton, Kingsley, & Dubey, 1986) have suggested the use of group anger control training programs over individual anger control training programs in that the role-played scenarios of conflict as well as the naturalistic provocation that occurs during any adolescent group training experience more closely approximates what the adolescent will find once that therapy hour is over. This has been discussed as an issue elsewhere (cf. Feindler, 1988). Additionally, the use of peer trainers is effective and efficient. Kendall and Williams (1986) indicate that peer involvement will only enhance the therapeutic interventions for adolescent behavior disorders. Peers may be used as role-playing confederates, as group assistants, and as assistants in the *in vivo* barb process. Indeed, Glenwick and Jason (1984) indicate that the use of natural change agents in intervention programs will enhance their effectiveness. They indicate that further study is needed on the selection, training, and supervision of naturalistic helpers and that the helper-therapy principle should be investigated.

The incorporation of self-management strategies also seems imperative. If we are to expect the adolescent to make the stimulus discriminations required for appropriate anger control in the naturalistic setting, he or she must be well skilled at self-observation, self-recording, self-reinforcement, and self-punishment strategies. Finally, strategies designed to enhance adherence and minimize relapse prevention in behavioral medicine may be helpful. Kendall and Braswell (1982) recommend that a part of any initial intervention program address the methods and skills and the desired cognitive interpretations for overcoming relapse and failure experience. Attribution retaining (Meichenbaum & Turk, 1987) focuses on enhancement of self-efficacy: the belief that one can respond effectively to a situation by using available skills. The adolescent must believe not only that the treatment will be effective to achieve the desired goals of improved interpersonal functioning (the outcome expectancy), but that he or she can actually implement the skills (the self-efficacy expectancy).

There are also specific training materials and methods that will improve generalization and maintenance behavior change. Certainly, we must appreciate the individual diversity of the adolescent (Glenwick & Jason, 1984) as not all children and adolescents learn in the same way. There are cognitive differences, cultural differences, developmental variables, and motivational differences that we must attend to when designing programs. Further, we need to look at alternative treatment settings. If anger control training is conducted in extratherapeutic environments, we will enhance generalization and behavior change to those environments. For example, in one study, anger control training took place in a summer camp (Kettlewell & Kausch, 1983) and in another, six boys from the age of 8 to 13 participated in a basketball program. During this program, the authors (Anderson, Rush, Ayllon, & Kandell, 1987) examined the training and generalization of social skills for these behaviorally disordered and socially isolated children. They did find increases in appropriate social behaviors that occurred in the context that was a leisurely, fun, sports-oriented activity. The authors indicate that motivation to acquire social skills may be enhanced by imbedding training in a pleasurable, natural setting away from the traditional structured therapeutic/classroom context. Other important generalization methods include a series of follow-up and booster sessions which will not only prompt but serve as an opportunity to reinforce anger control skills in a natural environment.

The use of contingency management techniques as a part of the cognitive–behavioral approach to adolescent anger control may also assist in the transfer and maintenance of behavior change. In the area of stimulus prompting, we can examine the use of the "barb" technique as a generalization strategy in addition to the use of homework assignments, such as reported by Goldstein, Glick, Zimmerman, and Reiner (1987). Other cues in the environment, such as an anger control club, motto, slogan, t-shirts, and so on, may also help to prompt the use of skills in the naturalistic environment.

Even though the anger control training program as originally designed by Feindler and her colleagues (Feindler et al., 1984; Feindler et al., 1986) was developed as a self-management program, external reinforcement of behavioral change may need to be programmed in order to get generalization of the skills to the naturalistic environment. In fact, Lochman and Lampron (1988) report that the goal-setting intervention, which was an additional contingency management component, enhanced transfer and maintenance of the anger control training program. Anger control may need to be a component of an already-existing token economy system for the management of aggressive behavior in a residential setting. Further, the uses of evaluation contingencies and contracting should be examined as a necessary ingredient to enhance generalization.

In addition to the incorporation of peer trainers, the use of alternative behavior change agents may be effective. Others who are more directly involved in naturalistic provocations will be more likely to prompt, model, and reinforce appropriate anger control skills as well as provide data on generalization to the naturalistic setting. As such, staff training is a crucial issue in the implementation of anger control programs. Goldstein et al. (1987) indicate that making and keeping staff as aware as possible of specific skills taught in the program is imperative. They need to know how, where, and why to reward increased competencies in anger control. This will require that they receive their own anger control training so they may become not only teachers of anger control but reinforcing agents for observed behavior changes.

Parents may also be a source of additional generalization agents. Clearly, family behavior therapy and parent contingency-management training may need to be a necessary component of any treatment program for conduct disorder or antisocial youth (Kazdin, 1987). Families of these children and adolescents typically are involved in numerous aversive control strategies and family anger control training may be necessary so that all can learn the required skills. The case study described in this chapter provides a clear example of the importance of parent training concurrent to adolescent anger control intervention. Kifer, Lewis, Green, and Phillips (1974) provided early empirical support for this effective strategy in their conflict negotiation training program for parents and adolescents.

Other sources of behavior change agents include probation counselors (Novaco, 1977), child-care workers, and any other persons in the child or adolescent environment. Certainly, teachers as well as administrative staff in the school systems may be included. Recently, Maher (1985) conducted a program for training five high school principals in problem solving with conduct disorder adolescents. Didactic presentation, role-playing exercises, performance feedback, and social reinforcement were used to teach them specific problem-solving skills to use when involved in a confrontation with an adolescent. Although this was not an experimentally analyzed study, all high school principals attained the skills which then generalized to their actual high school settings.

Finally, we must not overlook other possible persons that might provide additional reinforcement of anger control in the naturalistic environment. In their focus on community and societal interventions, Glenwick and Jason (1984) suggest a focus on not just the macrosystems (the educational or correctional systems within a community) but on the formal and informal support systems that an adolescent might be involved with. These would include voluntary associations, such as 4-H clubs, church youth groups, Girl Scouts, student council, self-help groups, and the like. Indeed, members of the support systems could all benefit from increased problem-solving and anger control abilities.

As a last point in the analysis of generalization issues, we need to take a look at the actual implementation of an anger control training program in the institutional setting. How the program is marketed (Levant, 1987) and positioned through the institution as well as to the clinical population will very often determine whether or not there is maintenance and generalization of treatment gains. If the program is positioned and packaged correctly, the children and adolescents in the residential setting will want to be a part of the anger control program and, therefore, will serve as reinforcing agents for increased anger control training skills. Graziano and Bythell (1983) indicate that some behavioral programs fail because the therapist fails to assess whether the context can provide the basic supports necessary to carry out behavioral programming.

FUTURE DIRECTIONS FOR ADOLESCENT ANGER CONTROL TRAINING

Much needs to be developed *vis-à-vis* a comprehensive assessment strategy to delineate clearly which cognitive distortions and deficiencies exist and which social skills are inappropriate or absent. The diagnostic dilemma entails not only clarification of which type of anger control problem a youth presents with (physiological arousal predominant, social/communication skills deficit, cognitive distortions/faulty attribution, or a more generalized context anger) but also which treatment approaches would work best. Data are required to support clinical observations that adolescents diagnosed with either conduct disorders or oppositional disorders seem best suited for the cognitive–behavioral approach to anger control.

Due to the nature of adolescent aggression and anger, as a low-frequency behavior outside the realm of adult supervision, direct methods of assessment are difficult to incorporate into research or treatment protocols. Recently, however, analogue methods, such as role-playing scenarios, have helped to assess the actual performance or behaviors during provocations. Tisdelle and St. Lawrence (1988) incorporated a type of barb procedure and Rabiner and Lochman (1988) videotaped a naturalistic dyadic interaction in which two youths discussed a hypothetical conflict situation. Hinshaw, Buhrmester, and Heller (1989) in an anger control program for attention-deficit hyperactive boys included an analogue group provocation (direct verbal taunting by a peer group) and a staged individual provocation to help assess the acquisition of anger control skills. Further development of these analogue assessment methods is encouraged for both assessment and treatment evaluation purposes.

Most of the time, however, the clinician must rely on self-report methods for assessment and there are numerous inventories available. However, care must be taken to assess responses in each area considered important in anger arousal: physiological/affective, cognitive, and behavioral. Table 3-2 presents a listing of self-report methods which can be used for adolescents exhibiting problems with anger and aggression control. Although not exhaustive, this listing is categorized according to the content assessed. Clinicians who work with adolescents are urged to assess not only the affect state of anger but more specific cognitive (deficits and distortions) and situational (i.e., family environment) variables. Much work, however, has yet to be done in the fine-tuned assessment of particular misattributions, outcome expectancies, and biases that have been suggested as causal in the occurrence of anger and aggression.

It would seem that there are five basic components of anger control training: (1) arousal reduction, (2) cognitive change, (3) behavioral skills development, (4) moral reasoning development, (5) appropriate anger expression; and at least six modalities in which treatment could be provided: (1) individual therapy, (2) group skills training, (3) family anger control, (4) dyadic anger control training, (5) parent only anger control, (6) classroom anger control training/affective education. A careful determination of which therapeutic components and which modalities would be most effective for these adolescents must be made following a comprehensive clinical assessment.

Treatment planning with the angry or aggressive adolescent involves the usual therapeutic decision-making step of hypothesis formulation: the stage when the therapist develops working hypotheses about variables (both

TABLE 3-2. Self-Report Measures Used in Anger Control Assessment

Affective Component
   Multidimensional Anger Inventory (Siegel, 1986)
   Children's Inventory of Anger (Finch & Nelson, 1978)
   STAXI (Spielberger, 1988)
   Imaginal and Role-Played Provocations (Novaco, 1975)

Cognitive Components
   Beliefs Supporting Aggression (Slaby & Guerra, 1988)
   Consequential Thinking Measure (Guerra, in press)
   Assessment of Self-Statements Test (Haynes–Clements & Avery, 1984)
   Adolescent Social Problem Solving Scale (Kennedy, 1982)
   Situation Self-Report Inventory (Saylor, Benson, & Einhaus, 1985)
   Causal Attribution Questionnaire (Schneider & Leitenberg, 1989)
   Interpersonal Problem Solving Analysis (Slaby & Guerra, 1988)
   Knowledge of Interpersonal Problem Solving Strategies (Asarnow & Callan,
     1985)
   Attributional Style Assessment (Asarnow & Callan, 1985)
   Self-Efficacy Questionnaire (Perry, Perry, & Rasmussen, 1986)
   Outcome Expectation Questionnaire (Perry, Perry, & Rasmussen, 1986)
   Irrational Beliefs Test (Zwemer & Deffenbacher, 1984).

Aggressive Behavior
   Children's Action Tendency Scale (Deluty, 1979)
   Achenbach CBCL—Self-Report (Achenbach & Edelbrock, 1987)
   Jesness Behavior Checklist (Jesness, 1971)
   Adolescent Assertion Expression Scale (Connor, Dann, & Twentyman, 1982)

Combination
   CARC: Children's Anger Response Checklist (Feindler, Stone, Bhumitra, &
     Cotronea, in preparation)
   Anger Control Inventory (Hoshmand & Austin, 1987)
   Ways of Coping Checlist (Hart, 1988)

Family Variables
   Parent–Adolescent Interaction Inventory (Robin & Weiss, 1980)
   Family Environment Scale (Moos & Moos, 1981)
   Family Beliefs Inventory (Vincent–Roehling, & Robin, 1986)

personal, situational, and historical) eliciting anger or aggression and external variables maintaining these patterns in addition to hypotheses concerning modes of thought (attributional style, locus of control, outcome, and response expectancies) contributing to provocation of anger and maintenance. Dodge (1985) indicates that an important initial determination be made as to whether a child's hostile attributional biases are a function of faulty formal information analyses or an affectively driven preemption since the treatment plan would be very different for either. Diagnostic interviewing as well as assessment instruments must be fine-tuned to determine not only the exact nature of the adolescent's anger control problem but the best treatment approach.

This chapter has emphasized cognitive mediational responses (specific distortions and deficiencies in thought) which seem to underlie problems in anger and aggression. A review of maintenance and generalization of change resulting from anger management interventions has indicated that changes in verbal behavior assessed via self-report and changes in cognitions (in particular, during hypothetical conflict negotiations) can be obtained. However, there is still an important note of caution: Few, if any, of these studies have produced change in actual rates and intensities of aggressive behavior as directly observed or as recorded in a reliable and continuous baseline fashion and most studies are too brief to assess maintenance adequately. Although I agree that some change, and certainly internal change, is noteworthy, these procedures are really only considered effective if we can impact rates of family violence, self-destructive behavior, property damage, interpersonal aggression, and any other by-product or end-product of anger arousal. Certainly, longer interventions and treatments which are interwoven into family, school, and community systems are needed.

Further research is needed in regard to cultural diversity and modality of treatment. What has been presented here entails an approach which, for the most part, has been evaluated in either a residential, delinquent, or psychiatric population, or in a white, middle-class, outpatient clinic. Further, much of the research on cognitive influences on anger control has been completed on either normal schoolchildren or incarcerated adolescents. Clearly, little comparative work has been done across age groups, cultural groups, or economic groups. The sex differences previously discussed (Cairns et al., 1989; Perry et al., 1989) also need examination in regard to client population and/or cultural variables. I encourage researchers to explore cultural diversity as it relates to the development of anger problems and the expression of anger and to incorporate these insights directly into treatment strategy.

CONCLUSIONS

It is apparent that the behavioral changes resulting from anger control training programs for children and adolescents do occur, but they do not necessarily generalize to extratherapeutic environments nor are the changes maintained across time. Explicit efforts to enhance generalization certainly should be included in the planning and implementation of any anger control training intervention (Feindler, 1988; Lochman & Lampron, 1988). Some authors have indicated that anger control programs may only be useful in demonstrating short-term reductions in aggressiveness and disruptiveness (Lochman & Lampron, 1988). Tramontana (1980) suggested that so long as costs are not prohibitive, interventions producing only temporary effects may have merit if only because improvement is greater or is achieved more quickly than without treatment. In fact, this standard applies in most medical practices. However, with the recent emphasis on cost-efficient as well as on therapeutic effectiveness and clinical significance, we need to examine which strategies will enhance maintenance and generalization most. Lochman and Lampron (1988) suggest that cognitive–behavioral interventions for aggressive behavior disorders are most effective when more operant behavior procedures, including reinforcement for goal attainment, are used to augment the training (see also Kendall, Chapter 1, this volume). Clearly, the interdependence between the cognitive skills training strategies and contingency management approaches needs further investigation.

Although not particular to adolescent anger control training, Kazdin (1987) indicates that we may need to look at alternative models of treatment, such as the high-strength intervention model or the broad-based intervention model, in order to effect change in this population. This would necessitate an increase in the amount and duration of treatment as well as incorporating multiple treatment modules in a comprehensive package. The diversity, seriousness, and durability of the problems of some adolescent delinquents, as well as deficiencies in their natural family, school, peer group, and vocational environments, are factors that have limited the success of short-term contingency management approaches (Wolf, Braukmann, & Ramp, 1987). In fact, evaluations of such token economy models like Achievement Place suggest that longer-term, supportive, and socializing environments may be more appropriate intervention goals for delinquent youth. The relationships between a more broadly based therapeutic program including environmental intervention, parent training, and cognitive–behavioral skills training with aggressive youth need further clarification.

Methodologically sound clinical research on the various transfer and generalization techniques that have been suggested by various authors is needed as is robust and comprehensive assessment packages for child and adolescent anger and aggression. Since Dodge and Coie (1987) have identified two general subtypes of aggressive behavior—reactive and proactive aggression—there may be different subtypes of children and adolescents displaying anger control problems. The impulsive aggressor may have very different cognitive biases, distortions, and dysfunctions than the adolescent who exhibits carefully mediated instrumental aggression and would, therefore, require different cognitive-restructuring techniques. Further, the exact impact of anger arousal on the performance of aggression in adolescents has yet to be empirically described. We *do* know that anger control training results in short-term changes in a variety of arousal management and prosocial skills and we can hypothesize changes in social information processing. However, we need to improve both our assessment strategies as well as our treatment strategies to promote generalization and maintenance of these skills in the adolescent's natural environment.

REFERENCES

Achenbach, T. M., & Edelbrock, C. (1986). *Manual for the Youth: Self-Report and Profile.* Burlington: University of Vermont, Department of Psychiatry.

Anderson, C. G., Rush, D., Ayllon, T., & Kandell, R. (1987). Training and generalization of social skills with problem children. *Journal of Child & Adolescent Psychotherapy, 4,* 294–298.

Asarnow, J. L., & Callan, J. W. (1985). Boys with peer adjustment problems: Social cognitive processes. *Journal of Consulting and Clinical Psychology, 53,* 1, 80–87.

Bandura, A. (1977). Self-efficacy: Toward a unifying theory of behavioral change. *Psychological Review, 84,* 191–215.

Baron, R. A. (1983). The control of human aggression: An optimistic perspective. *Journal of Social and Clinical Psychology, 1*(2), 97–119.

Berkowitz, L. (1989). Frustration–aggression hypothesis: Examination and reformulation. *Psychological Bulletin, 106,* 1, 59–73.

Cairns, R. B., Cairns, B. D., Neckerman, H. J., Ferguson, L. L., & Gariepy, J. L. (1989). Growth and aggression: 1. Childhood to early adolescence. *Developmental Psychology, 25,* 320–330.

Camp, B. W. (1977). Verbal mediation in young aggressive boys. *Journal of Abnormal Psychology, 86,* 145–153.

Connor, J. M., Dann, L. N., & Twentyman, C. T. (1982). A self-report measure of assertiveness in young adolescents. *Journal of Clinical Psychology, 38*(1), 101–106.

Deluty, R. H. (1979). Children's Action Tendency Scale: A self-report measure of aggressiveness, assertiveness, and submissiveness in children. *Journal of Consulting and Clinical Psychology, 47,* 1061–1071.

Dodge, K. A. (1985). Attributional bias in aggressive children. In P. C. Kendall (Ed.), *Advances in cognitive–behavioral research and therapy* (Vol. 4). Orlando, FL: Academic Press.

Dodge, K. A. & Coie, J. D. (1987). Social information-processing factors in reactive and proactive aggression in children's peer groups. *Journal of Personality and Social Psychology, 53,* 1146–1158.

Dodge, K. A., & Newman, J. P. (1981). Biased decision making processes in aggressive boys. *Journal of Abnormal Psychology, 90,* 375–379.

D'Zurilla, T. J., & Goldfried, M. R. (1971). Problem solving and behavior modification. *Journal of Abnormal Psychology, 78,* 107–126.

Eron, L. D. (1987). The development of aggressive behavior from the perspective of a developing behaviorism. *American Psychologist, 42,* 435–442.

Fagan, J. (1988). Types of violent delinquents. *Division of Child, Youth, and Family Services Newsletter, 11,* 2–16.

Feindler, E. L. (1988). *Anger arousal reduction via imaginal desensitization for an angry adolescent: A case study.* Unpublished report available from the author at Adelphi University, Garden City, NY 11535.

Feindler, E. L. (in press). Adolescent anger control: Review and critique. In M. Hersen, R. Eisler, & P. Miller (Eds.), *Progress in behavior modification* (Vol. 25). Newbury Park, CA: Sage.

Feindler, E. L., & Ecton, R. B. (1986). *Adolescent anger control: Cognitive–behavioral techniques.* Elmsford, NY: Pergamon Press.

Feindler, E. L., Ecton, R. B., Kingsley, D., & Dubey, D. (1986). Group anger control training for institutionalized psychiatric male adolescents. *Behavior Therapy, 17*, 109–123.

Feindler, E. L., Marriott, S. A., & Iwata, M. (1984). Group anger control training for junior high school delinquents. *Cognitive Therapy and Research, 8*(3), 299–311.

Feindler, E. L., Stone, K., Bhumitra, E., & Cotronea, R. (1990). *The Development and Validation of an Anger Response Checklist (CARC).* Unpublished manuscript available from the first author at Long Island University, Garden City, NY 11535.

Ferguson, T. J., & Rule, B. G. (1983). An attributional perspective on anger and aggression. In R. G. Green & E. I. Donnerstein (Eds.), *Aggression: Theoretical and empirical reviews* (pp. 41–74). New York: Academic Press.

Ferguson, T. J., & Rule, B. G. (1988). Children's evaluations of retaliatory aggression. *Child Development, 59*, 961–968.

Finch, A. J., & Nelson, W. M. (1978). *The Children's Inventory of Anger: A self-report measure.* Unpublished manuscript available from the author at the Medical University of South Carolina, Charleston, SC.

Glenwick, D. S., & Jason, L. A. (1984). Locus off intervention in child cognitive behavior therapy. In W. W. Meyers & W. E. Craighead (Eds.) *Cognitive behavior therapy with children.* New York: Plenum Press.

Goldstein, A. P., Glick, B., Zimmerman, D., & Reiner, S. (1987). *Aggression replacement training: A comprehensive intervention for the acting-out delinquent.* Champaign, IL: Research Press.

Graziano, A. M., & Bythell, D. I. (1983). Failures in child behavior therapy. In E. B. Foa & P. M. Emmelkamp (Eds.), *Failures in behavior therapy.* New York: Wiley Interscience.

Guerra, N. G. (in press). Consequential thinking and self-reported delinquency in high school youth. *Criminal Justice and Behavior.*

Guerra, N. G., & Slaby, R. G. (1989). Evaluative factors in social problem solving by aggressive boys. *Journal of Abnormal Child Psychology, 17*, 3, 277–289.

Guerra, N. G., & Slaby, R. G. (in press). *Cognitive mediators of aggression in adolescent offenders: 2. Intervention.*

Hayes, B., & Hesketh, B. (1989). Attribution theory, judgmental biases, and cognitive behavior modification: Prospects and problems. *Cognitive Therapy and Research, 13*, 211–230.

Haynes–Clements, L., & Avery, A. (1984). A cognitive–behavioral approach to social skills training with shy persons. *Journal of Clinical Psychology, 40*, 710–713.

Hinshaw, S. P., Buhrmester, D., & Heller, T. (1989). Anger control in response to provocation: Effects of stimulant medication for boys with ADHD. *Journal of Abnormal Child Psychology, 17, 4*, 393–407.

Hoshmand, L. T., & Austin, G. W. (1987). Validation studies of a multifactor cognitive–behavioral anger control inventory. *Journal of Personality Assessment, 51*, 417–432.

Huesmann, L. R., Eron, L. D., Lefkowitz, M., & Walder, L. (1984). Stability of aggression over time and generations. *Developmental Psychology, 20*, 1120–1134.

Jesness, C. F. (1971). *Manual for the Jesness Behavior Checklist.* Palo Alto, CA: Consulting Psychologists Press.

Kazdin, A. E. (1987). Treatment of antisocial behavior in children: current status and future directions. *Psychological Bulletin, 102*(2), 187–203.

Kendall, P. C. (1989). *Stop and Think Workbook.* Available from the author, 238 Meeting House Lane, Merion Station, PA 19066.

Kendall, P. C., & Braswell, L. (1982). Cognitive–behavioral self-control therapy for children: A components analysis. *Journal of Consulting and Clinical Psychology, 50,* 672–689.

Kendall, P. C., Ronan, K. R., & Epps, J. (1990). Aggression in children/adolescents: Cognitive–behavioral treatment perspectives. In D. Pepler & K. Rubin (Eds.), *Development and treatment of childhood aggression.* Hillsdale, NJ: Erlbaum.

Kendall, P. C., & Williams, C. L. (1986). Therapy with adolescents: Treating the "Marginal Man." *Behavior Therapy, 17,* 522–537.

Kennedy, R. E. (1982). Cognitive–behavioral approaches to the modification of aggressive behavior in children. *School Psychology Review, 11,* 1, 47–55.

Kettlewell, P. W., & Kausch, D. F. (1983). The generalization of the effects of a cognitive–behavioral treatment program for aggressive children. *Journal of Abnormal Child Psychology, 11,* 1, 101–114.

Kifer, R. E., Lewis, M. A., Green, D. R., & Phillips. E. L. (1974). Training predelinquent youths and their parents to negotiate conflict situations. *Journal of Applied Behavioral Analysis, 7,* 357–364.

Levant, R. F. (1987). The use of marketing techniques to facilitate acceptance of prevention program: Case example. *Professional Psychology: Research and Practice, 18*(6), 640–642.

Lochman, J. E. (187). Self and peer perceptions and attributional biases of aggressive and nonaggressive boys in dyadic interactions. *Journal of Consulting and Clinical Psychology, 55*(3), 404–410.

Lochman, J. E., & Lampron, L. B. (1988). Cognitive–behavioral interventions for aggressive boys: 7-month follow-up effects. *Journal of Child and Adolescent Psychotherapy, 2,* 21–25.

Maher, C. A. (1985). Effects of training high school principals in problem solving with conduct-disordered adolescents. *Journal of Child and Adolescent Psychotherapy, 5,* 15–23.

Meichenbaum, D. (1975). A self-instructional approach to stress management: A proposal for stress inoculation training. In C. Spielberger & I. Sarason (Eds.), *Stress and anxiety* (Vol. 2). New York: Wiley.

Meichenbaum, D., & Turk, D. C. (1987). *Facilitating treatment adherence.* New York: Plenum Press.

Moos, R. J., & Moos, B. S. (1981). *Family Environment Scale Manual.* Palo Alto, CA: Consulting Psychologists Press.

Novaco, R. W. (1975). *Anger control: The development and evaluation of an experimental treatment.* Lexington, MA: D. C. Heath.

Novaco, R. W. (1977). A stress inoculation approach to anger management in the training of law enforcement officers. *American Journal of Community Psychology, 5,* 327–346.

Novaco, R. W. (1985). Anger and its therapeutic regulation. In M. A. Chesney &

R. H. Rosenman (Eds.), *Anger and hostility in cardiovascular and behavioral disorders.* New York: Hemisphere Publishing Corp.

Novaco, R. W. (1986). Anger as a clinical and social problem. In R. J. Blanchard & D. C. Blanchard (Eds.), *Advances in the study of aggression* (Vol. 1). New York: Academic Press.

Olweus, D. (1979). Stability of aggressive reaction patterns in males: A review. *Psychological Bulletin, 86,* 825–875.

Olweus, D. (1984). Development of stable aggressive reaction: Patterns in males. In R. J. Blanchard & D. C. Blanchard (Eds.), *Advances in the study of aggression* (Vol. 1, pp. 103–137). New York: Academic Press.

Perry, D. G., Perry, L. C., & Rasmussen, P. (1986). Cognitive social learning mediators of aggression. *Child Development, 57,*(3), 700–711.

Perry, D. G., Perry, L. C., & Weiss, R. J. (1989). Sex differences in the consequences that children anticipate for aggression. *Developmental Psychology, 25,* 312–319.

Rabiner, D. L., & Lochman, J. E. (1988). *Assessing the relationship between distorted perceptions of aggression, aggressive behavior and behavior change following cognitive–behavioral intervention.* Presented at the Association for the Advancement of Behavior Therapy, New York.

Robin, A. L., & Weiss, J. G. (1980). Criterion-related validity of behavioral and self-report measures of problem-solving communication skills in distressed and nondistressed parent–adolescent dyads. *Behavioral Assessment, 2,* 337–352.

Saylor, C. F., Benson, B., & Einhaus, L. (1985). Evaluation of an anger management program for aggressive boys in inpatient treatment. *Journal of Child and Adolescent Psychotherapy, 2,* 5–15.

Schlicter, K. J., & Horan, J. J. (1981). Effects of stress inoculation on the anger and aggression management skills of institutionalized juvenile delinquents. *Cognitive Therapy and Research, 5,* 359–365.

Schneider, M. J., & Leitenberg, H. (1989). A comparison of aggressive and withdrawn children's self-esteem, optimism and pessimism and causal attributions for success and failure. *Journal of Abnormal Child Psychology, 17,* 2, 133–144.

Siegel, J. M. (1986). The Multidimensional Anger Inventory. *Journal of Personality and Social Psychology, 5*(1), 191–200.

Slaby, R. G., & Guerra, N. G. (1988). Cognitive mediators of aggression in adolescent offenders: 1. Assessment. *Developmental Psychology, 24,* 4, 580–588.

Smith, D. C., Adelman, H. S., Nelson, P., & Taylor, L. (1988). Anger, perceived control, and school behavior among students with learning problems. *Journal of Child Psychology, Psychiatry, and Allied Disciplines, 29,* 517–522.

Spielberger, C. D. (1988). *State–trait Anger Expression Inventory Professional Manual.* Odessa, FL: Psychological Assessment Resources.

Tisdelle, D. A., & St. Lawrence, J. S. (1988). Adolescent interpersonal problem solving skill training: Social validation and generalization. *Behavior Therapy, 19,* 171–182.

Tramontana, M. G. (1980). Critical review of research on psychotherapy outcome with adolescents: 1967–1977. *Psychological Bulletin, 19,* 171–182.

Vincent–Roehling, P., & Robin, A. L. (1986). Development and validation of the family beliefs inventory: A measure of unrealistic beliefs among parents and adolescents. *Journal of Consulting and Clinical Psychology, 54,* 693–697.

Wolf, M. M., Braukmann, C. J., & Ramp, K. A. 1987. Serious delinquent behavior as part of a significantly handicapping condition: Cures and supportive environments. *Journal of Applied Behavior Analysis, 20,* 347–359.

Zillman, D., & Cantor, J. R. (1976). Effect of timing of information about mitigating circumstances on emotional responses to provocation and retaliatory behavior. *Journal of Experimental Social Psychology, 12,* 38–55.

Zwemer, W. A., & Deffenbacher, J. L. (1984). Irrational beliefs, anger and anxiety. *Journal of Counseling Psychology, 31,* 391–393.

CHAPTER 4

Attention-deficit Hyperactivity Disorder

STEPHEN P. HINSHAW AND DREW ERHARDT
University of California, Los Angeles

Cognitive–behavioral treatment procedures for children received many of their initial trials with youngsters considered impulsive, hyperactive, or disruptive (e.g., Douglas, Parry, Marton, & Garson, 1976; Kendall & Finch, 1976; Meichenbaum & Goodman, 1971; Palkes, Stewart, & Kahana, 1968). Indeed, as intervention researchers increasingly eschewed the "uniformity myth" (Kiesler, 1966) that all therapies were of potentially equal value for all disorders and attempted to match specific treatment procedures to particular clients, considerable excitement was generated for the pairing of (1) cognitive–behavioral interventions designed to foster planful, self-regulated behavior, and (2) inattentive, overactive children, whose core problems were hypothesized to involve deficient self-regulation and impulsive cognitive styles (see Meichenbaum, 1977). It was specifically believed that self-instructional tactics would engender a more reflective problem-solving style and enhance sustained attention; direct involvement of the child in treatment would improve deficient motivation; such procedures as self-monitoring and self-evaluation would promote desired generalization and maintenance of cognitive and behavioral change; and social-problem solving strategies would help to remediate peer difficulties (e.g., Douglas, 1980).

In the past decade, however, a number of empirical investigations have diminished such initial enthusiasm for the application of cognitive–behavioral treatments to hyperactive children (for reviews, see Abikoff, 1987, in press; Whalen, Henker, & Hinshaw, 1985). In particular, outcomes of well-conducted, controlled trials have *not* led to significant cognitive, behavioral or achievement-related enhancements for hyperactive children receiving cognitive–behavioral intervention (e.g., Abikoff & Gittelman, 1985; Abikoff et al., 1988; Brown, Wynne et al., 1986). With regard to plausible reasons for such negative outcomes, growing emphasis has been placed on the diagnostic specificity of children who undergo cognitive–behavioral treatments. As opposed to the subclinical experimenter- or teacher-identi-

98

fied subjects used in many early investigations, more recent intervention trials have included samples that are clinically referred for hyperactivity. Such children are presumably more resistant to any but the most powerful interventions. Also, as opposed to laboratory measures of putatively salient constructs such as impulsivity, target goals for intervention have been expanded to include observed behavior, academic achievement, and other real-world outcomes. These dependent measures have been less amenable to clinically significant benefit. Furthermore, the response of hyperactive children to cognitive intervention strategies has been increasingly compared with their response to stimulant medication, with medication typically leading to greater gains. Thus, it is plausible that, as investigations have come to focus on (1) actual clinical samples, (2) real-world outcomes, and (3) comparisons with medication, results have become more humbling.

In light of these considerations and findings, a major question emerges as to how best to employ cognitive–behavioral interventions for hyperactive children. A key goal for the current chapter is to address this critical issue. To do so, we will first review several aspects of the nature and correlates of childhood hyperactivity, including its association with such features as aggression. Next, we will touch on some aspects of stimulant treatment for such youngsters, the most common treatment that they receive; and we will mention the use of more traditional operant behavioral procedures as well. We will then trace the development of cognitive treatment strategies for this child population, emphasizing both promising and disappointing results of clinical trials and lengthier descriptions of some specific techniques. It is stressed that no intervention strategies to date, whether employed singly or in combination, have proved clinically sufficient and durable for the troubling and troublesome problems of these youngsters, thus necessitating the continuing search for integrated components—cognitive, behavioral, and pharmacologic—that will constitute an adequate treatment package. Indeed, given the recent successes of cognitive–behavioral interventions for clinical samples of aggressive children (Kazdin, Bass, Siegel, & Thomas, 1989; Kazdin, Esveldt–Dawson, French, & Unis, 1987), and given promising small-scale applications of cognitive–behavioral treatments for selected problems of children with ADHD (to be reviewed below), it is too early to dismiss at least some cognitive–behavioral procedures from the search for a meaningful, multimodal treatment plan.

ATTENTION-DEFICIT HYPERACTIVITY DISORDER: DIAGNOSTIC ISSUES

Conceptualizations regarding the nature and classification of children considered "hyperactive" or "inattentive' have been in flux for many decades. Outdated terms such as minimal brain dysfunction (MBD) were quite broad, incorporating both large numbers of symptoms related to learning problems, impulsivity, aggression, inattention, motoric clumsiness, and the like, and unfounded notions about presumed neurologic etiology (Clements & Peters, 1962). More recent diagnostic conceptions are narrower. The terms "hyperkinesis" and "hyperactivity" came to replace MBD in the 1960s and 1970s, with emphasis on an impulsive and overactive behavioral style. By 1980, largely because of the seminal work of Douglas (1972), the core difficulty was assumed to be one of deficient sustained attention, leading to the new diagnostic category of attention deficit disorder (American Psychiatric Association, 1980).

The current revision of the official nomenclature, DSM-III-R, lists "Attention-deficit Hyperactivity Disorder" (ADHD) as one of the Disruptive Behavior Disorders, separable from Conduct Disorder and the controversial category of Oppositional Defiant Disorder (American Psychiatric Association, 1987).* Criteria for ADHD include the presence, for more than 6 months and since the age of 7 years, of developmentally inappropriate levels of a majority of 14 symptoms related to inattention, impulsivity, and motoric overactivity. Mental retardation, mood disorders, child-onset schizophrenia, and pervasive developmental disorders constitute exclusionary criteria. This categorical diagnosis is verified by increasing evidence from dimensional studies of child psychopathology that inattentive, immature, impulsive behavior is a viable facet of child psychopathology (Achenbach, Conners, Quay, Verhulst, & Howell, 1989; Quay, 1986). Furthermore, evidence is accumulating that ADHD is typically not a transitory disorder of childhood; rather, hyperactive youngsters are at risk for continued problems with impulse control and inattention and for such negative outcomes as substance abuse and delinquency (Gittelman, Mannuzza, Shenker, & Bonagura, 1985; Satterfield, Hoppe, & Schell, 1982; Weiss & Hechtman, 1986).

The nature of the "core deficit" in hyperactivity is the subject of intense speculation and debate. For one thing, ADHD is undoubtedly not a homogeneous syndrome or disorder; several etiologic routes may converge to result in a common pathway of extreme levels of inattentive, impulsive, and overactive behavior. Furthermore, the central areas of dysfunction are themselves heterogeneous constructs. That is, several subcomponents of attention and of impulsivity exist, rendering notions of a unitary "attentional deficit" or "problem in impulse control" overly simplistic (Milich & Kramer, 1984; Pelham, 1982; see also Chee, Logan, Schachar, Lindsay, & Wachsmuth, 1989, for recent data on the complexity of the sustained attention deficits in ADHD children). Also, despite its loss of status as the chief

---

*Because of the terminologic changes over the past several decades, multiple terms are currently in use to describe the syndrome now known as ADHD. Although "hyperactivity" technically refers to just one facet of the spectrum of ADHD behaviors, because of historical precedent, ADHD and hyperactivity are used interchangeably in this chapter.

feature of the disorder, hyperactivity per se is nontheless a salient feature (Porrino et al., 1983). If any overriding theme can be held to characterize recent conceptions, it is that ADHD comprises a behavioral style marked by deficiencies in higher order problem solving, in modulation of behavior to fit shifting environmental demands, and in overall self-regulation (e.g., Whalen, 1989; Douglas, Barr, Amin, O'Neill, & Britton, 1988).

Despite the growing consensus that a more narrowly defined disorder is viable and that inattention and overactivity are at least partly distinct from aggression/conduct problems and from academic underachievement (Hinshaw, 1987; Loney & Milich, 1982), it is important to realize that a number of difficulties are often associated with ADHD. The list of "secondary" or associated problems, in fact, includes low self-esteem, learning and achievement difficulties, negative peer status, labile mood, and aggression (APA, 1987; Barkley, 1982). Critically, peer difficulties, aggression, and low achievement are quite strongly associated with poor outcomes in later life (e.g., Parker & Asher, 1987). Because these types of "secondary" problems may therefore be crucial targets for intervention, the effects of cognitive–behavioral treatments on such domains should be examined.

One final comment regarding hyperactivity: As noted above, ADHD is separable from other disruptive or externalizing disorders, and dimensions of inattention versus aggression have divergent validity with respect to family history, classroom behavioral style, peer status, and, quite possibly, long-term outcome (see Hinshaw, 1987). Yet hyperactivity and aggressive behavior co-occur frequently, even with assessment tools that can meaningfully disentangle these aspects of externalizing behavior. Thus, as many as 50% of clinical samples of ADHD children may have noteworthy problems of aggression. Important here is the growing realization that the subgroup of youngsters with both hyperactivity and aggression evidences extreme problems in learning and achievement, peer reputation, and disruptive behavior (Milich & Landau, 1989; Walker, Lahey, Hynd, & Frame, 1987). It may well be that ADHD-aggressive youngsters are refractory to any but the most intensive and lengthy interventions.

INTERVENTIONS FOR ADHD

The most commonly employed intervention modality for children with ADHD is stimulant medication (Safer & Krager, 1984). Because of its prevalence as a primary treatment and because of its beneficial effects—at least in the short run—on the core symptoms of the disorder, it is a standard against which other interventions are often compared. Although even a cursory review of the research on stimulant treatment is beyond the scope of this chapter (see Klein, 1987; Young, Halperin, Leven, Shaywitz, & Cohen, 1987), in order to provide a better context for discussion of cognitive–behavioral interventions, we will present several issues regarding the use, benefits, and liabilities of this pharmacologic intervention.

First of all, in addition to their well-documented effects on attention, impulsivity, overactivity, and noncompliant behavior, stimulants have recently been shown to have meaningful impact on such important domains as complex problem solving (Douglas et al., 1988), academic productivity (Pelham, Bender, Caddell, Booth, & Moorer, 1985), aggressive behavior (Hinshaw, Henker, Whalen, Erhardt, & Dunnington, 1989; Murphy, Pelham, & Lang, 1986), and peer status (Whalen et al., 1989). Not all of these domains are fully normalized with medication; however, the findings that stimulants are efficacious with respect to such important "secondary" problems as peer reputation, aggression, and some aspects of learning difficulties mandate that any alternative interventions must transcend effects on ADHD's core symptoms alone.

Stimulant effects are extremely short-lived. Their benefits do not persist once they are excreted from the system, and evidence is extremely meager that stimulant treatment alters the long-term course of ADHD (e.g., Weiss & Hechtman, 1986). Furthermore, not all ADHD children are positive stimulant responders; 10%–30% do not benefit from these drugs. Also, side-effects are sometimes prohibitive; "palatability" and compliance are ever-present issues; and, because most dosing regimens are school-based, stimulants typically do not produce benefits when the child is at home. In short, the need for alternative or adjunctive intervention strategies is still paramount (Pelham & Murphy, 1986).

Although once commonly used as nonpharmacologic treatment for ADHD, individual counseling/therapy and dietary intervention have not shown much success for this population. The best-documented alternative intervention—and one that has been increasingly employed in community practice (Copeland, Wolraich, Lindgren, Milich, & Woolson, 1987)—involves behavior modification strategies. Operant behavioral treatments typically involve parent and teacher consultation to effect reductions in behavioral excesses and the promotion of alternative, adaptive responses (see Hinshaw & Erhardt, in press). Whereas operant behavioral programs can clearly lead to significant improvements in ADHD youngsters, usually with respect to rated and observed behavior at home and in the classroom, (1) They may not be quite so effective as moderate to high dosages of stimulant medication (Gittelman et al., 1980); (2) Considerable effort on the part of the involved adults is required; and (3) Their effects typically do not generalize to extratherapeutic environments or persist once the contingencies are lifted. In fact, one of the major motivations for the development and promotion of cognitive–behavioral strategies for hyperactive children was the lack of carryover of gains from operant approaches (Meichenbaum, 1977). Yet behavioral contingencies can be powerful tools in the treatment of ADHD children, and we argue strongly for their inclusion as a central facet of psychosocial intervention for these youngsters (see also Kendall, 1985).

COGNITIVE–BEHAVIORAL PROCEDURES: HISTORICAL DEVELOPMENT AND RATIONALE

Commendably, those who initially developed and investigated cognitive–behavioral treatments for hyperactive or impulsive children were explicitly guided by theory—not always the case in child (or adult) psychopathology. Indeed, in their groundbreaking reports, Palkes et al. (1968) and Meichenbaum and Goodman (1971) cited extensively the work of Vygotsky, Luria, and other Russian theorist/investigators, who contended that, in normative development, children acquire self-regulated behavior via internalization of guiding speech. Specifically, adult verbal commands initially direct the young child's behavior; such directions eventually become both internalized and covert, facilitating self-control. Given the salient dysregulation of hyperactive children's behavior, and given the impulsive (i.e., fast but inaccurate) cognitive tempo of such youngsters, the inference was made that such children may fail to follow the normal progression through which self-guiding private speech regulates cognition and behavior. Thus, an intervention strategy was advocated that explicitly instructed children to "talk to themselves" in order to slow down, approach a task logically, analyze task components, mediate careful performance, and self-reward. The early applications of these "cognitive–behavioral" training programs were multifaceted: Key aspects included cognitive modeling by the adult trainer, overt and covert rehearsal by the child, adult prompting and feedback, and social reinforcement.

The reports of Palkes et al. (1968), Palkes, Stewart, and Freedman (1972), and Meichenbaum and Goodman (1971) provided evidence that "cognitive self-instructional" training was successful in decreasing impulsive responding on such measures as the Porteus Mazes and the Matching Familiar Figures Test. Both investigative teams determined that explicit training in verbal self-instruction—and not modeling of cognitive strategies by an adult or silent reading of self-guiding commands by the child—was a central component of the successful outcomes, providing support for the underlying theoretical model. Yet, as noted above, the self-instructional procedures were still quite variegated. Furthermore, the samples used were not rigorously defined or diagnosed, and the outcome measures were largely restricted to cognitive analogue tasks. Critically, early investigators did not actually perform cognitive "task analyses" of hyperactive children's cognitive styles or use of covert speech; rather, deficiencies in these arenas were inferred from the disorganized behavioral style of the youngsters. Nevertheless, interest developed rapidly in the application of cognitive strategies to children with diverse externalizing problems.

During the busy formative years of cognitive–behavioral theory and therapy in the 1970s, several other themes were quite relevant to the development of treatment strategies for hyperactive children. First, Spivack and Shure (1974) outlined a model that implicated certain deficits in social problem solving as central to children's maladjusted behavior. Among other things, dysfunctional youngsters were found to produce a dearth of solutions to hypothetical interpersonal problems as well as to display deficient "means–end" problem solving—that is, a lack of proficiency in thinking through the mediating steps to solve a given social problem. Although Spivack and Shure's curriculum for interpersonal problem solving has been widely used over the ensuing years, the initial findings that enhanced cognitive-problem solving can promote improvement in overt behavior have not consistently been replicated (see Tisdelle & St. Lawrence, 1986). Second, literature on adult problem solving and self-control (e.g., D'Zurilla & Goldfried, 1971; Kanfer & Karoly, 1972) provided specific processes—establishing task goals, self-monitoring, self-evaluation, and self-reinforcement—that became integrated into children's cognitive–behavioral modification procedures. Early applications with disruptive children were quite promising (e.g., Drabman, Spitalnik, & O'Leary, 1973; Turkewitz, O'Leary, & Ironsmith, 1975). The explicit hope was that such procedures would produce generalizable and durable behavior change in the way that externally based reinforcement programs could not.

Working with clinical samples of hyperactive children, Douglas (1980) argued convincingly that the specific deficits of these children would be optimally matched by cognitive–behavioral procedures, rather than medication or operant strategies. Her comprehensive, disorder-specific cognitive training program was founded on the contention that the population's core deficiencies include of lack of investment of attention and effort in tasks, a failure to inhibit impulsive responding, and an inability to modulate arousal to meet shifting environmental demands. In scholarly and thoughtful fashion, she contended that if a training program operated at multiple levels (e.g., motivational, strategy-specific) and fostered internal rather than external control of behavior, it could promote self-awareness of deficit areas; strengthen motivation and participation; and teach specific task approach, organizational, arousal-modulating, and academic strategies.

The initial empirical application of this model was a controlled trial with a sample of 7–10-year-old hyperactive boys (Douglas et al., 1976). The 3-month training program included intervention to enhance self-awareness of problems; self-instructional guidance through academic-like and social games; explicit modeling of a problem-solving strategy intended to foster careful deliberation, self-monitoring, and self-reinforcement; and contingency management as needed. Evidence was found for gains in the domains of cognitive task performance, social-problem solving, and some academic measures at postintervention and 3-month follow-up assessments. No improvements in social behavior were noted, however, on standard rating scale measures. In addition to the individually administered cognitive training for the children, the total intervention program included parent training and teacher consultation in behavioral and self-control strategies, clearly exemplifying the type of "total push" program that may be required for ADHD youngsters, but rendering problematic the attribution of positive outcomes to the child cognitive training per se. With Douglas's theoretical and empirical efforts, the more "modern" era of application of cognitive–behavioral work to ADHD children had begun.

RECENT EMPIRICAL FINDINGS

Cognitive–behavioral procedures for ADHD children have been extended into the areas of academic skill enhancement, anger control, and attribution training, with promising results found in several short-term investigations. On the other hand, as foreshadowed earlier, larger-scale trials of cognitive–behavioral training procedures have not fared as well as either the initial reports or the promising, short-term studies, particularly when comparisons with stimulant medication have been made. Before we describe the implementation of clinical training procedures typically used in cognitive treatment programs for ADHD children, we will highlight results from some of the key studies of the 1980s (see Abikoff, 1987, in press, and Dush, Hirt, & Schroeder, 1989, for a more complete account of findings). We should point out that, like earlier studies, many of the current investigations continue to include multiple cognitive and behavioral elements in a comprehensive package. A matter of debate is whether intervention studies should attempt to parse active components (e.g., Varni & Henker, 1979; Hinshaw, Henker, & Whalen, 1984a, 1984b; Reid & Borkowski, 1987) before meaningful, durable results with clinical samples are obtained.

Promising Leads

Academic Performance

Proponents of cognitive training for ADHD children came to challenge the assumption that self-instruction in psychoeducational or perceptual-motor tasks—common in early applications of training—would automatically generalize to academic materials. Bolstered by applications with learning-disabled youngsters (e.g., Lloyd, 1980), investigators began to apply cognitive, self-instructional techniques directly to the learning of actual academic work. In an excellent single-case experimental investigation, Cameron and Robinson (1980) found that when self-instructions were performed with math problems, in the context of self-management and self-reinforcement procedures, math accuracy and on-task behavior improved in the classroom. Another single-case experimental design was employed by Varni and Henker (1979), who attempted to isolate active components of the cognitive–behavioral intervention. They found that only when "self-reinforcement" (involving the child's selecting and contingently receiving a major reinforcer) was combined with self-monitoring and self-instructions did gains in on-task and academic behavior occur in a classroom setting, emphasizing the role of behavioral contingencies in successful cognitive–behavioral programs. Overall, improvement in reflective cognitive style and enhancement of performance on laboratory tasks are not sufficient to promote academic gains; applications with academic materials appear to be crucial.

Social Competence and Anger Management

Given the early findings of Douglas et al. (1976) that cognitive therapy did not automatically ameliorate problematic social behavior, investigators have attempted to adapt or develop specific procedures that could promote social competence and reduce troublesome interpersonal behavior. In a series of studies initiated during after-school and summer-school research programs for hyperactive boys, Hinshaw et al. (1984a, 1984b) implemented cognitive–behavioral curricula to reduce angry and aggressive reactions to peer provocation and to extend the benefits of token reinforcement on positive social behavior through self-evaluation procedures.

Regarding anger management, the stress inoculation paradigm of Novaco (1979) was adapted for use with ADHD children in a controlled, experimental trial (Hinshaw et al., 1984b, Study 2). Via small training groups ($n = 4$), subjects were instructed in recognition of internal anger cues, generation of alternative strategies, and rehearsal of strategy use under increasingly strenuous verbal attack. When provoked by peers in videotaped provocation assessments, children trained in the rehearsal-based, stress inoculation treatment surpassed those receiving an exclusively problem-solving curriculum with respect to strategy implementation and to a global rating of self-control. Furthermore, rather low, naturally occurring doses of stimulant medication were not effective in enhancing anger control in this report. In a replication study, however, higher medication levels may have enhanced anger management training for ADHD boys (Hinshaw, Buhrmester, & Heller, 1989).

To promote the transfer of cognitive–behavioral procedures from the training group to the classroom and playground, Hinshaw et al. (1984a) trained ADHD boys in self-evaluation techniques (see Turkewitz et al.,

1975). Children were then assigned randomly to regular token reinforcement or cognitive–behavioral self-evaluation procedures, in which full token values were given only for accurate evaluation of one's own performance. The self-evaluation procedure led to greater reductions in negative social interactions on the playground, leading to the conclusion that a cognitive component might extend the effects of traditional operant programs. As in the Hinshaw et al. (1984b) studies, however, treatment and assessment periods were brief, and follow-up was not performed. Nonetheless, anger management and self-evaluation procedures may be beneficial components of larger-scale cognitive–behavioral intervention programs for ADHD children.

Attribution Training

One of the first perceived benefits of cognitive training with hyperactive children was that, because of its emphasis on active child participation and self-regulation, such intervention might help foster an "internal" attributional style—that is, one in which the child believes that his or her own actions are crucial for successful performance (Douglas, 1980; Henker, Whalen, & Hinshaw, 1980). Although attribution training programs have been designed for adults and for nonclinical samples of children (e.g., Dweck, 1975), and although the implicit attributional "messages" of cognitive–behavioral therapies for hyperactive children have been considered (e.g., Bugental, Whalen, & Henker, 1977), only recently has an integration of self-control intervention with specific attribution training procedures been attempted for ADHD youngsters.

In a four-session curriculum, Reid and Borkowski (1987) paired a cognitive–behavioral training curriculum based on the research of Meichenbaum, Kendall, and colleagues (see Kendall & Braswell, 1985) with instruction and coaching in effort attributions for both failure and success experiences. Specifically, when errors were made, children were encouraged to attribute the failure to a lack of use of the self-control strategies they had learned. Furthermore, they were coached to attribute subsequent successes to their active strategy use. Compared with self-control-only and control interventions, the self-control-plus-attribution condition fostered increased personal causality and a more reflective cognitive style; and at 10-month follow-up, a more clearly hyperactive subsample showed improved teacher ratings of social behavior with this intervention. The sample was not truly clinical, however, and some dependent measures were quite closely linked with the attribution training materials. Even so, the generalization and maintenance effects were promising, leading to the conclusion that explicit training regarding attributional style should be investigated further with ADHD children.

Larger-scale Trials

To evaluate more definitively the efficacy of cognitive–behavioral interventions for children with ADHD, several investigators have conducted trials with larger sample sizes, extended training periods, or both. Using group-comparison designs to ascertain the relative and combined efficacy of cognitive training and stimulant medication, Brown and colleagues (Brown, Borden, Wynne, Schleser, & Clingerman, 1986; Brown, Wynne, Borden et al., 1986; Brown, Wynne, & Medenis, 1985) performed twice-weekly, individually administered cognitive training for 3 months. Medication dosages were fixed at .3 mg/kg of methylphenidate. In order to enhance generalization, the cognitive training curricula allowed for the use of self-instructional problem-solving strategies with actual academic materials and with social problems, once the initial steps had been mastered. Outcome measures for these trials included cognitive performance assessments, academic achievement tests, and ratings of behavior at school and home.

Results from the reports of Brown and colleagues indicated that (1) Stimulant medication alone surpassed the results of cognitive therapy alone, and (2) Conbining cognitive therapy with medication did not add to the benefits of the latter. The overall picture is thus that cognitive therapy, even when extended for over 20 sessions of treatment, was not a particularly powerful intervention for ADHD children; its benefits were not equal to those of even relatively low dosages of stimulant medications, and it did not supplement medication effects in a combined treatment package.

Even more disheartening were findings from two major studies by Abikoff and colleagues (Abikoff & Gittelman, 1985; Abikoff et al., 1988). In the first report, carefully screened ADHD children, all of whom were receiving stimulant treatment, were assigned randomly to 16 weeks of (1) cognitive therapy, (2) attention control intervention, or (3) no psychosocial modality (Abikoff & Gittelman, 1985). The cognitive training comprised two phases: twice-weekly individual sessions ($n = 16$), focusing on self-instructional problem solving with cognitive analogue tasks, and twice-weekly, small-group sessions ($n = 16$), which emphasized interpersonal problem-solving skills. Social reinforcement was delivered for the children's use of covert speech and problem-solving skills, but token reinforcement was noncontingent. In addition, parents were involved in two meetings with the staff to discuss the problem-solving approach used in the child training.

Compared with the control intervention and no-treatment groups, the children receiving the cognitive training did not show any benefits with respect to measures of classroom behavior, home behavior, academic achievement, or cognitive performance (with the exception that they did develop longer response latencies on the Matching Familiar Figures Test, but without corresponding decreases in errors). Furthermore, during a follow-up period in which youngsters were placed on placebo, to determine whether cognitive training could facilitate medication withdrawal, it was found that the three intervention conditions were still essentially identical. Thus, in this study, the cognitive intervention neither supplemented the stimulant medication nor facilitated the discontinuance of the medication.

A criticism of the cognitive curriculum of Abikoff and Gittelman (1985) was that it did not include the explicitly behavioral component of contingent tangible reinforcement or response cost (see Kendall & Reber, 1987). Another critique, posed by Abikoff and Gittelman themselves, was that the cognitive problem-solving strategies were not applied to actual academic materials during the training. To remedy these gaps in the curriculum, Abikoff et al. (1988) devised an academic cognitive–behavioral training program, which included self-instructions, self-monitoring, self-reinforcement, and attack strategy training with reading and arithmetic academic materials (see Lloyd, 1980). Furthermore, contingent token rewards were given for the children's problem-solving strategies and their correct answers; response cost procedures were used as well.

The research design was similar to that of Abikoff and Gittelman (1985) in that 32, twice-weekly sessions of academic cognitive training were contrasted to an alternative treatment (remedial tutoring) and no psychosocial treatment in subjects receiving stimulants. Although children in all three conditions made some gains in academic achievement over the time course of the study, and although teachers perceived a greater benefit for the academic cognitive therapy group, there were no differential benefits on achievement tests. Furthermore, the academic cognitive training group showed a surprising tendency to display a *less* internal attributional style for academic failures after intervention. These results led the authors to the conclusion that self-instructionally based cognitive training—even when tailored to the specific academic and motivational deficits of ADHD children—did not provide incremental benefit over and above stimulant medication.

A pertinent issue related to these studies involves the medication procedures employed. In both Abikoff and Gittelman (1985) and Abikoff et al. (1988), stimulant dosages were incremented via clinical titration methods; the final dosages were in ranges considered moderate to high. In addition, Abikoff and Gittelman (1985) preselected children for a favorable medication response. Thus, it could be argued that the medication effects were sufficiently powerful to preclude significant supplementation by cognitive training. On the other hand, some children in Abikoff and Gittelman (1985) and all subjects in Abikoff et al. (1988) still had residual academic difficulties when successfully medicated, leading the authors to rebut the contention that "ceiling effects" had been reached with medication alone.

CLINICAL APPLICATIONS

With the sobering results in mind, we turn now to descriptions of the clinical applications of several cognitive–behavioral procedures typically used in training programs. We intend to give a "feel" for how cognitive–behavioral therapists put into practice the self-control strategies highlighted above. Following this section, we will conclude the chapter with an appraisal of such issues as the active components of cognitive–behavioral interventions, the actual cognitive deficits displayed by hyperactive children, and the role of cognitive strategies in the development of integrated intervention procedures for the serious problems of these youngsters.

Self-instructional Training

As noted earlier, self-instructional procedures were derived from the putative developmental sequence whereby children acquire self-control through the gradual internalization of guiding speech. The therapeutic focus of such procedures is on modifying, via "self-talk," the cognitions that precede and accompany overt behavior. Such internalized speech should orient the child to the task at hand, organize a behavioral strategy, and regulate performance until completion. It is critical to distinguish the *process* of self-instruction from the *content* of the self-statements that are made, with the latter constituting various steps or strategies to enhance planful behavior. When applied to youngsters with ADHD, self-instructional training is typically directed toward suppressing impulsive responding, enhancing the capacity to deploy and sustain attention, and facilitating self-monitoring and self-reinforcement.

Despite the variability of self-instructional training regimens across populations and tasks, most applications preserve the modeling, self-verbalization, and strategy training techniques developed by Meichenbaum and Goodman (1971). The usual training sequence is as follows: (1) The trainer first performs the task while talking aloud about the nature of the problem and the strategies he or she is using (cognitive modeling); (2) The child then performs the same task under the verbal direction of the adult (overt external guidance); (3) The child next performs the task while instructing him- or herself aloud (overt self-guidance); (4) The child performs the task again while whispering the instructions (faded overt self-guidance); (5) The child performs the task while guiding his or her behavior with private speech (covert self-instruction).

To be more concrete, we will give an example of the use of self-instructional procedures with arithmetic problems. Note that the problem-solving steps presented here include problem definition, planning, pacing oneself slowly during task performance, self-checking, error coping and correction, and self-reward for correct performance:

> OK, what is it that I have to do? I need to answer these math problems. I'll need to go slowly and carefully, I'll need to check the plus and minus signs, and I'll need to check over my work. Now, here's the first problem, $14+3$. It's a "plus" problem. I know that, it's 17. I'll write that down carefully. Wait, before I go on, I'll check myself. $14+3$ . . . right, do the one's column first, there's 7; the ten's column is a 1 . . . 17 is the answer. Great, I'm doing OK so far. Remember to keep going slowly. Next problem: $35-19$. This one looks tougher . . . right, it's a minus sign. So, first, I have to take away the numbers in the one's column. But look, 9 is bigger than 5, so I'll borrow from the 3. Now, $15-9$, that's 6. I'll write that here. What's next? Right, subtract the tens column. $3-1$ is 2; I'll write that here. So 26 is the answer. I'll check by adding the answer to the lower number. Wait a minute, that's not right! Don't worry, I'll check it carefully. Whoops, I must have forgot to change the 3 to a 2 when I borrowed. That's OK, I can erase my answer and do it right. $2-1$ is 1, so the answer is 16. Let's see if that checks. Good. Wow, even if I make a mistake, I can check it and make it right. Now I've finished. Nice job!

For different situations, the content of the problem-solving statements will be determined by the specific component tasks to be mastered. An older child's multifaceted school project, for example, might pull for thinking sequentially, organizing ideas, and gathering needed materials together. Social interactions, on the other hand, could emphasize the plans of sharing, taking turns, and/or being aware of the emotions and cues of the other children. Therapists must task analyze the problem to be solved and creatively devise statements that will enhance adaptive problem solving.

We should note that in Douglas's (1980) comprehensive cognitive training program, children are provided with an explicit rationale for their training in self-instructional, problem-solving techniques. The idea is to enhance children's motivation to employ the strategies. This issue is particularly important, given the embarrassment or mild stigma that children may experience when asked to self-instruct in classroom situations. In our concluding section, we will return to the issue of self-instructional training, taking a closer look at the clinical efficacy of these procedures for ADHD children and the theoretical rationale on which they are based.

Self-evaluation

Although self-monitoring and self-evaluation are components of the problem-solving approach incorporated in many cognitive–behavioral treatment packages, some separate discussion of these procedures is in order. Clinically, the behavioral style of ADHD children is marked by a seeming absence of accurate reflection over recently committed behavioral transgressions or over critical omissions in response style. Many such children seem genuinely perplexed, for example, over the trail of spilled materials left in the wake of their attempts to "help," or the disgruntled reactions of peers who do not wish to have the rules of a social game altered spontaneously. Indeed, investigators have commented on ADHD children's lack of careful checking of work or performance (e.g., Douglas, 1980). By incorporating explicit training in the establishment of goals or standards, monitoring of one's own behavior, and self-evaluation of such behavior in comparison with the standards, investigators are attempting to reverse the impulsive, careless, and inconsistent style of the ADHD youngster.

In treatment programs that have featured the explicit training of self-monitoring and self-evaluation, these skills are practiced on an ongoing basis. That is, as the children perform academic work, social problem solving, and other tasks, they are actively monitoring and evaluating their performance. The following description is taken form the script of Hinshaw, Henker, and Whalen (1981), who adapted procedures from Turkewitz et al. (1975) (for findings, see Hinshaw et al., 1984a). It is assumed that the participants in the small cognitive–behavioral training group to be described have been receiving 5-point behavioral ratings from the adult leaders throughout each session, with reinforcers distributed on the basis of the strength of the rating received (1 = "not at all good" behavior; 5 = "great" behavior).

Training in these skills begins with the leader's announcing a behavioral criterion for the next part of the day's curriculum. For instance, the trainer might state that children will receive reinforcement points for the next few minutes on the basis of their *paying attention*. A discussion is then held to define just what paying attention means, with the leader soliciting and modeling good and poor examples of paying attention. This part of the training is crucial: Unless the children have clear behavioral standards for the reinforcement criterion, their ability to self-monitor will be compromised. As the next task begins, the leader reminds the children to be thinking of how well they are paying attention.

After a few minutes of work, the leader stops the activity and shows the children a "Match Game" sheet (see Figure 4-1), explaining that the children will now attempt to guess or match the 5-point rating he or she will give to each of them. If there is more than one trainer, it is particularly helpful here to have the adults model a practice "Match Game." That is, one trainer, pretending to be a child, will "think out loud" as he or she tries to remember how he or she was performing with respect to the criterion.* For example: "Well, I was looking at my work and following the

---

*Other cognitive–behavioral programs employ self-evaluation programs similar to the Match Game, although such procedures are often identified by a different label.

FIGURE 4-1. "Match Game" form used for self-evaluation training.

problem-solving steps, but I did look out that window a couple of times and I did make noises with my papers. But I think that overall, I paid pretty good attention, so I'll give myself a 4—pretty good." The other adult, role playing the trainer, then says something like the following: "Sally did start out paying attention. I could tell by the way her hands were to herself and and eyes were on her work." (The trainer here should mention the criteria that went into the definition of paying attention.) "But there was a lot of time that she did look out the window, and she really didn't finish her problems. So, I'll rate her a 3—OK on paying attention." For this modeled Match Game, it is probably best for the "child" to overestimate her or his score in this way, to anticipate the overly generous evaluations that some children may give themselves.

Once the modeled Match Game is concluded and discussion is held, each child should complete a Match Game form, while the leaders privately consult to decide on their behavior ratings. The critical part of the training comes now, as the children announce, one by one, their self-evaluations, stating their reasons for the ratings they give. After each child's presentation, the leaders announce their rating for the child, again giving explicit behavioral reasons. In addition to the usual number of points the child receives, bonus points should be awarded for accurate self-evaluation. Initially, extra points can be given for self-ratings that are within a point of the adult rating; with time, the criteria can be tightened so that only percent "matches" receive extra reinforcement.

As it is being learned, the Match Game can be played several times within a given training session, so that the initial duration of self-monitoring periods is short. Eventually, the time span can be lengthened. Furthermore, whereas bonus reinforcers should initially be given for an accurate match even if the behavior is quite poor (a "1" rating), over time bonus points should be awarded for accuracy only if the behavior is at least at a level of "3." Otherwise, children could ensure an accurate match for continuous disruption or clowning. Also, the behavioral criterion for evaluations should be changed according to the training curriculum. For example, as training begins to deal with social problem solving, *cooperation* can be defined by the group and used as the matching criterion. Finally, once they have received initial consultation in behavioral and self-control principles, teachers and parents can use this self-evaluation exercise to promote the generalization of self-regulated behavior to school and home.

Anger Management

Although Feindler (Chapter 3, this volume) presents a thorough account of anger management principles and outcome findings, we will briefly discuss a documented application of anger control training for ADHD children, because of the salient interpersonal difficulties of this population. Hinshaw et al. (1981) devised a group curriculum for training in anger management skills, based, in part, on the work of Novaco (1979) for adults with anger control problems (see Hinshaw et al., 1984b, 1989, for empirical results). An essential aspect of this curriculum is the use of peers in both training and evaluation components. Also, the anger management curriculum does not constitute an isolated set of training procedures; rather, cognitive–behavioral skills for anger control are taught once the training group members have become well acquainted with one another and after they have learned basic cognitive–behavioral principles. Indeed, well before the anger control training begins, group members are asked to disclose, individually, the most bothersome or upsetting names or phrases that they are called by peers in their school or neighborhood. Leaders inform the children that such names will be used later to help practice self-control. Certainly, such open disclosure could engender embarrassment or ridicule (or could deteriorate into a forum for "bad words") unless leaders have established an open, helpful atmosphere that also incorporates firm limits. Each child's names/phrases are written on large poster paper for use in subsequent assessments.

The anger control curriculum involves several components. First, trainers bring up the issue of name calling, asking the children to generate as many alternative responses as possible to this occurrence. Second, the adult leaders engage, for the group, in a mock argument, during which one adult "provokes" the other while the second initially models a retaliatory response. This incident is stopped, and the group is encouraged to recall what happened and to see for themselves how a retaliatory response usually leads to escalation. Next, the leaders role play the argument, but this time the "target" cognitively models the use of an alternative strategy.

Another phase—and one that is quite difficult for young children—involves asking the children to reflect on their internal anger cues. That is, the trainers ask the children to search for feeling states or incipient behaviors (e.g., feeling hot, clenching a fist) that can let them monitor their developing anger. The critical component is now performed: Each youngster chooses, with guidance, a specific strategy to pair with the provocation and the impending anger he or she feels. Use of such plans is rehearsed under increasingly realistic threats from the adults and the group. For younger children, the plan may be quite concrete—for example, putting one's hands over one's ears—whereas for older youngsters more sophisticated self-talk may be adaptive. As noted earlier in the chapter, such specific strategy rehearsal appears to be the "active ingredient" in successful anger management, as assessed via videotaped group provocation exercises.

We should emphasize that such training procedures must be handled quite sensitively. If approached as a mere cognitive exercise, the curriculum will feel staged and will, in all likelihood, never be practiced in real-world, emotion-inducing circumstances. On the other hand, unless the adults are clear to enforce "no touching" rules and to contain overexuberant rehearsal, the procedures could backfire. As described earlier, stimulant medication, in sufficiently high dosages, may enhance the performance of such training practices. A clear research need is the evaluation of more extensive anger control interventions, applied to naturalistic provocations.

Attribution Training

The report of Reid and Borkowski (1987) constitutes an augmentation of cognitive–behavioral treatment strategies with explicit attribution training techniques for ADHD children. The inclusion of such a treatment component is based on the connection, in attribution theory, between external and uncontrollable causal ascriptions for personal outcomes, on the one hand, and decreased motivation, effort expenditure, and persistence in subsequent performance, on the other (Weiner, 1979). Such maladaptive attributions may be pertinent for hyperactive children (e.g., Linn & Hodge, 1982). Furthermore, interventions such as medication may continue to foster the attribution of successes to an agent outside personal control (Whalen & Henker, 1976; but see also Milich, Licht, Murphy, & Pelham, 1989). The promotion of causal attributions for successes and failures to controllable causes could conceivably enhance motivation and improve performance for ADHD children.

The four-session curriculum of Reid and Borkowski (1987) explicitly links self-control or specific strategy training procedures with attribution training. Initial sessions focus on "antecedent attributions," the child's pervasive and long-standing beliefs regarding learning ability and performance. Through a structured dialogue with the trainer, the child learns the importance of attributing both successes and failures to such controllable factors as effort and the use of self-control procedures. Visual aids in the form of cartoon characters who make controllable and uncontrollable attributional statements about both good and poor schoolwork are used to facilitate discussion. These characters make statements that "the teacher doesn't like me," "I am unlucky," "the task was too hard," or "I didn't use the strategy," following failure on a school task. Trainers model use of the latter, controllable effort attribution following modeled errors. They later make parallel effort attributions ("I tried hard and used the strategy") for correct performance.

The latter sessions address beliefs related specifically to the child's performance on training tasks. The aim here is to instill the link between (1) successful performance with training materials, and (2) the use of the specific self-control strategies that have just been taught. During the child's work with training materials, for example, trainers capitalize on naturally occurring errors to reinitiate attributional dialogue and to promote their attribution to a lack of use of the self-control strategy. Subsequent successes are also followed by attributional dialogue and by "coaching" in the explicit attribution of positive outcomes to the use of the training technique. Training tasks must be tailored to the level of the child so that errors—with their opportunity for appropriate attribution to a lack of effort and strategy use—can be made.

As noted, the Reid and Borkowski (1987) results must be viewed as preliminary, given the brevity of the intervention and the nonclinical nature of the sample. Yet the continued investigation of such attribution strategies as a concomitant to skill-based or cognitively based training procedures will be important to follow.

Response Cost

Response cost strategies are best classified as operant, and space does not permit a detailed description of these procedures here. We should note, however, that such techniques have been shown to be quite effective with externalizing children (Kendall & Braswell, 1985; Rapport, Murphy, & Bailey, 1982), whether used alone or paired with cognitive training procedures. They may be particularly important for motivating ADHD youngsters, whose performance seems to be best enhanced by the addition of prudent negative consequences to positive reinforcement programs (Rosen, O'Leary, Joyce, Conway, & Pfiffner, 1984). In brief, response cost involves the loss of previously earned reinforcers, contingent upon the display of a target behavior deemed unacceptable (e.g., off-task, disruption, aggression). Such procedures are always to be supplemented by direct reinforcement of alternative behaviors. The addition of response cost procedures to cognitive curricula is highly recommended for providing a truly integrated set of cognitive *and* behavioral procedures for children with significant attentional and behavioral difficulties.

CRITICAL ISSUES AND FUTURE DIRECTIONS

The chief issues from the preceding pages concern (1) the viability of cognitive training and of cognitive–behavioral treatments for children with ADHD, and (2) the role of such procedures in truly multimodal intervention packages. In reviewing these issues, we will highlight a recent meta-analysis of cognitive self-instructional treatments for children, comment on active treatment components within the broad range of cognitive–behavioral strategies, and discuss the debate regarding specific cognitive deficits or excesses of this population (see Kendall, 1985). We will conclude with the assertions that, although several cognitive strategies have a role in the treatment of children with ADHD, (1) self-instructional techniques alone have not been shown to constitute a valuable intervention for such children; and (2) cognitively oriented strategies cannot replace (but may be able to extend benefits from) the pharmacologic and behavioral treatments that are considered primary interventions.

Meta-analytic Findings

In a recent meta-analysis, Dush et al. (1989) reviewed the results of studies using "self-statement modification"—that is, procedures involving explicit intervention with covert self-statements, or self-instructional training—for behavior-disordered children. Across the sampled reports, the overall effect size was .35 (for all outcomes) or .47 (with studies equally weighted). Such effect sizes were greater than those from placebo treatment or no treatment conditions, leading to the conclusion that self-statement modification is a viable treatment modality. Effect sizes of this magnitude, however, are smaller than those found with adult applications of cognitive–behavioral therapy, and they are "contaminated" by the many additional techniques incorporated within the treatment procedures. In addition, when Dush et al. (1989) subcategorized the effect sizes by reports with (1) truly clinical samples or (2) follow-up data, the effect sizes dropped considerably. In short, the initially positive picture regarding self-statement modification approaches is tempered when one examines clinical samples or when one is interested in durable effects. Self-instructions may be a useful component of a comprehensive program but cannot be considered a viable intervention when used alone.

Such meta-analytic results parallel those that we have discussed in the preceding pages regarding cognitive–behavioral, and particularly self-instructional, treatments for children with specific problems of hyperactivity. That is, the promise of the procedures is diminished when one considers actual clinical samples, overt behavioral outcomes, durable effects, or comparisons with medication. Even with more recent investigations that have incorporated longer training periods of up to 32 sessions, the clinical efficacy of the procedures is found to be wanting (e.g., Abikoff & Gittelman, 1985; Abikoff et al., 1988). In all, the use of self-instructionally based, cognitive training procedures (without the behavioral components) for children with ADHD cannot be advocated.

Cognitive–Behavioral Interventions: Active Components

We noted earlier that several well-controlled reports of recent origin point to statistically, if not clinically, significant benefits of cognitive–behavioral intervention for aggressive, conduct-disordered children (e.g., Kazdin et al., 1989; see also Lochman, White, & Wayland, Chapter 2, this volume).*

---

*That low SES, aggressive children have responded favorably to (but not been normalized with) cognitive–behavioral therapy, when ADHD children have not benefited from major

We also described the promising (albeit short-term) applications of self-control training for ADHD children with respect to social competence, anger management, and the altering of maladaptive attributions. Whereas the treatments deployed in these reports incorporated self-instructions to some extent, they also included other key facets of the broad spectrum of cognitive–behavioral procedures, including social skills/problem-solving training, anger management strategies, response cost, and explicit intervention regarding self-evaluation. The issue here is the identification of those elements that show the most promise for clinical samples. In other words, many techniques are included in intervention programs labeled "cognitive" or "cognitive–behavioral," and more specificity regarding active components is required.

Yet, as foreshadowed in an earlier section, component analyses or dismantling studies that could potentially ascertain active ingredients may be premature before the field has documented clinically meaningful gains with *any* treatments or treatment combinations. Furthermore, it can be argued that extant treatments for ADHD, including both cognitive–behavioral and medication interventions, are rather exclusively focused on the individual child's problems and that the contextual determinants of behavior are neglected. That is, components that address couple or family conflict, the peer network, or wider systems support for families may be mandated for the sufficient treatment of ADHD youngsters. Also, given the chronic nature of externalizing behavioral disorders, treatment procedures may have to be extended well beyond the 3–4-month periods that now constitute lengthy interventions (Kazdin, 1987).

Perhaps the optimal strategy would be to use results of reports that point to promising components, integrate these into an intervention program of sufficient duration to be of real potential benefit, and only then perform the necessary dismantling studies to ascertain truly active procedures. Indeed, such an approach is exemplified in three large-scale projects that have either recently begun or will soon begin in the United States and Canada. To delineate some specific plans regarding the integration of cognitive components with behavioral, family, and pharmacologic interventions for ADHD children, we will briefly describe the clinical procedures to be employed in these new investigations.

Integrative Intervention Programs

First, Hinshaw will work with clinically referred ADHD children who are receiving stimulant medication. Following intensive summer research programs, children and families will be assigned randomly to 9 months of (1)

---

trials, is puzzling. Abikoff (in press) raises the issue of diagnostic specificity, arguing that results with one disorder may not generalize to other diagnostic categories.

behavioral and cognitive–behavioral parent training *plus* small-group, self-control intervention groups for the children, versus (2) regular community treatment. Youngsters in both conditions will continue to receive medication treatment. Parent and child groups will be scheduled on a weekly basis for 4 months, followed by home visits, school consultation, and booster sessions. The child training will deemphasize self-instructional procedures, focusing instead on rehearsal-based interpersonal problem solving, anger management, and self-evaluation procedures, with particular emphasis on promotion of generalization to home and school. Although the parent intervention will be largely behavioral, parents will receive instruction in the techniques learned by their children and will attempt to coach and reinforce self-controlled behavior at home. The hope is to determine whether intensive parent and child intervention can supplement stimulant medication, with particular interest in outcomes related to social competence.

Second, in a remarkably thorough multimodality intervention study, for which Howard Abikoff and Lily Hechtman serve as principal investigators, a clinical sample of ADHD children and their families will participate in an intensive package of psychosocial interventions in addition to stimulant medication. The three-group design is similar to those reported by Abikoff and Gittelman (1985) and Abikoff et al. (1988): Medication-responsive ADHD children, all of whom will receive optimal dosages of stimulants, will be assigned randomly to (1) an intensive multimodality treatment package, (2) attention placebo treatment, or (3) regular community intervention. The multimodality condition will comprise individual child therapy, academic tutoring, group parent training, individual family counseling, and small-group social skills training for 1 year, with booster sessions conducted in the second year (H. Abikoff, personal communication, October, 1989).

Although the child training curriculum is directed toward shaping social skills rather than toward modifying private speech, external reinforcement procedures during the groups will be systematically faded via self-evaluation procedures that are similar to those described above in the section on clinical applications. Thus, the "cognitive" feature of self-evaluation will be used to fade from external rewards, but cognitive problem-solving strategies are not the focus of the curriculum. The study is noteworthy for the intensive coordination required for the home–school reinforcement program that will be established: Parents will provide home rewards contingent upon the child's points earned both at school and within the social skills groups. In all, this study will attempt to extend and solidify the findings of the uncontrolled multimodality investigation of Satterfield, Satterfield, and Cantwell (1981), in which children receiving multiple treatment components, including medication, fared better than expected over extended follow-up periods.

Third, working with a younger population, Russell Barkley and colleagues will randomly assign kindergarten children meeting criteria for ADHD to special enriched classroom settings versus regular kindergarten placements for a full school year. Medication treatment is not a central focus of this study, although medication assessments will be performed if indicated. The intensive, multifaceted, special classroom programs will contain a wide variety of behavioral and cognitive components, including contingency management procedures (token rewards, time out, and differential attention for positive behaviors), direct instruction via computers, self-instructional problem solving, anger management, and behavioral parent training. Follow-up measures through first and second grade in a variety of behavioral and academic domains will be collected; the intention is clearly to treat the core classroom, social, and home-based manifestations of ADHD before the grade-school years begin, in order to prevent the typically worsening course of the disorder throughout childhood.

All three of these recently planned programs include multiple treatment components; in addition, all include at least 9 months of active intervention as well as procedures to promote generalization. Although results will obviously not be available for some time, such investigations may begin to determine whether integrative treatments can alter the core symptoms, associated features, and short-term course of ADHD. However, none makes the assumption that cognitive procedures alone can provide clinically sufficient benefit.

Final Issues

It will be recalled that the initial impetus for the use of cognitive techniques with hyperactive children came from developmental theorizing and evidence regarding the origins of self-controlled behavior via internalized self-verbalizations. One issue that arises in light of the weak effects of self-instructional training for children with ADHD is whether this model is actually appropriate for explaining the cognitive and behavioral deficits of this population. That is, even if the Russian linguistic model mentioned previously has validity for normally developing children, it is still indeterminate whether the multiple difficulties of ADHD children originate from a failure or delay in the internalization of guiding speech. Furthermore, even if hyperactive youngsters do evidence such a delay, it is unclear whether training procedures that recapitulate the putative developmental sequence—the steps of trainer cognitive modeling through child covert self-instruction (see section on clinical applications)—will ameliorate deficient self-regulation. In short, the validity of the underlying model providing the rationale for self-instructional training with ADHD children is far from certain.

Related to this issue is the continuing need for research on the cognitive mechanisms and processes of ADHD youngsters. The kinds of "task

analyses" of environmental cues and consequences that are routinely performed by operant behavioral practitioners are still relatively unexplored in
the cognitive realm (Whalen, et al., 1985). We need to know more precisely the actual cognitive deficits or excesses displayed by ADHD youngsters in various academic or social demand situations. With respect to
aggression, the seminal work of Dodge and colleagues (see Dodge, 1985)
has shown that aggressive children display several levels of cognitive processing deficiencies (e.g., cue underutilization regarding ambiguous interpersonal situations) and excesses (e.g., overattribution of hostile intent to
peers), which may be related to the display of reactive (but not proactive)
aggression (Dodge & Coie, 1987). Presumably, intervention can be increasingly tailored to such processes.* In spite of the impressive work of Douglas and others aimed at pinpointing the cognitive deficiencies of ADHD
children, debate continues as to which types of attentional, strategic, metacognitive, self-regulatory, motoric, and/or motivational deficits are primary (e.g., Van der Meere, van Baal, & Sergeant, 1989). In short, a ver-
idical theoretical rationale for effective cognitive procedures may still be
lacking.

We suggest that the optimal role for "cognitive" strategies in the treatment of ADHD children may be related to one of the original motivations
for their development: to extend the benefits of more traditional operant
behavioral treatments.** Although the field has clearly moved away from
contentions that cognitive techniques alone can supplant behavioral interventions, the intentional use of cognitive strategies such as self-evaluation
to fade token reward programs or to extend their benefits to nonpro-
grammed settings is an underresearched area. Overall, we contend that optimal psychosocial interventions for ADHD youngsters should blend behavioral and cognitive elements. That is, with the basis of intervention located
in a strong, behavioral motivational system, cognitive strategies can be used
to (1) increase initial motivation for participation and persistence, (2) fade
the external reinforcers via self-evaluation procedures, (3) help to program
for refractory domains, such as anger management or development of prosocial behavior, and (4) enhance optimal attributions for successful outcomes.

To amplify this last point, we point out further that the boundary between "behavioral" and at least some "cognitive" strategies is an increasingly fuzzy one. Practitioners of good behavior management systems have
typically included implicit (if not explicit) cognitive procedures, by actively
involving the child in the selection of reinforcers, gradually allowing the

---

*It is noteworthy that Milich and Dodge (1984) localized such cognitive deficiencies and
excesses in a subgroup composed of hyperactive plus aggressive children, and not in a purely
aggressive group.
**Discussions with William Pelham were central to the development of these ideas.

child a greater role in his or her management program, thinning reinforcement schedules, and the like. Furthermore, the most promising cognitive interventions for ADHD children have routinely included overtly behavioral components (e.g., rehearsal-based anger management training; direct reinforcement for accurate self-evaluation or for classroom application of academic strategies; response cost procedures that are integrated into training groups). The salient question is whether the integration of cognitive and behavioral strategies—with each other and with pharmacologic treatment—can provide significant long-term benefit for the difficult problems of ADHD children.

REFERENCES

Abikoff, H. (1987). An evaluation of cognitive behavior therapy for hyperactive children. In B. B. Lahey & A. E. Kazdin (Eds.), *Advances in clinical child psychology* (Vol. 10, pp. 171–216). New York: Plenum Press.

Abikoff, H. (in press). Cognitive training in ADHD children: Less to it than meets the eye. *Journal of Learning Disabilities.*

Abikoff, H., Ganeles, D., Reiter, G., Blum, C., Foley, C., & Klein, R. G. (1988). Cognitive training in academically deficient ADHD boys receiving stimulant medication. *Journal of Abnormal Child Psychology, 16,* 411–432.

Abikoff, H., & Gittelman, R. (1985). Hyperactive children treated with stimulants: Is cognitive training a useful adjunct? *Archives of General Psychiatry, 42,* 953–961.

Achenbach, T. M., Conners, C. K., Quay, H. C., Verhulst, F. C., & Howell, C. T. (1989). Replication of empirically derived syndromes as a basis for taxonomy of child/adolescent psychopathology. *Journal of Abnormal Child Psychology, 17,* 299–323.

American Psychiatric Association. (1980). *Diagnostic and statistical manual of mental disorders* (3rd ed.). Washington, DC: Author.

American Psychiatric Association. (1987). *Diagnostic and statistical manual of mental disorders* (3rd ed., rev.). Washington, DC: Author.

Barkley, R. A. (1982). Guidelines for defining hyperactivity in children: Attention deficit disorder with hyperactivity. In B. B. Lahey & A. E. Kazdin (Eds.), *Advances in clinical child psychology* (Vol. 5, pp. 137–180). New York: Plenum Press.

Brown, R. T., Borden, K. A., Wynne, M. E., Schleser, R., & Clingerman, S. R. (1986). Methylphenidate and cognitive therapy with ADD children: A methodological reconsideration. *Journal of Abnormal Child Psychology, 14,* 481–497.

Brown, R. T., Wynne, M. E., Borden, K. A., Clingerman, S. R., Geniesse, R., & Spunt, A. L. (1986). Methylphenidate and cognitive therapy in children with attention deficit disorder. A double-blind trial. *Developmental and Behavioral Pediatrics, 7,* 163–172.

Brown, R. T., Wynne, M. E., & Medenis, R. (1985). Methylphenidate and cognitive therapy: A comparison of treatment approaches with hyperactive boys. *Journal of Abnormal Child Psychology, 13,* 69–87.

Bugental, D. B., Whalen, C. K., & Henker, B. (1977). Causal attributions of hyperactive children and motivational assumptions of two behavior change approaches: Evidence for an interactionist position. *Child Development, 48,* 874–884.

Cameron, M. I., & Robinson, V. M. J. (1980). Effects of cognitive training on academic and on-task behavior of hyperactive children. *Journal of Abnormal Child Psychology, 8,* 405–419.

Chee, P., Logan, G., Schachar, R., Lindsay, P., & Wachsmuth, R. (1989). Effects of event rate and display time on sustained attention in hyperactive, normal, and control children. *Journal of Abnormal Child Psychology, 17,* 371–391.

Clements, S. C., & Peters, J. E. (1962). Minimal brain dysfunction in the school-aged child. *Archives of General Psychiatry, 6,* 185–197.

Copeland, L., Wolraich, M., Lindgren, S., Milich, R., & Woolson, R. (1987). Pediatricians' reported practices in the assessment and treatment of attention deficit disorders. *Developmental and Behavioral Pediatrics, 8,* 191–197.

Dodge, K. A., & Coie, J. D. (1987). Social information-processing factors in reactive and proactive aggression. *Journal of Personality and Social Psychology, 53,* 1146–1158.

Douglas, V. I. (1972). Stop, look, and listen: The problem of sustained attention and impulse control in hyperactive and normal children. *Canadian Journal of Behavioral Science, 4,* 259–282.

Douglas, V. I. (1980). Treatment and training approaches to hyperactivity: Establishing internal or external control. In C. K. Whalen & B. Henker (Eds.), *Hyperactive children: The social ecology of identification and treatment* (pp. 283–317). New York: Academic Press.

Douglas, V. I., Barr, R. G., Amin, K., O'Neill, M. E., & Britton, B. G. (1988). Dosage effects and individual responsivity to methylphenidate in attention deficit disorder. *Journal of Child Psychology and Psychiatry, 29,* 453–475.

Douglas, V. I., Parry, P., Marton, P., & Garson, C. (1976). Assessment of a cognitive training program for hyperactive children. *Journal of Abnormal Child Psychology, 4,* 389–410.

Drabman, R., Spitalnik, R., & O'Leary, K. D. (1973). Teaching self-control to disruptive children. *Journal of Abnormal Psychology, 82,* 10–16.

Dush, D. M., Hirt, M. L., & Schroeder, H. E. (1989). Self-statement modification in the treatment of child behavior disorders: A metaanalysis. *Psychological Bulletin, 106,* 97–106.

Dweck, C. S. (1975). The role of expectations and attributions in the alleviation of learned helplessness. *Journal of Personality and Social Psychology, 31,* 674–685.

D'Zurilla, T. J., & Goldfried, M. R. (1971). Problem solving and behavior modification. *Journal of Abnormal Psychology, 78,* 107–126.

Gittelman, R., Abikoff, H., Pollack, E., Klein, D. F., Katz, S., & Mattes, J. (1980). A controlled trial of behavior modification and methylphenidate in hyperactive children. In C. K. Whalen & B. Henker (Eds.), *Hyperactive children: The social ecology of identification and treatment* (pp. 221–243). New York: Academic Press.

Gittelman, R. Mannuzza, S., Shenker, R., & Bonagura, N. (1985). Hyperactive boys almost grown up. *Archives of General Psychiatry, 42,* 937–947.

Henker, B., Whalen, C. K., & Hinshaw, S. P. (1980). The attributional contexts of cognitive intervention strategies. *Exceptional Education Quarterly, 1*, 17–30.

Hinshaw, S. P. (1987). On the distinction between attentional deficits/hyperactivity and conduct problems/aggression in child psychopathology. *Psychological Bulletin, 101*, 443–463.

Hinshaw, S. P., Buhrmester, D., & Heller, T. (1989). Anger control in response to verbal provocation: Effects of stimulant medication for boys with ADHD. *Journal of Abnormal Child Psychology, 17*, 393–407.

Hinshaw, S. P., & Erhardt, D. (in press). Behavioral treatment of attention deficit-hyperactivity disorder. In V. B. Van Hasselt & M. Hersen (Eds.), *Handbook of behavior therapy and pharmacotherapy for children: A comparative analysis*. Orlando, FL: Grune & Stratton.

Hinshaw, S. P., Henker, B., & Whalen, C. K. (1981). *Self-regulation for hyperactive boys: A training manual*. Unpublished manuscript, University of California, Los Angeles.

Hinshaw, S. P., Henker, B., & Whalen, C. K. (1984a). Cognitive–behavioral and pharmacologic interventions for hyperactive boys: Comparative and combined effects. *Journal of Consulting and Clinical Psychology, 52*, 739–749.

Hinshaw, S. P., Henker, B., & Whalen, C. K. (1984b). Self-control in hyperactive boys in anger-inducing situations: Effects of cognitive–behavioral training and of methylphenidate. *Journal of Abnormal Child Psychology, 12*, 55–77.

Hinshaw, S. P., Henker, B., Whalen, C. K., Erhardt, D., & Dunnington, R. E. (1989). Aggressive, prosocial, and nonsocial behavior in hyperactive boys: Dose effects of methylphenidate in naturalistic settings. *Journal of Consulting and Clinical Psychology, 57*, 636–643.

Kanfer, F. H., & Karoly, P. (1972). Self-control: A behavioristic excursion into the lion's den. *Behavior Therapy, 3*, 398–416.

Kazdin, A. E. (1987). Treatment of antisocial behavior in children: Current status and future directions. *Psychological Bulletin, 102*, 187–203.

Kazdin, A. E., Bass, D., Siegel, T., & Thomas, C. (1989). Cognitive–behavioral therapy and relationship therapy in the treatment of children referred for antisocial behavior. *Journal of Consulting and Clinical Psychology, 57*, 522–535.

Kazdin, A. E., Esveldt–Dawson, K., French, N. H., & Unis, A. S. (1987). Problem-solving skills training and relationship therapy in the treatment of antisocial behavior. *Journal of Consulting and Clinical Psychology, 55*, 76–85.

Kendall, P. C. (1985). Toward a cognitive–behavioral model of child psychopathology and a critique of related interventions. *Journal of Abnormal Child Psychology, 13*, 357–372.

Kendall, P. C., & Braswell, L. (1985). *Cognitive–behavioral therapy for impulsive children*. New York: Guilford Press.

Kendall, P. C., & Finch, A. J., Jr. (1976). A cognitive–behavioral treatment for impulsivity: A case study. *Journal of Consulting and Clinical Psychology, 44*, 852–857.

Kendall, P. C., & Reber, M. (1987). Cognitive training in treatment of hyperactivity in children [Letter to the editor]. *Archives of General Psychiatry, 44*, 296.

Kiesler, D. J. (1966). Some myths of psychotherapy research and the search for a paradigm. *Psychological Bulletin, 65*, 110–136.

Klein, R. G. (1987). Pharmacotherapy of childhood hyperactivity: An update. In

H. Y. Meltzer (Ed.), *Psychopharmacology: The third generation of progress* (pp. 1215–1224). New York: Raven Press.

Linn, R. T., & Hodge, G. K. (1982). Locus of control in childhood hyperactivity. *Journal of Consulting and Clinical Psychology, 50,* 592–593.

Lloyd, J. (1980). Academic instruction and cognitive behavior modification: The need for attack strategy training. *Exceptional Education Quarterly, 1,* 53–56.

Loney, J., & Milich, R. (1982). Hyperactivity, inattention, and aggression in clinical practice. In M. Wolraich & D. K. Routh (Eds.), *Advances in developmental and behavioral pediatrics* (Vol. 2, pp. 113–147). Greenwich, CT: JAI Press.

Meichenbaum, D. H. (1977). *Cognitive behavior modification: An integrative approach.* New York: Plenum Press.

Meichenbaum, D. H., & Goodman, J. (1971). Training impulsive children to talk to themselves: A means of developing self-control. *Journal of Abnormal Psychology, 77,* 115–126.

Milich, R., & Dodge, K. A. (1984). Social information processing in child psychiatric populations. *Journal of Abnormal Child Psychology, 12,* 471–489.

Milich, R., & Kramer, J. (1984). Reflections on impulsivity: An empirical investigation of impulsivity as a construct. In K. D. Gadow (Ed.), *Advances in learning and behavioral disabilities* (Vol. 3, pp. 57–94). Greenwich, CT: JAI Press.

Milich, R., & Landau, S. (1989). The role of social status variables in differentiating subgroups of hyperactive children. In L. M. Bloomingdale & J. Swanson (Eds.), *Attention deficit disorder* (Vol. 4). Oxford, England: Pergamon Press.

Milich, R., Licht, B. G., Murphy, D. A., & Pelham, W. E. (1989). ADHD boys' evaluations of and attributions for task performance on medication vs. placebo. *Journal of Abnormal Psychology, 98,* 280–284.

Murphy, D. A., Pelham, W. E., & Lang, A. R. (1986, August). *CNS stimulant effects on aggression in ADD and ADD/aggressive children.* Paper presented at the annual meeting of the American Psychological Association, Washington, DC.

Novaco, R. W. (1979). The cognitive regulation of anger and stress. In P. C. Kendall & S. D. Hollon (Eds.), *Cognitive–behavioral interventions: Theory, research, and procedures* (pp. 241–285). New York: Academic Press.

Palkes, H., Stewart, M., & Freedman, J. (1972). Improvement in maze performance of hyperactive boys as a function of verbal-training procedures. *Journal of Special Education, 5,* 337–342.

Pelkes, H., Stewart, M., & Kahana, B. (1968). Porteus Maze performance of hyperactive boys after training in self-directed verbal commands. *Child Development, 39,* 817–826.

Parker, J. G., & Asher, S. R. (1987). Peer relations and later personal adjustment: Are low-accepted children at risk? *Psychological Bulletin, 102,* 357–389.

Pelham, W. E. (1982, August). Laboratory measures of attention in the diagnosis of hyperactivity/attention deficit disorder. In W. Pelham (Chair), *Identification and diagnosis of children with attention deficit disorder/hyperactivity.* Symposium presented at the annual meeting of the American Psychological Association, Washington, DC.

Pelham, W. E., Bender, M. E., Caddell, J., Booth, S., & Moorer, S. H. (1985). Methylphenidate and children with attention deficit disorder: Dose effects on classroom and social behavior. *Archives of General Psychiatry, 42,* 948–952.

Pelham, W. E., & Murphy, H. A. (1986). Attention deficit and conduct disorders.

In M. Hersen (Ed.), *Pharmacological and behavioral treatments: An integrative approach* (pp. 108–148). New York: Wiley.

Porrino, L. J., Rapoport, J. L., Behar, D., Sceery, W., Ismond, D. R., & Bunney, W. E. (1983). A naturalistic assessment of the motor activity of hyperactive boys: I. Comparison with normal controls. *Archives of General Psychiatry, 40,* 681–687.

Quay, H. C. (1986). Classification. In H. C. Quay & J. S. Werry (Eds.), *Psychopathological disorders of childhood* (3rd ed., pp. 1–34). New York: Wiley.

Rapport, M. D., Murphy, H. A., & Bailey, J. S. (1982). Ritalin vs. response cost in the control of hyperactive children: A within-subject comparison. *Journal of Applied Behavior Analysis, 15,* 205–216.

Reid, M. K., & Borkowski, J. G. (1987). Causal attributions of hyperactive children: Implications for teaching strategies and self-control. *Journal of Educational Psychology, 79,* 296–307.

Rosen, L. A., O'Leary, S. G., Joyce, S. A., Conway, G., & Pfiffner, L. J. (1984). The importance of prudent negative consequences for maintaining the appropriate behavior of hyperactive students. *Journal of Abnormal Child Psychology, 12,* 581–604.

Safer, D. J., & Krager, J. M. (1984). Trends in medication therapy for hyperactivity: National and international perspectives. In K. D. Gadow (Ed.), *Advances in learning and behavioral disabilities* (Vol. 3, pp. 125–149). Greenwich, CT: JAI.

Satterfield, J. H., Hoppe, C. M., & Schell, A. M. (1982). A prospective study of delinquency in 110 adolescent boys with attention deficit disorder and 88 normal adolescent boys. *American Journal of Psychiatry, 139,* 795–798.

Satterfield, J. H., Satterfield, B. T., & Cantwell, D. P. (1981). Three-year multimodality treatment study of 100 hyperactive boys. *Journal of Pediatrics, 98,* 650–655.

Spivack, G., & Shure, M. B. (1974). *Social adjustment of young children: A cognitive approach to solving real-life problems.* San Francisco: Jossey–Bass.

Tisdelle, D. A., & St. Lawrence, J. S. (1986). Interpersonal problem-solving competency: Review and critique. *Clinical Psychology Review, 6,* 337–356.

Turkewitz, H., O'Leary, K. D., & Ironsmith, M. (1975). Generalization and maintenance of appropriate behavior through self-control. *Journal of Consulting and Clinical Psychology, 43,* 577–583.

Van der Meere, J., van Baal, M., & Sergeant, J. (1989). The additive factor method: A differential diagnostic tool in hyperactivity and learning disability. *Journal of Abnormal Child Psychology, 17,* 409–422.

Varni, J. W., & Henker, B. (1979). A self-regulation approach to the treatment of three hyperactive boys. *Child Behavior Therapy, 1,* 171–192.

Walker, J. L., Lahey, B. B., Hynd, G. W., & Frame, C. L. (1987). Comparison of specific patterns of antisocial behavior in children with conduct disorder with or without coexisting hyperactivity. *Journal of Consulting and Clinical Psychology, 55,* 910–913.

Weiner, B. (1979). A theory of motivation for some classroom experiences. *Journal of Educational Psychology, 71,* 3–25.

Weiss, G., & Hechtman, L. T. (1986). *Hyperactive children grown up.* New York: Guilford Press.

Whalen, C. K. (1989). Attention-deficit hyperactivity disorder. In T. H. Ollendick

& M. Hersen (Eds.), *Handbook of child psychopathology* (2nd ed., pp. 131–169). New York: Plenum.

Whalen, C. K., & Henker, B. (1976). Psychostimulants and children: A review and analysis. *Psychological Bulletin, 83,* 1113–1130.

Whalen, C. K., Henker, B., Buhrmester, D., Hinshaw, S. P., Huber, A., & Laski, K. (1989). Does stimulant medication improve the peer status of hyperactive children? *Journal of Consulting and Clinical Psychology, 57,* 545–549.

Whalen, C. K., Henker, B., & Hinshaw, S. P. (1985). Cognitive–behavioral therapies for hyperactive children: Premises, problems, and prospects. *Journal of Abnormal Child Psychology, 13,* 391–410.

Young, J. G., Halperin, J. M., Leven, L. I., Shaywitz, B. A., & Cohen, D. J. (1987). Developmental neuropharmacology: Clinical and neurochemical perspectives on the regulation of attention, learning, and movement. In L. L. Iversen, S. D. Iversen, & S. H. Snyder (Eds.), *Handbook of psychopharmacology* (Vol. 19, pp. 59–121). New York: Plenum Press.

PART III
INTERNALIZING DISORDERS

CHAPTER 5

Treating Anxiety Disorders in Children and Adolescents

PHILIP C. KENDALL, TAMAR ELLSAS CHANSKY,
MICHAEL FREIDMAN, RAY KIM,
ELIZABETH KORTLANDER, FRANCES M. SESSA,
AND LYNNE SIQUELAND
Temple University

NATURE OF ANXIETY IN CHILDREN AND ADOLESCENTS

Fear is a universal human experience; for children, adolescents, and adults it can serve as an adaptive response in many situations. Fears in youngsters are common, they are usually transitory and their appearance and resolution can be seen as a part of a normal developmental process. Thus, the mere presence of fears is not an indicator of psychopathology and, in fact, often may be a necessary concomitant to normal development. At other times, fearful or anxious reactions may be a deterrent to development, impinging on mastery and growth. Such developmental factors and normative data on children's fears and anxieties must be considered when making decisions about diagnosis and treatment.

Differences among fear, phobia, and anxiety have been posited and can assist in clarifying the diagnostic picture. Fear is seen as a discrete response to a circumscribed experience of threat, as opposed to anxiety, which is considered a less differentiated response to diffuse stimuli—what Johnson and Melamed (1979) described as "apprehension without apparent cause" (p. 107). Phobias are fears which are severe, persistent behavioral patterns of avoidance (Barrios & Hartmann, 1988; Miller, Barrett, & Hampe, 1974; Morris & Kratochwill, 1983). Fears are part of normal development and emerge and recede throughout childhood and adolescence. To distinguish normal and developmental fears from pathological ones, a clearer demarcation of normal fears is needed (Graziano & Mooney, 1984). Early efforts in this direction established the prevalence of fears in normal samples and have suggested a developmental sequence in the content of these fears.

A separate category of childhood anxiety disorders was first introduced in DSM-III (American Psychiatric Association, 1984). Three subtypes were identified: Separation Anxiety Disorder, Avoidant Disorder, and Overanxious Disorder. Although the disorders may overlap (Gittelman, 1986), each subtype has distinct features. Separation Anxiety involves anxiety to the point of panic upon separation from, or for older children in anticipation of separation from, an attachment figure. Concerns include impending danger and preoccupation with death which result in curtailed activity away from home. Extreme shyness and withdrawal from new situations or people characterizes Avoidant Disorder; stranger anxiety continues beyond the developmental timetable. Overanxious Disorder is generalized anxiety, including fear of evaluation, self-consciousness, and rumination about past or future behavior. Given the clinical, as opposed to empirical, derivation of these categories (Francis, 1988), many consider them to be tentative distinctions and subject to change (e.g., Gittelman, 1985).

The need to establish the validity of childhood anxiety disorders by determining developmentally relevant criteria (Last, 1988) has yet to be fully amplified. An exception, Strauss, Lease, Last, and Francis (1988), examined developmental differences in Overanxious Disorder. No significant demographic differences emerged, but older children (12–19) presented with a larger total number of symptoms than did younger children (5–11), and older children were more likely to have concurrent major depression and simple phobia while younger children were more likely to have concurrent Separation Anxiety or Attention Deficit Disorder.

The importance of correctly determining developmental anomalies is inextricably linked to diagnostic validity. Changes that appear in DSM-III-R (APA, 1987), compared with DSM-III, reflect this concern. For example, DSM-III-R contains more stringent criteria for giving a diagnosis of Separation Anxiety. Ostensibly, the revised criteria differentiate pathological from normally occurring separation anxiety. Given the newness of the category, changes in diagnostic criteria may be expected as data are gathered and reported.

Studies of fears in normal children reveal their prevalence, emergence, and resolution throughout childhood and adolescence. For instance, in one sample, 90% of the children evidenced a least one fear between the ages of 2 and 14. Jersild and Holmes (1936) reported that on the average children had 4.64 fears. Examining maternal report of their children's fears throughout childhood (2–14), McFarlane, Allen, and Honzik (1954) found that 90% of the children experienced at least one fear. And Lapouse and Monk (1959) found that 43% of their sample had seven or more fears. It is important to note that in this study, fears were not correlated with other indicators of psychopathology (Orvaschel & Weissman, 1986).

Normative data suggest that the changing content of fears over time reflects the child's growing experience in the world and increasing perception of reality (Campbell, 1986). Children's fears evolve from global, imaginary, uncontrollable powerful content (e.g., monsters, the dark), to more specific, differentiated, and realistic content, such as social acceptance and school achievement (Bauer, 1976). The fears themselves may be a way for the child to deal with challenges which he or she confronts (Campbell, 1986; Morris & Kratochwill, 1983). For example, the prevalent stranger response in infants may occur concurrently with mastery of the concept of the familiar (Campbell, 1986). A five-factor structure of the content areas of children' fears has been outlined on the basis of the widely used Fear Survey Schedule for Children (FSSC-R; Ollendick, 1983; Ollendick, Matson, & Helsel, 1985). These areas include: fear of failure and criticism, the unknown, minor injury and small animals, danger and death, and medical fears. While age and gender difference exist, the factors themselves appear to be robust across age, gender and even nationality (Ollendick, King, & Frary, 1989).

In addition to developmental changes in fear content, quantitative changes also occur. In general, research suggests a decrease in number of fears with increasing age (Bauer, 1976; Draper & James, 1985; Jersild & Holmes, 1936; Lapouse & Monk, 1959). But even older adolescents (16–18) report an average of 11.6 fears (Ollendick et al., 1985).

Sex differences in the number of childhood fears have been found. Both maternal and self-report show more prevalent fears among girls (Bauer, 1976; Lapouse & Monk, 1959; Ollendick et al., 1985). However, sex-role expectations or other sociocultural factors may impinge on both child and parent reports (Bauer, 1976; Ollendick et al., 1985).

While age and developmental level dictate some dimensions of a child's response to fears, individual difference exist. Campbell (1986) argued that given such influences as temperament, context, and past experience, a fear response may take such disparate forms as "nightmares, bed-wetting, temper-tantrums, social withdrawal or aggressive behavior with peers" (p. 25).

Clinicians and researchers view childhood anxiety as a multidimensional construct manifested at physiological, behavioral, and cognitive levels. Despite criticisms (e.g., Campbell, 1986), motoric responses in anxiety are important and have received much research attention (Barrios & Hartmann, 1988). Common motoric components of anxiety responses include, most prominently, avoidance, as well as, shaky voice, rigid posture, crying, nail biting, and thumb sucking (Barrios & Hartmann, 1988).

Physiological reactions include: increase in automatic nervous activity, perspiration, diffuse abdominal pain ("butterflies in the stomach"), flushed face, urgent need to urinate, trembling, and gastrointestinal distress (see also Barrios & Hartmann, 1988). The physiological assessment of anxiety in adults has received wide attention (see Himadi, Boice, & Barlow, 1985), yet little empirical data on these indicators in children exist (Barrios & Hartmann, 1988; Beidel, 1988) even though these are considered a necessary and promising area of research (Barrios, Hartmann, & Shigetomi, 1981; Miller, 1983). An exception is a recent study by Beidel (1988), where significant differences in autonomic activity were found in anxious children, compared with nonanxious controls, during a test-taking task. Overall, test-anxious children had significantly higher heart rates than nonanxious controls; however, no differences were found in systolic or diastolic blood pressure. Such results confirm cautions by some (e.g., Haynes, 1978) who advocate monitoring more than one physiological indicator, because concurrent indicators may not correlate.

A variety of anxious children's thoughts have been described; these include thoughts of being scared or hurt, self-critical thoughts, or thoughts of danger (see Barrios & Hartmann, 1988). However, until recently, little empirical work has examined cognitions in clinically anxious children. Francis (1988), in her recent review of cognitions of anxious children, concluded that "no definitive statements about the cognitions of anxious children can be made" (p. 276). Studies using nonclinical samples on circumscribed fears, such as test anxiety (Zatz & Chassin, 1983, 1985) diving anxiety (Prins, 1986), or dental anxiety (Prins, 1985), have found that high anxiety is associated with negative self-referent cognitions. Examples include: "I'm going to mess up," "I'm going to get hurt again." Also, low anxiety in children is associated with a lower frequency of negative thoughts, what Kendall (1984) has called the "power of nonnegative thinking." Using a recently developed scale (discussed later in this chapter), Kendall and Ronan (1990b) have identified a set of self-statements that characterize anxious as opposed to nonanxious children.

Kendall (1985) proposed distinguishing between cognitive *distortions* and cognitive *deficiencies* in conceptualizing child psychopathology. Deficiencies refer to an absence of thinking where it would be beneficial (e.g., acting before thinking). Deficits in information processing involve a child's failure to engage in forethought and planning. Distortions refer to dysfunctional thinking process (e.g., exaggeration of threat to self). In distorted information processing, the individual is attending to social or environmental cues and is actively processing these data, but the processing itself is dysfunctional (crooked) and maladaptive. Separations based on cognitive deficiencies versus cognitive distortions help clarify the nature of cognitive dysfunction in several psychological disorders. For example, anxious children seem preoccupied with concerns about evaluations by self and others and the likelihood of severe negative consequences. They seem to misperceive characteristically the demands of the environment and routinely add stress to a variety of situations. Consistent with the differentiation being

proposed, anxious children seem not to be deficient in information processing, but rather evidence an information-processing style that is distorted.

ASSESSMENTS

Measuring childhood anxiety is a relatively new and developing area. Although many of the assessment strategies employed with children have been
derived from work with adults, the assessment of childhood disorders has a
unique feature: The assessment process must address the extensive developmental changes occurring during this life-stage. Cognitive, socioemo-
tional, and biological changes mean that a child of 8 or 9 may be very
different from a child of 12 or 13.

Corresponding changes in children's expressive and comprehension
abilities influence the suitability of particular assessment strategies, as well
as the normative data against which behaviors will be judged developmentally appropriate (Barrios & Hartmann, 1988; Bierman, 1984; from Edelbrock, Costello, Duncan, Kalas, & Conover, 1985). To date, there is no
single approach to the assessment of childhood disorders that is consistently
reliable and valid. Consequently, multimethod assessment, obtaining information from multiple settings (school and home) and multiple perspectives
(parent, child, and teacher), is necessary (Achenbach, McConaughy, &
Howell, 1987; Kendall, Pellegrini, & Urbain, 1981).

While a multimethod, developmentally sensitive approach is recommended for the assessment of most childhood disorders, the assessment of
anxiety is further constrained by questions of diagnostic validity of anxiety
in children. Some mental health professionals oppose the DSM-III-R classification of anxiety for children, arguing instead that childhood disorders
can only be differentiated into narrow-band (overcontrolled) or broad-band
(undercontrolled) behaviors (Achenbach & Edelbrock, 1978; Quay, 1977).
The nature of anxiety as an overcontrolled behavior has also contributed to
the reported inconsistency, across source, of this diagnosis. Parents and
teachers are less likely to be aware of the often subtle symptoms of childhood anxiety and these may be perceived as less problematical than some
of the symptoms of conduct disorder or oppositionalism. Indeed, when the
behavioral symptoms of anxiety, such as fidgeting, appear troublesome to
adults, they may be mislabeled as symptoms of undercontrolled behavior
such as Attention Deficit Disorder. This problem emphasizes the need for
multiple sources of information when assessing childhood anxiety and stresses
the need to obtain the child's perception of his or her difficulties.

Drawing from Lang's tripartite model, fear and anxiety can have cognitive, behavioral, and physiological components (Lang, 1968), and should
be assessed across all three response channels. Clinical interviews, self-
report, parent and teacher ratings, behavioral observations, physiological

recordings, and family assessment are strategies that can be employed to elicit expressions of anxiety across response channels. This section will briefly review the available childhood anxiety assessment methods and provide an overview of the advantages and disadvantages of each (see also Barrios & Hartmann, 1988; Kendall & Ronan, 1990a; Rutter, Tuma, & Lann, 1988).

Clinical Interviews

The clinical interview remains one of the most common methods for assessing childhood anxiety. Numerous interview schedules designed to be administered to both children and parents have been developed and empirically tested. They range from a highly structured format to an unstructured one, and have the advantage of gleaning information about the child's developmental history from both the child and parent's perspective. The more structured interviews, such as the Schedule for Affective Disorders and Schizophrenia for School-age Children (K-SADS; Puig–Antich & Chambers, 1978), the Diagnostic Interview for Children and Adolescents (DICA; Herjanic & Reich, 1982), the Diagnostic Interview Schedule for Children (DISC; Costello, Edelbrock, Kalas, Kessler, & Klaric, 1982), and the Anxiety Disorders Interview Schedule for Children (ADIS-C; Silverman, 1987), establish diagnosis according to established classification systems (e.g., the DSM-III-R) and the Research Diagnostic Criteria (RDC; Spitzer, Endicott, & Robins, 1985).

Although most of these interviews are designed to elicit general diagnoses in children, not all have been found to be empirically reliable and valid for diagnosing anxiety. For general diagnoses, concordance between parent and child report during the clinical interview ranges from moderate to good, but concordance for the diagnosis of anxiety disorders is much lower (Chambers et al., 1985; Edelbrock, Costello, Duncan, Conover, & Kalas, 1985; Edelbrock et al., 1986; Hodges, McKnew, Burbach, & Roebuck, 1987). Questions concerning factual, unambiguous and concrete information produce the highest agreement between parent and child report (Herjanic, Herjanic, Brown, & Wheatt, 1975; Herjanic & Reich, 1982); questions concerning subjective information and internalizing symptoms related to depression and anxiety produce the lowest (Herjanic et al., 1975; Herjanic & Reich, 1982; Verhulst, Althaus, & Berden, 1987). Developmental differences have also been shown to affect the reliability of parent and child report on the clinical interview. As children age, the reliability of their reports tends to increase, while conversely the reliability of parent reports tends to decrease (Edelbrock et al., 1985).

Self-reports

The most widely used method for assessing childhood anxiety is the self-report inventory. Numerous inventories exist; three that are frequently employed and have demonstrated adequate reliability and validity are the Revised Children's Manifest Anxiety Scale (RCMAS; Reynolds & Richmond, 1978), the State–Trait Anxiety Inventory for Children (STAIC; Spielberger, 1973), and the revised Fear Survey Schedule for Children (FSSC-R; Ollendick, 1983).

Self-report measures have the advantage of being economical in both time and expense, but are limited in several ways. They do not adequately address the situation specificity of childhood anxiety disorders, and some do not capture the fears and anxieties specific to the child (Kendall & Ronan, 1990a). This limitation is potentially serious since without such information treatment cannot be individualized nor address a child's unique behavioral dysfunction. The present inability of self-report inventories to account for developmental differences is another disadvantage. Few inventories have adequate normative data for different developmental stages, and many inventories are not modified for variations in children's comprehension abilities. For example, it is unclear whether the differences between "never worried," "rarely worried," "sometimes worried," and "often worried" represent the same meaning for children at different stages of cognitive development or if children at different stages of development are capable of making such distinctions.

A relatively unexplored, though promising, area of self-report in childhood anxiety is that of cognitive assessment. Cognitive contents, schemata, processes, and products have been implicated in the maintenance and etiology of anxiety (e.g., Ingram & Kendall, 1987; Kendall & Ingram, 1987, 1989) but have received little empirical attention with children (Kendall & Ronan, 1990a). Preliminary investigations of "think aloud" tasks and thought-listing techniques with anxious children have shown differences between the cognitions of anxious and nonanxious children as well as among the cognitions of children with differing levels of anxiety (Prins, 1986; Zatz & Chassin, 1983).

Although the cognitive assessment of children with anxiety disorders is a promising area, few scales exist. Kendall and Ronan (1990b) developed the Children's Anxious Self-Statement Questionnaire (CASSQ) to assess the cognitive content of anxious children. Preliminary reliability and validity analyses are favorable and have supported the CASSQ's ability to differentiate among the cognitions of both psychometrically defined and clinic cases of anxious and nonanxious children between 8 and 15 years old. Two factors have emerged from the CASSQ: Positive Self-Concept and Expectations, and Negative Self-Focused Attention. Anxious children tend to score higher on the Negative Self-focused Attention factor and lower on the other factor, which includes more positive self-statements. Because negative self-statements about the self are associated with other internalizing disorders, such as depression, additional analyses are ongoing to determine the specificity of the CASSQ to anxiety. These analyses are especially necessary, given the high correlation between anxiety and depression.

Behavioral Observations

The behavioral assessment of childhood anxiety includes many structured and unstructured observational techniques. Throughout the assessment process, especially during the clinical interview, diagnosticians observe the child and note any behaviors characteristic of anxiety, such as fidgeting, fingernail biting, avoiding eye contact, and speaking softly. Parent and teacher rating scales, discussed below, are based on unstructured observations of the child's behavior in naturalistic settings. These observations are important but can be limited by observer bias and, especially in the case of parent and teacher ratings, lack of appropriate observer training.

More structured observation strategies are employed in Behavioral Avoidance Tasks (BATs) and direct observation by trained raters in naturalistic settings such as the school room or playground. Although the structured behavioral assessment methods are advantageous because trained raters assess a child's behavior against a list of operationalized behaviors, they are limited by the absence of standardized procedures. This problem hinders the comparability across studies of data obtained with these techniques. Further, neither unstructured nor structured behavioral observations are sufficient assessment techniques because no single behavior appears to be pathognomonic to childhood anxiety. As noted above, there appears to be symptom overlap among the internalizing disorders (see also Kendall & Watson, 1989).

Parent and Teacher Rating Scales

Parent and teacher rating scales can be considered a subset of behavioral observation techniques because they assess children's observably anxious symptomatology in different settings. Like the child self-report measures, they are economical to administer. Unfortunately, they have a number of potential disadvantages (Saal, Downey, & Lahey, 1980), including the retrospective nature of the observations and the possibility of rater bias. Also, many of the rating scales are not designed to assess the general expression of anxiety in childhood (Morris & Kratochwill, 1983).

The most widely used rating scale is the Child Behavior Check List (CBCL; Achenbach & Edelbrock, 1983), which has acceptable reliability, validity, and normative data. The CBCL provides adequate discrimination between broad-band, externalizing disorders and internalizing disorders, but does not differentiate among the subtypes of anxiety suggested by DSM-III-R. There are rating scales to assess specific childhood anxieties and fears, such as Separation Anxiety or test anxiety, but they are less useful in trying to assess or diagnose anxiety in general. The reader is referred to the comprehensive list of these other scales compiled by Barrios and Hartmann (1988).

Physiological Recordings

Although the physiological assessment of anxiety in adults has been explored (e.g., Himadi et al., 1985), similarly extensive work has not been conducted on childhood anxiety (Johnson & Melamed, 1979). Opponents of this method of assessing anxiety in children have cited the large imbalance between the extensive cost, in time and money, of gathering such information, and its relative yield (Barlow & Wolfe, 1981). Further, the most commonly used physiological techniques, (cardiovascular and electrodermal measures), lack adequate normative data for children. Children also appear to show idiosyncratic patterns of response during physiological assessment. Further, measures can be influenced by expectancy effects, emotions other than anxiety, and incidental motoric and perceptual activity (Wells & Virtulano, 1984; Werry, 1986).

Despite these somewhat daunting limitations, the physiological assessment of childhood anxiety should not be totally abandoned. Biological as well as cognitive and behavioral assessment techniques can be employed to gain a comprehensive picture of the expression of anxiety. Empirical investigations of autonomic responsivity in anxious children should be conducted as such data would increase our understanding of the psychophysiological expression of anxiety and help to develop normative data in this area. There is some evidence suggesting that the physiological activity of anxious children is somewhat similar to that of anxious adults (Beidel, 1988).

Family Assessment

Family assessment is an essentially unexplored method of assessing childhood anxiety. Since the cognitive–behavioral model acknowledges the influence of the family and other social contexts on childhood anxiety (Kendall, 1985; Kendall, Chapter 1, this volume), the absence of established techniques to assess the family of the anxious child is a serious oversight. This situation is not surprising, however, given the limited research that has been conducted on the family correlates of childhood anxiety. We encourage research in this important area.

Summary

The assessment of anxiety in children requires a multimethod approach, drawing information from clinical interviews, child self-report, parent and teacher ratings, behavioral observations, physiological indices, as well as family history and patterns of interaction. Each method has advantages and disadvantages that limit the efficacy of using a single assessment technique for diagnostic purposes. Further work on these assessment strategies will improve the current resources of standardized and normative data, address the developmental changes occurring during the childhood, and expand our understanding of the cognitive and physiological contributions to anxiety.

COGNITIVE–BEHAVIORAL TREATMENT STRATEGIES

Although a great deal of research has been committed to adult anxiety disorders during the past two decades (see Barlow, 1988; Kendall & Watson, 1989; Michelson & Ascher, 1987), little attention has been paid to childhood anxiety, until recently. Clinicians have drawn from the adult anxiety literature in order to provide treatments for children. For example, various forms of behavior therapy have been found to treat generalized anxiety successfully in adults (Barrios & Shigetomi, 1979) and are used in treating anxious youths. In addition, the adult literature has suggested a cognitive component to anxiety (Beck & Emery, 1986; Ingram & Kendall, 1987; Kendall & Ingram, 1989; Meichenbaum, 1986), which is important in treatment. Through a developmentally sensitive synthesis of behavioral and cognitive treatment approaches, therapeutic gain may result for the anxious child (see Kendall, Howard, & Epps, 1988). The following discussion highlights six features of cognitive–behavioral treatment: (1) relaxation, (2) building a cognitive coping template, (3) problem solving, (4) contingent reinforcement, (5) modeling, and (6) imaginal and *in vivo* exposure. Following these discussions, our integrated cognitive–behavioral therapy for anxious children (see Kendall, Kane, Howard & Siqueland, 1989; Kendall, 1990) will be presented.

Relaxation

Relaxation training is a valuable cognitive–behavioral technique for the treatment of anxiety. In this procedure, major muscle groups of the body are progressively relaxed through systematic tension-releasing exercises (King, Hamilton, & Ollendick, 1988). By tensing and relaxing various muscle groups, the individual learns to perceive sensations of bodily tension and to use these sensations as the stimuli to relax. It has been suggested that children learn a maximum of three muscle groups in each session and practice the relaxation exercises twice daily at home (Strauss, 1988).

Cue-controlled relaxation can be introduced to the client. This process involves a repeated association of the relaxed state with a self-produced cue word, such as "relax" or "calm." So while the client is totally relaxed, the cue word is subvocalized with each exhalation. As a result, the word can be used to combat feelings of anxiety. When teaching these progressive and cue-controlled techniques, relaxation training scripts are usually incorporated. Although most of the scripts have been written for adults (Bernstein & Borkovec, 1973; Rimm & Masters, 1974), formats for children have also been developed (Koeppen, 1974; Ollendick & Cerny, 1981).

Weisman, Ollendick, and Horne (1978) demonstrated the effectiveness of muscular relaxation procedures with normal 6- and 7-year-old children. They found that the procedures of both Ollendick and Cerny (1981) and Koeppen (1974) resulted in significantly reduced muscle tension levels, as measured by EMG recordings (both groups were superior to an attention-control group but did not differ from one another). These findings suggest that muscular relaxation procedures may be effective counterconditioning agents for young children; however, as Ollendick (1986) noted, well-controlled evaluations of their efficacy with diagnosed cases are lacking and needed.

Building a Cognitive Coping Template

Cognitive restructuring is an important strategy used in the treatment of anxiety. Cognitive-based therapies highlight the role of maladaptive thinking in maladaptive behavior and by changing distorted (faulty) cognitive processing the therapist can effect constructive behavior change.

Building a cognitive coping template entails the identification and modification of maladaptive self-talk, along with the building of a new way to view situations—a new structure that is based on coping. That is, the therapist works with the child to (1) remove characteristic misinterpretations of environmental events and (2) gradually and systematically build a frame of reference that includes strategies for coping. Not that the perceptions of stress will disappear forever, but the formerly distressing misperceptions and arousal, when seen through the cognitive coping structure, will serve as reminders for the use of coping strategies. Cognitive-based treatment of anxiety-disordered children has shown considerable promise (e.g., Kane & Kendall, 1989), but more investigation is necessary before the utility of these procedures can be firmly supported (e.g., Meador & Ollendick, 1984; Neilans & Israel, 1981).

Problem Solving

Another component of our cognitive–behavioral approach to anxiety is problem solving. D'Zurilla and Goldfried (1971) outlined a five-stage problem-solving sequence (see also Spivack & Shure, 1974; D'Zurilla, 1986). In the first stage, general orientation, the individual begins to prepare for the solution of a problem. In the second stage, problem definition and formulation, the problem and the major goals are described. The individual can then generate alternative solutions, and the process of decision making takes place. Once a decision is made, it is implemented. Finally, the success of this choice is verified (see Kendall & Braswell, 1985; Kendall &

Siqueland, 1989 for discussion). Through this process of resolving anxiety-related problems a child or adolescent can achieve an ability to cope with and manage future problems.

Kleiner, Marshall, and Spevack (1987) demonstrated that problem solving prevents posttreatment relapses of anxiety disorders. Twenty-six agoraphobic patients were randomly assigned to either an *in vivo* exposure treatment or *in vivo* exposure plus a problem-solving skills training program. All of the patients improved significantly after 12 treatment sessions. However, while those in the *in vivo* only procedure either failed to show further gains at follow-up or relapsed, those receiving training in problem solving continued to improve at follow-up. Thus problem solving may enhance the therapeutic gains of treatment strategies such as *in vivo* exposure (e.g., Arnow, Taylor, Agras, & Telch, 1985; Jannoun, Munby, Catalan, & Gelder, 1980).

Contingent Reinforcement

Contingent reinforcement involves a number of treatment procedures that are derived from the principles of operant conditioning. According to operant theory, environmental response to a particular behavior determines whether or not that response is repeated. Reinforcement occurs when an event that follows a behavior increases the probability of that behavior occurring again. Contingent reinforcement has been successful in modifying a wide variety of behavior, such as school phobic behavior, (e.g., Ayllon, Smith, & Rogers, 1970). Since that study was only preliminary evidence for the utility of contingent reinforcement in the treatment of anxious children, further application and investigation is warranted (e.g., Rines, 1973; Leitenberg & Callahan, 1973). Nevertheless, rewards work, and anxious children do benefit from rewards.

Modeling

Derived from an observational learning paradigm (Bandura, 1969, 1986), modeling offers another valuable cognitive–behavioral strategy when treating anxiety. Nonfearful behavior is demonstrated in the fear-producing situation, therefore illustrating an appropriate response to the fearful situation. As a result, fear may be reduced and appropriate skills acquired. Additionally, the child is instructed to imitate the model. Regular feedback and reinforcement is provided for performance that matches that of the model. Operant principles are used to maintain the desired behaviors (Ollendick & Francis, 1988).

Ross, Ross, and Evans (1971) successfully used modeling procedures in treating a 6-year-old boy who feared interaction with his peers. Generalized imitation, participant modeling, and social reinforcement were the main treatment procedures. Directly following treatment and upon follow-up, the child could interact positively with his peers and displayed few avoidance behaviors. In sum, modeling procedures have shown considerable clinical utility in treating anxious and fearful children (e.g., Lewis, 1974; Melamed & Siegel, 1975) as well as helping children placed in stressful situations (e.g., medical procedures, Peterson, 1989).

Exposure

Exposure, an oft-used component of anxiety treatments (Wilson, 1985), entails placing the subject in the fear-evoking experience, either imaginally or *in vivo* (King et al., 1988). The rationale for this behavioral procedure is noted by Marks (1975): "An important mechanism shared by all of these methods is exposure of the frightened subject to a frightening situation until he acclimatizes." It is important to note that to the extent to which the subject can discriminate between threatening and nonthreatening stimuli is linked to fear reduction. Also, careful planning of exposure must be involved so that exposure is not so aversive that it actually reinforces the fear. Exposure is considered a fundamental and active ingredient in behavioral programs. For instance, desensitization is the combination of graduated exposure and responses incompatible with anxiety (Hatzenbuehler & Schroeder, 1978).

Foa, Steketee, and Grayson (1985) demonstrated the efficacy of both imaginal and *in vivo* exposure. They found that exposure treatment was moderately effective in ameliorating obsessive–compulsive symptoms. Although research has shown merit in the use of exposure in the treatment of adult anxiety disorders, the relative efficacy of imaginal and *in vivo* exposure with child and adolescent cases awaits further empirical evaluation.

INTEGRATED COGNITIVE–BEHAVIORAL THERAPY FOR ANXIOUS CHILDREN

The cognitive–behavioral treatment of anxiety disorders in children and young adolescents integrates the demonstrated efficiencies of the behavioral approach (e.g., exposure, relaxation training, role plays) with an added emphasis on the cognitive information-processing factors associated with each individual's anxieties (see treatment manual; Kendall et al., 1989). The overall goal is to teach children and teenagers to recognize signs of unwanted anxious arousal and to let these signs serve as cues for use of anxiety management strategies. Identifying the cognitive processes associated with excessive anxious arousal, training in cognitive strategies for anxiety management, and behavioral relaxation and performance-based practice opportunities are sequenced within the treatment program to build skill upon skill. The greatest emphasis within the treatment program provided at the Child and Adolescent Anxiety Disorders Clinic (CAADC) at Temple University is placed upon the following general strategies:

- coping modeling
- identification and modification of anxious self-talk
- exposure to anxiety-provoking situations
- role playing and contingent reward procedures
- homework assignments ("Show That I Can" [STIC] tasks)
- affective education
- awareness of bodily reactions and cognitive activities when anxious
- relaxation procedures
- graduated sequence of training tasks and assignments
- application and practice of newly acquired skills in increasingly anxiety-provoking situations

The program is divided into two segments: Skills training occurs in the first eight sessions and skills practice in the second eight. In the latter segment, the children begin to use the required skills in anxiety-provoking situations.

Throughout the treatment, concepts and skills are introduced in a sequential order from the most basic to the more difficult. As each new skill is introduced, the therapist functions as a coping model, demonstrating the skill in each new situation. The child is then invited to participate with the therapist in role playing (tag along; Ollendick, 1983). As the therapist role plays a situation, the child follows along with him or her. Describing what he or she is feeling or thinking, the therapist asks the child if he or she is experiencing the same thing or something different. Finally, the child is encouraged to role play scenes alone, practicing the newly acquired skills by himself or herself. All or some of these variations in role playing are used, depending on the child's skill level and understanding of the concept being introduced. With adolescence, the tag-along procedure is often unnecessary. Within each session and throughout the training program, the level of anxiety is gradually increased, beginning with nonstressful situations to help reinforce what has been addressed during the session, and gradually incorporating increasing levels of anxiety. STIC tasks (also known as homework) are assigned as tasks to be completed outside of the therapy session.

The training sessions focus on four basic skill areas: awareness of bodily reactions to feelings and those physical symptoms specific to anxiety; recognition and evaluation of "self-talk" or what the child thinks and says to himself or herself when anxious; problem-solving skills, including modifying anxious self-talk and developing plans for coping; and self-evaluation and reward.

To introduce the concept of physical feelings, the therapist and child discuss how different facial expressions and postures are related to different emotions. All concepts are first introduced in the abstract or by referring to other people, rather than focusing on the child or adolescent's own experience. The client looks at pictures or drawings from magazines, books, or educational materials and is asked to identify different facial expressions and body postures. Following this, the therapist discusses how the child knows what different friends or family members are feeling, based on their facial expressions and postures. Various emotions and their expression can be role played by the therapist. Finally, the child is asked about his or her own physical reactions to emotions. Often, anxious youths appear to have difficulty distinguishing different feelings, especially fear, sadness, and anger. The following is a transcript from part of a session with a 12-year-old boy diagnosed with Overanxious Disorder.*

> THERAPIST: You said you sometimes get confused about when you're sad and when you're angry. How do you carry yourself when you're angry or what is your body like?
>
> CHILD: I get agitated, but the sadness and anger go hand in hand.
>
> T: Does one come first?
>
> C: The sadness, I guess.
>
> T: Do you get mad about being sad.
>
> C: Sort of. Well when things haven't been going my way. Sometimes when I'm so angry, I start crying, like if things have been going badly all day.
>
> T: Can you tell when you're in the sad part or the angry part from the way your body feels?
>
> C: Not really, but when I'm sad I just sit around and listen and when I'm angry I start moving around.
>
> T: So when you're angry you're active and when you're sad you're kind of passive. Does your body get tense when you're angry?
>
> C: Sometimes I get tense and sometimes I get a headache.

By disclosing her own bodily reactions to anxiety, the therapist can then model recognition of anxiety symptoms and ask how anxious symptoms are the same or different for the child.

> T: How about when you get nervous or worried? When I have to give a talk and I get a little nervous, my face gets really red and hot, I

---

*All cases referred to in this chapter were assessed via multiple methods of measurement, including structured diagnostic interviews for parent and child. All cases received a diagnosis of Overanxious Disorder (OAD).

talk fast, I start to get a little sweaty, and my heart starts pounding. Sometimes my stomach starts to hurt and makes noises.

C: Yeah, my hands start sweating sometimes. I start sweating all over sometimes, and sometimes a lump gets in my throat like THUMP right there.

T: You mean you can't swallow. I get that sometimes. So you get sweaty, and you get a lump in your throat. Does your heart start pounding?

C: Sometimes, and I get a queasy stomach. If I get really nervous, sometimes I feel like I get dizzy.

T: Any other things you can think of?

C: My voice starts quavering or cracks.

T: Mine does too, it gets weak sometimes. So those are all signs for you that you are nervous or worried. Once you know what those signs are, you can begin to figure out what to do about them.

This child, bright and articulate, can label his own reactions, unlike younger or lower functioning children, who often have more difficulty. To help, the therapist can make up stories about an imaginary group of kids or a basketball team and have the child, with the therapist's aid, talk about various physical symptoms the imaginary characters might experience. A discussion of how these reactions are similar to the child's experience can follow.

Once the children begin to identify their own physical symptoms of anxiety, they are taught to use these physical reactions as *cues* to begin cognitive coping and relaxation (see also Meichenbaum, 1986). The children are taught a modified, progressive muscle relaxation, which first focuses on the three or four muscle groups most affected by their anxiety. The therapist can then model and discuss with the child times when using the relaxation might be useful. For the younger child, a script which puts the exercises in a story-like scenario (for example, Koeppen, 1974) encourages participation. A script by Ollendick and Cerny (1981) is recommended for the older child. An audiotape of the therapist going through the relaxation procedure can be given to the child, enabling him or her to practice at home. In addition, the child can demonstrate the procedure to his or her parents, who might like to practice with the child, or help find a time and a place to practice at home.

The notion of self-talk, the things children say to themselves when they are anxious, is the second concept introduced in this training program. Self-talk includes the child's expectations and attributions about oneself, others, and situations. For the anxious child these expectations seem to focus on negative self-evaluation, perfectionistic standards for performance, heightened self-focused attention or concern about what others are thinking, and concerns about failure or not coping. The following is a transcript of a 12-year-old overanxious child talking about his thoughts before a music recital.

> THERAPIST: What were you thinking to yourself before the concert?
> CHILD: I was thinking I was going to make a mistake, if you make a mistake, it sticks with you and you feel stupid.
> T: Why does making a mistake make you feel stupid?
> C: Because you could have prevented it. You have a feeling of failure. I hate failure.
> T: What if you make mistakes sometimes like everybody else?
> C: That's the whole point, you are not like everybody else.
> T: Why can't you be like everybody else?
> C: Some people have more expected of them than others.
> T: Why do you have more expected of you?
> C: Because I'm supposed to be smart.
> T: So if you are smart, you are not allowed to make mistakes.
> C: No, and you drive yourself nuts, thinking of ways you could have done it better and you didn't do it; you drive yourself crazy, and it's not easy.

Children are often unaware that they might be thinking things to themselves when they are nervous; they may initially find this concept difficult to understand. Cartoons with empty thought bubbles can be used to introduce the concept. Children are asked to generate various alternatives for what the character might be thinking in the situation. The cartoons portray fairly simple, nonthreatening scenes in which the character's thoughts are likely to be fairly obvious. More ambiguous or anxiety-provoking situations can then be introduced. With the therapist's help, the child generates both anxiety-provoking and anxiety-reducing thoughts for the characters. Also, the therapist points out for the child that the way the child thinks about things affects what he or she might feel or do in that situation. The following is a 9-year-old's responses to a variety of cartoons that depict possible anxiety-producing situations.

> CARTOON 1: One boy sitting down playing trumpet looking at another kid on stage playing trumpet.
> THERAPIST: What could be in that boy's thought bubble?
> CHILD: I'll never play as good as him.
> T: And how would that boy feel if he were thinking that?
> C: Nervous and bad.
> T: What's another possibility of what he could be thinking?
> C: I think I play good.

T: That's a good one. Or he could think, that other boy has been playing a long time, maybe I can play like that if I keep on trying.

CARTOON 2: Kid sitting in classroom with teacher at blackboard which reads Math Test tomorrow.

T: What could he be thinking? What's in his thought bubble?

C: I'll never pass that math test.

T: What's another kind of thought?

C: I could probably do it—I have tonight to study.

T: What will happen do you think if he's thinking "I'll never pass" when he goes to study. Would he be able to study?

C: He'd probably be all worried.

T: What if he thought "I'll do okay, I have tonight to study."

C: He'd probably start to study.

T: Would he be able to ask for help if he needed to?

C: I think so.

Problem solving is the third concept or skill focused on in our program. The therapist helps the child begin to generate various alternative solutions to cope with a difficult situation and to select the most appropriate solution. Failing to believe there is anything they can do to make a situation less frightening, anxious children's only coping response is to withdraw from the anxiety-provoking situation. Discussion of nonthreatening situations can be used for introducing the problem-solving concept. For example, you've lost your shoes in the house. What are some ways you could go about trying to find them. The therapist provides other examples of situations and helps the child to generate alternatives, to evaluate these possibilities, and to decide what is the preferred solution.

At this point in the program, the children have already been introduced to two different coping strategies: relaxation and changing anxiety-producing thoughts into coping thoughts. The child is reminded that in an anxious situation, he or she could take some deep breaths to calm down and begin to relax those parts of the body that might become tense. By asking what he or she is expecting to happen or what he or she fears will happen, the therapist also helps the child to recognize his or her thoughts. The therapist helps the child to challenge any distortions in thinking and to evaluate the likelihood that what one is fearing will actually happen by beginning to ask: How likely is it that that will happen? Has that happened before? What if what I fear actually happens? Finally, by asking the child how else he or she might think about the situation, the therapist helps the child to begin replacing maladaptive thoughts with coping thoughts.

Other coping strategies are more specific to individual problems. Often possible solutions involve enlisting friends or family members for support or advice, thinking about or watching how others cope with situations, or rehearsing and practicing various skills in academic, performance, or social situations. For example, a child who was afraid of going into the snake house at the zoo (on a school trip) came up with the following possibility to deal with the situation: take deep breaths, say everything is okay, listen to my tape player and think about the music, or be with a friend who is not scared and will not tease me. The child both generates and evaluates the different possibilities as much as he or she can and decides which solution feels best.

Especially with younger children and sometimes with older children, it is helpful to have the child choose a cartoon (TV, movie) character or hero whom he or she admires or believes can cope with difficult situations. The therapist can encourage the child to think about how that character might handle anxiety-provoking situations. As a problem-solving strategy, the child can pretend to be that character or take that character along into scary situations for support. A 10-year-old-boy who was afraid to walk home from school for 9 months following a confrontation with an older child who pushed him off his bike used this method as one of his coping strategies. He decided that he could take deep breaths when he was walking, think "nothing will happen to me" or "I can handle this," or go into a store or to someone's doorstep. He also brought "X-man" (a superhero figure) along with him on the walk and imagined that he would be right behind if he needed him. Older children or adolescents can also identify imaginary or real people who they feel cope with difficult situations in a manner they admire and can use them as models. If the child cannot generate coping thoughts by oneself or is unwilling to consider other possibilities, he or she can think about how the hero might think differently. The following, from a session with a 12-year-old-boy, demonstrates this strategy.

CHILD: I don't think there's any other way to think about it for me.

THERAPIST: Do you have a hero or is there someone who handles things differently than you, that you like how they think about things?

C: Yeah, like Eddie Murphy or Michael J. Fox—they seem like they don't care what anybody thinks. They are just themselves. I don't think they are like that really but maybe acting is the way they get out their anxiety.

T: But you might like to feel like that sometimes—like you don't care what everybody thinks. Maybe right now you can't figure out how you might think differently but how would one of them think about a social situation?

C: He would think everything is a joke. He'd make something funny out of something that's not.

T: How would he make it funny?

C: It doesn't seem possible but he makes basic things funny by laughing at himself.

T: If you can laugh about something, you are well on your way to handling it.

The idea of self-evaluation and reward is the fourth concept introduced in this program. Anxious children often have difficulty evaluating themselves accurately and/or set extremely high standards for success. The therapist can help the child begin to think about possibly evaluating situations based on partial success. The child can learn to identify what things they liked about how they handled the situation and what things they would like to do differently. The idea of rewarding oneself for accomplishments one is proud of is also introduced. Finally the child can learn to generate a list of possible self-rewards, ranging from spending more time in an activity he or she likes (e.g., riding bikes or reading), giving oneself a pat on the back, telling oneself "I've done a good job," to spending time with family and friends.

The four skills taught in the sessions are represented in an acronym, FEAR, as a way of helping children remember what things to do when they get nervous. FEAR stands for the following:

F—Feeling frightened? (recognizing physical symptoms of anxiety)

E—Expecting bad things to happen? (recognizing self-talk and what you are worried about)

A—Actions and attitudes that will help (different behaviors and coping statements the child can use in the anxiety provoking situation based on problem-solving)

R—Results and rewards (self-evaluation and self-rewards)

Even after the children have been taught many of these skills, they do not always use them in anxiety-provoking situations. The second half of the treatment program involves imaginal and *in vivo* exposure to anxiety-provoking situations. In our program at CAADC, imaginal exposure to anxiety-provoking situations has helped children to begin thinking through various coping strategies which they might use in these situations; however, imaginal exposure does not always produce much visible anxiety except in the most anxious children. For these children, imaginal exposure can be used before moving on to the *in vivo* situations. Initially a low-anxiety situation is introduced, followed by a gradual progression to higher anxiety-producing situations.

The therapist presents the situation to be encountered, remarks about aspects of the situation that are likely to be troubling, and models behavior, using the different approaches in coping with the situation. The therapist then helps the child think through the steps to use when approaching the situation. He or she also helps the child to practice using these steps until the child feels calmer and is ready actually to try the situation. Following the *in vivo* exposure, the child is helped to evaluate his or her performance and to think of a reward.

Various *in vivo* situations can be set up in the office, such as taking a math test, giving a speech, reading a poem in front of a small audience or video camera, or introducing oneself to office personnel. Other *in vivo* exposures involve taking the child to a site outside the office, for example, to a graveyard, zoo, or shopping center. Many naturally occurring academic and social situations can be arranged in schools with the help of teachers and guidance personnel. Following the first successful *in vivo*, the child often experiences a new sense of competency and more willingly engages in other anxiety-provoking situations. Given the new set of skills that the child can call on if feeling anxious, much of the treatment encourages risk taking. In large part, the therapist also frequently normalizes anxiety, stressing that it is not necessarily abnormal.

In the following transcript a 13-year-old overanxious boy describes how, with the help of the "Fear Force," he used the four steps he learned to approach and talk with a girl he liked.

> THERAPIST: So (child's name), how did you get through the situation of talking to that girl?
> CHILD: By using the Fear Force.
> T: Terrific, how did the Fear Force help?
> C: Well, Captain Nervous and Lieutenant Expect let me know I was anxious and expecting her to make a fool of me. So Attitude von Action came in to help me calm down by telling me to take a deep breath and to think before I speak. Even though I was nervous, it went okay and Sergeant Result and Rewards then said I should reward myself with some time listening to the radio.
> T: So the Fear Force helps you remember the plan for dealing with anxiety?
> C: Yeah, the Fear Force is just really my common sense which helps me get through times when I get nervous. I realize I can rely on what I think about the situation.
> T: Well your common sense sounds pretty on the ball.
> C: Yeah I think so.

Another child, worried that he would get lost, feared going into new places alone. When taken to a shopping mall, he came up with his plan.

> T: So are you feeling nervous now.
> C: I don't know, not really.

T: How would you know you were starting to get nervous?

C: My heart would start beating faster.

T: What about your breathing? (therapist remembers about his getting short of breath)

C: I might start breathing faster.

T: And what would you be thinking to yourself?

C: I might get lost or I don't know where I am.

T: And what are some things you could do if you start getting nervous?

C: I could take deep breaths and say everything is going to be okay.

T: That's good, but what if you were unsure where you were or got lost?

C: I could ask somebody.

T: Yes, you could ask somebody, would it be a good idea to ask one of the guards or policemen? How are you feeling—do you think you are ready to give it a try?

Then, the therapist and child agreed on a number of trips to make within the mall, varying in distance and degree of familiarity. During one trip, the child was to ask the guard for directions so that he could feel comfortable doing this in the future.

A number of the children treated at CAADC show concern about their parents' health or safety. For these children, whose mothers may be ill (for example, diabetic or asthmatic), the *in vivo* exposure entails the therapist helping the mother and child to talk about the illness. For the children, some basic information, discussing the mother's self-care, and even what the child can do if he or she is feeling worried about the mother can offer a great deal of relief. Other *in vivo* exposures can be planned and talked about within the office; then, with parental help, these can be carried out as they naturally occur. Parental involvement allows the therapist to have greater flexibility in planning, though the degree of flexibility largely depends on the parents' abilities and motivation.

Our program closes with the child contributing to the creation and production of a "commercial" about his or her experiences at the clinic. that is, the client is asked to help put together a video, booklet, or cassette tape to help tell other children about the clinic. We have produced "rap" tapes and video cassettes, which are both humorous and impressively informative. It is our goal to set the stage for the client to be an endorser of the program and the making of a tape, for example, gives clear evidence of our interest in their support, provides a demonstration of their success, offers a tangible reward at the end of the program, and, we suspect, helps to buttress the maintenance of the treatment-produced gains.

Working with Families

We recognize the importance of parental involvement in helping the child to overcome disproportionate anxiety. While the cognitive–behavioral nature of the program focuses on helping the individual learn to think and behave differently, we also encourage parents to participate in a supportive role. Though the normal treatment program does not include "family" therapy, parents are actively involved from the outset. For instance, unless the parental responses to inventories and structured interview lead to a diagnosis of Overanxious Disorder, the child is not accepted into the program. Prior to the fourth session with the child, parents are required to meet with the therapist. There are several purposes to this meeting. First, we provide additional information about the treatment via an outline of the program and detail where the child is in the program. Specifically, the parent is told not to expect an immediate reduction in the child's anxiety, but to be encouraging as the youth begins to apply the coping skills that are learned during the first eight sessions. Second, we give the parents an opportunity to discuss their concerns about the child and provide further information that might be helpful to the therapist. Third, we share impressions about what specific situations provoke the child's anxiety, and how the child typically reacts. Lastly, we offer specific ways that the parents can become involved in the program. For instance, the parents are invited to sit in on part of the child's next session so that they can help the child to practice relaxation skills. Also, they are invited to call the therapist if they can think of any further information that might be helpful or if they have any questions. Depending on the age of the child and the quality of parental support, the therapist may ask the parents to help in other specific tasks assigned to the child in upcoming weeks.

Given the important role that parents can play in their child's treatment, therapists should be aware of the particular problems that families of anxious children may be experiencing. These problems may range from increased rates of anxiety disorders as well as other types of pathology (for a review of increased anxiety disorders among relatives of anxiety probands, see Carey & Gottesman, 1981) to particular problems in parenting such as overprotectiveness and guilt about the problems that their children are experiencing.

A number of studies have examined rates of anxiety in the relatives of anxiety disorder probands. Overall, strong evidence has emerged for a familial pattern in rates of panic disorder among relatives of individuals with this disorder (Cloninger, Martin, Clayton, & Guze, 1981; Crowe, Noyes, Pauls & Slymen, 1983; Crowe, Pauls, Slymen, & Noyes, 1980; Harris, Noyes, Crowe, & Chaudery, 1983; Torgersen, 1983). Moreover, there is some indication that female relatives are more susceptible than males, while male relatives have been shown to have a somewhat increased rate of alcoholism (Crowe et al., 1980).

Studies comparing relatives of individuals with a broad range of anxiety disorders with those of normal controls (Noyes, Clancy, Crowe, Hoenk, & Slymen, 1978; Solyom, Beck, Solyom, & Hugel, 1974) show significantly higher rates of pathology (e.g., alcoholism, depression, and anxiety) among the relatives of the anxious probands. Other studies have looked more closely at rates of pathology among parents and children. Children of affective disorder parents (i.e., depression) have shown an increased risk for anxiety disorder or related symptoms (Conners, Himmelhock, Goyette, Ulrich, & Neil, 1979; Cytryn, McKnew, Bartko, Lamour, & Hamovitt, 1982; McKnew, Cytryn, Efron, Gershon, & Bunney, 1979; O'Connell, Mayo, O'Brien, & Misrsheidaie, 1979). However, in comparison to children of dysthymic parents, children of anxious parents have been found to be at an increased risk for receiving a DSM-III diagnosis of an anxiety disorder (Turner, Beidel, & Costello, 1987). And children of depressed and panic disorder parents have shown higher rates of depression and anxiety and poorer rates of adjustment than children of controls (Sylvester, Hyde, & Reichler, 1987). Somewhat inconclusive results exist on whether mothers of children with various anxiety disorders are themselves at risk for increased levels of anxiety or whether there is simply a general increased rate of pathology among mothers of children receiving any type of diagnosis (Berg, Butler, & Pritchard, 1974; Last, Hersen, Kazdin, Francis, & Grubb, 1987). Finally, there is some evidence that different types of parental anxiety disorders (e.g., agoraphobia versus generalized anxiety disorder) have a varying impact on the rates of clinical diagnosis and/or receiving a CBCL score in the clinical range (Silverman, Cerny, & Nelles, 1988).

While research suggests that families with anxious children may have increased rates of pathology, these typically correlational studies provide little insight into what to expect when working with parents in a clinical setting. Given the dearth of research in this area, many of the following suggestions stem directly from our clinical work and observations. It is our experience that parental involvement with overanxious youth ranges from underinvolved, in which parents appear to be unaware of their children's problems, to extreme overprotectiveness. Underinvolvement can lead to problems with keeping appointments or helping the child to keep his or her therapy-related material organized. Parents benefit from being informed of the negative impact that this can have on therapy. Overprotectiveness* can interfere with the child's performing important tasks that are designed to build the child's sense of confidence. For example, one mother

---

*Overprotectiveness and overdependence on the child have been cited in the etiology of school phobia (Coolidge & Brodie, 1974; Davidson, 1961; Eisenberg, 1958; Waldron, Shrier, Stone, & Tobin, 1975).

of a 12-year-old girl who had suffered from cancer as a young child expressed concern when the therapist said that she and the girl were going to leave the building and go to a nearby bookstore. The parent wanted to go along! Rather than getting into a power struggle with the concerned parent, the therapist simply announced that she and the girl were going together, and kept on walking out the door. When dealing with such an overprotective parent, the therapist needs to strike a delicate balance between helping the child to become more independent while at the same time not increasing the parent's own anxiety and hence risking alienation from the treatment. One tactic may be to get the parent initially involved in suggesting or participating in some of the *in vivo* experiences that the child will complete. This allows the parent to maintain initial involvement with child, while soon encouraging the child's independent behavior since the parent does not continue with the *in vivo* experiences.

Studies of school-phobic children have also indicated that a high rate have experienced a death or illness in a parent or other relative (Davidson, 1961; Waldron, Shrier, Stone, & Tobin, 1975), and it has been suggested that certain types of school phobia represent the child's fear that something will happen to the parent if the child leaves them (Waldron et al., 1975). Our observations support the idea that a number of the members of overanxious youth express concern about some type of illness. The children in treatment have reported restricting their activities, or frequently calling home, because of the parent's illness. Thus, the therapist may want to discuss any fears that the child might have about his or her parents' well-being. This could involve helping the parent to tell the child realistically about any dangers and helping the child to see that he or she is not responsible for the parent's physical health.

Parents of anxious children may also express guilt about the child's anxiety. Helping them to cope with these feelings may involve pragmatic confrontation that how the problem developed is not the issue, rather it is important to focus on how they can contribute to helping their child cope at the present time. If the parent's own anxiety or other problems appear to be genuinely contributing to the child's anxiety, it is discussed with the parent. Such a discussion may involve observations and suggestions about how to change the "parent–child" situation, and even recommendations for the parent's own treatment. More specifically, it may be helpful to find out what kinds of expectations the parents hold for their children—both academically and behaviorally. For instance, are they overconcerned with academic performance and therefore placing a lot of pressure on their child to achieve? Parents may also have inaccurate expectations about what is appropriate behavior, given their child's developmental level. Helping parents to clarify what is and is not within the normal range of behavior may prevent inappropriate and anxiety-provoking responses to their child's normal behavior. Finally, it is important to help parents learn new ways of responding to their child's anxious behavior. The stress of dealing with an anxious child may lead parents to become sensitized to any signs of anxiety in their children. They may be hypervigilant and strongly react to any indication of anxiety—for example, becoming anxious themselves or depressed as they feel helpless about what to do.

Given the important role that parents play in the success of child-focused treatment for childhood anxiety disorders, and given the hypothesized roles family members may play in the genesis and maintenance of anxiety disorders, the time is ripe for the development of *family* cognitive–behavioral treatment strategies for child anxiety disorders. Cognitive–behavioral treatment for families has begun to be proposed in some problem areas (e.g., Epstein, Schlesinger, & Dryden, 1988) such as conduct disorder (DiGiuseppe, 1988), child abuse (Morton, Twentyman, & Azar, 1988) and addictions (Schlesinger, 1988). Our proposed model concerns the interactive influence of family members cognitions on behavior—their own and each other's. Thus, treatment strategies would address the cognitive distortions and behavioral skill deficits of the family members which contribute to the presenting problem.

For example, treatment for a separation-anxious child might concurrently address the child's need for greater independence by working on age-appropriate problem-solving or assertiveness skills in situations in which he or she may have previously unnecessarily relied on a parent, and for the parent, examining and correcting (testing out *in vivo*) their misperceptions of their child's competencies or their equating good parenting with overinvolved parenting. One can imagine that without coordinating efforts between parents and children, a child's gains toward greater independence and management of fears may be mislabeled as disobedience or may contribute to depression in the parent because they misattribute this change to their no longer being needed. Such responses could threaten the maintenance of the child's gains. By coordinating efforts, the new behavior in the child is concomitant with new beliefs or expectancies in the parents. Inversely, a depressed parent's acquisition of new coping skills and overt behaviors such as going to work rather than sleeping all day will be coupled with the child's new attributions of strength to the parent, and will be less fearful for their safety. While cognitive–behavioral treatment strategies for families have begun to be incorporated into our clinical research and practice, there is great need for empirical evaluation of their efficacy in treating anxiety disorders in children and adolescents.

SUMMARY

Our cognitive–behavioral treatment (Kendall et al., 1989), as we have described, integrates behavioral and cognitive coping skills in a graduated fashion. Exposure experiences provide real challenges and therapist-supported practice helps to arrange success. Our child and adolescent clients are taught to identify anxiety cues, employ coping skills, and manage or overcome their anxiety and avoidance. While all anxiety disorders are not totally cured, evidence does support the efficacy of an integrated program for the management of formerly anxiety-producing situations (Kane & Kendall, 1989; Kendall, 1989).

ACKNOWLEDGEMENTS

The authors wish to thank those who have been actively involved in the Child and Adolescent Anxiety Disorders Clinic. Therapists, writers, schoolteachers and counselors, and especially the children and their parents, are offered a collective thank you for their efforts and cooperativeness throughout. Preparation of this report was facilitated by support from the National Institute of Mental Health, grant number 1 RO1 MH44042-01A1. Temple University, especially the Department of Psychology, is also commended for its support of the CAADC and its research mission.

REFERENCES

Achenbach, T. M., & Edelbrock, C. S. (1978). The classification of child psychology: A review and analysis of empirical efforts. *Psychological Bulletin, 85*, 1275–1301.

Achenbach, T. M. & Edelbrock, C. S. (1983). *Manual for the Child Behavior Checklist and Revised Child Behavior Profile*. Burlington, VT: University Associates in Psychiatry.

Achenbach, T. M., McConaughy, S. H., & Howell, C. T. (1987). Child/adolescent behavioral and emotional problems: Implications of cross-informant correlations for situational specificity. *Psychological Bulletin, 101*, 213–232.

American Psychiatric Association. (1984). *Diagnostic and statistical manual of mental disorders 2nd ed., rev*. Washington, DC: Author.

American Psychiatric Association. (1987). *Diagnostic and statistical manual of mental disorders 3rd ed., rev*. Washington, DC: Author.

Arnow, B. A., Taylor, C. B., Agras, W. S., & Telch, M. J. (1985). Enhancing agoraphobia treatment outcome by changing couple communication patterns. *Behavior Therapy, 16*, 452–467.

Ayllon, T., Smith, D., & Rogers, M. (1970). Behavioral management of school phobia. *Journal of Behavior Therapy and Experimental Psychiatry, 1*, 125–138.

Bandura, A. (1969). *Principles of behavior modification*. Englewood Cliffs, NJ: Prentice–Hall.

Bandura, A. (1986). *Social learning theory*. Englewood Cliffs, NJ: Prentice–Hall.

Barlow, D. (1988). *Anxiety and its disorders: The nature and treatment of anxiety and panic*. New York: Guilford Press.

Barlow, D., & Wolfe, B. E. (1981). Behavioral approaches to anxiety disorders: A report on the NIMH–SUNY, Albany, Research Conference. *Journal of Consulting and Clinical Psychology, 49*, 448–454.

Barrios, B. A., & Hartmann, D. B. (1988). Fears and anxieties. In E. J. Mash & L. G. Terdal (Eds.), *Behavioral assessment of childhood disorders.* (2nd ed., pp. 196–264). New York: Guilford Press.

Barrios, B. A., Hartmann, D. B., & Shigetomi, C. (1981). Fears and anxieties in children. In E. J. Mash & L. G. Terdal (Eds.), *Behavioral assessment of childhood disorders* (pp. 259–304). New York: Guilford Press.

Barrios, B. A., & Shigetomi, C. C. (1979). Coping skills training for the management of anxiety: A critical review. *Behavior Therapy, 10,* 491–522.

Bauer, D. (1976). An exploratory study of developmental changes in children's fears. *Journal of Child Psychology and Psychiatry, 17,* 69–74.

Beck, A. T., & Emery, G. (1985). *Anxiety and phobias: A cognitive perspective.* New York: Basic Books.

Beidel, D. C. (1988). Psychophysiological assessment of anxious emotional states in children. *Journal of Abnormal Psychology, 97,* 80–82.

Berg, I., Butler, A., & Pritchard, J. (1974). Psychiatric illness in the mothers of school-phobic adolescents. *British Journal of Psychiatry, 125,* 466–467.

Bernstein, D. A., & Borkovec, T. D. (1973). *Progressive relaxation training: A manual for helping professions.* Champaign, IL: Research Press.

Bierman, K. L. (1984). Cognitive development and clinical interviews with children. In B. B. Lahey & A. E. Kazdin (Eds.), *Advances in clinical child psychology* (Vol. 6, pp. 217–250). New York: Plenum Press.

Campbell, S. B. (1986). Developmental issues. In R. Gittelman (Ed.), *Anxiety disorders of childhood* (pp. 24–57). New York: Guilford Press.

Carey, G., & Gottesman, I. (1981). Twin and family studies of anxiety, phobic, and obsessive disorders. In D. F. Klein & J. Rabkin (Eds.), *Anxiety: New research and changing concepts* (pp. 117–133). New York: Raven Press.

Chambers, W. J., Puig–Antich, J., Hirsch, M., Paez, P., Ambrosini, P. J., Tabrizi, M. A., & Davies, M. (1985). The assessment of affective disorders in children and adolescents by semistructured interview. *Archives of General Psychiatry, 42,* 696–702.

Cloninger, C. R., Martin, R. L., Clayton, P., & Guze, S. B. (1981). A blind follow-up and family study of anxiety neurosis: Preliminary analysis of the St. Louis 500. In D. F. Klein & J. Rabkin (Eds.), *Anxiety: New research and changing concepts* (pp. 137–148). New York: Raven Press.

Conners, C. K., Himmelhock, J., Goyette, C. H., Ulrich, R., & Neil, J. F. (1979). Children of parents with affective illness. *Journal of the American Academy of Child Psychiatry, 18,* 600–607.

Coolidge, J. C., & Brodie, R. D. (1974). Observatiions of mothers of 49 school phobic children. *Journal of the American Academy of Child Psychiatry, 13,* 275–285.

Costello, A. J., Edelbrock, C., Kalas, R., Kessler, M. D., & Klaric, S. (1982). *The NIMH Diagnostic Interview Schedule for Children (DISC).* Pittsburgh: Costello et al.

Crowe, R. R., Noyes, R., Pauls, D. L., & Slymen, D. (1983). A family study of panic disorder. *Archives of General Psychiatry, 40,* 1065–1069.

Crowe, R. R., Pauls, D. L., Slymen, D. J., & Noyes, R. (1980). A family study of anxiety neuroris. *Archives of General Psychiatry, 37,* 77–79.

Cytryn, L., McKnew, D. H., Bartko, J. J., Lamour, M., & Hamovitt, J. (1982).

Offspring of parents with affective disorders: II. *Journal of the American Academy of Child Psychiatry, 21*, 389–391.

Davidson, S. (1961). School phobia as a manifestation of family disturbance: Its structure and treatment. *Journal of Child Psychology and Psychiatry, 1*, 270–287.

DiGiuseppe, R. (1988). A cognitive–behavioral approach to the treatment of conduct disorder children and adolescents. In N. Epstein, S. E. Schlesinger, & W. Dryden (Eds.), *Cognitive–behavioral treatment with families* (pp. 183–214). New York: Brunner/Mazel.

Draper, T. W., & James, R. S. (1985). Preschool fears: Longitudinal sequence and cohort changes. *Child Study Journal 15*, 147–155.

D'Zurilla, T. (1986) *Problem-solving approaches to therapy*. New York: Springer.

D'Zurilla, T. J., & Goldfreid, M. R. (1971). Problem-solving and behavior modification. *Journal of Abnormal Psychology, 78*, 107–126.

Edelbrock, C., Costello, A. J., Duncan, M. K., Conover, N. C., & Kalas, R. (1986). Parent–child agreement on child psychiatric symptoms assessed via structured interview. *Journal of Child Psychology and Psychiatry, 27*, 181–190.

Edelbrock, C., Costello, A. J., Duncan, M. K., Kalas, R., & Conover, N. C. (1985). Age differences in the reliability of the psychiatric interview of the child. *Child Development, 56*, 265–275.

Eisenberg, L. (1958). School phobia: A study in the communication of anxiety. *American Journal of Psychiatry, 114*, 712–718.

Epstein, N., Schlesinger, S. E., & Dryden, W. (1988). Concepts and methods of cognitive–behavioral family treatment. In N. Epstein et al. (Eds.), *Cognitive–behavioral therapy with families* (pp. 5–83). New York: Brunner/Mazel.

Foa, E. B., Steketee, G., & Grayson, J. B. (1985). Imaginal and *in-vivo* exposure: A comparison with obsessive–compulsive checkers. *Behavior Therapy, 16*, 292–302.

Francis, G. (1988). Assessing cognitions in anxious children. *Behavior Modification, 12*, 167–281.

Gittelman, R. (1985). Anxiety disorders in children. In B. B. Lakey & A. E. Kazdin (Eds.) *Advances in clinical child psychology* (Vol. 8, pp. 53–79). New York: Plenum Press.

Gittelman, R. (1986). (Ed.). *Anxiety disorders of childhood*. New York: Guilford Press.

Graziano, A. M., & Mooney, D. C. (1984). *Children and behavior therapy*. Hawthorne, NY: Aldine.

Harris, E. L., Noyes, R., Crowe, R. R., & Chaudery, M. D. (1983). A family study of agoraphobia. *Archives of General Psychiatry, 40*, 1061–1064.

Hatzenbuehler, L. C., & Schroeder, H. (1978). Desensitization procedures in the treatment of childhood disorders. *Psychological Bulletin, 85*, 831–844.

Haynes, S. N. (1978). *Principles of behavioral assessment*. New York: Gardner Press.

Herjanic, B., Herjanic, M., Brown, F., & Wheatt, T. (1975). Are children reliable reporters? *Journal of Abnormal Child Psychology, 1*, 41–48.

Herjanic, B., & Reich, W. (1982). Development of a structured psychiatric interview for children: Agreement between child and parent on individual symptoms. *Journal of Abnormal Child Psychology, 10*, 307–324.

Himadi, W. G., Boice, R., & Barlow, D. H. (1985). Assessment of agoraphobia: Triple response measurement. *Behavior Research and Therapy, 23*, 311–323.

Hodges, K., McKnew, C., Burbach, D. J., & Roebuck, L. (1987). Diagnostic concordance between the Child Assessment Schedule (CAS) and the Schedule for Affective Disorders and Schizophrenia for School-age Children (K-SADS) in an outpatient sample using lay interviewers. *Journal of the American Academy of Child and Adolescent Psychiatry, 26*, 654–661.

Ingram, R. & Kendall, P. C. (1987). The cognitive side of anxiety. *Cognitive Therapy and Research, 11*, 523–536.

Jannoun, L., Munby, M., Catalan, J., & Gelder, M. (1980). A home-based treatment program for agoraphobia: Replication and controlled evaluation. *Behavior Therapy, 11*, 294–305.

Jersild, A. T., & Holmes, F. B. (1936). Children's fears. *Child Development Monograph* (No. 20).

Johnson, S. B., & Melamed, B. G. (1979). The assessment and treatment of children's fears. In B. B. Lahey & A. E. Kazdin (Eds.), *Advances in clinical child psychology* (Vol. 2, pp. 107–139). New York: Plenum Press.

Kane, M. T., & Kendall, P. C. (1989). Anxiety disorders in children: A multiple-baseline evaluation of a cognitive–behavioral treatment. *Behavior Therapy, 20*, 499–508.

Kendall, P. C. (1984). Behavioral assessment and methodology. In G. T. Wilson, C. M. Franks, K. D. Brownell, & P. C. Kendall, *Annual review of behavior therapy: Theory and practice* (Vol. 9). New York: Guilford Press.

Kendall, P. C. (1985). Toward a cognitive–behavioral model of child psychopathology and a critique of related interventions. *Journal of Abnormal Child Psychology, 13*, 357–372.

Kendall, P. C. (1989). Maintenance and generalization of behavior change: Comments, considerations, and the "no-cure" criticism. *Behavior Therapy, 20*, 357–364.

Kendall, P. C. (1990) *Coping cat workbook.* Available from the author, 238 Meeting House Lane, Merion Station, PA 19066.

Kendall, P. C., & Braswell, L. (1985). *Cognitive–behavioral therapy for impulsive children.* New York: Guilford.

Kendall, P. C., & Braswell, L. (1986). Medical applications of cognitive–behavioral interventions with children. *Developmental and Behavioral Pediatrics, 7*, 257–264.

Kendall, P. C., Howard, B. L., & Epps, J. (1988). The anxious child: Cognitive–behavioral treatment strategies. *Behavior Modification, 12*, 281–310.

Kendall, P. C., & Ingram, R. (1987). The future of the cognitive assessment of anxiety: Let's get specific. In L. Michelson & M. Ascher (Eds.), *Anxiety and stress disorders: Cognitive–behavioral assessment and treatment.* New York: Guilford Press.

Kendall, P. C., & Ingram, R. (1989). Cognitive–behavioral perspectives: Theory and research on depression and anxiety. In P. C. Kendall & D. Watson (Eds.), *Anxiety and depression: Distinction and overlapping features.* New York: Academic Press.

Kendall, P. C., Kane, M., Howard, B., & Siqueland, L. (1989) *Cognitive–behavioral therapy for anxious children: Treatment manual.* Available from the first author, Department of Psychology, Temple University, Philadelphia, PA 19122.

Kendall, P. C., Pellegrini, D., & Urbain, E. (1981). Assessment strategies for cognitive–behavioral procedure with children. In P. C. Kendall & S. D. Hollon (Eds.), *Assessment strategies for congitive–behavioral interventions.* New York: Academic Press.

Kendall, P. C. & Ronan, K. R. (1990a). Assessment of children's anxieties, fears, and phobias: Cognitive–behavioral models and methods. In C. R. Reynolds & R. W. Kamphaus (Eds.), *Handbook of psychological and educational assessment of children: Personality, behavior, and context.* New York: Guilford Press.

Kendall, P. C. & Ronan, K. R. (1990b) Children's Anxious Self-Statement Questionnaire (CASSQ). Unpublished manuscript, Department of Psychology, Temple University, Philadelphia, PA. 19122.

Kendall, P. C., & Siqueland, L. (1989). Child and adolescent therapy. In A. M. Nezu & C. M. Nezu (Eds.), *Clinical decision making in behavior therapy: A problem-solving perspective.* Champaign, IL.: Research Press.

Kendall, P. C., & Watson, D. (1989). (Eds.), *Anxiety and depression: Distinctive and overlapping features.* New York: Academic Press.

King, N. J., Hamilton, D. I., & Ollendick, T. H. (1988). *Children's phobias: A behavioral perspective.* Chichester, England: Wiley.

Kleiner, L., Marshall, W. L., & Spevack, M. (1987). Training in problem-solving and exposure treatment for agoraphobics with panic attacks. *Journal of Anxiety Disorders, 1,* 219–238.

Koeppen, A. S. (1974). Relaxation training for children. *Elementary School Guidance and Counseling, 9,* 14–21.

Lang, P. J. (1968). Fear reduction and fear behavior: Problems in treating a construct. In J. M. Schleen (Ed.), *Research in psychotherapy.* Washington, DC: American Psychological Association.

Lapouse, R., & Monk, M. A. (1959). Fears and worries in a representative sample of children. *American Journal of Orthopsychiatry, 29,* 223–248.

Last, C. G. (1988). Introduction. *Behavior Modification, 12,* 163–164.

Last, C. G., Hersen, M., Kazdin, A. E., Francis, G. & Grubb, H. J. (1987). Psychiatric illness in the mothers of anxious children. *American Journal of Psychiatry, 144*(12), 1580–1583.

Leitenberg, H., & Callahan, E. J. (1973). Reinforced practice and reduction of different kinds of fears in adults and children. *Behavior Research and Therapy, 11,* 19–30.

Lewis, S. A. (1974). A comparison of behavior therapy techniques in the reduction of fearful avoidance behaviors. *Behavior Therapy, 5,* 648–655.

Marks, I. M. (1975) Behavioral treatments of phobic and obsessive–compulsive disorders: A critical appraisal. In M. Hersen, R. M. Eisler, & P. M. Miller (Eds.), *Progress in behavior modification.* New York: Academic Press.

McFarlane, J. W., Allen, L., & Honzik, M. P. (1954). *A developmental study of the behavior problems of normal children between 21 months and 14 years.* Berkeley: University of California Press.

McKnew, D. H., Cytryn, L., Efron, A. M., Gershon, E. S., & Bunney, W. E. (1979). Offspring of patients with affective disorders. *British Journal of Psychiatry, 134,* 148–152.

Meador, A., E., & Ollendick, T. H. (1984). Cognitive behavior therapy with children: An evaluation of its efficacy and clinical utility. *Child and Family Behavior Therapy, 6,* 25–44.

Meichenbaum, D. (1986). *Stress inoculation training.* New York: Pergamon Press.

Melamed, B. G., & Siegel, L. J. (1975). Reduction of anxiety in children facing hospitalization and surgery by way of filmed modeling. *Journal of Consulting and Clinical Psychology, 43,* 511–521.

Michelson, L., & Ascher, L. M. (Eds.) (1987). *Anxiety and stress disorders: Cognitive–behavioral assessment and treatment.* New York: Guilford Press.

Miller, L. C. (1983). Fears and anxiety in children. In C. E. Walker & M. C. Roberts (Eds.), *Handbook of clinical child psychology* (pp. 337–380). New York: Wiley.

Miller, L. C., Barrett, C. L., & Hampe, E. (1974). Phobias of childhood in a pre-scientific era. In A. Davids (Ed.), *Child personality and psychotherapy: Current topics.* New York: Wiley.

Morris, R. J., & Kratochwill, T. R. (1983). *Treating children's fears and phobias: A behaviorial approach.* New York: Pergamon Press.

Morton, T. L., Twentyman, C. T., & Azar, S. T. (1988). Cognitive–behavioral assessment and treatment of child abuse. In N. Epstein, S. E. Schlesinger, & W. Dryden (Eds.). *Cognitive–behavioral therapy with families* (pp. 87–117). New York: Brunner/Mazel.

Neilans, T. H., & Israel, A. C. (1981). Towards maintenance and generalization of behavior change: Teaching children self-regulation and self-instructional skills. *Cognitive Therapy and Research, 2,* 189–195.

Noyes, R., Clancy, J., Crowe, R., Hoenk, P. R., & Slymen, D. J. (1978). The familial prevalence of anxiety neurosis. *Archives of General Psychiatry, 35,* 1057–1059.

O'Connell, R. A., Mayo, J. A., & O'Brien, J. D., & Misrsheidaie, F. (1979). In J. Mendlewicz & B. Shopsin (Eds.), *Genetic aspects of affective illness* (pp. 55–68). New York: Medical and Scientific Books.

Ollendick, T. H. (1983). Reliability and validity of the Revised Fear Survey Schedule for Children (FSSC-R). *Behavior Research and Therapy, 21,* 685–692.

Ollendick, T. H. (1986). Behavior therapy with children and adolescents. In S. L. Garfield & A. E. Bergen (Eds.), *Handbook of psychotherapy and behavior change* (3rd ed.). New York: Wiley.

Ollendick, T. H., Cerny, J. A. (1981). *Clinical behavior therapy with children.* New York: Plenum Press.

Ollendick, T. H., & Francis, G. (1988). Behavioral assessment and treatment of childhood phobias. *Behavior Modification, 12,* 165–204.

Ollendick, T. H., King, N. J., & Frary, R. B. (1989). Fears in children and adolescents: Reliability and generalizability across gender, age and nationality. *Behavior Research and Therapy, 27,* 19–26.

Ollendick, T. H., Matson, J. L., & Helsel, W. J. (1985). Fears in children and adolescents: Normative data. *Behavior Research and Therapy, 23,* 465–467.

Orvaschel, H., & Weissman, M. M. (1986). Epidemiology of anxiety disorders in children: A review. In R. Gittelman (Ed.), *Anxiety disorders of childhood* (58–72). New York: Guilford Press.

Peterson, L. (1989). Coping by children undergoing stressful medical procedures: Some conceptual, methodological, and therapeutic issues. *Journal of Consulting and Clinical Psychology, 57,* 380–387.

Prins, P. J. (1985). Self-speech and self-regulation of high- and low-anxious children in the dental situation: An interview study. *Behavioral Research and Therapy, 23,* 641–650.

Prins, P. J. (1986). Children's self-speech and self-regulation during a fear-provoking behavioral test. *Behavior Research and Therapy, 24,* 181–191.

Piug–Antich, J., & Chambers, W. (1978). *The Schedule for Affective Disorders and Schizophrenia for School-age Children (K-SADS).* Pittsburgh: Western Psychiatric Institute and Clinic.

Quay, H. C. (1977). Measuring dimensions of deviant behavior: The Behavior Problem Checklist. *Journal of Abnormal Child Psychology, 5,* 277–289.

Reynolds, C. R., & Richmond, B. O. (1978). "What I think and feel": A revised measure of children's manifest anxiety. *Journal of Abnormal Child Psychology, 6,* 271–280.

Rimm, D. C., & Masters, J. C. (1974). *Behavior therapy: Techniques and empirical findings.* New York: Academic Press.

Rines, W. B. (1973). Behavior therapy before institutionalization. *Psychotherapy: Theory, Research, and Practice, 10,* 281–283.

Ross, C., Ross, S., & Evans, T. A. (1971). The modification of extreme social withdrawal by modificatioin with guided practice. *Journal of Behavior Therapy and Experimental Psychiatry, 2,* 273–279.

Rutter, M., Tuma, A. H., & Lann, I. S., (Eds.), (1988). *Assessment and diagnosis in child psychopathology.* New York: Guilford Press.

Saal, F. E., Downey, R. G., & Lahey, M. A. (1980). Rating the ratings: Assessing the psychometric quality of rating data. *Psychological Bulletin, 88,* 413–428.

Schlesinger, S. E. (1988). Cognitive–behavioral approaches to family treatment of addictions. In N. Epstein, S. E. Schlesinger, & W. Dryden (Eds.), *Cognitive-behavioral therapy with families* (pp. 254–291). New York: Brunner/Mazel.

Silverman, W. K. (1987). *Anxiety Disorders Interview Schedule for Children (ADIS-C).* Albany, NY: Center for Stress and Anxiety Disorders.

Silverman, W. K., Cerny, J. A., & Nelles, W. B. (1988). Familial influence in anxiety disorders: Studies on the offspring of patients with anxiety disorders. In B. B. Lahey & A. E. Kazdin (Eds.), *Advances in child clinical psychology* (Vol. 16, pp. 223–248). New York: Plenum Press.

Solyom, M. D., Beck, P., Solyom, C., & Hugel, R. (1974). Some etiological factors in phobic neurosis. *Canadian Psychiatric Association Journal, 19,* 69–78.

Spielberger, C. C. (1973). *Manual for the State-trait Anxiety Inventory.* Palo Alto, CA: Consulting Psychologists Press.

Spitzer, R. L., Endicott, J., & Robins, E. (1985). *Research Diagnostic Criteria (RDC) for a Selected Group of Functional Disorders.* New York: New York State Psychiatric Institute.

Spivack, G., & Shure, M. (1974). *A problem-solving approach to children's adjustment.* San Francisco: Jossey–Bass.

Strauss, C. C. (1988). Behavioral assessment and treatment of overanxious disorder in children and adolescents. *Behavior Modification, 12,* 234–250.

Strauss, C. C., Lease, C. A., Last, C. G., & Francis, G. (1988). Overanxious disorder: An examination of developmental differences. *Journal of Abnormal Child Psychology, 16*(4), 433–443.

Sylvester, C., Hyde, T. S., & Reichler, R. J. (1987). The Diagnostic Interview for

Children and Personality Interview for Children in studies of children at risk for anxiety disorders and depression. *Journal of the American Academy of Child and Adolescent Psychiatry, 26,* 668–675.

Torgersen, S. (1983). Genetic factors in anxiety disorders. *Archives of General Psychiatry, 40,* 1085–1089.

Turner, S. M., Beidel, D. C., & Costello, A. (1987). Psychopathology in the offspring of anxiety disorders patients. *Journal of Consulting and Clinical Psychology, 55,* 229–235.

Verhulst, F. C., Althaus, M., & Berden, G. F. M. G. (1987). The child assessment schedule: Parent–child agreement and validity measures. *Journal of Child Psychology and Psychiatry, 28,* 455–466.

Waldron, S., Shrier, D. K., Stone, B., & Tobin, F. (1975). School phobia and other childhood neuroses: A systematic study of the children and their families. *American Journal of Psychiatry, 132,* 802–808.

Weisman, D., Ollendick, T. H., & Horne, A. M. (1978). *A comparison of muscle relaxation techniques with children.* Unpublished manuscript, Indiana State University, Terre Haute, IN.

Wells, K. C., & Virtulano, L. A. (1984). Anxiety disorders in childhood. In S. E. Turner (Ed.), *Behavioral theories and treatment of anxiety.* New York: Plenum Press.

Werry, J. S. (1986). Diagnosis and assessment. In R. Gittelman (Ed.), *Anxiety disorders of childhood.* New York: Guilford Press.

Wilson, G. T. (1985). Fear reduction methods and the treatment of anxiety disorders. In C. M. Franks, G. T. Wilson, P. C. Kendall, & K. D. Brownell, *Annual review of behavior therapy* (Vol. 10, pp. 87–122). New York: Guilford.

Zatz, S., & Chassin, L. (1983). Cognitions of test-anxious children. *Journal of Consulting and Clinical Psychology, 51,* 524–534.

Zatz, S., & Chassin, L. (1985). Cognitions of test-anxious children under naturalistic test-taking conditions. *Journal of Consulting and Clinical Psychology, 53,* 393–401.

CHAPTER 6

Treatment of Depression During Childhood and Adolescence: Cognitive–Behavioral Procedures for the Individual and Family

KEVIN D. STARK, LAWRENCE W. ROUSE, AND
RONALD LIVINGSTON
University of Texas

In this chapter, we describe a treatment program for depressed youths that has evolved from years of empirical scrutiny and clinical experience. The program combines behavioral, self-control, and cognitive procedures that are used with the child, with related procedures used in family therapy. The behavioral and self-control procedures are used primarily as a means of helping the children learn how to cope with their depressive symptoms, gain some distance from their depressive thinking, and produce some cognitive change. The cognitive procedures are used to change the schemata and core schemata that underly the depressive symptoms and maladaptive behavior patterns. The family therapy procedures are used to alter the maladaptive patterns of interaction and verbal communications within the family that often lead to, and/or maintain, the child's maladaptive behavior and cognition.

The treatment program has grown as a result of treatment outcome research and clinical experience; procedures have been added, others have been dropped and/or modified. For instance, our early treatment efforts (e.g., Stark, Reynolds, & Kaslow, 1987) followed a programmatic approach in which the youngsters participated in a preplanned multiprocedure program that taught the youngsters a set of coping skills that they could use to control depressive symptomatology. Based upon that experience, cognitive restructuring and family therapy procedures have been added. In addition, attempts at attribution retraining have been dropped as the children

165

found this procedure to be too abstract to understand and apply. Moreover, the format of the treatment program has changed. First, as relevant assessment procedures have appeared in the literature, the treatment program has become more individually tailored as the choice of treatment procedures has been increasingly guided by assessment results. Secondly, and perhaps of greater therapeutic import, attempts have been made to devise more engaging modes for teaching children the skills and therapeutic constructs. Since *involvement* in treatment is one of the best predictors of treatment outcome (Braswell, Kendall, Braith, Carey, & Uye, 1985), and since at least one study has shown that earlier cognitive–behavioral treatments were not particularly engaging for depressed children (Butler, Miezitis, Friedman, & Cole, 1980), this concern has received much attention.

GUIDING RATIONALE FOR TREATMENT

It is important for the potential user of this treatment program to understand the underlying theoretical model that guides the choice and implementation of treatment procedures (see Kendall, Chapter 1, this volume). The treatment program is based on a combined *skills deficit* and *cognitive distortion* model of depression. In other words, it is believed that the client's depressive symptoms are a result of an interaction among a lack of coping, self-control, interpersonal skills, and a dysfunctional style of thinking. Furthermore, it is hypothesized that these behavioral and cognitive deficits, and the distortion in thinking, are produced and maintained by disturbances in family interaction patterns and communications. The model is depicted in Figure 6-1, which was adapted from Ingram and Kendall (1986). The central terms of the model are defined below and their significance for the treatment of depression is discussed.

Cognitive products are the thoughts, images, symbolic words, and gestures that occur in an individual's stream of consciousness, and can be made conscious through introspection. These cognitive events are the products of the interaction of environmental information, cognitive operations, and schemata (Ingram & Kendall, 1986). It is important to note that the cognitive events reported are the result of an individual's thinking and may not be an accurate representation of the actual thoughts or process of thinking (Guidano & Liotti, 1983).

The stream of consciousness of depressed children is dominated by negative thoughts about the self, the world, and the future. The children are preoccupied with such thoughts. In fact, they have a very difficult time getting these thoughts out of their mind. Even when the child tries to rid him or herself of these thoughts, they reoccur. Another problem is that the child believes that the thoughts are true.

Schemata are hypothesized to underlie the consistency that is observed

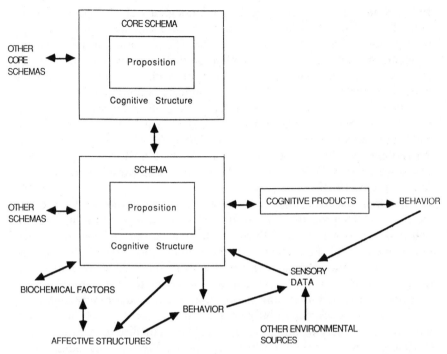

FIGURE 6-1. Skills deficit and cognitive distortion model of depression.

in an individual's behavior, emotions, and thinking (Meichenbaum, 1977). A *schema* is comprised of structure and content. The structural aspect is referred to as cognitive structure. The content is referred to as a proposition. A cognitive structure stores information in some fashion. It is not a physical structure, but rather a functional unit, such as long-term memory (Ingram & Kendall, 1986). A proposition is comprised of memorial representations of a domain including general knowledge and specific exemplars of the domain, and a specification of the relationships among the primary attributes of the domain (Turk & Salovey, 1985). Schemata have been referred to as "filters" (Meichenbaum, Bream, & Cohen, 1985) and "templates" (Kendall, 1985) because they directly influence the way an individual derives meaning from his or her world. Schemata affect what the individual attends to, perceives, recalls, and views as important (Kendall, 1985). They direct the focus, structure, and sequence of encoding, and the storage and retrieval of information (Turk & Salovey, 1985). Thus, they provide the guidelines for processing information.

Schemata appear to be organized hierarchically. The higher level schemata are referred to as *core schemata*, and develop earlier in life. Schemata elaborate progressively over the course of development (Guidano & Liotti,

1983). Schemata at all levels are linked through a web of cognitive operations. Due to their developmental primacy, core schemata appear to shape the formation of the subordinate schemata. The proximity of the schemata, both core and subordinate, is dependent on the similarity in content. Thus, they are organized in interconnected clusters with the core schema at the directive pinnacle and the subordinate schemata fanning out from it.

The information processing of depressed children appears to be dominated by schemata that distort information in a negative direction (Kendall, Stark, & Adam, in press). At a core level, the depressed child's thinking is dominated by core schemata that include, à la Beck's theory (1967), a negative view of the self, the world, and the future (Kaslow, Stark, Printz, & Livingston, 1990).

Cognitive operations, also commonly referred to as cognitive processes, are the rules for processing information that shape and transform information into cognitive products. They also serve as the procedures that enable the components of the system to interact. These processes are both driven and shaped by the schemata, and they construct the cognitive representatioins that comprise the proposition (cognitive content). Cognitive operations determine how incoming information is encoded, stored, combined, and altered with respect to information and structures already in the system, and how the existing structures are engaged, disengaged, or altered (Hollon & Kriss, 1984). When maladaptive schemata are operating, errors are evident in the rules that appear to be guiding information processing.

Beck (1967) has identified a number of systematic errors that appear to characterize the processing of information by depressed individuals. Included are (1) magnification and minimization, (2) overgeneralization, (3) selective abstraction, (4) arbitrary inference, and (5) dichotomous thinking. Turk and Salovey (1985), after reviewing the literature, identified a number of additional processing errors that may be present in depression, including (1) selective attention, (2) confirmatory bias, (3) availability and representativeness bias, (4) egocentric bias, and (5) false consensus.

Behavior is viewed within this model as both a product and an initiator of cognition and environmental events. Thus, Bandura's (1977) principle of reciprocal determinism is embraced. This is especially important to keep in mind when working with the depressed child's family. The child is not simply a victim of a dysfunctional system; rather he or she may be an unwitting participant in the construction of that system.

One of the areas of behavior that has been symstematically studied in depressed children is social skills (Linn & Stark, 1989). Depressed children have greater deficits in both social skills knowledge and behavior than their nondepressed peers. In addition, upon entering social situations, depressed children experience heightened aversive physiological arousal. This arousal is accompanied by a plethora of negative thoughts, which seem to further heighten arousal and discourage the child from interacting. It is hypothesized that dysfunctional thinking accompanies the behavioral disturbances found among depressed children.

EXPRESSION OF DEPRESSION DURING CHILDHOOD AND ADOLESCENCE

How is depression manifested during childhood? Effective treatment is based in part on an understanding of the range of possible manifestations of depression. It appears as though depression during childhood is manifested in much the same way that it is during the adult years (Kaslow & Rehm, 1983). It is a syndrome that is comprised of a number of symptoms that reliably co-occur (Cantwell & Carlson, 1979) and are manifested in the affective, cognitive, motivational, and physical realms (Kovacs & Beck, 1977). Relative to adults, there are some age-appropriate developmental differences in the expression of the symptoms, and some age-specific associated features (American Psychiatric Association, 1987). Table 6-1 contains a list of the symptoms that we have systematically assessed in depressed youths. The table reports the frequency that each symptom occurs in public school children 10 to 12 years old who were diagnosed with Major Depression (MD), Dysthymic Disorder (DD), Depressive Disorder Not Otherwise Specified (DNOS), and in the general school population.

From the data presented in Table 6-1, it appears that dysphoria is the primary mood disturbance reported by our sample of depressed schoolchildren. When it occurred, many children reported that it was a distinctly different feeling of sadness which frequently was associated with environmental events, but was not reactive to environmental interventions. Among those children who reported a diurnal variation in mood, most of them felt worse during the afternoon or evening. Anhedonia was reported by about half of the children experiencing MD, while it was relatively uncommon among the other two diagnostic groups. Anger, which has proven somewhat resistant to change, was reported by about 33% of the children who had been diagnosed as having a depressive disorder. The angry children tended to experience this feeling in the afternoon or evening, and once they were angry, it was difficult to cheer them up. Another of the affective symptoms, feeling unloved, was reported by approximately half of the children diagnosed with MD, while it was less common among the other children.

A number of cognitive symptoms were quite common among depressed youths. Almost all of the children with MD reported a negative self-image and two-thirds of the DD children reported a negative self-image, while this problem was reported by approximately one-third of the DNOS children. Over half of the depressed children had difficulty concen-

TABLE 6-1. Percentage of Depressed Children From Grades 4–7 Who Report Clinically Relevant Levels of Depressive Symptoms

Symptom Special characteristic	Major depression ($n = 11$)	Dysthymic ($n = 15$)	Depressive disorder N.O.S. ($n = 35$)	General population ($n = 179$)
Dysphoric mood	91	70	40	1
Quality of mood	40	27	57	2
Association	10	0	14	1
Reactivity	50	27	100	1
Morning	10	9	0	0
Afternoon	36	18	84	0
Irritability/anger	45	30	23	2
Association	20	9	37	0
Reactivity	100	9	75	4
Morning	0	9	0	0
Afternoon	60	18	75	3
Excessive guilt	36	13	20	1
Negative self-image	91	60	37	7
Feeling unloved	54	33	20	1
Hopeless	36	33	0	1
Self-pity	18	27	9	1
Aches and pains	54	67	37	8
Hypochondriasis	9	20	7	1
Anhedonia	54	7	6	0
Fatigue	73	53	31	6
Difficulty concentrating	73	60	40	4
Psychomotor agitation	36	7	9	3
Cannot sit still	100	100	66	2
Pacing	50	100	33	0
Hand wringing	50	100	33	2
Pulling/rubbing	50	100	0	1
Talking	25	0	66	1
Psychomotor retardation	18	20	3	1
Slowed speech	100	33	100	1
Increased latencies	0	33	100	1
Monotonous	100	66	100	0
Decreased speech	75	66	100	0
Slowed movements	25	33	100	0
Stupor	0	0	0	0
Social withdrawal	73	27	11	1
Social isolation	18	13	6	1
Insomnia	64	60	17	4
Initial	57	66	100	3
Middle	28	22	17	1
Terminal	14	11	34	1
Reversal	0	0	0	0
Nonrestorative	42	33	50	2
Daytime	28	44	34	3
Hypersomnia	18	13	3	1
Anorexia	27	13	6	4
Weight loss	0	0	0	1
Increased appetite	9	7	9	2

(cont.)

TABLE 6-1. (*cont.*)

Symptom Special characteristic	Major depression ($n=11$)	Dysthymic ($n=15$)	Depressive disorder N.O.S. ($n=35$)	General population ($n=179$)
Crave sweets	27	20	9	3
Weight gain	0	0	6	0
Suicidal ideation	27	7	11	1
Acts	0	0	0	0
Seriousness	0	0	0	0
Lethality	0	0	0	0
Self-damage	0	0	3	0

Notes. Depressive Disorder N.O.S. = Depressive Disorder Not Otherwise Specified. It is important to explain that the lower rate of dysphoria noted for children who received a diagnosis of DNOS is somewhat misleading. The prevalence rte of 40% represents the percentage of these children who reported as severe a level of mood disturbance as those youngsters who received one of the other two diagnoses. The remaining 60% actually reported a chronic low-grade sense of dysphoria.

trating, a factor that could be contributing to their academic difficulties (Stark, Livingston, Laurent, & Cardenas, 1989). Hopelessless was not a common characteristic of this sample of depressed youths.

The motivational symptom of social withdrawal was reported by nearly three of four children with MD, suggesting that this may need to be a target of intervention. Suicidal ideation was uncommon among the depressed youngsters, although 27% of the MD children reported clinically relevant levels. None of the children were actively suicidal, and only one reported acts of self-damage.

The physical symptoms of psychomotor agitation and retardation, and eating disturbances were relatively uncommon. However, sleep disturbance, fatigue, and aches and pains were relatively common. Insomnia was reported by more than half of the children with MD and DD. The most common disturbance was initial insomnia. Many of the children also reported feeling tired or weighted down during waking hours. Aches and pains, most commonly headaches and stomachaches, were reported by about half of the depressed children.

PREVALENCE OF DEPRESSION DURING CHILDHOOD

The prevalence of depression during childhood varies greatly across research studies for a variety of reasons (Lobovits & Handal, 1985). Epidemiological studies of the prevalence of depression in the general population have reported figures as low as 1.9% (Kashani & Simonds, 1979) to as high as 13.9% (Pfeffer, Zuckerman, Plutchik, & Mizruchi, 1984). Over the past 3 years we have screened more than 1,400 public school children from grades 4 through 7. Our results (Stark, Rouse, Laurent, Printz, 1990) indicate that approximately 4.2% of this population exhibit a diagnosable mood disorder. Of these youngsters, 1% received diagnoses of MD, 1% DD, and 2.2% DNOS. This latter group reported a long-standing, low-grade experience of dysphoria, accompanied by a number of additional symptoms, such as low self-esteem. It is important to note that the prevalence rate seems to be much lower for preschool-aged children (e.g., Kashani & Ray, 1983). In this group, depression appears to be associated with extreme chaos, drug or alcohol abuse, family violence, and neglect (Kashani & Ray, 1983).

It appears that higher prevalence rates are found among children from a variety of special populations. Children who are referred for educational problems appear to suffer from higher rates of depression. Weinberg, Rutman, Sullivan, Penich, and Dietz (1973) reported that 49% of the children from an educational diagnostic clinic were depressed. Lobovits and Handal reported a prevalence rate of 34% for youngsters who were referred to a psychiatric clinic for behavioral and academic problems. Children with a variety of medical problems including headaches (40%; Ling, Oftedal, & Weinberg, 1970), orthopedic patients (23%; Kashani, Venzke, and Millar, 1981b), cancer patients (17%; Kashani & Hakami, 1982), and general medical patients (Kashani et al., 1981) experience higher rates of depression, than with children in the general population. The prevalence rate of depression among elementary-age children from psychiatric clinics ranged in the literature from 2.1% (Christ, Adler, Isacoff, & Gershansky, 1981) to 61% (Weinberg et al., 1973).

SYMPTOMS THAT IMPACT TREATMENT

Depressed youngsters pose a number of unique problems for the cognitive–behavorial therapist since many of the symptoms that they experience can have an adverse impact on treatment strategies. While each of the symptoms noted in Table 6-1 would be problematic by itself, they become even more of a problem when they occur in combination. Cognitive–behavioral treatments are based on the assumption that the client can, and will be, an active participant in the therapeutic process. This assumption underlies the collaborative approach to treatment and the incorporation of therapeutic homework assignments. A number of symptoms of depression undermine this assumption. The socially withdrawn child interacts at a minimal level, which greatly inhibits the verbal interchange between the child and the therapist. Thus, the child's participation and the opportunity for collaboration may be reduced. Hopelessness affects both collaboration and the independent completion of homework. The child believes that nothing will work; so why bother with homework? Some depressed children become overly dependent on the therapist. Their reliance on the therapist to "make them better" can adversely affect collaboration. Due to the impact on memory, difficulty concentrating can result in the child's not completing homework assignments. Indecision and fatigue are additional symptoms that can interfere with assignments.

Depressed children can be difficult to engage in therapy. Their belief that things will not improve, or get worse, also applies to their expectations for treatment. Thus they may see no reason to become involved in treatment. The child may merely go through the motions during the sessions or want to stop coming to treatment. The socially withdrawn child is very quiet, does not spontaneously volunteer information, and responds minimally. Consequently, the therapist has to work to get the child engaged in treatment and to draw out information. Open-ended questions are unproductive since the child often responds with "I don't know" or some other minimal response that leaves the therapist in the dark. Depressed youngsters who are anhedonic are bored most of the time and fail to derive pleasure from many things. This, too, pervades their reaction to treatment—they find it boring. At times they complain about not having any fun. Their failure to become engaged in therapy, as a result of any of the previously mentioned symptoms, can be devastating. Furthermore, some treatments have a didactic component. Depressed children can find this to be quite uninteresting (Butler et al., 1980) and, as a result, fail to learn the coping skills. In order to combat the adverse effect of depressive symptoms, a number of steps can be taken. The treatment approach is also designed to address some of the developmental differences between children and adults in cognitve–behavioral therapy.

A number of principles guide the treatment format. First, the child is taught the therapeutic concepts and procedures in a fun and engaging manner. Therapy benefits from an engaging positive affective tone, as heightened emotional intensity has a meaningful impact on cognitive process and structural features (see Kendall, Chapter 1, this volume). This is accomplished by using games, activities, stories, and cartoons. Another principle that is followed is that the children learn best through their own experience, rather than through listening to a therapist. For example, when illustrating and explaining to a child that thoughts can often guide behavior, the exercise involves having the child listen to his or her own thoughts while working on a puzzle.

It is very important for the discussions about the therapeutic concepts and coping skills to be directly tied to the children's lives and problems. Discussions are individualized, making them more meaningful and real—a factor that seems to increase involvement.

The establishment of a solid thereaputic relationship, as held by clinical wisdom, can help motivate the youngster and promote compliance. A variety of procedures are used to enhance the client–therapist relationship including (1) collaboration, (2) conveying a sense of concern, (3) active listening, (4) displaying a sense of humor, and (5) arranging a rich schedule of reward and positive atmosphere in the therapeutic environment.

A final goal is helping the child understand the therapeutic rationale. This is accomplished through a series of activities designed to teach the relationships among thought, behavior and affect, and about one's own emotions. These activities are detailed later, in the section on Affective Education.

TREATMENT OUTCOME RESEARCH

Prior to describing in detail the treatment procedures recommended for use with depressed children, we briefly discuss the recommendations that others have made in the literature and review the existing treatment outcome research.

Proposed Treatment Models

Behavioral and cognitive–behavioral treatment approaches to childhood depression have received attention in the form of model development, case studies, and empirical investigations of treatment efficacy. Cognitive–behavioral models of treatment have centered on the concepts of self-control (Rehm, 1977), learned helplessness (Abramson, Seligman, & Teasdale, 1978), social reinforcement (Lewinsohn, 1975), and Beck's notion of cognitive distortions (Beck, 1967). Kaslow and Rehm (1983) have examined behavioral and cognitive procedures that have been successful in treating adult depression. They recommended that training in social skills, activity scheduling, production of positive self-statements, problem solving, reattribution, and self-control be included in the treatment of childhood depression. Clarizio (1985) has outlined a similar approach to treatment and noted that an eclectic approach with a blending of both cognitive and behavioral strategies may be most effective. Clarizio suggested that the choice of procedures is dictated by the choice of behaviors targeted for intervention. Nissen (1986) describes an "indirect therapy," based on the use of initial pharmacotherapy, reinforcement of general activity, agreement to engage in specific activities, and training in social skills. Additionally, Frame, Johnstone, and Giblin (1988) have provided a case report of the treatment of depression that included social problem solving, self-control training, social skills training, and academic remediation.

Case Studies

Two case studies that employed behavioral treatments have been published. Petti, Bornstein, Delamater, and Conners (1980) described a multimodal treatment for a 10-year-old girl with a chronic depressive disorder. The treatment consisted of individual, group, family, and pharmacological therapy. Over the course of treatment, the severity of the youngster's depressive symptoms was assessed twice a day by the hospital staff.

The initial treatment regimen consisted of using the therapeutic relationship to resolve some issues involving her parents and to improve self-esteem. In addition, she received remedial help in areas of academic deficiencies. A creative dramatics group was used to help her learn about her interpersonal behavior. Concurrently, the client and her foster family were involved in family therapy. Since an improvement in her hospital behavior was not noted, she received imipramine treatment, which produced a marked reduction in her overt manifestations of depression. She also noted subjective improvements. Finally, she received social skills training that was directed toward increasing the amount of eye contact, frequency and duration of smiles, duration of speech, and assertive behaviors. The skills training consisted of education, modeling, rehearsal, and feedback. This training, which was conducted in nine 15-minute sessions over 3 weeks, produced desired improvements on the targeted behavior. Despite the fact that this case evidenced improvements, the use of many different strategies without a research design to tease apart their separate effects reduces the conclusions that can be reached based on these data.

Frame, Matson, Sonis, Fialkov, and Kazdin (1982) evaluated a behavioral treatment for a 10-year-old boy with borderline intellectual ability who had been hospitalized for depression and a number of related problems. A skills training regimen consisting of instruction, modeling, rehearsal, and feedback was used to try to improve eye contact, volume and amount of speech, facial expressions, and body position. The training was conducted in twenty 20-minute sessions over a 4-week period. In this report, a multiple baseline design across behaviors was used to evaluate treatment effectiveness, and the results suggested that a systematic relationship existed between change in behavior and implementation of the skills training.

Group Comparison Studies

Only a few group-comparison treatment-outcome studies designed to evaluate the efficacy of cognitive–behavioral procedures have appeared in the literature. It is important to note that all of these investigations have been completed with depressed children selected from the public schools. Thus, the procedures have promise for clinical populations, but there is, as yet, no empirical support for their efficacy with this group of children.

In an early investigation, Butler and colleagues (1980) evaluated the efficacy of a role-playing treatment, cognitive-restructuring, and attention placebo control, relative to a waiting-list condition. Subjects were 56 children from grades 5 and 6 of the public schools. The children were assessed for depression and a number of related constructs using a battery of self-report measures and an unstructured teacher interview.

Each of the treatment conditions had a different emphasis. Children who received the role-playing treatment were taught social skills, and they were sensitized to their thoughts and feelings as well as those of others. In addition, they were taught to generate alternative solutions when facing stressful situations. The skills were taught through role playing, followed by feedback, and applied through homework. Children who received the cognitive restructuring treatment were taught the relationship between thoughts and feelings, and to identify and change maladaptive ones. They also were taught listening skills, and given therapeutic homework assignments. The authors noted that this program was didactic in nature and did not have the "appeal" of role playing.

The attention placebo condition consisted of teaching the children to solve academic problems as a group through sharing research and pooling information. Youngsters assigned to the three previously mentioned conditions met ten times, once a week, for an hour each meeting. The waiting-list subjects completed the pre- and posttreatment measures.

Results of the Butler et al. study indicated that all of the children across the four groups reported significant improvement from pre- to post-treatment assessment on the Children's Depression Inventury (CDI; Kovacs, 1981). The greatest improvement on self-report and teacher report measures was evident for children who received the role play treatment. Children who received the cognitive restructuring treatment showed the next best gain.

Reynolds and Coats (1986) evaluated the efficacy of a cognitive–behavioral and relaxation therapy for the treatment of 30 depressed adolescents in public high schools. The cognitive–behavioral treatment was an amalgamation of self-control and behavioral procedures, including training in self-monitoring, self-evaluation, and self-reinforcement. Once the skills had been learned, they were combined by the youngsters and used to promote personal change. The relazation treatment consisted of training in progressive muscle relaxation and emphasis on using the relaxation as a coping skill when faced with stress. One-third of the subjects were assigned to a waiting-list condition in which they completed the assessment battery at pre, post, and follow-up assessments but did not receive either treatment.

Results indicated that both active treatments were effective at reducing depression across a battery of self-report measures. Improvements were maintained at a 5-week follow-up assessment.

In the first of our treatment studies with depressed children (Stark et al., 1987), a downward extension of Rehm's self-control treatment (Rehm, Kaslwo, & Rabin, 1987) was compared with a behavioral intervention based loosely on Lewinsohn's treatment program (e.g., Lewinsohn, Sullivan, & Grosscup, 1980), and a waiting-list control condition. Subjects were 29 schoolchildren from grades 4–6 who reported elevated levels of depressive symptomatology on two separate administrations of the CDI (2 weeks apart) as well as in a semistructured clinical interview. Subjects completed a battery of self-report measures at pre, post, and 8-week follow-up assessments.

Children in the two active treatments met in small groups of four or five at their school for twelve 45–50-minute meetings completed over 5 weeks. The self-control treatment was designed to teach the children more adaptive skills for self-monitoring, self-evaluation, attributing the causes of good and bad outcomes, and self-consequating. The skills were taught through didactic presentations and in-therapy activities, and they were applied through extratherapy homework assignments. In the later sessions, the skills were combined as a means of working toward self-improvement. Self-monitoring was taught during the first four sessions and was applied to the children's daily lives through "pleasant events." The latter were scheduled daily throughout the treatment program. To increase the probability that the children would complete their self-monitoring assignments and other homework, the children contracted for tangible rewards. During sessions five and six, the focus of the self-monitoring was on the long-term consequences of their behavior.

The later portion of session six and all of session seven were devoted to teaching the youngsters a more adaptive attributional style. This was accomplished through education and role playing. Children were taught a more adaptive means of evaluating their own performances and abilities through a combination of an educational exercise and cognitive restructuring during sessions eight and nine. In addition, at this time the children began setting goals and subgoals for self-improvement and they combined their new skills (self-monitoring, a new attributional style, and self-evaluating) as a means of working toward goal attainment. Overt and covert forms of self-reinforcement were taught during the final three sessions.

The behavioral problem-solving therapy consisted of education about feelings and interpersonal behavior, and a combination of training in problem-solving skills, self-monitoring of pleasant events, activity scheduling, and social skills training. The skills were taught through didactic presentations and in-therapy exercises and applied through homework. Self-monitoring and group problem solving were used to increase pleasant activity level. To help ensure therapeutic compliance, these children contracted for tangible rewards, which were received intermittently.

Results indicated that children in both treatment conditions reported a significant reduction in depression at posttesting across depression measures and reported significantly less depressive symptomatology than children in the waiting-list condition. Children in the waiting-list condition reported only a minimum of change, suggesting that depressive symptoms do not spontaneously remit. A look at the clinical significance of the changes revealed that 78% of the children in the self-control treatment and 60% of the children in the behavioral problem-solving treatment scored in the nondepressed range on the CDI, and that all of the children scored in the nondepressed range on the semistructured interview. The improvements noted by the children in both active treatments at posttesting were maintained at 5-week follow-up. Moreover, children in the self-control condition improved and reported significantly less depression than the children in the behavioral problem-solving condition on the interview. The results of this initial investigation were encouraging and led to a second study that was designed to evaluate a revised cognitive–behavioral treatment.

Approximately 700 children from grades 4 to 7 were screened for depression, using a multiple-gate assessment procedure. This procedure involves screening the children twice with a self-report measure. Those children who score in the depressed range on both administrations of the self-report measure go on to complete a semistructured interview. In this assessment process, 26 youngsters reported elevated levels of depressive symptomatology, including major depression ($n = 3$), dysthymic disorder ($n = 10$), depressive disorder not otherwise specified ($n = 2$), and adjustment disorder with depressed mood ($n = 2$). The other 9 children reported elevated levels of symptomatology, but it was either not severe enough, or of long enough duration to warrant a diagnosis. The depressed children and their parents were invited to participate in the treatment program: All but 2 participated.

The 24 children were randomly assigned to a cognitive–behavioral treatment or a traditional counseling condition. The treatments were conducted in school and at home with the child and parents. The children met in groups of 4 with a pair of therapists. Both treatments consisted of 24 to 26 sessions lasting 45–50 minutes conducted over a 3 ½-month period. The groups met two times a week for 8 weeks, and once a week thereafter. In addition to the group sessions, there were monthly family meetings. Each family meeting lasted between 1 and 1½ hours.

The cognitive–behavioral treatment consisted of training in self-control skills, social skills, and cognitive restructuring. More specifically, the self-control training consisted of teaching the children more adaptive self-consequation (self-reinforce more and self-punish less), self-monitoring (pay attention to positive thoughts, good things that happen, and enjoyable things that you do), and self-evaluation (set less perfectionistic standards). Assertiveness training focused on interactions with significant others, including asking someone to do something fun, giving positive feedback, and telling someone to stop doing something that is annoying. Social skills training emphasized initiating interactions, maintaining interactions, and handling conflict. Relaxation training and imagery were used to help prepare the children for using their skills. Cognitive restructuring (e.g., "What's the evidence?") was employed by the therapists throughout treatment. In addition, a number of sessions were entirely devoted to the acquisition of the cognitive restructuring techniques, and a couple more sessions were devoted to teaching the children problem solving. During family sessions, the parents were taught how to encourage their child to use his or her new skills and to engage in more pleasant family activities.

The traditional counseling condition was designed to control for meeting with a group of peers who have similar problems, meeting with warm and emphathic adults, being given a rationale for what causes depression and how to overcome it, talking about problems, development of a support group, being given the expectation that they will get better, completing tasks, and the demand characteristics of the situation that work for the children to say that they are feeling better. The group interactions, discussions, and suggestions served as the therapeutic vehicle. During ecah session the therapists also involved the children in an exercise that would either help them learn more about emotions, or enhance self-esteem. When the children raised a specific problem, the therapists brought it to the groups' attention, and it was then discussed. The therapists worked in an empathic and nondirective fashion. The objective of the family sessions was to improve communication and increase engagement in pleasant family activities.

Depressed children in both treatment conditions reported significantly less depressive behavior at posttreatment relative to pretreatment. In addition, the youngsters reported significantly fewer depressive cognitions. Comparisons of the posttreatment and 7-month follow-up data indicated that the improvements were maintained. Perhaps of greater interest are the results of the between group analyses. While there were no significant between-group differences prior to treatment (on any of the measures,) subjects in the cognitive–behavioral treatment reported significantly less depression on a semistructured posttreatment interview, and significantly fewer depressive cognitions. At 7-month follow-up, the differences were no longer significant, but this was in part due to attrition in the subjects. Only five of the children from the traditional counseling condition could be found and only seven of the children from the cognitive–behavioral condition were located. The children's scores on the measures had not changed, rather, the composition of the groups had changed with a few of the children who had reported the most improvement at posttesting in the cognitive–behavioral group not being included at follow-up and a few of the youngsters from the traditional counseling group who had reported the least improvement not being located at follow-up.

In summary, numerous authors have proposed cognitive–behavioral models of treatment for childhood depression. While there are relatively few treatment outcome studies, we have briefly reviewed the existing case and group comparison studies available. With the exception of the two case studies, the outcome studies involved depressed children selected from public schools and not clinical populations. The cognitive–behavioral techniques employed included training in social skills, cognitive restructuring, self-control, problem solving, and relaxation. In all of the studies reviewed, cognitive–behavioral strategies were successfully used with school-aged children or adolescents. In general, while further treatment outcome studies are needed, it appears that cognitive–behavioral techniques are effective in reducing depressive symptomatology in this clientele.

TREATMENT ASSESSMENT LINK

Our treatment model is based on a skills deficit and cognitive distortion model of depression in children and adolescents. Thus, the main goal of treatment is to increase skill level and promote realistic, adaptive thinking. Two important operations seem necessary in order to accomplish these goals. These operations inherently tie treatment and assessment together into an intimate relationship, each having an effect on the other as the intervention progresses. First, an initial diagnostic assessment identifies those skills and cognitive distortions in need of attention, promoting the development of general objectives for therapy. Second, ongoing monitoring of cognitive distortions and skills provides feedback to the therapist and child which assists in fine-tuning the intervention to meet the characteristics of the particular client and situation.

The initial assessment is linked to treatment in that it allows a diagnosis of depression to be made with the general goal being to decrease depressive symptoms and provide preventative strategies to decrease the likelihood of further episodes. In addition, an initial assessment of the depressed child's cognitive processing yields information that is used to develop a treatment plan for changing the child's processing errors, maladaptive schemata, and depressogenic cognitive products as described by Beck (1967) and Turk and Salovey (1985). Furthermore, an initial assessment of skills provides information related to any deficits in problem solving, assertiveness, self-control skills, and family interaction. For example, if the result of assessment indicates that the child displays a social skills deficit and unfounded negative cognitions about his or her peers, then cognitive restructuring and social skills training might be emphasized during treatment planning. On the other hand, if assessment indicates that the child experiences negative cognitions about others, but has acceptable social skills, then social skills training would become less central during treatment planning. The initial assessment can also provide the therapist and child with an initial standard against which future assessments can be compared to evaluate the overall effect of treatment.

It is recommended that the therapist incorporate a semistructured interview such as the Schedule of Affective Disorders and Schizophrenia for School-Age Children (Kiddie SADS; Puig–Antich & Ryan, 1986) into the initial assessment. The interview can provide the therapist with information about the child's perceptions of his or her thoughts, feelings, behaviors, and interactions with others. It also offers the opportunity to ask probe questions that may reveal the child's constructions of her or his self, the world, and future, as well as other therapeutically relevant information. After assessing for the presence and severity of depressive symptoms, the evaluation necessarily turns to the assessment of related and therapeutically relevant constructs such as hopelessness, self-esteem, automatic thoughts, schemata, social skills, self-control skills, and family interaction (for a review of the assessment of childhood depression, see Kendall, Cantwell, & Kazdin, 1989).

Assessment is also closely linked to treatment through ongoing evaluation of treatment effectiveness. This can be accomplished through monitoring the child's spontaneous disclosures, homework, and in-session activities. In our treatments we have asked the children to keep diaries in which they record their thoughts, behaviors, and mood. We have found diaries useful for rating performance as well as the number and quality of scheduled activities. This material provides feedback to the child and therapist about the fit of the child to the cognitive–behavior–affect model (see Kendall, Chapter 1, this volume). For example, diary entries related to automatic thoughts in target situations can identify those behaviors and affective states that follow negative cognitions. An evaluation of homework can also identify areas in need of more work such as modifying schemata or building new coping schematas. In this vein, an analysis of diaries can reveal themes in the child's thoughts which helps the child and therapist identify prevailing schema or the change in these schemata across sessions. The assessment of in-session exercises may also be used to gain useful information. For example, the child and therapist might rate the child's level of skill proficiency after role playing a task that pulls for an assertive response.

If the outcome of the ongoing assessment indicates the child is not improving, then the therapist re-evaluates the present treatment plan and considers using alternative procedures. Furthermore, the therapist would question the therapeutic validity and relevance of the current targets of cognitive restructuring, and try to identify alternative, possibly more core cognitive structures, to target for change. If the child continued to be nonresponsive to treatment, then a referral for an alternative treatment modality such as pharmacotherapy would be considered.

Treatment and assessment are also linked in other ways. The behavioral underpinnings of the treatment approach at first blush seems to pose an assessment problem as the client might simply learn to respond in a socially desirable way to the measures presented by the therapist. For example, in teaching positive self-statements, the client might simply parrot these self-statements while responding to an automatic thoughts questionnaire, which would invalidate this measure. The therapist should be alert for such responses. In order to avoid the pitfalls of this situation a couple of therapeutic strategies might be considered. First, the validity of the initial (and possible posttreatment) and ongoing assessments are dependent upon honest, accurate reporting of symptoms by the child. In order to increase the likelihood of a valid assessment, treatment must include the development of a level of rapport between therapist and client that is effective enough to establish a therapeutic alliance. The therapist should use basic rapport-building techniques such as reflection of feeling and thought content and collaboration in order to create a nonthreatening, supportive treatment atmosphere. Second, the direction of the treatment sessions of each client will dictate the nature of the ongoing assessments as each client will present unique situations and responses. These assessments will most likely be less standardized and more spontaneous and thus less susceptible to response sets or simple regurgitation of material learned during the course of therapy. Third, ongoing assessments will be less comparable across sessions in contrast to a standardized assessment battery. In this case, it is up to the therapist and client, through collaboration, to establish the meaningfulness of these evaluations. The in-session, ongoing assessments, however, do offer a chance for validation as the therapist rates performance or evaluates situations along with the client. Lastly, the therapist may consider using alternate forms of available standardized measures or administering a knowledge test to assist the client in distinguishing simple knowledge and application of new processing steps and skills from diagnostic inquiries into his or her level of depressive symptoms.

THE TREATMENT PROGRAM

Building on an understanding of the nature and causes of the child's depression, the therapist strives to establish a relationship with the child and his or her family. In addition, the therapist establishes the ground rules for treatment. The child is informed that he or she and the therapist will work as a "team" to help the child learn how to feel better. This collaborative approach to treatment is one of the characteristics of cognitive–behavioral interventions. The child is actively involved in the assessment and treatment and encouraged to understand the reasons for it. This involves the therapist working with the child to develop a common conceptualization of the child's problems and how to overcome and/or cope with them.

During the process of conceptualizing the problem, the therapist educates the client about the cognitive–behavioral conceptualization of depression, and the client, with the therapist's guidance, educates the therapist about how he or she fits this model. It is believed that this educational and collaborative process (see Kendall, Chapter 1, this volume) will lead to greater treatment adherence.

Affective Education

Recently, cognitive–behavioral therapists have paid greater attention to the role of maladaptive affect in psychological disorders, and methods are appearing for modifying this affect. The primary mode of intervention that seems to be gaining widespread use is affective education. Given that the quintessential symptom of depression is a mood disturbance, it makes sense that this procedure has potential utility for the treatment of depressed youths. Affective education is the first therapeutic procedure that we employ in the treatment of depressed children. In addition, it is a procedure that is employed with all youngsters, since it also helps the youngsters gain an understanding of the relationship between their thoughts, feelings, and behaviors. Thus, it helps the youngsters learn the cognitive–behavioral conceptualization of depression. Furthermore, it is used as a means of helping them develop a sense of trust in the therapist.

A series of games is used to teach the youngsters about their emotions. The youngsters learn the names for a wide variety of pleasant and unpleasant emotions; in addition, they learn that emotions are experienced along a continuum according to the intensity of their experience (e.g., happy to sad to so sad that it hurts). The youngsters learn how to recognize when they are experiencing various emotions as well as signs of what others look like when they are experiencing these emotions. The actual content of the activities are designed to address the child's specific needs. For example, some children may not recognize the spectrum of emotions that they experience nor the continuum of severity. This would then become the primary focus of the activities. In contrast, another child may not be able to recognize how others are feeling. Then, teaching the child how to recognize the behavioral cues that are associated with various emotions become the focus of the activities. A series of activities that are designed to remediate the aforementioned deficits is described below.

A series of five games that we refer to as Emotional Vocabulary, Emotional Vocabulary II, Emotion Charades, Emotion Statues, and Emotion Expression are used as the medium for teaching the children about their emotions. The activities begin by teaching the children the basics about emotions and then progressively build upon this knowledge. Progressively more complex skills are taught and finer distinctions between the emotions are made.

During Emotional Vocabulary, a set of cards is constructed so that each card has the name of an emotion on it. The number of cards created and the sophistication of the emotions on the cards should vary, depending on the age of the child. With younger and less mature clients, we use fewer cards with more basic emotions on them (e.g., scared, sad, happy). The game is played by placing the deck of cards in the middle of the table. The players take turns drawing cards from the deck. After picking a card, the player states the name of the emotion, and then describes how the emotion feels and what was happening the last time he or she felt that emotion. The game can be played a number of times until the child has learned how each of the emotions is experienced.

The therapist starts to teach the child the cognitive–behavioral perspective during Emotional Vocabulary II. More specifically, through this game the child begins to learn about the relationships among thought, behavior, and emotion. The deck of cards is once again used and the game is played in much the same way as the first one. However, this time, after picking a card, reading it aloud, and describing how it feels, the child also describes what a person who is feeling that way might be thinking and how the person might be behaving. The objective is to help the child see that his or her feelings do not arise from nowhere, but are associated with what the child is thinking.

During Emotional Charades, the links among thoughts, feelings and behaviors are strengthened, and the child learns how to identify the emotional state of others. Once again, the players take turns drawing cards from the deck, only this time they do not read the name of the emotion aloud; instead they read it to themselves and think about what a person who is feeling that emotion might look like. Then, the child acts out the emotion while the other players try to guess its name. Once an emotion is identified, the player states what the actor did that clued him or her into the name of the emotion, what was happening the last time he or she felt that way, and what he or she was thinking at that time.

Emotion statues is a game that has to be played with more than two persons. The players take turns being the statue, the sculptor, and the audience. The child who is the sculptor chooses a card from the deck and does not let the audience know what it is. Then, the sculptor works with the statues to shape his or her facial expression, posture, and so on, so that he or she looks like a person who is experiencing that emotion. Once the emotion is correctly identified, the player states the cues that he or she used to identify the emotion, and what a person experiencing that emotion might be thinking, how they might be behaving, and what might have been happening.

Emotion Expression is the final activity. This time after drawing a card from the deck without divulging the name of the emotion, the actor expresses the emotion through his or her voice—through sounds without words. The player who correctly identifies the emotion, states what he or she used to identify the emotion, describes the last time he or she felt that way, the thoughts he or she had, and what was happening.

Self-control, Behavioral, and Cognitive Procedures

After completion of the affective education training, the therapist typically begins to employ a number of self-control and behavior therapy procedures to help the therapist learn more about the child and to help the child acquire skills for controlling the depressive symptoms. The self-control procedures have been adapted from those developed by Rehm (e.g., Rehm et al., 1987) for the treatment of depressed adults. The behavioral procedures have been adapted from a variety of sources, most notably Beck, Rush, Shaw, and Emery (1979), and Lewinsohn (e.g., Lewinsohn & Graf, 1973).

Included among the self-control procedures are training in self-monitoring, self-evaluation, and self-reinforcement. The procedure that is taught first depends on the assessment. Typically, it has varied between self-monitoring and self-reinforcement. There is some debate about which of these two procedures should be taught first. When self-reinforcement is taught first, it is used as a means of creating a system of rewards for acquiring additional skills. This is important because depressed children lack motivation; they expect that nothing they do will help, and are anhedonic. Thus, there is a need to create some incentives to get the child to work toward change. On the other hand, it has been argued that a prerequisite skill for self-reinforcement is accurate self-monitoring. Thus, self-monitoring could be taught first. However, depressed children, unlike impulsive children, can self-monitor. What they are taught is to redirect the focus of their attention. They are not taught *how* to self-monitor, rather they are taught *what* to self-monitor. Thus, they are capable of completing the self-monitoring that is involved in self-reinforcement training without needing to be taught to self-monitor first.

A variety of additional behavioral procedures are used in the treatment of depressed children. Many of these procedures including education, modeling, feedback, role playing, and social reinforcement are used spontaneously and in most sessions. They are used to teach the children many of the self-control and behavioral skills. These procedures are so commonly used that the steps involved in implementing them will not be described here. However, a few important points will be made. First, the therapy environment is characterized by a rich schedule of reinforcement, which creates a positive atmosphere and enhances the self-esteem of the youngster. Secondly, role playing is used whenever possible to increase the involvement in treatment and helps the child to be more active. Most children find role playing to be fun. It seems to increase the probability that the child will engage in the desired behavior outside of the treatment setting.

All of the aforementioned procedures are used to help the child gain some control over his or her depressive symptoms and environment. Thus, they are used relatively early in the treatment process. Perhaps as a result of the improvement in the severity of depressive symptoms that accrues from using these procedures, the depressed child is able to gain some distance from his or her thinking and examine one's thoughts from a more objective perspective. This enhances the effectiveness of the cognitive restructuring procedures.

The goal of treatment is change at the level of core schemata. The cognitive procedures described later in this chapter are used to produce this change. A variety of cognitive procedures are used throughout treatment as opportunities arise, and a number of sessions should be devoted to teaching the youngster how to use the procedures independently. Included among the procedures used with depressed youths are cognitive restructuring, cognitive modeling, behavioral assignments, problem solving, and self-instructional training.

Prior to using the cognitive procedures, it is necessary to identify the targets for change. A variety of assessment procedures can be used, including the interview, projectives, and self-report measures. Due to space limitations, these procedures will not be described here. The interested reader is referred to Stark (in press) for a description of these assessment procedures.

A number of rules are followed when using the cognitive techniques. First, the therapist begins using the techniques in a tentative, probing fashion as the therapist tests to see if the child is ready to change his or her thinking. Secondly, in the beginning of treatment, the therapist is primarily responsible for identifying and restructuring the child's thinking. As treatment progresses, the child is taught to identify maladaptive thoughts and schemata, and to restructure them. Third, the therapist and child move from identifying and restructuring individual maladaptive thoughts to identifying themes in the child's thoughts that are reflective of depressogenic schemata or core schemata. Fourth, the most powerful way to produce cognitive change is through behavioral assignments.

In the following section, we will describe the implementation of the aforementioned self-control, behavioral, and cognitive procedures with depressed children.

Self-reinforcement

Self-reinforcement is the process of presenting rewards to oneself contingent upon successful performance of a desired behavior. It may be one of the most effective treatment procedures with a vareity of behavior disorders (O'Leary & Dubey, 1979), and it seems to have the same impact on behavior that externally administered rewards has; it increases the probability that the behavior will occur in the future. In its use as an incentive, self-reinforcement serves as a bridge between acquiring and utilizing new skills, and the natural reinforcement of symptom improvement. Its primary use is as a procedure that ensures that the child is rewarded after using one of the coping skills (behavioral and cognitive) that the therapist is trying to teach the child to use. Thus, the child is taught to self-reinforce whenever he or she tries to complete a therapeutic homework assignement, or uses one of the coping skills.

Depressed children have a very difficult time reinforcing themselves. Perhaps it is due to their generally low level of self-esteem ("I don't deserve it") or their tendency to evaluate themselves negatively ("I didn't do well enough"). Thus, it commonly is necessary to use other procedures concurrently, such as cognitive restructuring and self-evaluation training.

The first step in the process of self-reinforcement training is the identification of possible rewards for the child. This can be an especially difficult task to accomplish with anhedonic youngsters. Furthermore, some of the more severely depressed youths have a very difficult time identifying any possible rewards; in this case, the therapist tries to identify things that were rewarding in the past. During this assessment, which can be completed through a self-report questionnaire (Stark, in press) or through an interview, the therapists tries to identify activities, favorite snacks and beverages, people, objects, and thoughts that are rewarding for the child. While identifying these rewards, it is important for the therapist to gauge whether the identified rewards are readily available in the child's environment and whether they can be self-administered. Since the emphasis is on self-administration, it is necessary to identify rewards that are readily available and are under the child's control. As rewards are identified, they are compiled into a menu-like list.

Since children commonly do not have independent access to, or control over the delivery and choice of many rewards, it is often necessary to involve the parents in the identification and administration process. The parents also are interviewed to identify rewards for the child, and any additional rewards are added to the child's menu. Gaining parental support is a prerequisite to the success of the procedure. A commitment should be made by the parents to try to provide their child with access to rewards. Often the parents are quite restrictive, even resistant, in their use of rewards to manage their child's behavior.

After identifying possible rewards and getting parental support, the training process begins by educating the child. Reinforcement and punishment are defined for the child, and concrete examples (e.g., teaching a pet to do tricks) are used to help the youngster gain an understanding of the impact of rewards. The importance of immediacy, contingent administration, and continuous schedules of reinforcement are discussed and illustrated through examples from the child's everyday life. In addition, the emotional impact of rewards should be discussed with the child. The point to be made is that rewarding oneself feels good while punishment feels bad.

The relationship between emotion and self-consequation is an important link for the child to understand. It is especially important for the youngster to recognize that postive self-statements, especially self-evaluative statements, can be rewards and lead to positive affect while negative self-statements can be self-punitive and lead to unwanted aversive affect. For example, thinking "Wow you did great!" feels good while thinking "You jerk, how could you be so stupid?" leads to negative affect. Many depressed youths display a propensity for self-punishment and a deficit in the use of self-reinforcement. The problem with self-punishment is alleviated through self-evaluation and cognitive restructuring procedures described below. However, the children are taught to increase the frequency of self-reinforcement.

The next characteristic of reinforcement to be taught is that rewards vary along a continuum of potency, which is gauged by how much pleasure is derived from each one. This idea is then applied to the youngster's menu of possible self-rewards. The child and therapist work together to rank order the rewards based upon their potency, and hypothetical values between 0 and 100 are assigned to each reward. Next, the child is taught to self-administer highly valued rewards for difficult or demanding tasks, medium rewards for moderately demanding tasks, and less valuable rewards for simple tasks.

Once the child understands all of the aforementioned characteristics of reinforcement, the therapist works for a model pulling all of these ideas together for reinforcement. The therapist describes how he or she has reinforced him or herself in the recent past. Then, the therapist asks the child to describe how he or she would use self-reinforcement for various hypothetical situations. For example, "How would you reward yourself for completing all of your homework for 1 week?" Next, the child may be instructed to choose a behavior that will occur during the session and to demonstrate his or her use of self-reinforcement following the behavior. Finally, the child is given homework to record use of self-reinforcement.

As the sessions progress, the therapist instructs the child to self-reinforce for use of a coping skill or completion of some other therapeutic assignment. The therapist inquires on a regular basis about the child's use of self-reinforcement. Any problems are identified and a collaborative problem-solving approach is taken to developing a solution. Then the child is instructed to try the procedure again.

Self-monitoring

Self-monitoring is the purposeful and conscious act of observing oneself and the situations one enters. The individual may be taught to observe his or her overt behavior, thoughts, feelings, or physiological reactions and make a judgment about the occurrence or nonoccurrence. In addition, the youngster may be instructed to monitor some other information, such as what is happening when he or she has a target thought (e.g., when thinking "I hate myself.") Similarly, this child may be instructed to monitor other situational information such as who was present and what they did. Typically, the youngster is also asked to record the information in some manner.

Self-monitoring is used both as an assessment and treatment procedure. This distinction may be somewhat artificial since self-observation can, in and of itself, lead to change. Nonetheless, when self-monitoring is used as an assessment procedure, it is used as a means of gathering therapeutically relevant information. As a treatment procedure, self-monitoring is used as a way to redirect the child's attention.

Self-monitoring as an assessment tool serves a variety of purposes throughout treatment. Since the procedure can be used to collect virtually any information, it is an integral part of the assessment and treatment process. It also gives the therapist access to the child's perceptions of self, the world, and the future. Often the target of assessment (e.g., the child's thoughts) may only be accessible during a certain situation. Thus, traditional procedures could not capture it. While self-monitoring has the advantage of being able to capture the youngster's constructions of daily life, it is important to recognize that the information reported is a reflection of these perceptions, which are not free of the child's distortions in constructing reality.

During the early sessions, self-monitoring serves as an adjunctive assessment tool to the more traditional forms of assessment. It is used as a way to understand what is happening in the child's life. It is used to identify the stressors in the child's life as well as for identifying maladaptive thoughts. As treatment progresses, self-monitoring is also used as a method for assessing the effectiveness of treatment. The child is instructed to monitor use of the coping skills as well as any impediments to their successful use. Thus, it is used as a guide to treatment as it helps to identify targets for change as well as effective procedures. In addition, as the child monitors the use of various procedures, and the child sees the change that results from use of the skills, a sense of self-efficacy is built.

Teaching a child to self-monitor is relatively easy. Typically the procedure begins by collaboratively defining the phenomena to be monitored and the value of self-monitoring that phenomena. This includes developing examples and nonexamples of the target. When first teaching the child to self-monitor, it is wise to begin with a behavior that is likely to occur during the session. Thus, the therapist can check for accuracy, model if necessary, and reward the child for successful and accurate self-monitoring.

After identifying a target for self-monitoring and defining it, the child and therapist devise a method for recording its occurrence or nonoccurrence. The parameters of both self-monitoring and self-recording need to be stated in concrete terms that are clearly understood by the child. The child needs to not only know what is going to be self-monitored and how it is going to be recorded (e.g., narrative or slash mark), he or she also needs to be taught when and how often to do both of these tasks. The importance of immediacy in self-recording for accuracy is emphasized.

Next, the child is given practice at self-monitoring during the sessions. It is useful to do this anytime the child is being taught to self-monitor a new target. When the child seems to be self-monitoring accurately during the session, he or she is then instructed to self-monitor *in vivo* as a homework assignment. However, prior to such an assignment, the child and therapist collaborate to identify potential impediments to the homework. After a block has been identified, the child and therapist use problem solving (see forthcoming discussion of cognitive procedures) to develop a plan for overcoming these impediments. The child is encouraged to use this same problem-solving procedures during the homework. Finally, the child and therapist review the assignment to be sure that the child understands it. At the beginning of each subsequent session, the child and therapist review the child's efforts and develop plans to overcome any difficulties.

The content of the self-monitoring varies according to therapeutic goals. One of the more common targets of self-monitoring is engagement in pleasant events, which helps identify activities, thoughts, and events that are associated with elevated mood (see Activity Scheduling). This also serves a number of therapeutic functions noted below. Other common targets are thoughts, behaviors, situations, and behaviors of others.

As a treatment procedure, self-monitoring also serves a number of functions. It is used as a procedure for increasing activity level and promoting cognitive restructuring. It serves as a method for directing the child's attention to more positive things, thus breaking the cycle of negative attention. Self-monitoring of engagement in pleasant activities often leads to an increase in activity level, which leads to an improvement in mood, and consequently more activity. It helps the child see that there are some positive things going on in his or her life. When self-monitoring is used as a means of producing cognitive restructuring, the child is instructed to self-monitor specific events that directly counter misbeliefs or provide the child with other positive information. For example, the child might be asked to self-monitor evidence of positive qualities.

Self-evaluation

Negative self-evaluation is one of the most common symptoms of depression. Depressed children evaluate their performances, possessions, and personal qualities more negatively, as research has indicated (Kendall et al., 1990). Self-evaluation training may be used at any time during treatment. It is useful to begin this training relatively early in treatment so that the youngster will recognize improvement as a result of positively evaluating his or her use of the therapeutic skills. The first object of self-evaluation training is to teach the child to evaluate him or herself less harshly. The second objective is to teach skills that will lead to self-improvement in deficient areas.

Self-evaluation training is a form of cognitive restructuring in which children learn how to evaluate themselves more optimistically and rationally. It also helps them recognize their positive attributes, outcomes, and possessions. The first step is to identify the existence and nature of the disturbance. This can be accomplished through an informal assessment or through the My Standards Questionnaire–Revised (Stark, 1990). If the child sets unrealistically stringent standards for his or her performance, then cognitive restructuring procedures (see below) are used to help the child set and accept more reasonable standards. When the child sets realistic standards, but evaluates him or herself negatively, cognitive restructuring and self-monitoring are used. The cognitive restructuring procedures of "What's the evidence?" and cognitive modeling may be used. Self-monitoring would be used as a means of solidifying the new self-evaluations as the child is instructed to self-monitor the evidence that supports it. Over the course of treatment, the therapist and child review the evidence that supports the new self-evaluation.

In some instances, where the child could benefit from change, the goal of self-evaluation training is to help the child translate personal standards into realistic goals, and then, to develop and carry out a plan for attaining the goals. Typically, this training occurs late in treatment after the child has acquired the other self-control procedures and has gained some distance from the negative thinking; this enables the child to make and recognize the changes. Following the translation process, the child prioritizes the areas where he or she is working toward self-improvement. Initially, a plan is formulated for producing improvement in an area where success is probable. Problem solving is used to help develop the plan. The long-term goal is broken down into subgoals and problem solving is used to develop a plan that will lead to subgoal and eventually goal attainment. Prior to enacting the plan, the child and therapist try to identify possible impediments to carrying out the plan. Once again, problem solving is used to develop contingency plans for overcoming the impediments. Once the plan, including the contingency plans, has been developed, the child is instructed to self-monitor his or her progress toward change. Alterations in the plan are made along the way.

Activity Scheduling

Activity scheduling involves the scheduling of enjoyable and goal-directed activities into the child's day. This helps the youngster combat the withdrawal, passivity, and sedentary life-style associated with an episode of depression. In addition, the activities provide the child with a distraction from his or her preoccupation with negative thinking. Finally, it may lead to some cognitive restructuring as the child rediscovers that he or she can complete some important tasks (e.g., school projects).

One class of activities that is a primary target for scheduling is mood-enhancing activities. Enactment of these activities is a powerful coping skill that can be used to moderate depressive affect. The training procedure begins by helping the child recognize the relationship between engagement in pleasant activities and improvement in mood. Most children can readily understand that they feel good when they do fun things. The next step involves the identification of mood-enhancing activities and those activities that have to be completed for the child to successfully adapt to his or her environment. For example, the youngster may have to complete various school assignments or chores around the house.

Once the activities have been identified, the child and therapist collaboratively plan the youngster's daily activities for a day on an hour-by-hour basis. The activities are written down so that the child has something to refer to. Next, the child and therapist try to identify any impediments to carrying out the plan. As impediments are identified, problem solving is used to develop plans for overcoming the impediments. It also is important for the child to recognize that unforeseen things will occur that will make it difficult for the plan to be carried out as initially conceived. An honest effort toward carrying out the plan is all that can be expected. Finally, the child is instructed to self-monitor completion of the activities.

In order to increase the likelihood that the child will complete the plan, a number of additional steps may be taken. The child may be asked to sign a contract agreeing to try to carry out the plan. Another procedure that can be used is cognitive rehearsal; the child is led through an imagery exercise in which he or she completes the activity plan. While imaging the plan, the child is asked to try to experience the feelings that are associated with enactment of the activities.

Social Skills Training

Social skills training is an important part of the treatment program since many depressed children report social withdrawal and unsatisfying interpersonal relationships. Social skills training also provides an opportunity to engage the depressed child in an "action"-oriented activity, provides "concrete," observable situations for self-monitoring, evaluation, and reinforcement, and provides material for the analysis of the child's perception of his or her social world. Overall, the re-engagement of the depressed child in the social milieu is important as socialization is a major source of opportunities for reinforcement and learning.

The content and teaching techniques that we originally used in our programmed treatment package with depressed children are similar to traditional social skills training approaches. We have taught basic assertiveness, including microskills such as eye contact and facial expression, and advanced assertiveness skills, such as giving compliments, asking others to stop annoying behavior, conversation, and conflict resolution. Training procedures we have used include education, modeling, role playing, coaching, feedback, homework, and relaxation skills combined with coping imagery.

The emphasis of social skills training, however, should be tailored to meet the characteristics of the child. The clinician should take into account the child's level of micro- and global social skills, social cognition, and self-control skills. For example, a depressed child's social withdrawal may be due to feeling bored and a low level of motivation to engage with others as opposed to displaying deficient skills. On the other hand, a child's social withdrawal may be due to a history of employing social behaviors that result in rejection or a low rate of reinforcement from others. In this case, the child may benefit from learning more adaptive behaviors. Another scenario might include a child who believes he or she has no right to obtain needs. In this case, cognitive restructuring may be used to help the youngster accept his or her social rights. In a case such as this, the child may have the necessary skills, but believes he or she has no right to use them.

Assertiveness training can be accomplished through using several techniques. We have started the process by using a series of cartoons to demonstrate the differences among passive, assertive and aggressive people. During the presentation of the cartoons, the behavioral characteristics of the cartoon characters are noted along with the reaction of others and results of their behaviors. The therapist and the child then take turns role playing the different behaviors. The session then turns to having the child provide an example of a fun activity they would like to do with someone and then role-play using assertive behaviors in asking the person to engage in the activity. The therapist and the child then take turns in each role. During this time, the therapist provides the child with instruction and demonstration of behaviors, feedback, and coping statements, combined with relaxation and imagery techniques, to decrease any apprehension. Self-instructional training procedures can also be used to teach the child to use verbal mediators to accomplish the role-playing. Similar procedures can be used for teaching the other assertive behaviors, such as giving compliments and asking others to stop annoying behaviors.

These behavioral activities naturally lead to self-control and cognitive restructuring. Self-control training can be practiced within and outside of sessions. After role playing in the session, the child can be asked to describe what took place. Then the child can rate him or herself on a simple Likert scale and indicate what kind of reward he or she might deserve. This data can be compared with the therapist's descriptions, ratings, and rewards and any discrepancies between the child and therapist would be discussed. Cognitive restructuring can also take place during social skills training. With role playing the therapist can elicit automatic thoughts from the child through asking about his or her impressions, the use of guided imagery, or asking the child for reactions to the scene with an emphasis on thoughts. The data obtained from these procedures can be used to identify the self-statements, schemata, and possible core schemata that are active during social interactions. The data obtained through self-monitoring can then be used to provide evidence for the appropriateness of the schemata. These self-control, cognitive restructuring, and social activities can be practiced and become more fully developed through the use of homework assignments negotiated by the therapists and the client.

Relaxation Combined with Positive Imagery

Relaxation training is used to accomplish a number of objectives in the treatment of depressed youths. Relaxation is taught as a coping skill that the child can use as needed. Children are taught to use it to cope with the anxiety that commonly co-occurs with depression. The state of relaxation that is achieved through completion of a deep muscle relaxation exercise is a positive feeling and peaceful state that provides depressed youths with a respite. It also is used in combination with imagery to provide mental rehearsal of homework assignments. The child completes an exercise and, when a state of relaxation is achieved, is led through an imagery activity in which he or she successfully carries out the assignment.

Ollendick and Cerney (1981) have suggested how to modify relaxation procedures for children. The child is taught relaxation during the sessions and is encouraged to practice using relaxation at home on a regular basis until mastering it. Once the child has achieved the ability to obtain a state of relaxation, the therapist combines it with positive coping imagery related to the child's assignment. For example, the child may be working on being more assertive with one's parents. In this case, the therapist would lead the child through a relaxation exercise, followed by an imagery activity in which the child successfully asserts him or herself, as rehearsed with the therapist. The child is asked to then focus on the good feeling that accompanies successful completion of the imaginal activity.

Behavioral Assignments

Perhaps the most potent way to change a child's thinking is to alter strategically behaviors that serve as a confirmatory or disconfirmatory base of evidence for the child's thoughts. The alteration in behavior provides the child with immediate, direct, and concrete evidence. This process of giving homework assignments requires a good deal of creativity as the therapist has to be able to identify first a maladaptive thought or schema, bring it to the child's recognition, work with the child to establish the necessary evidence to support or refute the thought or schema, and then devise a behavioral assignment that directly tests the validity. Finally, the therapist works with the child to process the results of the assignment.

A very simple example is coaching a child who believes that he or she can no longer do schoolwork. In this case, success was assured since the therapist was with the child and could help as roadblocks appeared. It is useful to follow the rule of trying to develop assignments in the early part of treatment that can be accomplished during the session. Since many assignments just do not lend themselves to being completed in the office, assignments have to be given for enactment at home or in the classroom. In these cases, it is necessary to achieve compliance and to be sure that the child understands the assignment prior to sending the youngster off to do it. For example, one socially withdrawn youngster who spent her time in her room, believed that if she came out, her parents would just get angry with her, was given the assignment to come out of her room for 30 minutes one evening to see what would happen. The therapist had already spent time talking with the youngster's parents as well as the whole family so that he knew that the odds were against the child's fear coming true. In reality, it was a "no lose" situation, since the assignment was posed as an experiment, and if the parents had become angry, it would have provided further helpful information for treatment. This was a somewhat more difficult task for the youngster to complete since there was a strong push to avoid her fear. Thus, the therapist relied on collaboration and the strength of the relationship to produce compliance. In some instances, role playing ahead of time, walking through the assignment using imagery, or writing a contract may be used to aid in the assignment.

Cognitive Restructuring

Cognitive restructuring procedures are designed to modify the client's thinking and the premises, assumptions, and attitudes underlying the client's thoughts (Meichenbaum, 1977). A number of the cognitive restructuring procedures developed by Beck and colleagues (1979) can be used with depressed children. Children are taught to be "Thought Detectives" who identify maladaptive thoughts and (1) evaluate the evidence for the thought,

(2) consider alternative interpretations, or (3) think about what really would happen if the undesirable event occurred. These procedures are used throughout treatment and a number of sessions are devoted to teaching the child specifically to use the procedures independently.

With depressed children, the timing of the use of the cognitive restructuring procedures is important. Cognitive restructuring procedures require attention to one's thoughts. This increased attention can lead to an exacerbation of the child's depressive symptoms if the child has not acquired skills for regulating depressive symptoms. In addition, early in treatment the child holds these thoughts to be true, and he or she cannot achieve the necessary distance from the thoughts to evaluate them objectively. Thus, it is important to determine when the child has acquired some coping skills and can use them to moderate the impact of depressive symptoms. In addition, the client must trust the therapist and see the cognitive–behavioral model of depression as credible prior to the use of the cognitive restructuring procedures.

What's the Evidence?

Asking what's the evidence? is a very useful technique that the children readily understand. It involves asking the child to work with the therapist to find evidence that supports or refutes the youngster's automatic thoughts and the schemata underlying them. The first step involves defining the premise that encompasses the child's maladaptive thoughts. Once this has been defined, the therapist works with the child to establish the evidence that he or she believes is necessary to support or disconfirm the underlying premise. After agreeing on the necessary and sufficient evidence, the therapist and child evaluate the existing evidence and establish a procedure for collecting additional evidence. Subsequently, the therapist and child review the evidence and process the outcome. Finally, the child is given a homework assignment to collect evidence that supports the revised, more adaptive premise.

Alternative Interpretations

Depressed children have a narrow and negativistic way of processing information. Alternative interpretations is a procedure that can be used to broaden the focus of the child's thinking. In this case, the way that the child is interpreting events is altered as the therapist and child work together to identify alternative interpretatioins for what has happened. They collaboratively generate a number of plausible, more adaptive, and *realistic* interpretations for what has happened. Next, they evaluate the evidence for the alternative interpretations, and then the most plausible one is chosen.

What If?

Depressed children are often in disappointing situations, in which they exaggerate the significance of the situation and/or predict unrealistically dire outcomes. "What if?" can be used to help the child obtain a more realistic understanding of the meaning of the situation and to see that the probable outcome is not going to be so bad.

When using "what if?" the therapist acknowledges the child's distressing situation. However, the therapist also listens for instances of thinking that reflect an exaggerated interpretatioin of the significance of the event. These exaggerations are then countered and the child is helped to see that he or she can survive.

As the child learns to use the three previously noted cognitive restructuring techniques, they usually begin to ask the same questions of themselves spontaneously. The therapist encourages this and gives the child homework assignments to identify maladaptive thoughts independently and then to use the cognitive restructuring procedures. With older children, the skill is extended to identifying and restructuring the themes that underly the child's thoughts.

Cognitive Modeling and Self-instructions

Cognitive modeling is a subtle and continually used treatment procedure. It involves the therapist verbalizing his or her thoughts, or verbalizing more adaptive thoughts, that the child might have the next time he or she faces the same situation. In the first instance, the therapist simply thinks aloud whenever confronting a problem or some other situation that enables him or her to model relevant thoughts for the child. For example, the therapist might tell a story about a problem situation that he or she faced over the week, and then state aloud the thoughts that represent the problem-solving steps. Likewise, the therapist might use an interpersonal situation that is occurring within the session as an opportunity to think aloud as a way to demonstrate how one copes with anger that is expressed by someone else. The therapist might also observe the child's reactions to the interpersonal exchange and model thoughts that the child might have used to guide more appropriate behavior.

Self-instruction

Self-instructional training (Meichenbaum, 1977) is used to help a child internalize a set of self-statements that guide the child's thinking and/or behavior. In our work with depressed children, we have used Kendall's (e.g., 1977) adaptation of Meichenbaum's procedure. The content of the thoughts that the children are taught can be anything. For example, we have used it in the traditional way to help the children acquire the problem solving sequence of self-instructions noted above. A child may be taught a set of coping statements such as "Remember, I'm okay, they're just fooling around" in response to other children's cutting horseplay. Prior to starting assignments, a child was taught to say "Just take a deep breath, relax, concentrate, all I have to do is the best I can. It doesn't have to be perfect."

Problem Solving

Training in problem solving is designed to counteract a number of characteristics of depressed youths. It counteracts the rigidity in the depressed child's thinking as it forces them to consider alternative solutions to situations. It also helps the children overcome a sense of hopelessness as they see that there may be some options that they were unaware of. In some cases, the child becomes empowered as he or she experiences some success and sense of mastery over the environment. For those children who actually are in an unpleasant situation, it helps them develop plans for overcoming, avoiding, or lessening the impact of an undesirable situation.

The problem-solving procedure that we have used is a modification of the one used by Kendall (1981). The children are taught a series of seven problem-solving steps through education, modeling, coaching, rehearsal, and feedback. The first step is problem definition. Identifying and placing a label on the problem provides the child with some sense of control, since he or she finally knows what the problem is. Since depressed children often face a multitude of problems, this first step may be repeated a number of times, and then the problems are prioritized and worked on in order of priority.

Generation of alternative solutions is the second step. The child is taught to brainstorm as many possible solutions as possible without evaluating them. It is especially important to teach the child not to evaluate the alternatives, since depressed youths have a tendency to believe that nothing will work. Thus, the youngster will short-circuit the process. Early in treatment, the therapist collaborates with the child.

The third step is focusing of attention and mustering of energy to enable completion of the task. Included at this stage may be coping statements to relax and keep trying. Step four involves projection of the outcomes for each possible solution. The therapist and child evaluate the outcome of each possible solution relative to the desired goals. The fifth step involves reviewing the possible solutions, choosing the one that is most consistent with the child's goals, and beginning to enact the plan. The sixth step is evaluating the outcome of the enactment of the chosen solution. If the outcome is goal-consistent, the child self-reinforces as enactment of step seven. If the outcome is inacceptable, the youngster reconsiders the possible solutions.

FAMILY INTERVENTION PROCEDURES

When treating depressed children, it is important to involve the family in the treatment process. The type of involvement is dependent on the characteristics of the family. If the family is healthy, the parents will be taught to cooperate and facilitate the therapy for their child. If the family system is unhealthy, then the family system will be one of the targets of intervention.

In the case of the healthy family, the parents are brought into the treatment process as a way to promote the acquisition of skills and the generalization of treatment effects. As noted earlier, the parents may be asked to help the child self-reinforce. They may be educated about how they can gently remind their child to complete his or her homework assignments. In addition, they may be instructed how they can help their child use the skills that the therapist is teaching the child during therapy sessions. The parents also can be taught to identify depressogenic thoughts for their child and then to help him or her to restructure those thoughts.

Since depressed youths are inactive, the child's parents may be asked to encourage their child to do things either with the family or with his or her friends. When the child is working toward self-improvement, the parents may be asked to help the child carry out his or her plan.

When the family system is disturbed, the therapist tries to idenfiy and help the family alter interaction patterns, communications, and family rules that support the child's maladaptive behavior and thinking. Intervention begins with education about the cognitive–behavioral perspective and how it applies to the family. The therapist observes the family during sessions for examples of maladaptive interactions and points them out to the relevant family members. In addition, the therapist explores the cognitions of the individuals who participated in the interaction. Then the family may be asked to monitor the occurrence of specific interactions between sessions.

The subtle and not so subtle messages that family members send to each other are a major focus of intervention (see Stark, 1990). These messages that are communicated both verbally and nonverbally, are pointed out to the family. Since this may be a difficult task, the therapist listens and watches for examples and then points them out. The therapist may have to model the thinking that goes into identifying the messages. In addition, the impact of the messages on the recipient are illustrated.

The therapist may use a variety of procedures to change the behaviors and communications that lead to and maintain the depressogenic thinking of the child. The therapist may give the family directives, educate, coach, model, provide feedback, or ask the family to rehearse new behaviors. Problem-solving and negotiation skills may be taught to the family members. These procedures may be applied to family conflict, and to increasing the pleasant activity level of the family. Activity scheduling also may be used to accomplish this.

Parent training may be used to help the parents learn how to manage their child's behavior through more positive means. In addition, they may be taught how to involve their child in the decision-making process.

INTEGRATION OF THE PROCEDURES AND APPLICATION TO SPECIFIC SYMPTOMS

We have described a vareity of procedures that can be used to treat depressed children. While we have described how each procedure is trained in isolation, the children typically combine the skills to cope with the symptoms they are experiencing. The therapist and child approach symptoms as problems to be solved and use problem solving as a strategy for identifying possible procedures for coping with the symptom. Several examples of this process are described below.

Anger has proven to be one of the more difficult symptoms of depression to help the child client overcome. Our research (Hill & Stark, 1989) indicates that there is a significant difference in the cognitive products of depressed, depressed and angry, and nondistressed children. The angry youngsters reported significantly more angry cognitions. These cognitions and the schemata that give rise to them are one of the primary focuses of treatment. Another focus is the physical arousal that accompanies the anger, as well as the interaction patterns that are associated with the onset of anger.

In order to achieve each of the previously noted objectives, a variety of procedures are used. Self-monitoring is used to identify anger-engendering cognitions and situations. In addition, it is used to monitor the implementation of the other procedures, as well as symptom change. Cognitive restructuring is used to change the child's constructions of others' behavior as a personal affront. Self-instructional training and cognitive modeling are used to provide the child with a set of self-statements that he or she can employ to control anger during different stages of the provocative situations. In addition, the child is taught to use relaxation to cope with the physical reaction to anger. Imagery of successfully using the procedures to cope with the anger-provoking situations is used to provide the child with a chance to rehearse the use of the skills. Self-reinforcement is used by the child as a means of consequating his or her use of the other coping skills. Activity scheduling is used to help the child avoid anger-provoking situations and as a way to distract the child during times when the youngster is already angry. Role playing, problem solving, and social skills training would be used to help the youngster behave differently in anger-producing situations so that he or she can terminate the aversive interaction. In addition, pro-social skills would be taught to help the youngster get along better with his or her peers.

Sleep disturbance is a problem that many of the more severely depressed youths face. It appears as though the prevalence of sleep disorders increases with age (Lahmeyer, Poznanski, & Bellur, 1983). A number of pharmacological interventions can be used (Turner, 1986), although tricyclic antidepressants may be most beneficial with depressed youths, given the potentially lethal affect of barbiturates (Williams & Karacan, 1985). The psychological treatment of sleep disturbance may involve a number of behavioral and cognitive procedures. The child and therapist may brainstorm things that can be done to improve sleep behavior. Activity scheduling may be used to help the youngster maintain a regular activity level and to establish an exercise routine. Right before going to bed, the youngster can schedule an enjoyable and relaxing activity. Since hunger may interfere with sleep, the youngster may schedule a snack in the evening. Progressive relaxation may be used to reduce autonomic arousal and muscular activity, thus permitting sleep.

Many youngsters who suffer from sleep disorders report that anxious concerns, hypervigilance, and ruminative thoughts are closely associated with their inability to fall asleep. Cognitive restructuring procedures can be used to help the youngsters deal with their cognitive concerns. In addition, positive imagery may be used to help overcome anxious thoughts (see also Kendall et al., Chapter 5, this volume.)

The child's parents also might become involved in the treatment process. They may be asked to help establish a quiet and relaxed atmosphere prior to and during bedtime. Positive reinforcement for use of the other skills may also be used to encourage the use of the child's coping skills. They also may become involved in ensuring that the child sleeps only during certain hours, not during normal waking hours.

SUMMARY

Our comprehensive treatment program is based on a synthesis of the cognitive distortion (e.g., Beck et al., 1979) and skills deficit (e.g., Rehm, 1977) models of depression, while considering the impact of the family system on the depressed youngster. Our model suggests that the child's depressive symptoms are the result of an interaction among a lack of coping, self-control, and interpersonal skills, and a dysfunctional cognitive style.

Furthermore, it is believed that the dyfunctional cognitions and behaviors are often produced and maintained by maladaptive patterns within the family system. Based on this underlying model, the present program combines individual therapy with the child (i.e., behavioral, self-control, and cognitive procedures) with family therapy procedures. Recent trends guiding the development of the present program include: (1) the intervention being tailored to the individual youth by assessing the specific characteristics of the child's depression, and (2) therapeutic techniques and presentation modes being designed to be age-appropriate and engaging.

As is characteristic of most cognitive–behavioral interventions, the present program is based on a collaborative relationship. Initially, the therapist develops an understanding of the dynamics of the case and establishes a relationship with both the child and his or her family. Affective education is usually the first therapeutic procedure employed. This procedure helps children recognize the full spectrum of their emotions, the varying degrees in which they experience their emotions, and the relationship between their thoughts, feelings, and behaviors. Subsequently, the therapist introduces various self-control (i.e., self-reinforcement, self-monitoring, and self-evaluation) and behavioral procedures (e.g., activity scheduling, social skills training, relaxation training, etc.). These procedures are intended to: (1) help the youths develop skills for controlling their depressive symptoms and environment, (2) gain distance from their depressive thinking, therefore allowing a more objective perspective, and (3) produce some cognitive change and enhance the effectiveness of the cognitive restructuring procedures.

Cognitive procedures also comprise a major aspect of the program. These procedures have the goal of producing change at the level of core schemata and several techniques have proven to be effective with this population. First, cognitive restructuring procedures can be introduced to modify the client's cognitions and the underlying assumptions and attitudes. Second, behavioral assignments, or the strategical modification of behaviors supporting or contradicting the evidence for the client's cognitions, can also be a very potent procedure for producing cognitive change. Third, cognitive modeling allows the therapist to model adaptive thoughts that the child can incorporate and utilize in subsequent situations. Fourth, problem-solving training can be beneficial in a number of ways as it encourages the client to recognize and consider alternative solutions to situations. Lastly, self-instructional training can be used to help the child internalize self-statements that can guide his or her thinking and/or behavior.

Additionally, the importance of involving the family in the treatment of depressed children is recognized. However, the degree and form of family involvement is variable. For example, in the case of a relatively healthy family, it may only be necessary to engage the parents as "co-therapists" to promote skill acquisition and generalization. However, in the case of a more pathological family system, the therapist may find it necessary to identify and modify dyfunctional interaction and communication patterns that are supporting the client's maladaptive cognitions and behavior.

REFERENCES

Abramson, L. Y., Seligman, M. E. P., & Teasdale, J. (1978). Learned helplessness in humans: Critique and reformulation. *Journal of Abnormal Psychology, 87,* 49–74.

American Psychiatric Association. (1987). *Diagnostic and statistical manual of mental disorders* (3rd ed., rev.). Washington, DC: Author.

Bandura, A. (1977). Self-efficacy: Toward a unifying theory of behavior change. *Psychological Review, 84,* 191–215.

Beck, A. T. (1967). *Depression: Clinical, experimental and theoretical aspects.* New York: Hoeber.

Beck, A. T., Rush, A. J., Shaw, B. F., & Emery, G. (1979). *Cognitive therapy of depression.* New York: Guilford Press.

Braswell, L., Kendall, P. C., Braith, J., Carey, M. P., & Uye, C. S. (1985). "Involvement" in cognitive–behavioral therapy with children: Process and its relationship to outcome. *Cognitive Therapy and Research, 9,* 611–630.

Butler, L., Miezitis, S., Friedman, R., & Cole, E. (1980). The effect of two school-based intervention programs on depressive symptoms in preadolescents. *American Educational Research Journal, 17,* 111–119.

Cantwell, D. P., & Carlson, G. A. (1979). Problems and prospects in the study of childhood depression. *Journal of Nervous and Mental Disease, 167,* 522–529.

Christ, A. E., Adler, A. G., Isacoff, M., & Gershansky, I. S. (1981). Depression: Symptoms versus diagnosis in 10,412 hospitalized children and adolescents (1957–1977). *American Journal of Psychotherapy, 35,* 400–412.

Clarizio, H. F. (1985). Cognitive–behavioral treatment of childhood depression. *Psychology in the Schools, 22,* 308–322.

Frame, C. L., Johnstone, B., & Giblin, M. S. (1988). Dysthymia. In M. Hersen & C. G. Last (Eds.), *Child behavior therapy casebook.* New York: Plenum Press.

Frame, C., Matson, J. L., Sonis, W. A., Fialkov, M. J., & Kazdin, A. E. (1982). Behavioral treatment of depression in a prepubertal child. *Journal of Behavior Therapy and Experimental Psychiatry, 3,* 239–243.

Guidano, V. F., & Liotti, G. (1983). *Cognitive processes and emotional disorders: A structural approach to psychotherapy.* New York: Guilford Press.

Hill, S. J., & Stark, K. D. (1989). *The cognitions of angry and depressed children: A test of the cognitive specificity hypothesis.* Manuscript in preparation.

Hollon, S. D., & Kriss, M. R. (1984). Cognitive factors in clinical research and practice. *Clinical Psychology, Review, 4,* 35–76.

Ingram, R. E., & Kendall, P. C. (1986). Cognitive clinical psychology: Implications of an information processing perspective. In R. E. Ingram (Ed.), *Information processing approaches to clinical psychology* (pp. 3–21). New York: Academic Press.

Kashani, J. M., & Hakami, N. (1982). Depression in children and adolescents with malignancy. *Canadian Journal of Psychiatry, 27,* 474–477.

Kashani, J. H., & Ray, J. S. (1983). Depressive related symptoms among preschool-age children. *Child Psychiatry and Human Development, 13,* 233–238.

Kashani, J. H., & Simonds, J. F. (1979). The incidence of depression in children. *American Journal of Psychiatry, 136,* 1203–1205.

Kashani, J. H., Venzke, R., & Millar, E. A. (1981). Depression in children admitted to hospital for orthopaedic procedures. *British Journal of Psychiatry, 138,* 21–25.

Kaslow, N. J., & Rehm, L. P. (1983). Childhood depression. In R. J. Morris & T. R. Kratochwill (Eds.), *The practice of child therapy.* New York: Pergamon Press.

Kaslow, N. J., Stark, K. D., Printz, B., & Livingston, R. B. (1990). *The Cognitive Triad Inventory for Children: Development and relationship to depression and anxiety disorders in children.* Manuscript submitted for publication.

Kendall, P. C. (1977). On the efficacious use of verbal self-instructional procedures with children. *Cognitive Therapy and Research, 1,* 331–341.

Kendall, P. C. (1981). Cognitive–behavioral interventions with children. In B. B. Lahey & A. E. Kazdin (Eds.), *Advances in clinical child psychology* (Vol. 4). New York: Plenum Press.

Kendall, P. C. (1985). Toward a cognitive–behavioral model of child psychopathology and a critique of related interventions. *Journal of Abnormal Child Psychology, 13,* 357–372.

Kendall, P. C., Cantwell, D. P., & Kazdin, A. E. (1989). Depression in children and adolescents: Assessment issues and recommendations. *Cognitive Therapy and Research, 13,* 109–146.

Kendall, P. C., Stark, K. D., & Adam, T. (1990). Cognitive deficit or cognitive distortion in childhood depression? *Journal of Abnormal Child Psychology, 18,* 267–283.

Kovacs, M. (1981). Rating scales to assess depression in school aged children. *Acta Paedopsychiatrica, 46,* 305–315.

Kovacs, M., & Beck, A. T. (1977). An empirical-clinical approach toward a definition of childhood depression. In J. G. Schulterbrandt & A. Raskin (Eds.), *Depression in childhood: Diagnosis, treatment and conceptual models* (pp. 1–25). New York: Raven Press.

Lahmeyer, H. W., Poznanski, E. O., & Bellur, S. N. (1983). Sleep in depressed adolescents. *American Journal of Psychiatry, 140,* 1150–1153.

Lewinsohn, P. M. (1975). The behavioral study and treatment of depression. In M. Hersen, R. M. Eisler, & P. M. Miller (Eds.), *Progress in behavior modification (Vol. 1),* (pp. 16–64). New York: Academic Press.

Lewinsohn, P. M., & Graf, M. (1973). Pleasant activities and depression. *Journal of Consulting and Clinical Psychology, 41,* 261–268.

Lewinsohn, P. M., Sullivan, J. M., & Grosscup, S. J. (1980). Changing reinforcing events: An approach to the treatment of depression. *Psychotherapy: Theory, Research and Practice, 17,* 322–334.

Ling, W., Oftedal, G., & Weinberg, W. (1970). Depressive illness in childhood presenting as severe headaches. *American Journal of Diseases of Children, 120,* 122–124.

Linn, J. L. & Stark, K. D. (1989). *Social functioning of depressed and anxious children.* Manuscript in preparation.

Lobovits, D. A., & Handal, P. J. (1985). Childhood depression: Prevalence using DSM-III criteria and validity of parent and child depression scales. *Journal of Pediatric Psychology, 10,* 45–54.

Meichenbaum, D. (1977). *Cognitive–behavior modification: An integrative approach.* New York: Plenum Press.

Meichenbaum, D., Bream, L. A., & Cohen, J. S. (1985). A cognitive–behavioral perspective of child psychopathology: Implications for assessment and training. In B. McMahon, & R. Peters (Eds.), *Childhood disorders: Behavoiral-developmental approaches* (pp. 65–115). New York: Brunner-Mazel.

Nissen, G. (1986). Treatment for depression in children and adolescents. *Psychopathology, 19,* 156–161.

O'Leary, S. G., & Dubey, D. R. (1979). Applications of self-control procedures by children: A review. *Journal of Applied Behavior Analysis, 12,* 449–465.

Ollendick, T. H., & Cerney, J. A. (1981). *Clinical behavior therapy with children.* New York: Plenum Press.

Petti, T. A., Bornstein, M., Delamater, A., & Conners, C. K. (1980). Evaluation and multimodality treatment of a depressed prepubertal girl. *Journal of the American Academy of Child Psychiatry, 19,* 690–702.

Pfeffer, C. R., Zuckerman, S., Plutchik, R., & Mizruchi, M. S. (1984). Suicidal behavior in normal school children: A comparison with child psychiatric inpatients. *Journal of the American Academy of Child Psychiatry, 23,* 416–423.

Puig–Antich, J., & Ryan, N. (1986). *Schedule for Affective Disorders and Schizophrenia for School-Age Children (6–18 years)—Kiddie SADS.* Unpublished manuscript. Western Psychiatric Institute and Clinic, Pittsburgh.

Rehm, L. P. (1977). A self-control model of depression. *Behavior Therapy, 8,* 787–804.

Rehm, L. P., Kaslow, N. J., & Rabin, A. S. (1987). Cognitive and behavioral targets in a self-control therapy program for depression. *Journal of Consulting and Clinical Psychology, 55,* 60–67.

Reynolds, W. M., & Coats, K. I. (1986). A comparison of cognitive–behavioral therapy and relaxation training for the treatment of depression in adolescents. *Journal of Consulting and Clinical Psychology, 54,* 653–660.

Stark, K. D. (1990). *Childhood depression: School-based intervention.* New York: Guilford Press.

Stark, K. D., Livingston, R. B., Laurent, J. L., & Cardenas, B. (1989). *Childhood depression: Relationship to academic achievement and scholastic performance.* Manuscript submitted for publication.

Stark, K. D., Reynolds, W. M., & Kaslow, N. J. (1987). A comparison of the relative efficacy of self-control therapy and a behavioral problem-solving therapy for depression in children. *Journal of Abnormal Child Psychology, 15,* 91–113.

Stark, K. D., Rouse, L., Printz, B. & Laurent, J. L. (1990). *Prevalence, symptom picture, and demographic characteristics of depression during childhood.* Manuscript in preparation.

Turk, D. C., & Salovey, P. (1985). Cognitive structures, cognitive processes, and cognitive–behavior modification: I. Client issues. *Cognitive Theory and Research, 9*, 1–17.

Turner, R. M. (1986). Behavioral self-control procedures for disorders of initiating and maintaining sleep (DIMS). *Clinical Psychology Review, 6*, 27–38.

Weinberg, W. A., Rutman, J., Sullivan, L., Penich, E. C., Dietz, S. G. (1973). 51pression in children referred to an educational diagnostic center: Diagnosis and treatment. *Journal of Pediatrics, 83*, 1065–1072.

Williams, R. L., & Karacan, I. (1985). Recent developments in the diagnosis and treatment of sleep disorders. *Hospital and Community Psychiatry, 36*, 951–957.

PART IV

SPECIAL POPULATIONS

CHAPTER 7

Cognitive–Behavioral Interventions for Children with Chronic Illnesses

GARY A. WALCO
Schneider Children's Hospital of Long Island Jewish Medical Center and the Albert Einstein College of Medicine

JAMES W. VARNI
University of Southern California and Orthopaedic Hospital Los Angeles, California

As a group, children with chronic illnesses and physical handicaps have been found to be at risk for psychological and social adjustment problems (Wallander, Varni, Babani, Banis, & Wilcox, 1988). The typical methodology of the previous decade involved comparisons on some psychosocial parameter between children and adolescents with chronic illnesses and what were deemed to be appropriate control groups (e.g., healthy peers, outpatient clinic samples). Such comparisons usually indicated higher levels of psychological maladjustment and functional limitation among the chronically ill groups of (cf. Battle, 1972; Matteson, 1972; Pless & Roghmann, 1971). However, there is considerable variability in individual children's adaptation to their chronic physical condition, with some children functioning quite well psychologically, while other children exhibit psychological and social maladjustment (Wallander et al., 1988).

Russo (1986) argued that the psychological effects of chronic illness must be viewed from the perspective of "normalcy" and "chronicity." Thus, an individual with a chronic illness should be viewed as a normal person who must learn to develop behaviors that foster adaptation to a long-standing and difficult situation. As a result, he and others (e.g., Varni, 1987) have advocated the exploration of specific stressors which systematically affect children and their families as well as mediating variables that lead to positive adjustment (relative resilience to the stress) or maladjustment (relative vulnerability to the stress).

A complete review of factors affecting adjustment to chronic illness in children is well beyond the scope of this chapter. Instead, we will examine two major areas in depth to exemplify the theoretical and empirical base upon which cognitive–behavioral models are used for interventions in this group: the assessment and management of recurrent and chronic pain in children with chronic illnesses and social support and cognitive problem solving in chronically ill and handicapped children.

It should be noted that, unlike other chapters in this text, in which a specific form of psychopathology and its accompanying cluster of problem behaviors is the focus of treatment, this chapter examines two major stressors that may affect children with chronic illnesses, and not necessarily maladaptive behavior. Thus, the goal of cognitive–behavioral interventions in this population is to help children identify specific stressors associated with their chronic illness and to implement a set of behaviors that may moderate those stressors and to prevent the development of maladaptive behavior patterns. As will be described, interventions for chronic pain focus on teaching children a new set of skills aimed at modifying their subjective experience and enhancing function and life-style. Social–cognitive problem-solving skills are utilized to facilitate chronically ill children's re-entry into the school setting as a means of minimizing the stresses associated with this transition.

RECURRENT AND CHRONIC PAIN IN CHILDREN WITH CHRONIC ILLNESSES

Pain in children represents a complex cognitive–developmental phenomenon, involving a number of biobehavioral components that synergistically interact to produce differential levels of pain perception and verbal and nonverbal manifestations (Varni, 1983). In marked contrast to the rather extensive literature on adult chronic pain assessment and management, the systematic investigation of pediatric chronic and recurrent pain from a cognitive–biobehavioral perspective represents a relatively new area of inquiry (Varni, Jay, Masek, & Thompson, 1986; Varni, Katz, & Dash, 1982).

Given children's various cognitive–developmental stages, conceptualizations of pain and discomfort must be taken into consideration (Thompson & Varni, 1986). Thus, an accurate understanding of pain perception in children cannot be gleaned from simply applying downward the knowledge of pain perception in adults; rather, research and clinical practice in pediatric pain assessment and management must develop a separate, if not parallel database from the adult field which is sensitive to the unique characteristics of children. In the past several years a growing number of investigators have begun generating a substantial database from which the clinical potential of cognitive–biobehavioral techniques in managing pediatric chronic and recurrent pain has become clear (McGrath, 1987a; Varni, Walco, & Wilcox, 1990).

Varni (1983) has identified four primary categories of pediatric pain: (1) pain associated with a disease state (e.g., hemophilia, arthritis, sickle cell disease); (2) pain associated with an observable physical injury or trauma (e.g., burns, lacerations, fractures); (3) pain not associated with a well-defined or specific disease state or identifiable physical injury (e.g., migraine and tension headaches, recurrent abdominal pain); and (4) pain associated with medical and dental procedures (e.g., lumbar punctures, bone marrow aspirations, surgery, injections, venipuncture, tooth extractions). We will focus exclusively on chronic and recurrent pain associated with the pediatric chronic diseases of hemophilia, juvenile rheumatoid arthritis, and sickle cell disease. In discussing interventions for such pain syndromes, we will emphasize cognitive–biobehavioral techniques that have received empirical attention over the last several years (Varni, Walco, & Wilcox, 1990), and minimize descriptions of pharmacological treatments (see Lovell & Walco, 1989; and Dampier, Walco, & Zimo, 1990, for details of pharmacological interventions in juvenile rheumatoid arthritis and sickle cell disease, respectively).

In the cognitive–biobehavioral assessment and management of pediatric pain, it is essential to distinguish among acute, chronic, and recurrent pain (McGrath, 1987b; Varni, 1983; Varni, Walco, & Wilcox, 1990). Acute pain serves an adaptive biological warning signal, directing attention to an injured part or disease condition, functioning within an avoidance paradigm to encourage escape or avoidance of harmful stimuli and indicating the need for rest, immobilization, or treatment of the injured area. While neurophysiological processes may distinguish acute from chronic pain (Bonica, 1977), it is often the intensity of acute pain and its associated anxiety reaction that most parsimoniously differentiate acute from chronic pain expression (Varni, 1983).

Pediatric chronic pain, on the other hand, is typically characterized by the absence of an anxious component, with a constellation of reactive features such as compensatory posturing, lack of developmentally appropriate behaviors, depressed mood, and inactivity or restriction in the normal activities of daily living. These chronic pain behaviors may eventually be maintained independently of the original nociceptive impulses and tissue damage, being reinforced by socioenvironmental influences (Crue, 1985; P. A. McGrath, 1986; Varni, Bessman, Russo, & Cataldo, 1980). Acute pain, in contrast, typically occurs in temporal proximity with a pathogenic agent or noxious stimulus.

In pediatric chronic diseases, the chronic musculoskeletal pain (pain arising from the system of muscles and bone) associated with juvenile rheumatoid arthritis and hemophilic arthropathy (joint disease) correspond to the chronic pain model described above. In the recurrent, episodical pain of acute bleeding episodes in hemophilia and of vaso-occlusive crises (blockages in the small blood vessels) in sickle cell disease, the clear distinction between acute and chronic pain is not evident. The following sections will describe further the differential assessment and management strategies inherent in chronic and recurrent pain comprehensive care.

PEDIATRIC CHRONIC AND RECURRENT PAIN ASSESSMENT

Central to the assessment of pediatric chronic or recurrent pain is children's conceputalizations of their illness. We know of no studies specifically addressing the relationship between cognitive development, concepts of illness, and pain experience in children with any of the chronic illnesses under discussion. In fact, in cases where these issues were ignored, pain assessment data may be quite misleading. For example, two early studies focused on pain intensity in subjects with arthritis using simple visual analogue scales or four-point descriptive scales (Laaksonen & Laine, 1961; Scott, Ansell, & Huskisson, 1977). Results showed relatively low levels of pain in children, and it was concluded that children with juvenile rheumatoid arthritis (JRA) experience less pain than adults with rheumatoid arthritis. However, these authors did not adequately attend to developmental factors (a number of children were unable to respond appropriately to visual analogue scales, for example), and thus the reliability of these data is questionable.

Beales, Keen, and Holt (1983) took cognitive–developmental issues into account to a greater degree and found that children with JRA were able to describe discomfort in their joints. These authors subsequently divided their sample based on chronological age (6 to 11 yrs, 12 to 17 yrs) and performed midpoint splits on visual analogue scores for pain intensity, yielding a finding that older children tended to report higher levels of pain. It is not clear why the data were analyzed in this manner; however, it was concluded that with increasing age comes greater understanding of key concepts related to illness and disease, leading to increased significance of pain and discomfort and thus reports of greater pain intensity. Although this notion was not tested directly, it is likely that children's concepts of illness and pain affect coping strategies.

Thompson and Varni (1986) discussed the relationship between pain assessment and the stages of children's concepts of illness as described by Bibace and Walsh (1980). Briefly, as the manner in which children comprehend the concept of illness develops, it is likely that similar changes occur in conceptualizations of pain and its relationship to disease. Because such developmental issues precluded the use of adult pain measures in young children, a comprehensive pain questionnaire for chronic and recurrent pain in children was constructed.

The Varni–Thompson Pediatric Pain Questionnaire

For adult chronic pain patients, the most widely used and respected assessment instrument has been the McGill Pain Questionnaire (MPQ; Melzack, 1975). Subsequent to its publication, other investigators have further shown the reliability, validity, and clinical utility of the MPQ across a diversity of adult pain syndromes (cf. Reading, 1983). Modeled after the MPQ but designed to be sensitive to the cognitive–developmental conceptualizations of children, the Varni–Thompson Pediatric Pain Questionnaire (PPQ; Varni & Thompson, 1985) is a comprehensive multidimensional assessment instrument specifically designed for the study of acute, chronic, and recurrent pain in children, with child, adolescent, and parent forms.

The PPQ-Child Form addresses the intensity of pain through visual analogue scales and colors (representing relative levels of pain) on a body outline (through which specific sites are also identified). Verbal descriptors are also used to help delineate the sensory, evaluative, and affective qualities of pain perception. The PPQ-Adolescent Form additionally addresses potential socioenvironmental influences on pain perception. The PPQ-Parent Form consists of similar components to the PPQ-Child and PPQ-Adolescent forms to allow for cross-validation. A comprehensive family history section addresses the child's pain history and the family's pain history with questions pertaining to symptomatology, past and present treatments for pain, and socioenvironmental situations that may influence pain perception.

Thus far, the published reliability and validity of components of the PPQ are available for chronic musculoskeletal pain in juvenile rheumatoid arthritis (Thompson, Varni, & Hanson, 1987; Varni, Thompson, & Hanson, 1987; Varni, Wilcox, Hanson, & Brik, 1988). Data are emerging on the psychometric properties and clinical utility of the PPQ for children and adolescents with sickle cell disease (Walco, Dampier, & Djordjevic, 1987; Walco & Dampier, in press) and there are ongoing studies by Varni and other investigators at different sites on its applicability to a range of pediatric acute, chronic, and recurrent pain syndromes. In the following sections, details of certain aspects of the PPQ will be described.

Visual Analogue Scale

Present pain and worst pain intensity for the previous week are assessed in the PPQ by a visual analogue scale (VAS). Each VAS is a 10-cm line with no numbers, marks, or descriptive vocabulary words along its length. The child VAS is anchored with developmentally appropriate pain descriptors (e.g., "not hurting," "hurting a whole lot") and happy and sad faces. The adolescent and parent VAS are anchored by the phrases "no pain" and "severe pain" in addition to the descriptors "hurting" and "discomfort." The instructions for the VAS ask the child or parent to place a mark through the VAS line which represents the intensity of pain along the continuum.

The assessment of pediatric pain must fulfill the requirements for any measurement instrument, including reliability, validity, minimum inherent bias, and versatility necessary for an objective pain measure in a vareity of experimental and clinical pain studies. (Beyer & Knapp, 1986; P. A. McGrath, 1986; P. J. McGrath, 1986; Varni, Thompson, & Hanson, 1987). As reviewed by P. A. McGrath (1986), the VAS, although deceptively simple, has demonstrated these features. Historically, the VAS has been used extensively with adult pain subjects because of its sensitivity and reproducibility (Huskisson, 1983). As a continuous measurement scale, the VAS avoids the spurious clustering of pain reports that occur with stepwise or categorical pain-scaling methods (Levine, Gordon, Smith, & Fields, 1981).

In both children and adults, the VAS has demonstrated excellent construct validity in postoperative medication studies, showing the expected reduction in pain subsequent to analgesia intake (Aradine, Beyer, & Tompkins, 1988; Levine et al., 1981; O'Hara, McGrath, D'Astous, & Vair, 1987; Taenzer, 1983), and in chronic musculoskeletal pain, demonstrating the expected increase in perceived pain intensity with greater rheumatic disease activity (Thompson et al., 1987; Varni et al., 1987). Finally, it was found that in children and adolescents with sickle cell disease, VAS scores were related to physician estimates of disease severity, increased dramatically with the onset of severe vaso-occlusive episodes, and were sensitive to analgesic effects in patients hospitalized for uncomplicated vaso-occlusive crises (Walco & Dampier, in press).

From the psychophysical measurement perspective, the VAS is considered a direct scaling method and a form of cross-modality matching in which the length of a line is adjusted to match the intensity of pain (Huskisson, 1983; P. A. McGrath, 1986). P. A. McGrath has investigated the measurement properties of the VAS in a series of psychophysical studies with both children and adults (McGrath & de Veber, 1986; McGrath, de Veber, & Hearn, 1985; Price, McGrath, Rafii, & Buckingham, 1983) and demonstrated that the VAS has ratio rather than interval scale properties. Interval scales reflect equal distances in the variables being quantitatively ordered where the zero point is arbitrarily determined and does not represent the complete absence of the variable being measured. Ratio scales are the same as interval scales except that there is a true zero point. Clearly, for the measurement of pain, the latter is highly desirable.

In a study of chronic musculoskeletal pain in juvenile rheumatoid arthritis by Varni et al. (1987) using the PPQ, the child's report of pain on the child VAS correlated highly with both parental ($r=.72$, $p<.001$) and physician ($r=.65$, $p<.001$) ratings of the child's pain independently recorded on the adult VAS. Parent and physician ratings also correlated highly ($r=.85$, $p<.001$). In a similar study of vaso-occlusive pain in sickle cell disease (Walco & Dampier, in press), these respective correlation coefficients were $r=.21$ ($p>.05$), $r=.67$ ($p<.001$), and $r=.62$ ($p<.001$). Finally, focusing on pediatric postoperative pain, P. J. McGrath and colleagues (1985) found a correlation of $r=.91$ between observer and nurse ratings on the VAS. The nurse and observer ratings on the VAS also correlated highly with a pain behavior checklist, $r=.81$ and $r=.86$, respectively.

The high correlations between the observer and nurse VAS ratings and the pain behavior checklist suggest that the paths of decision making regarding pediatric pain perception by observers may be the same for the observer VAS and the checklist; that is, manifestation of overt verbal and nonverbal pain behaviors by the child is a necessary (but not sufficient) condition for the ratings of pediatric pain perception by objective observers. However, it is clear that a child can experience pain without necessarily exhibiting overt pain behaviors, consequently resulting in considerable measurement error for adult observation techniques.

This point was discussed by Walco and Dampier (in press) with respect to the correlations reported above for pediatric sickle cell pain. In assessing the intensity of children's pain, physicians and parents appear to rely heavily on observations of overt pain behaviors (and thus their estimates intercorrelate). Additionally, physicians possess knowledge of disease characteristics and severity, which also likely contributes to their estimates of pain. Neither, however, have access to the private subjective experience of the child, and thus correlations with the child's pain estimates may be rather low (as was the case for child and parent VAS scores for present pain). This effect may be especially so when pain is episodic (such as with sickle cell disease) in contrast to chronic and ongoing pain (as is often the case for the musculoskeletal pain of juvenile rheumatoid arthritis).

It is important to note that Walco and Dampier (in press) did not question the validity of the children's self-reported pain intensity on the VAS. Indeed, the VAS has been shown to be a reliable and valid measure of pain perception for children as young as 5 (McGrath & de Veber, 1986; P. A. McGrath et al., 1985; Varni et al., 1987). To question children's self-report of pain because of a lack of significant correlations with observer estimates is an erroneous concept. Pain is a subjective phenomenon and it cannot be expected that another individual can accurately and without measurement error assess another person's private experience of it. In a study of adult pain, for example, the correlatioin between patients' VAS scores and nurses' VAS scores was only $r=.38$ (Teske, Dart, & Cleeland, 1983). This finding did not lead these investigators to question subsequently the validity of these adults to assess their pain! We strongly feel that children should be accorded the same degree of consideration; that is, they are the best judges of their pain experience. Throughout the rest of this chapter we hope to make this point further by providing both research and clinical findings which support the validity of children's self-reports of their pain experience.

Pain Threshold and Chronic Clinical Pain

As one traces the history of the literature on the assessment of clinical pain in children, initial emphasis was placed on the accurate assessment of the subjective pain experience. More recently, greater attention has been paid to the various factors which may affect that experience. Details of a comprehensive predictive model of disease-related and socioenvironmental factors related to joint pain in juvenile rheumatoid arthritis will be presented below. One recent study, however, has focused on a little-studied aspect of pediatric pain—pain threshold.

In the adult literature, experimental pain measures include threshold (the lowest level of stimulation labeled as "pain"), tolerance (the maximal level of noxious stimulation which the subject can tolerate), and reactivity (an index of a specific response to painful stimuli). Pain threshold is generally thought to be a sensory event which is physiologically loaded, while pain tolerance and reactivity are the result of one's physiological sensitivity (pain threshold) in tandem with psychological variables (Merskey, 1973; Sternbach, 1975; Wolff, 1983). While the latter two factors are probably most closely related to clinical pain experience, for ethical reasons, research involving experimentally induced pain at tolerance or reactance levels in pediatric populations is limited.

Walco and his colleagues (Walco, Dampier, Hartstein, Djordjevic, & Miller, 1990) investigated the relationship between pain threshold levels and clinical pain experience in four groups of children between 5 and 16 years of age: (1) Children with juvenile rheumatoid arthritis (a chronic illness in which chronic and recurrent pain is a feature); (2) Children with sickle cell disease (a chronic illness in which recurrent episodes of acute pain is a common feature); (3) Asthma (a chronic illness in which pain is typically not a feature), and (4) Healthy controls. Pain threshold was measured through direct pressure to a joint and through circumferential pressure stimulation, while present clinical pain was assessed through visual analogue scales. Although no direct relationship was observed between these two measures, it was found that children with juvenile rheumatoid arthritis and sickle cell disease had significantly lower pain thresholds than did their healthy peers. Furthermore, pain threshold values were found to be internally consistent over repeated trials and across stimulus modes, and were not found to be significantly related to measures of psychological adaptation or perceived self-competence and did not predict behavioral indices such as school attendance. Thus, it was concluded that pain threshold is a factor worthy of further consideration and that it may not be principally physiologically determined. It is also possible that experience with recurrent pain sensitizes children to future pain stimulation. Clearly, chronic pain in children is not a unidimensional construct and thus requires the assessment of a number of intrapersonal and socioenvironmental factors, a conceptualization which will be described in more detail for each of the major chronic illnesses to be described below.

COGNITIVE–BIOBEHAVIORAL TREATMENT

The primary cognitive–biobehavioral treatment techniques utilized in the management of pediatric chronic and recurrent pain have been categorized by Varni (1983) into (1) *Pain perception regulation* modalities through such self-regulatory techniques as progressive muscle relaxation, meditative breathing, and guided imagery, and (2) *Pain behavior regulation*, which identifies and modifies socioenvironmental factors that influence pain expression and rehabilitation. The following sections will describe the utilization and clinical research findings of cognitive–biobehavioral assessment and management techniques for three pediatric chronic diseases: hemophilia, juvenile rheumatoid arthritis, and sickle cell disease.

Hemophilia

Whereas recurrent acute pain in the hemophiliac is associated with a specific bleeding episode, chronic musculoskeletal pain as a result of hemophilic arthropathy (similar to osteoarthritis and caused by repeated hemorrhages into the joint areas) represents a sustained condition over an extended period of time. Thus, pain perception in the hemophiliac truly represents a complex psychophysiological event, complicated by the existence of both recurrent bleeding pain and chronic arthritic pain, requiring differential treatment strategies. More specifically, acute pain of hemorrhage provides a functional signal, indicating the necessity of intravenous infusion of factor replacement, which temporarily replaces the missing clotting factor, converts the clotting status to normal, and allows a functional blood clot to form. Arthritic pain, on the other hand, represents a potentially debilitating chronic condition which may result in impaired life functioning and analgesic dependence (Varni & Gilbert, 1982). Consequently, the development of an effective alternative to analgesic dependency in the reduction of perceived chronic arthritic pain secondary to hemophilic arthropathy that does not interfere with the essential functional signal of acute recurrent bleeding pain has been the goal of the behavioral medicine approach to hemophilia pain management (Varni, 1981a).

Varni and his associates (Varni, 1981a, 1981b; Varni & Gilbert, 1982;

Varni, Gilbert, & Dietrich, 1981) have reported on a series of studies investigating chronic arthritic pain management in both child and adult hemophiliacs. Instruction in the cognitive–biobehavioral self-regulation of arthritic pain perception consists of three sequential phases. The child is first taught a 25-step progressive muscle relaxation sequence involving the alternative tensing and relaxing of major muscle groups (see Varni, 1983, for more details). Then meditative breathing exercises are taught, consisting of medium deep breaths inhaled through the nose and slowly exhaled through the mouth. While exhaling, the child is instructed to say the word "relax" silently to himself or herself and initially to describe aloud and subsequently visualize the word "relax" in warm colors, as if written in colored chalk on a blackboard. Finally, the child is instructed in the use of guided imagery techniques, consisting of pleasant, distracting scenes selected by the child. Initially, the child is instructed to imagine himself or herself actually in the scene, not simply to observe himself or herself there. The scene is evoked by a detailed multisensory description by the therapist and subsequently described aloud by the child. Once the scene is clearly visualized, the therapist instructs the child to experiment with other, different scenes to maintain interest and variety. The child is instructed to practice these techniques on a regular basis at home, and to return for sessions with the therapist to maintain technique and for encouragement and problem solving. Data have demonstrated the successful utilization of these techniques with both child and adult patients in controlling chronic musculoskeletal pain secondary to hemophilic arthropathy.

Juvenile Rheumatoid Arthritis

In children with chronic musculoskeletal pain, the prototype for inflammatory chronic arthropathy is juvenile rheumatoid arthritis (Varni & Jay, 1984). The disease typically manifests itself before 16 years of age, with peak onset in the age groups 1 to 3 and 8 to 12. In general, girls are affected twice as often as boys. Although the precise mechanisms of joint pain in juvenile rheumatoid arthritis are not fully understood, it is clear that the effects are substantial and, from a clinical standpoint, pain is seen as the major mediating factor in one's ability to cope with the disease (Lovell & Walco, 1989).

Varni and his colleagues (Thompson et al., 1987; Varni et al., 1987; Varni, Wilcox, Hanson, & Brik, 1988) have developed an empirical model using multiple regression analysis to predict statistically pain perception and functional status in children with juvenile rheumatoid arthritis. The criterion variable (dependent measure) for pain was the child VAS, and the predictor variables included child psychological adjustment, family psychosocial environment, and disease parameters. This empirical model was able to statistically predict 72% of the variance in child perception and report of worst pain for the previous week (Thompson et al., 1987). Taking the model one step further, Varni entered into the multiple regression analysis worst pain for the previous week in addition to the other predictor variables, this time to predict the criterion variable of functional status. The model accounted for 57% of the variance in activities of daily living (Varni, Wilcox, Hanson, & Brik, 1988). This multidimensional assessment battery (see Thompson et al., 1987, for a complete description of all the instruments used) provides a comprehensive basis for developing pediatric chronic and recurrent pain management interventions. By using such a developmentally appropriate instrument as the PPQ, intensity, location, and the qualitative aspects of the pain experience can be obtained from the child, as well as potentially modifiable psychological and socioenvironmental factors.

In an ongoing study of cognitive–biobehavioral interventions for pain associated with juvenile rheumatoid arthritis (Walco, Varni, Hartstein, & Ilowite, 1988), the PPQ is used for initial assessment and components are being employed to assess both immediate as well as long-term effects of the intervention. Children between 5 and 16 years are seen for a total of eight sessions in which they are taught progressive muscle relaxation, meditative breathing, and guided imagery in an attempt to moderate joint pain and increase adaptive functioning. In addition, parents are seen for two sessions in which pain behavior regulation is discussed.

Although the general paradigm is similar to that described above for patients with hemophilia, the specific contents of images and means of inducing relaxation vary to some degree, depending on the age and interests of the particular child. It is here that data gathered on the PPQ are so essential to the implementation of specific interventions. For example, in addition to self-regulatory techniques used to distract children from their pain, are images aimed at "undoing" the pain. If among the verbal descriptors, the child uses "hot" to describe the pain, then images involving cooling may be ideal. Similarly, if "squeezing" is chosen as a descriptor, the child may be asked to elaborate on a metaphor for this pain (e.g., "My knee feels like it is in a vise"), and then this metaphor may be applied to an image involving a reversal of the pain process (e.g., the vise opening).

Data from the body outlines, in which young children use specific colors to identify relative levels of pain intensity, may also be used to generate images. For example, a child may choose red to represent the most intense level of pain and use it to color in a specific joint. Once relaxed, the child is asked to picture that area of the body and to visualize it painted red. Images are then invoked in which the red area continually shrinks, with healthy, pain-free tissue replacing those that had previously been painful.

Preliminary data indicate that there is tremendous short-term benefit of these strategies, as virtually all subjects have been able to dramatically reduce their level of subjective pain. Audiotapes are provided for rehearsal at home and instructions to practice the techniques on a regular basis are given. Although descriptive data indicate that generalization from clinic sessions to strategies employed at home is possible, few subjects spontaneously use these skills outside of the clinic setting.

Within the PPQ, there are also questions focusing on behavioral sequelae of the child's pain, psychosocial factors which may mediate the pain, and outcomes related to the child's pain. These data are incorporated into discussions with parents on pain behavior regulation. Essentially, this is an operant paradigm aimed at increasing "well behaviors" while minimizing "pain behaviors." Using specific issues and examples previously provided by the child or parent appears to facilitate parents comprehending these issues and then modifying stimuli that may be eliciting or reinforcing maladaptive pain behaviors. Preliminary analyses of 6- and 12-month follow-up data indicate improved adaptive daily functioning (physical activities, etc.) and data continue to be gathered.

Sickle Cell Disease

The need for careful assessment of pain associated with sickle cell disease is very important as so little is known about its specific causes and course. Reversible microvascular occlusion at the arteriolar or capillary level affecting bone or bone marrow circulation causes the characteristic painful "crisis" (painful episode) which is the hallmark of sickle cell disease. Although a variety of biochemical (Karayalcin, Lanzkowsky, & Kazi, 1981; Lawrence & Fabry, 1986) or hemotological (Warth & Rucknagel, 1984) variables are altered during acute painful episodes, most are nonspecific and thus are not diagnostic for this event.

The frequency and severity of pain due to vaso-occlusive episodes varies greatly both across and within individuals. Recent data indicate that the average pediatric sickle cell patient experiences one to two severe episodes per year (Dampier et al., 1990). The variation is great, however; some patients may experience no pain in a year, while others experience pain more than once a week. Furthermore, within a given individual, there may be extended periods that are pain-free followed by a number of vaso-occlusive episodes over a relatively short period of time.

There are few reliable hemotological parameters by which the severity of a vaso-occlusive episode may be gauged. Thus, unlike the pain associated with acute bleeds in hemophilia or joint flare-ups in arthritis in which there are objective indices of medical factors related to pain, in sickle cell disease one is limited to subjective reports of the patient and behavioral observations as a means of evaluating the intensity of pain due to vaso-occlusion.

A study has been conducted utilizing the PPQ to assess sickle cell pain

(Walco & Dampier, in press). Thirty-five subjects between the ages of 5 and 15 years were evaluated in the outpatient clinic. Results indicated that the relative infrequency of vaso-occlusive episodes apparently limited the number of opportunities parents had to evaluate their child's pain, and thus retrospective accounts of pain intensity were poor. Significant relationships between physician estimates of disease severity, restrictions in activity, impact on daily functioning, and reported levels of present pain were consistenty shown. Furthermore, it was clear that pain adjectives, colors (for younger children), and body outlines could be used meaningfully to describe pain.

As a second aspect of the study, the present pain VAS and pain adjective checklist were used on a daily basis with patients admitted to the hospital for uncomplicated painful episodes. Findings indicate that the VAS was quite useful in this situation as patients were able to express different levels of discomfort throughout the course of their hospitalization and VAS ratings correlated with dosage of analgesic (an independent criterion as the house physician was not privy to VAS ratings). In addition, patients utilized the adjective checklist in a meaningful way throughout the hospitalization. It was noted that a large number of pain descriptors were selected at the beginning of the hospital stay, and steadily dropped as days passed. This trend was especially obvious for the affective and evaluative pain descriptors. Finally, body outlines proved to be worthwhile as patients labeled specific pain sites and to a large extent differentiated relative levels of pain intensity among the sites.

These assessment data are essential information in planning both pharmacological and psychological treatment strategies. Studies are currently under way in which optimal analgesic regimens are being matched to individual patients' reported pain experiences. In addition, attempts are being made to identify those patients who may benefit most from learning self-regulatory techniques, as well as those who may require behavioral programs aimed at enhancing daily functioning.

Treatment of Sickle Cell Pain

Vaso-occlusion and Recurrent Acute Pain. By and large, sickle cell crises may be conceptualized as recurrent acute painful episodes. Thus, the average patient appears to maintain a relatively normal life style, which is interrupted periodically by vaso-occlusive episodes. At these times, rest and immobilization are encouraged, and analgesic treatments range from aspirin or acetaminophen (Tylenol) for less severe episodes to parenterally administered (intramuscular or intravenous) narcotics given during hospitalizations (Cole, Sprinkle, Smith, & Buchanon, 1986; Scott, 1982). In the latter situations, a fixed dosing schedule adjusting for dosage of analgesic is much preferred to either p.r.n. or variable-schedule dosing. Fixed dosing facilitates the maintenance of therapeutic levels of the analgesic, thereby reducing the severe peaks and valleys experienced as the drug is metabolized. This facet, in tandem with the fact that the patient receives the analgesic without having to ask for it, reduces the tendency of constantly attending to one's level of discomfort. In addition, recent data indicate that in adolescents with sickle cell disease, patient controlled analgesia is an efficient means of delivering therapeutic doses of narcotic analgesics (Schechter, Berrien, & Katz, 1988).

Zeltzer, Dash, and Holland (1979) described two cases in which self-regulatory techniques were shown to be of benefit to adolescent and young adult patients experiencing painful episodes. Hypnosis was induced through the use of eye fixation and progressive muscle relaxation techniques. Images were used in which the patients placed themselves in a favorite place, engaged in an enjoyable activity, free of pain. Subsequent images focused on body warmth and vasodilation (a reversal of the vaso-occlusive state), and thermal biofeedback was employed to monitor changes in peripheral temperature. Instructions were given to use these techniques at the perceived onset of a sickle cell crisis. Reductions in the frequency and intensity of pain crises, the need for heavy analgesia, the frequency of emergency room visits, and the frequency and length of hospitalizations were shown.

Similar techniques and results were obtained in a larger study conducted with 15 adults between 22 and 35 years of age (Thomas, Koshy, Patterson, Dorn, & Thomas, 1984). Finally, in a study with 8 patients between 10 and 20 years, Cozzi, Tryon, and Sedlacek (1987) demonstrated the immediate short-term effectiveness of biofeedback training (e.g., frontalis muscle tension, digital temperature, frequency of headache as a crisis symptom, analgesic use, perceived pain intensity), but no significant effect on emergency room or inpatient utilization. Clearly much more systematic research is needed on the efficacy of both pharmacological and nonpharmacological interventions for recurrent pain in sickle cells disease.

Sickle Cell Disease and Chronic Pain. The key assumption underlying an acute pain model of intervention is that the pain is principally peripheral in its origin (Crue, 1985). Implicit here is the notion that once the condition resolves, the pain will dissipate, and the patient will return to a normal routine. Also implicit is that psychological factors play a relatively small part in the patient's pain experience and thus these issues are often ignored. For most pediatric and adolescent sickle cell disease patients, the acute pain model is valid (Dampier et al., 1990). There is a minority, however, for whom psychological and social issues play a major role in affecting their pain experience, and thus these issues should not be ignored. As discussed by Walco and Dampier (1987), these patients are typically adolescents whose life-style is marked by maladaptive coping patterns, poor psychological adjustment, inadequate family and social support, and school absenteeism and failure. Clearly, to ignore these factors and continue hospitalizing such patients for pain only contributes to the cycle of dependency on the medical system and withdrawal from prosocial activities.

Although it seems that these psychological factors parallel those found in adults with chronic pain syndromes, devising appropriate assessment and treatment strategies is difficult. For example, when such a patient presents in the emergency room complaining of severe pain, medical professionals are faced with the truly impossible task of determining the extent to which that pain is due to vaso-occlusion or to psychosocial factors. In actuality, such a strict dichotomization cannot be made and is rarely productive. However, for many professionals, this distinction exists and carries the incorrect implication that the former is "real" pain, while the latter is "all in the patient's head." As a result, antagonistic relationships develop between patients and caregivers, which often lead to manipulation and malingering. Furthermore, in that treatment of pain follows from assessment, medical professionals are faced with another conflict. As mentioned above, if pathophysiological factors are emphasized while psychological and social issues are ignored, the maladaptive pattern is reinforced. On the other hand, if one assumes that the pain is purely psychological, there is a strong chance of undertreating a severe vaso-occlusive episode.

As described by Walco and his colleagues (Varni et al., 1990; Walco & Dampier, 1987), in order to treat such patients adequately, biomedical, psychological, and social factors must be addressed. Behaviorally based interventions, usually in the form of behavioral contracts, include protocols specifying the frequency and duration of hospitalizations (for uncomplicated painful episodes), inpatient analgesic dosing schedules, frequency of emergency room visits, and availability of narcotics for outpatient use, have been used. Each of these variables are modified over time to successively approximate norms for matched peers and all medical personnel are provided with these protocols so that responses are standardized and few relevant decisions are made on a subjective basis.

These behavioral contracts have been successful in curbing inappropriate health care utilization and the frequency and intensity of manipulative or malingering behavior has decreased. Quality of life outside of the hospital, however, does not improve dramatically until other interventions are introduced to address specifically psychological maladjustment. Our clinical work here has included facilitating re-entry to school, building social skills, working to improve the family system, and in some cases psychopharmacological interventions. A controlled study is currently in progress in which these variables, and possible related interventions, are being examined systematically.

Summary

The comprehensive assessment and management of chronic and recurrent pain associated with chronic illness in children involves a range of psychosocial variables amenable to cognitive–behavioral interventions. A key assumption here is that for many children pain is a stressor that, if managed and mediated, has less of a negative impact on psychosocial adjustment to chronic illness. Although the literature on multidimensional pain assessment in children continues to expand, systematic studies of techniques aimed at modifying pain perception and pain behavior in children remain few. This is difficult research due to, among other reasons, the unpredictable course of chronic illness and its related pain, as well as the relatively small number of subjects available in a single setting. Nonetheless, we feel that such work is imperative and should be pursued.

SOCIAL SUPPORT AND SOCIAL COGNITIVE PROBLEM SOLVING IN CHRONICALLY ILL AND HANDICAPPED CHILDREN

One prominent factor receiving empirical attention as a potential mediator of the psychological adaptation to pediatric chronic disorders is perceived social support (Varni, 1987; Varni, Rubenfeld, Talbot, & Setoguchi, 1989a). From one perspective (Thoits, 1986), social support may be viewed as part of the coping process in living with a chronic strain, such as pediatric chronic illness and physical handicap (Varni, Babani, Wallander, Roe, & Frasier, 1989; Varni, Wilcox, & Hanson, 1988; Wallander & Varni, 1989).

In the adult stress literature, chronic strains (e.g., chronic illness) have been defined as persistent objective conditions that require continual readjustment, repeatedly interfering with the adequate performance of ordinary role-related activities (Pearlin, Lieberman, Menaghan, & Mullan, 1981). Thus the ongoing chronic strains of pediatric chronic disorders, such as the potential limitations in the activities of daily living and functional independence and the psychological and social effects of being physically different from one's peers, may interact synergistically to produce a negative impact on psychological and social adjustment. However, given our previous findings (Wallander et al., 1988), this negative impact does not appear to be consistent across chronically ill and handicapped children. Consequently, the chronic strain–psychological adjustment relationship may be mediated by a factor such as perceived social support (Varni, Rubenfeld et al., 1989a).

As viewed by Cohen and Wills (1985), social support has been found to function within two theoretical models. The buffering or interaction effects model proposes that social support buffers or protects individuals from the potentially pathogenic influence of stressful life events or chronic strains. The main or direct effects model posits that social support has a beneficial effect, irrespective of whether individuals are under stress. Cohen and Wills (1985) conclude that empirical evidence exists for both models.

In research with children with congenital or acquired limb deficiencies, Varni and associates (Varni, Rappaport, Talbot, & Setoguchi, 1989a; Varni, Rubenfeld et al., 1989a) found support for the direct effects model of perceived social support on psychological symptomatology, and no evidence for an interaction between social support and hassles or microstressors. Given the direct effects of perceived social support (cf. Alloway & Bebbington, 1987), it may be beneficial to determine empirically the various hypothesized antecedents and consequences of perceived social support domains as a first step toward cognitive–behavioral interventions to enhance perceived social support (Varni, Rappaport, Talbot, & Setoguchi, 1989b). Such an empirical approach requires a theoretical reconceptualization of perceived social support from simply a stable mediating variable to a potentially modifiable factor.

Recently, models of social support other than the stress-buffering model have been proposed (Barrera, 1986). Social support has been hypothesized to have a multiplicity of linkages to stress, psychological symptomatology, and various intervening variables, as well as hypothesized reciprocal relationships with these variables. In a review, Barrera (1986) has identified three major concepts of social support, designated as *perceived social support* (satisfaction with perceived availability and adequacy of social support), *social embeddedness* (social support network size), and *enacted support* (frequency of helping behaviors from others). Measures of these social support constructs generally show only modest correlations with each other.

Perceived social support has emerged as a prominent concept that delineates social support as the *cognitive appraisal* of an individual's valued connections to others (Barrera, 1986). This cognitive–appraisal model of social support is compatible with the stress and coping cognitive model developed by Lazarus and his colleagues (Lazarus & Folkman, 1984). Consistent with this model, it is one's cognitive appraisal of the availability and adequacy of social support that is hypothesized to have the greatest impact on psychological symptomatology, rather than social network size or the number of helping behaviors from others (Barrera, 1986).

Further, Heller, Swindel, and Dusenburg (1986) suggest that the cognitive appraisal of social support satisfaction may develop from routine socializing and companionship more than from a history of stress-related helping transactions, with the first experiences of perceived support for children usually occurring within the context of the family, that is, parental social support, and in some situations, older sibling social support (Bruhn & Phillips, 1987). Thus, the term *perceived social support* refers to the cognitive appraisal by individuals that they are cared for and valued, that significant others are available to them if needed, and that they are satisfied with their interpersonal relationships (Heller et al., 1986). This suggests that it is not social connections is per se that are protective against psychological maladjustment, but rather how the individual perceives and interprets his or her social network that determines the protectivve function of social support.

In the literature review by Barrera (1986), perceived social support was the most frequently assessed social support concept, typically demonstrating negative relationships to psychological distress and life stress/chronic strain measures across both cross-sectional and prospective longitudinal investigations. Although perceived social support has been consistently linked both concurrently and prospectively to psychological symptomatology, little empirical evidence exists regarding the possible *determinants* of the perception that one is receiving adequate social support (Cutrona, 1986). Both intrapersonal and interpersonal factors may determine the amount and quality of social support which children receive, and various domains of social support may relate more effectively to various dimensions of psychological adaptation to stressful life events and chronic strains (Varni, Babani et al., 1989; Varni, Wilcox, & Hanson, 1988; Wallander & Varni, 1989; Wolchik, Sandler, & Braver, 1987).

Studying the possible antecedents and consequences of perceived social support may not only lead to a better understanding of the resilience some chronically ill and handicapped children exhibit, but may also provide the empirical heuristic guidance needed in the development of cognitive–behavioral interventions within a prevention model to facilitate these children's psychological and social adaptation to their chronic physical condition by modifying the determinants of perceived social support. Theoretically, the understanding of the mechanisms through which perceived social support functions as a protective factor against the chronic strain of pediatric chronic illness and physical handicap cannot advance until the variables that engender a sense of support are clearly delineated (Cutrona, 1986). In order to generate effective preventive interventions to increase social support in at-risk children, a clearer understanding of the determinants of perceived social support must be empirically investigated (Varni, Rappaport et al., 1989b).

Thus, the empirical challenge is to identify the factors that contribute to the perception that one is supported by others. Two categories of variables are now beginning to receive empirical investigation in this regard: interpersonal factors and intrapersonal characteristics (Cutrona, 1986; Dunkel–Schetter, Folkman, & Lazarus, 1987; Varni, Rappaport et al., 1989b). From a theoretical perspective, an understanding of whether certain intrapersonal characteristics and behaviors are typical of those high and low in social support may further advance our conceptualizations of social support processes (Sarason & Sarason, 1986). Most of the research thus far on social support has emphasized either the relationship between social support and psychological and physical symptomatology, or the measurement of social support per se.

Sarason and Sarason (1986) recently suggested that perceived social support be considered as an *individual difference variable* as much or more than merely a function of the individual's environment or happenstance. Much of the prior research assumed that social support was an environmental provision, something that the individual receives from interpersonal relationships. However, the Sarasons and others have now begun the process of accumulating empirical evidence that an individual's perceived social support level is an attribute that has intrapersonal characteristics, rather than as simply an environmental provision (B. R. Sarason, Shearin, Pierce, & Sarason, 1987; I. G. Sarason & B. R. Sarason, 1986; Sarason, Sarason, Hacker, & Basham, 1985; Sarason, Sarason, & Shearin, 1986).

Thus, there may be certain intrapersonal characteristics which are necessary to gain and retain social support, or put another way, "the stimulus qualities of individuals who differ in levels of social support are sufficiently distinct to account for some of their differences in social support" (Sarason et al., 1986, p. 853). From this perspective, individuals are not passive recipients of social support, but are essential contributors to the development of their social support networks and in eliciting enacted support (Heller et al., 1986).

Social Support and Coping Style

Research studies on child and adolescent coping have demonstrated that cognitive and behavioral efforts to alter sources of stress, as well as attempts to regulate the negative emotions associated with stressful circumstances, are important in reducing the adverse effects of a myriad of stressful events, including interpersonal problems and academic achievement-related stressors (cf. Compas, 1987). Theoretically, the coping styles of children experiencing the chronic strain of chronic illness or physical handicap may determine in part their development of social support networks and their eliciting enacted support.

Lazarus and Folkman (1984) have distinguished between *problem-focused coping*, defined as efforts to act on the source of stress to change it, and *emotion-focused coping*, defined as efforts to regulate emotional states that are associated with or result from stressful events. Adult subjects have been found to use more problem-focused coping in situations that they cognitively appraised as changeable and used more emotion-focused coping in situations that they appraised as unchangeable realities that they must accept (Folkman, Lazarus, Dunkel–Schetter, DeLongis, & Gruen, 1986).

Compas, Malcarne, and Fondacaro (1988) found that both problem-

and emotion-focused coping strategies are used by older children and young adolescents in response to both interpersonal problems and academic stressors. Furthermore, they found that the number of problem-focused alternative solutions generated and strategies used for interpersonal stressors were related to both self-reports and maternal reports of internalizing and externalizing emotional or behavioral problems. Additionally, the number of problem-focused alternative solutions the children generated was adjusted to match their appraisals of the controllability of the cause of interpersonal stressors. Whereas the problem-focused alternatives generated and strategies used were negatively related to emotional or behavioral problems, emotion-focused alternatives generated and strategies used were positively related. Finally, coping with academic stress was not related.

The pattern of results from the Compas et al. (1988) study suggests that the type of coping style utilized by children for interpersonal problems may have an impact on their psychological adjustment. Varni, Rappaport et al. (1989b) have hypothesized that children who utilize social–cognitive problem-solving strategies in their interpersonal encounters will be better able to access and maintain social support from peers. The Compas et al. (1988) study demonstrates that problem-focused coping with interpersonal problems, rather than emotion-focused coping, results in lower emotional or behavioral problems. Whether this is a direct effect, or one which is mediated by increased access to social support, remains to be empirically determined. Nevertheless, the findings suggest that coping style as it relates to interpersonal problems and controllability does influence adjustment, and may have relevance for the adjustment of children having to cope with chronic disorders.

Social Support and Social Skills

Since perceived classmate social support has been shown to be a significant predictor of both depressive symptomatology and self-esteem in children with physical handicap (Varni, Rappaport et al., 1989a; Varni, Rubenfeld et al., 1989a, 1989b), then social skills training may potentiate chronically ill and handicapped children's access to and maintenance of peer social support.

Partial support for the concept that social skills may facilitate the development and maintenance of peer social support may be gleaned from a study by Cohen, Sherrod, and Clark (1986) with first-year college students (mean age = 18.7 yrs). In prospective analyses based on testing at the beginning of the school year and 11- and 22-week follow-ups, Cohen et al. (1986) found that higher levels of social skills predicted the development of both perceived social support and friendship formation. While this investigation is best viewed as exploratory, it nevertheless provides preliminary empirical evidence for the heuristic concept that *social skills training may facilitate access to peer social support* (Varni, Rubenfeld et al., 1989a).

Thus social skills may be viewed as contributing to the development of social networks, perceptions of support availability, and the mobilization and maintenance of social support. It should be noted that in the Cohen et al. study, both social competence and self-disclosure were social skills measures that positively predicted perceived social support. In contrast, social anxiety negatively predicted perceived social support. This distinction suggests that in teaching children the social skills to access social support better, a cognitive–behavioral intervention must also include a cognitive relaxation procedure for those children experiencing social anxiety, which might inhibit them from performing the social skills in their behavioral repertoire.

Social Skills and Social Competence

Social competence is an evaluative term based upon global judgments of the general quality of a child's typical performance as rated by parents, teachers, peers, or significant others (Gresham, 1986; Kennedy, 1988). In addition to these global judgments by significant others, social competence evaluations are also based upon comparisons with explicit criteria, including the number of social tasks performed correctly in relation to some criterion, or reference to some normative sample. For example, the social competence summary scale of the Child Behavior Checklist (Achenbach & Edelbrock, 1983) is based on three subscales measuring such constructs as interpersonal relations, school performance, and activities such as clubs, sports, and hobbies.

Thus, *social competence* represents an evaluative judgment that the child performs age-appropriate adaptive behavior in those areas that are considered socially important by significant others. In contrast, *social skills* are the specific behaviors that a child engages in when faced with an interpersonal situation (e.g., eye contact, voice intonation, asking open-ended questions, complimenting). Thus, social skills are the observable behaviors upon which the global evaluations are, in part, based (Gresham, 1986; Kennedy, 1988).

Social Skills Training

Children with chronic physical disorders often experience a disruption in their social relations with peers, siblings, teachers, and parents secondary to illness/disability-imposed limitations and medical treatments (Varni, 1983). The potential of social skills training in overcoming these disruptions in normal social development may result not only in improved relationships in the present, but may also prevent later psychological and social adjustment problems. Chronically ill and handicapped children may not only be taught the requisite social skills for effective social interaction and peer acceptance, but may even excel in interpersonal skills beyond the level of their physically healthy peers (Varni, 1983).

Social skills training typically involves some form of modeling, behavioral rehearsal, corrective feedback, and reinforcement of selected prosocial behaviors. Social skills selected for intervention may include improving conversation skills and increasing cooperative play, positive peer interactions, peer acceptance, and making friends (cf. Ladd, 1984). As summarized by Ladd (1984), "Based on what is known, it seems reasonable to conclude that early peer rejection is an important predictor of later maladjustment and thus a compelling justification for early detection and intervention." Furthermore, because academic instruction takes place in a social context, peer relationship difficulties may undermine academic progress as well (Parker & Asher, 1987). To go to school each day without looking forward to interacting with classmates either individually or in group activities might be a sufficient cause for avoiding school, regardless of academic achievement. Children who are poorly accepted by their peers are more likely to drop out of school than children who are better accepted (cf. Parker & Asher, 1987).

This evidence indicating a relationship between problematic peer relations during childhood and academic and later psychosocial maladjustment has been a major contributor to the empirical investigation of social skills training, a behaviorally oriented strategy designed to facilitate children's social competence with peers, and is one of the most promising and effective methods of treatment (Ladd, 1984). The basic premise of social skills intervention is that unaccepted or rejected children lack the requisite skills to develop and maintain peer relationships. By teaching children these requisite social skills, one can improve peer relationships and ultimately enhance long-term development on such adjustment domains as school achievement, self-esteem, shyness/withdrawal, and depressive symptoms (Furman & Gavin, 1989). Since peer relationship difficulties place children at increased risk for long-term adjustment problems, children for whom social skills training is successful should experience fewer subsequent adjustment problems than those who do not receive explicit social skills instruction (cf. Parker & Asher, 1987).

Children are hypothesized to exhibit deficits in interpersonal skills for three possible reasons: (1) a lack of specific behavioral abilities; that is, a social skills behavioral deficit or underdeveloped social repertoire, (2) a lack of opportunity for peer interaction or prolonged or intermittent periods of social isolation, and (3) emotional or cognitive factors that interfere with social skills performance (e.g., social anxiety, negative self-appraisals). Hence, social skills training may be a means of transmitting new skills, strengthening or enhancing existing skills, and eliminating psychological barriers to social skills.

Increasing the social skills of school-age children has typically involved direct training in the components of appropriate social interaction, with or without some form of modeling. For example, LaGreca and Santogrossi (1980) identified eight skill areas for training: smiling or laughing, greeting others, joining ongoing activities, extending invitations, conversational skills, sharing and cooperation, verbal complimenting, and physical appearance/grooming. The main treatment procedures they utilized were coaching and behavioral rehearsal with corrective feedback and reinforcement within a group format. Role-playing situations were based on the real-life experiences that the children reported encountering. The children were given immediate feedback on their role playing, with suggestions for improvement. To encourage the children to use the skills with their peers, they were given homework assignments that focused on practicing the social skills with peers outside the group sessions (e.g., greeting a classmate at least once a day for the next week). In comparison to an attention-placebo group and a waiting-list control group, the social skills training group demonstrated increased skill in a role-playing situation, a greater verbal knowledge of how to interact with peers, and more initiation of peer interactions in the school setting.

Ladd (1984) suggested the development of a social skills training curriculum that has the potential for promoting social skills that are ecologically valid (i.e., identifying types of social tasks that specific groups of children must competently perform in order to achieve desired social outcomes). This ecological approach is especially appropriate in revising social skills training curricula to be particularly relevant to the social challenges faced by chronically ill and handicapped children.

Social–Cognitive Problem Solving

In addition to being taught the behavioral social skills needed to initiate and maintain social interactions effectively, children need to be taught how to apply those skills, that is, they need a *metacognitive approach* to social situations. Social–cognitive problem solving represents such a metacognitive orientation. *Social–cognitive problem-solving strategies* include being able to plan practical ways to meet others, develop plans for increasing the number of people one meets during the day, discriminate when and with whom to initiate conversations, and (particularly important for children with visible physical differences who may experience teasing) generate effective methods for resolving interpersonal conflicts. Thus, social–cognitive problem-solving interventions include not only social skills training, but also instruction in the metacognitive strategies necessary for the optimal utilization of the social skills in the child's behavioral repertoire.

A growing number of studies have identified the correlates of children's social–cognitive problem solving skills (e.g., Fischler & Kendall, 1988; Hopper & Kirschenbaum, 1985; Kendall & Fischler, 1984; Mullins, Siegel, & Hodges, 1985; Richard & Dodge, 1982). In general, these typically cross-sectional correlational analyses have found that higher levels of social–cognitive problem-solving *component* skills (e.g., quality versus quantity of alternative solutions generated) are positively related to various indices of psychological and social adjustment. Most of these cross sectional analyses have tested the Interpersonal Cognitive Problem Solving (ICPS) model, as originally formulated by Spivack, Platt, and Shure (1976).

The ICPS model consists of at least five component skills: problem recognition, alternative thinking, means–end thinking, consequential thinking, and evaluative thinking. In recent studies, one of the more consistent findings has been the relative superiority of *quality* versus *quantity* of alternative solutions generated as predictive of positive adjustment. As cogently stated by Hopper and Kirschenbaum (1985, p. 698),

> When differences in adjustment between groups are not extreme, quantity becomes less important and quality of problem solving becomes more important as a mediator of adjustment. This assertion is supported by the sheer number of real-life situations in which it is reasonable to assume that generating more alternatives would not necessarily prove helpful and, in fact, could hinder social performance. . . . rapidly selecting a good alternative, instead of merely generating many possibilities, should be most advantageous.

The few published intervention studies with children utilizing various derivatives of social–cognitive problem-solving training have generally demonstrated a therapeutic effect on psychological adjustment (e.g., Shure & Spivack, 1982; Stark, Reynolds, & Kaslow, 1987; Yu, Harris, Solovitz, & Franklin, 1986); however, some variability may exist across socioeconomic groups of children (e.g., Weissberg et al., 1981). The social–cognitive problem-solving model as originally formulated by D'Zurilla and Goldfried (1971) has received considerable recent empirical validation in the adult literature, as exemplified by the series of investigations by Nezu and his associates (described below).

Specifically, D'Zurilla and Goldfried (1971) delineated a five-component problem-solving model: (1) *problem orientation* (the cognitive and motivational set with which one approaches and recognizes problems in general); (2) *problem definition and formulation* (the delineation of a problem into concrete and specific terms and the identification of specific goals); (3) *generation of alternative solutions* (the production of an extensive list of possible appropriate solutions through brainstorming); (4) *decision making* (the systematic evaluation of a range of alternative solutions regarding possible consequences and the selection of the most optimal choices); and (5) *solution implementation and verification* (the monitoring and evaluation of the actual solution outcome after its implementation).

In a series of studies, Nezu and his associates have tested social–cognitive problem-solving components and theoretical models in predicting depressive symptomatology and anxiety. Within a life stress conceptual framework of depressive symptomatology, social–cognitive problem solving was hypothesized to function as a mediator variable for depressive symptomatology for individuals experiencing high levels of stress emanating from negative life events. According to this hypothesis, individuals who are unable to resolve effectively the problems inherent in negative life events will experience more depressive symptomatology than individuals characterized by effective problem-solving skills. In both concurrent cross-sectional and prospective longitudinal correlational analyses, Nezu found that social–cognitive problem-solving skills (as measured by a standardized questionnaire) served as a moderator of stress-related depressive symptomatology and anxiety (Nezu, 1986a; Nezu, Nezu, Saraydarian, Kalmar, & Ronan, 1986; Nezu & Ronan, 1985, 1988). More definitive causal evidence of the efficacy of the social–cognitive problem-solving therapy approach for unipolar depression has also been demonstrated (Nezu, 1986b; Nezu & Perri, 1989).

Collectively, these findings provide conceptual support for current theories of depression that emphasize problem-focused coping ability, social competence, and cognitive appraisal. As such, this five-component social–cognitive problem-solving model was selected for a clinical trial as described below.

Social–Cognitive Problem Solving and Childhood Cancer

With increasing survival and potential for cure in children with cancer, the qualitative nature of life experience has become an area of growing concern. This has resulted in a shift in psychological emphasis from confronting imminent death to facilitating coping and adjustment to serious chronic disease and its consequences (Varni & Katz, 1987).

In order to promote optimal rehabilitation and adjustment to disease and medical treatment chronic strain, newly diagnosed children with cancer are encouraged to return to their normal premorbid school and social experiences as soon as medically feasible (Katz, Rubinstein, Hubert, & Blew, 1988). Unfortunately, these children face multiple impediments to a smooth return to school and ongoing socialization. Following a diagnosis of cancer, these children are frequently absent from school and peers. They must endure the visible side-effects of cancer and its medical treatment, such as hair loss, weight gain or loss, and physical disfigurement, all of which can result in significant negative reactions from peers. Specialized academic needs may interact with school staff misconceptions regarding cancer and its medical treatment. Reports of social isolation and separation anxiety have also been documented (cf. Katz, Dolgin, & Varni, 1990). Thus, the complex medical management requirements of childhood cancer, along with the acute crisis and the potentially fatal prognosis, may all interact synergistically to produce a negative impact on the child's psychological and social adjustment. Because of their exposure to numerous negative life experiences with the potential for impairing social relationships and social competence, children with cancer have been hypothesized and demonstrated to be at risk for problems in these domains (cf. Katz et al., 1988; Varni & Katz, 1987).

It seems plausible that children without social support from peers would be at risk for school avoidance and feelings of loneliness, depression, and poor self-esteem. In order to address these concerns, Katz et al. (1988) developed, implemented, and empirically evaluated a comprehensive hospital-based school reintegration intervention for newly diagnosed children with cancer. The intervention package developed was comprised of the following major components:

1. *Early preventive education and support* for patients, parents, medical and school staffs about the importance of rapid return to school when medically feasible. This included individual and family counseling regarding the importance of early school return and how this could be accomplished, along with school personnel phone contacts and arrangement for special school services when needed.
2. *School and classroom presentations* to demystify the cancer experience for peers and school personnel, with direct patient participation, whenever possible.
3. *Regular follow-up* with all concerned to ensure that progress was maintained.

An intervention group comprised of 49 children ages 5–17 years (mean = 9.8) was assessed at diagnosis and again following intervention and their return to school. A comparison group was comprised of 36 children, diagnosed within 3 years of the study's inception who had not received the intervention; this group was assessed once on the same measures as the intervention group. Children in the intervention group demonstrated significant increases in parent-rated social competence following the school reintegration intervention and return to school. At posttesting, the intervention subjects were also significantly higher than the comparison subjects on the social competence measures. Additionally, the intervention subjects demonstrated a significant improvement in their self-perceived social acceptance ratings, and were again higher after intervention than the comparison group.

Although the intervention subjects scored higher on parent-rated social competence and self-rated social acceptance than the comparison subjects, the relatively large standard deviations on these measures suggested the presence of substantial individual differences between subjects. These data suggest that the school reintegration intervention was, on the average, helpful in bolstering the social competence and social acceptance of newly diagnosed children with cancer. However, the comparison group was not actually a control group, and therefore differences between the groups may have been a function of the passage of time and not necessarily the intervention itself. Other methodological difficulties with this initial investigation included a wide age range, and the lack of a randomized, controlled design.

In an ongoing project, Katz and Varni (1988) are building on this earlier research by expanding the subject pool, using a randomized clinical trial design, and focusing on children in kindergarten through the 8th grade. The project is investigating the incremental efficacy of a standardized social–cognitive problem-solving intervention over and above the standardized school reintegration program. Although the study by Katz et al. (1988) included components of social skills training in its intervention, such as role playing and practical discussions, no specific social skills training package was tested. Additionally, the design of that study did not allow for a direct evaluation of the social skills component from the overall school reintegration intervention approach utilized.

The research project by Katz and Varni (1988) assesses the children on standardized self-report, parent-report, and teacher-report measures within 1 month, 6 months, and 9 months of diagnosis. In addition to the standard school reintegration intervention, children randomly assigned to the social–cognitive problem-solving intervention receive a standardized approach to solving interpersonal problems. Based on a metacognitive model, the social–cognitive problem-solving intervention follows in part the premise that

> It seems reasonable to assert that, because there are an infinite number of potential problem situations and an infinite list of discrete solutions, interventions are best focused not on teaching specific responses but on *training the cognitive processes* involved in problem solving. The ability to achieve successful problem solutions across various situations is the desired therapeutic outcome. Specific skills may be effective under discrete conditions, but greater generalization of the benefits of training will accrue when the focus is on the cognitive problem-solving process. (Kendall, 1984, p. 118)

The children in the experimental intervention group are first taught the five-component, social–cognitive problem-solving approach, originally delineated by D'Zurilla and Goldfried (1971). Specifically, the children are taught to problem-solve concerns related to peers, teachers, parents, and siblings, as they arise. These strategies are incorporated throughout the intervention, but are highlighted during the first part of the intervention. Steps in the problem-solving model are: (1) recognizing that interpersonal problems can be solved; (2) emphasizing the importance of identifying the problem; (3) considering what happened to create the problem; (4) exploring options to resolve the problem; and (5) options to prevent future occurrences are explored, along with methods for implementation.

After introducing the general cognitive set of solving interpersonal problems, the children are then taught how to express effectively their thoughts, wishes, and concerns to others through specific assertiveness training. They are taught the differences among being assertive, aggressive, and passive. Emphasis is placed upon situations involving medical care and treatment, school concerns (e.g., making up missed school assignments because of clinic appointments, hospitalizations, or disease-related incapacity), and dealing with possible parental overprotectiveness at home.

Next, the children are taught specifically how to cope with verbal and physical teasing and name calling associated with changes in their personal appearance (e.g., hair loss, weight gain or loss, surgical disfigurement). Strategies such as extinguishing inappropriate peer responses through lack of behavioral response, giving age-appropriate explanations for physical changes, as well as going to an authoritative adult for support and assistance are emphasized. Finally, the children receive relaxation training (meditative breathing and muscle relaxation training) to counteract social anxiety that might inhibit social skills performance in the child's social environment.

Excerpts from Social Skills Training Manual

Explain what social skills are, for example: "What I mean by social skills are things that can help you make new friends, solve problems, handle teasing, say how you feel, and get along better with other kids, your parents, and teachers."

Describe the five *basic steps* to be used, for example: "First, I'll tell you exactly what social skill you'll learn during the lesson" (define social skill). "Then, I'll show you the way to do it" (modeling). "Then you'll try it" (behavioral rehearsal). "Next, we'll talk about what you did well and some things you could do to make it even better" (performance feedback). "Finally, we'll work together to plan on ways you can practice your new social skill at home and school" (generalization and maintenance).

Further describe social skills training procedures by *comparing* them to the way kids learn *any new game* or physical activity, for example:

Learning how to use social skills is like learning anything new. Think about the first time you learned to play baseball, basketball, or volleyball (ask child what his or her favorite sport is). In order to get good at (favorite sport), you had to practice. Practice is important because when you're in a big game, you really need to know what to do when you can do it. Practicing your social skills is like practicing to get better at (favorite sport). That way when you really need to use your social skills with someone, you know what to do and how to do it.

Now we are going to talk about solving problems. A problem is something that makes you feel bad or bothers you. Once you have a problem, you can either do things to make the problem worse for you, or you can do things to make it better for you, that is, solve it. To solve a problem and make it better for you: (1) Take a deep breath to get calm. (2) Think about what the problem is that is bothering you. (3) Think of at least three different things you can do to solve the problem, so that it does not bother you as much or make you feel as bad. (4) Choose the best one for you to try first. (5) Try your best choice. (6) If your best choice doesn't work, take a deep breath to stay calm, and try another choice.

Specific vignettes were developed based on clinical experience which reflected the kinds of problems children frequently face when re-entering school. These vignettes served as the stimulus situations for role playing, setting the stage for subsequent *in vivo* practice in the school setting.

SUMMARY

The above review demonstrates the multiple levels at which cognitive–behavioral interventions may be used to mediate some of the recurrent stresses confronted by children with chronic illnesses. On an immediate basis, children may use such techniques in the context of self-regulation as a means of reducing levels of pain intensity, which may ultimately lead to enhanced psychosocial functioning. On a much broader level, once one recognizes the power of peer relationships and social supports in mediating adjustment to chronic illness, social–cognitive problem-solving techniques become central. It is essential to recognize that the systematic investigation of stressors related to psychosocial adjustment in children with chronic illnesses is a relatively new area of investigation. Certainly as other factors mediating the stress–psychological adjustment relationship are identified, innovative cognitive–behavioral strategies for assessment and intervention will be devised and tested.

REFERENCES

Achenbach, T. M., & Edelbrock, L. S. (1983). *Manual for the Child Behavior Checklist and Revised Child Behavior Profile.* Burlington: University of Vermont.
Alloway, R., & Bebbington, P. (1987). The buffering theory of social support: A review of the literature. *Psychological Medicine, 17,* 91–108.

Aradine, C. R., Beyer, J. E., & Tompkins, J. M. (1988). Children's pain perception before and after analgesia: A study of instrument construct validity and related issues. *Journal of Pediatric Nursing, 3*, 11–23.

Barrera, M. (1986). Distinctions between social support concepts, measures, and models. *American Journal of Community Psychology, 14*, 413–445.

Battle, C. U. (1972). The role of the pediatrician as ombudsman in the health care of the young handicapped child. *Pediatrics, 50*, 916–922.

Beales, J. G., Keen, J. H., & Holt, P. J. L. (1983). The child's perception of the disease and experience of pain in juvenile chronic arthritis. *Journal of Rheumatology, 10*, 61–65.

Beyer, J. E., & Knapp, T. R. (1986). Methodologic issues in the measurement of children's pain. *Children's Health Care, 14*, 233–241.

Bibace, R., & Walsh, M. (1980). Development of children's concepts of illness. *Pediatrics, 66*, 912–917.

Bonica, J. J. (1977). Neurophysiologic and pathologic aspects of acute and chronic pain. *Archives of Surgery, 112*, 750–761.

Bruhn, J. G., & Phillips, B. U. (1987). A developmental basis for social support. *Journal of Behavioral Medicine, 10*, 213–229.

Cohen, S., Sherrod, D. R., & Clark, M. S. (1986). Social skills and the stress-protective role of social support. *Journal of Personality and Social Psychology, 50*, 963–973.

Cohen, S., & Wills, T. A. (1985). Stress, social support, and the buffering hypothesis. *Psychological Bulletin, 98*, 310–357.

Cole, T. B., Sprinkle, R. H., Smith, S. J., & Buchanon, G. R. (1986). Intravenous narcotic therapy for children with severe sickle cell pain crisis. *American Journal of Diseases of Children, 140*, 1255–1259.

Compas, B. E. (1987). Coping with stress during childhood and adolescence. *Psychological Bulletin, 101*, 393–403.

Compas, B. E., Malcarne, V. L., & Fondacaro, K. M. (1988). Coping with stressful events in older children and young adolescents. *Journal of Consulting and Clinical Psychology, 56*, 405–411.

Cozzi, L., Tryon, W. W., & Sedlacek, K. (1987). The effectiveness of biofeedback-assisted relaxation in modifying sickle cell crisis. *Biofeedback and Self-Regulation, 12*, 51–61.

Crue, B. L. (1985). Multidisciplinary pain treatment programs: Current status. *Clinical Journal of Pain, 1*, 31–38.

Cutrona, C. E. (1986). Objective determinants of perceived social support. *Journal of Personality and Social Psychology, 50*, 349–355.

Dampier, C. D., Walco, G. A., & Zimo, D. A. (1990). *Therapy of pain syndromes in children and adolescents with sickle cell disease.* Manuscript submitted for publication.

Dunkel–Schetter, C., Folkman, S., & Lazarus, R. S. (1987). Correlations of social support receipt. *Journal of Personality and Social Psychology, 53*, 71–80.

D'Zurilla, T. J., & Goldfried, M. R. (1971). Problem-solving and behavior modification. *Journal of Abnormal Psychology, 78*, 107–126.

Fischler, G. L., & Kendall, P. C. (1988). Social cognitive problem solving and childhood adjustment: Qualitative and topological analyses. *Cognitive Therapy and Research, 12*, 133–153.

Folkman, S., Lazarus, R. S., Dunkel–Schetter, C., DeLongis, A., & Gruen, R. J. (1986). Dynamics of a stressful encounter. Cognitive appraisal, coping, and encounter outcomes. *Journal of Personality and Social Psychology, 50*, 992–1003.

Furman, W., & Gavin, L. (1989). Peers' influence on adjustment and development. A view from the intervention literature. In T. J. Berndt & G. W. Ladd (Eds.), *Peer relationships in child development* (pp. 319–340). New York: Wiley.

Gresham, F. M. (1986). Best practices in social skills training. In A. Thomas & J. Grimes (Eds.), *Best practices in school psychology* (pp. 181–192). Kent, OH: National Association of School Psychologists.

Heller, K., Swindle, R. W., & Dusenburg, L. (1986). Component social support process: Comments and integration. *Journal of Consulting and Clinical Psychology, 54*, 466–470.

Hopper, R. B., & Kirschenbaum, D. S. (1985). Social problem solving and social competence in preadolescents: Is inconsistency the hobgoblin of little minds? *Cognitive Therapy and Research, 9*, 685–701.

Huskisson, E. C. (1983). Visual analogue scales. In R. Melzack (Ed.), *Pain measurement and assessment* (pp. 33–37). New York: Raven Press.

Karayalcin, G., Lanzkowsky, P., & Kazi, A. B. (1981). Serum alpha-hydroxybutyrate dehydrogenase levels in children with sickle cell disease. *American Journal of Pediatric Hematology/Oncology, 3*, 169–171.

Katz, E. R., Dolgin, M. J., & Varni, J. W. (1990). Cancer in children and adolescents. In A. M. Gross & R. S. Drabman (Eds.), *Handbook of clinical behavioral pediatrics* (pp. 129–146). New York: Plenum Press.

Katz, E. R., Rubinstein, C. L., Hubert, N. C., & Blew, A. (1988). School and social reintegration of children with cancer. *Journal of Psychosocial Oncology, 6*, 123–140.

Katz, E. R., & Varni, J. W. (1988). *The impact of social skills training on coping and adjustment in newly diagnosed children with cancer.* American Cancer Society, Grant No. PBR-31.

Kendall, P. C. (1984). Social cognition and problem solving: A developmental and child–clinical interface. In B. Gholson & T. Rosenthal (Eds.), *Applications of cognitive–developmental theory* (pp. 115–148). New York: Academic Press.

Kendall, P. C., & Fischler, G. L. (1984). Behavioral and adjustment correlates of problem solving: Validational analyses of interpersonal cognitive problem solving measures. *Child Development, 55*, 879–892.

Kennedy, J. H. (1988). Issues in the identification of socially incompetent children. *School Psychology Review, 17*, 276–288.

Laaksonen, A. L., & Laine, V. (1961). A comparative study of joint pain in adult and juvenile rheumatoid arthritis. *Annals of the Rheumatic Diseases, 20*, 386–387.

Ladd, G. W. (1984). Social skills training with children: Issues in research and practice. *Clinical Psychology Review, 4*, 317–337.

LaGreca, A. M., & Santogrossi, D. A. (1980). Social skills training with elementary school students: A behavioral group approach. *Journal of Consulting and Clinical Psychology, 48*, 220–227.

Lawrence, C., & Fabry, M. E. (1986). Erythrocyte sedimentation rate during steady state and painful crisis in sickle cell anemia. *American Journal of Medicine, 81*, 801–809.

Lazarus, R. S., & Folkman, S. (1984). *Stress, appraisal, and coping.* New York: Springer.

Levine, J. D., Gordon, N. C., Smith, R., & Fields, H. L. (1981). Analgesic responses to morphine and placebo in individuals with post-operative pain. *Pain, 10,* 379–389.

Lovell, D. J., & Walco, G. A. (1989). Pain associated with juvenile rheumatoid arthritis. *Pediatric Clinics of North America, 36,* 1015–1027.

Matteson, A. (1972). Long-term physical illness in childhood: A challenge to psychosocial adaptation. *Pediatrics, 50,* 801–811.

McGrath, P. A. (1986). The measurement of human pain. *Endodontics and Dental Traumatology, 2,* 124–129.

McGrath, P. A. (1987a). The management of chronic pain in children. In G. D. Burrows, D. Elton, & G. V. Stanley (Eds.), *The handbook of chronic pain management* (pp. 205–216). Amsterdam: Elsevier Press.

McGrath, P. A. (1987b). The multidimensional assessment and management of recurrent pain syndromes in children. *Behaviour Research and Therapy, 25,* 251–262.

McGrath, P. A., & de Veber, L. L. (1986). The management of acute pain evoked by medical procedures in children with cancer. *Journal of Pain and Symptom Management, 1,* 145–150.

McGrath, P. A., de Veber, L. L., & Hearn, M. T. (1985). Multidimensional pain assessment in children. In H. L. Fields, R. Dubner, & F. Cervero (Eds.), *Advances in pain research and therapy* (Vol. 9, pp. 387–393). New York: Raven Press.

McGrath, P. J. (1986). The clinical measurement of pain in children: A review. *Clinical Journal of Pain, 1,* 221–227.

McGrath, P. J., Johnson, G., Goodman, J. T., Schillinger, J., Dunn, J., & Chapman, J. (1985). The Children's Hospital of Eastern Ontario Pain Scale (CHEOPS): A behavioral scale for rating post-operative pain in children. In H. L. Fields, R. Dubner, & F. Cervero (Eds.), *Advances in pain research and therapy* (Vol. 9, pp. 395–402). New York: Raven Press.

Melzack, R. (1975). The McGill Pain Questionnaire: Major properties and scoring methods. *Pain, 1,* 277–299.

Merskey, H. (1973). The perception and measurement of pain. *Journal of Psychosomatic Research, 17,* 251–255.

Mullins, L. L., Siegel, L. J., & Hodges, K. (1985). Cognitive problem-solving and life event correlates of depressive symptoms in children. *Journal of Abnormal Child Psychology, 13,* 305–314.

Nezu, A. M. (1986a). Negative life stress and anxiety: Problem solving as a moderator variable. *Psychological Reports, 58,* 279–283.

Nezu, A. M. (1986b). Efficacy of a social problem-solving therapy approach for unipolar depression. *Journal of Consulting and Clinical Psychology, 54,* 196–202.

Nezu, A. M., Nezu, C. M., Saraydarian, L., Kalmar, K., & Ronan, G. F. (1986). Social problem solving as a moderating variable between negative life stress and depressive symptoms. *Cognitive Therapy and Research, 10,* 489–498.

Nezu, A. M., & Perri, M. G. (1989). Social problem solving therapy for unipolar depression: An initial dismantling investigation. *Journal of Consulting and Clinical Psychology, 57,* 408–413.

Nezu, A. M., & Ronan, G. F. (1985). Life stress, current problems, problem solving, and depressive symptoms: An integrative model. *Journal of Consulting and Clinical Psychology, 53,* 693–697.

Nezu, A. M., & Ronan, G. F. (1988). Social problem solving as a moderator of stress-related depressive symptoms: A prospective analysis. *Journal of Counseling Psychology, 35,* 134–138.

O'Hara, M., McGrath, P. J., D'Astous, J. D., & Vair, C. A. (1987). Oral morphine versus injected meperidine (Demerol) for pain relief in children after orthopedic surgery. *Journal of Pediatric Orthopedics, 7,* 78–82.

Parker, J. G., & Asher, S. R. (1987). Peer relations and later personal adjustment: Are low-accepted children at risk? *Psychological Bulletin, 102,* 357–389.

Pearlin, L. I., Lieberman, M. A., Menaghan, E. G., & Mullan, J. T. (1981). The stress process. *Journal of Health and Social Behavior, 22,* 337–356.

Pless, I. B., & Roghmann, K. J. (1971). Chronic illness and its consequences: Observations based on three epidemiologic surveys. *Journal of Pediatrics, 79,* 351–359.

Price, D. D., McGrath, P. A., Rafii, A., & Buckingham, B. (1983). The validation of visual analogue scales as ratio measures of experimental and chronic pain. *Pain, 17,* 45–56.

Reading, A. E. (1983). The McGill Pain Questionnaire: An appraisal. In R. Melzack (Ed.), *Pain measurement and assessment* (pp. 55–61). New York: Raven Press.

Richard, B. A., & Dodge, K. A. (1982). Social maladjustment and problem solving in school-aged children. *Journal of Consulting and Clinical Psychology, 50,* 226–233.

Russo, D. C. (1986). Chronicity and normalcy as the psychological basis for research and treatment in chronic disease in children. In N. A. Krasnegor, J. D. Arasteh, & M. F. Cataldo (Eds.), *Child health behavior: A behavioral pediatrics approach* (pp. 521–536). New York: Wiley.

Sarason, B. R., Shearin, E. N., Pierce, G. R., & Sarason, I. G. (1987). Interrelations of social support measures: Theoretical and practical implications. *Journal of Personality and Social Psychology, 52,* 813–832.

Sarason, I. G., Levine, H. M., Basham, R. B., & Sarason, B. R. (1983). Assessing social support: The Social Support Questionnaire. *Journal of Personality and Social Psychology, 44,* 127–139.

Sarason, I. G., & Sarason, B. R. (1986). Experimentally provided social support. *Journal of Personality and Social Psychology, 50,* 1222–1225.

Sarason, B. R., Sarason, I. G., Hacker, T. A., & Basham, R. B. (1985). Concomitants of social support: Social skills, physical attractiveness, and gender. *Journal of Personality and Social Psychology, 49,* 469–480.

Sarason, I. G., Sarason, B. R. & Shearin, E. N. (1986). Social support as an individual difference variable: Its stability, origins, and relational aspects. *Journal of Personality and Social Psychology, 50,* 845–855.

Schechter, N. L., Berrien, F. B., & Katz, S. M. (1988). The use of patient controlled analgesia in adolescents with sickle cell pain crisis. *Journal of Pain and Symptom Management, 3,* 1–5.

Scott, P. J., Ansell, B. M., & Huskisson, E. C. (1977). Measurement of pain in juvenile chronic polyarthritis. *Annals of the Rheumatic Diseases, 36,* 186–187.

Scott, R. B. (1982). The management of pain in children with sickle cell disease. In R. B. Scott (Ed.), *Advances in the pathophysiology, diagnosis, and treatment of sickle cell disease* (pp. 47–58). New York: Liss.

Shure, M. B., & Spivack, G. (1982). Interpersonal problem solving in young children: A cognitive approach to prevention. *American Journal of Community Psychology, 10*, 341–356.

Spivack, G., Platt, J. J., & Shure, M. B. (1976). *The problem-solving approach to adjustment.* San Francisco: Jossey–Bass.

Stark, K. D., Reynolds, W. M., & Kaslow, N. J. (1987). A comparison of the relative efficacy of self-control therapy and a behavioral problem-solving therapy for depression in children. *Journal of Abnormal Child Psychology, 15*, 91–113.

Sternbach, R. A. (1975). Psychophysiology of pain. *International Journal of Psychiatry in Medicine, 6*, 63–73.

Taenzer, P. (1983). Post-operative pain: Relationships among measures of pain, mood, and narcotic requirements. In R. Melzack (Ed.), *Pain measurement and assessment* (pp. 111–118). New York: Raven Press.

Teske, K., Dart, R. L., & Cleeland, L. S. (1983). Relationships between nurses' observations and patients' self-reports of pain. *Pain, 16*, 289–296.

Thoits, P. A. (1986). Social support as coping assistance. *Journal of Consulting and Clinical Psychology, 54*, 416–423.

Thomas, J. E., Koshy, M., Patterson, L., Dorn, L., & Thomas, K. (1984). Management of pain in sickle cell disease using biofeedback therapy: A preliminary study. *Biofeedback and Self-Regulation, 9*, 413–420.

Thompson, K. L., & Varni, J. W. (1986). A developmental cognitive–biobehavioral approach to pediatric pain assessment. *Pain, 25*, 282–296.

Thompson, K. L., Varni, J. W., & Hanson, V. (1987). Comprehensive assessment of pain in juvenile rheumatoid arthritis: An empirical model. *Journal of Pediatric Psychology, 12*, 241–255.

Varni, J. W. (1981a). Behavioral medicine in hemophilia arthritic pain management. *Archives of Physical Medicine and Rehabilitation, 62*, 183–187.

Varni, J. W. (1981b). Self-regulation techniques in the management of chronic arthritic pain in hemophilia. *Behavior Therapy, 12*, 185–194.

Varni, J. W. (1983). *Clinical behavioral pediatrics: An interdisciplinary biobehavioral approach.* New York: Pergamon Press.

Varni, J. W. (1987, August). *Stress, moderator variables, and psychological adaptation in pediatric chronic disorders.* Invited address presented at the annual meeting of the American Psychological Association, New York.

Varni, J. W., Babani, L., Wallander, J. L., Roe, T. F., & Frasier, S. D. (1989). Social support and self-esteem effects on psychological adjustment in children and adolescents with insulin-dependent diabetes mellitus. *Child and Family Behavior Therapy, 11*, 1–17.

Varni, J. W., Bessman, C. A., Russo, D. C., & Cataldo, M. F. (1980). Behavioral management of chronic pain in children. *Archives of Physical Medicine and Rehabilitation, 61*, 375–379.

Varni, J. W., & Gilbert, A. (1982). Self-regulation of chronic arthritic pain and long-term analgesic dependence in a hemophiliac. *Rheumatology and Rehabilitation, 22*, 171–174.

Varni, J. W., Gilbert, A., & Dietrich, S. L. (1981). Behavioral medicine in pain and analgesia management for the hemophilic child with factor VIII inhibitor. *Pain, 11*, 121–126.

Varni, J., & Jay, S. M. (1984). Biobehavioral factors in juvenile rheumatoid arthritis: Implications for research and practice. *Clinical Psychology Review, 4*, 543–560.

Varni, J. W., Jay, S. M., Masek, B. J., & Thompson, K. L. (1986). Cognitive–behavioral assessment and management of pediatric pain. In A. D. Holzman & D. C. Turk (Eds.), *Pain management: A Handbook of psychological treatment approaches* (pp. 168–192). New York: Pergamon Press.

Varni, J. W., & Katz, E. R. (1987). Psychological aspects of cancer in children: A review of research. *Journal of Psychosocial Oncology, 5*, 93–119.

Varni, J. W., Katz, E. R., & Dash, J. (1982). Behavioral and neurochemical aspects of pediatric pain. In D. C. Russo & J. W. Varni (Eds.), *Behavioral pediatrics: Research and practice* (pp. 177–224). New York: Plenum Press.

Varni, J. W., Rappaport, L. R., Talbot, D., & Setoguchi, Y. (1989a). *Stress, social support and self-esteem effects on depressive symptomatology in children with congenital/acquired limb deficiencies.* Manuscript submitted for publication.

Varni, J. W., Rappaport, L. R., Talbot, D., & Setoguchi, Y. (1989b). *Concomitants of perceived social support in children with congential/acquried limb deficiencies.* Manuscript submitted for publication.

Varni, J. W., Rubenfeld, L. A., Talbot, D., & Setoguchi, Y. (1989a). Stress, social support, and depressive symptomatology in children with congenital/acquired limb deficiencies. *Journal of Pediatric Psychology, 14*, 515–530.

Varni, J. W., Rubenfeld, L. A., Talbot, D., & Setoguchi, Y. (1989b). Determinants of self-esteem in children with congenital/acquired limb deficiencies. *Journal of Developmental and Behavioral Pediatrics, 10*, 13–16.

Varni, J. W., & Thompson, K. L. (1985). *The Varni/Thompson Pediatric Pain Questionnaire.* Unpublished manuscript.

Varni, J. W., Thompson, K. L., & Hanson, V. (1987). The Varni/Thompson Pediatric Pain Questionnaire: I. Chronic musculoskeletal pain in juvenile rheumatoid arthritis. *Pain, 28*, 27–38.

Varni, J. W., Walco, G. A., & Wilcox, K. T. (1990). Cognitive–biobehavioral assessment and treatment of pediatric pain. In A. M. Gross & R. S. Drabman (Eds.), *Handbook of clinical behavioral pediatrics* (pp. 83–109). New York: Plenum Press.

Varni, J. W., Wilcox, K. T., & Hanson, V. (1988). Mediating effects of family social support on child psychological adjustment in juvenile rheumatoid arthritis. *Health Psychology, 7*, 421–431.

Varni, J. W., Wilcox, K. T., Hanson, V., & Brik, R. (1988). Chronic musculoskeletal pain and functional status in juvenile rheumatoid arthritis: An empirical model. *Pain, 32*, 1–7.

Walco, G. A., & Dampier, C. D. (1987). Chronic pain in adolescent patients. *Journal of Pediatric Psychology, 12*, 215 –225.

Walco, G. A., & Dampier, C. D. (in press). Pain in children and adolescents with sickle cell disease: A descriptive study. *Journal of Pediatric Psychology.*

Walco, G. A., Dampier, C. D., & Djordjevic, D. (1987, September). *Pain assessment in children and adolescents with sickle cell disease.* Paper presented at the conference on Sickle Cell Disease in the Next Decade: Innovative Therapeutic Approaches, Washington, DC.

Walco, G. A., Dampier, C. D., Hartstein, G., Djordjevic, D., & Miller, L. (1990). The relationship between recurrent clinical pain and pain threshold in children. In D. C. Tyler & E. J. Krane (Eds.), *Advances in pain research and therapy* (pp. 333–340). New York: Raven Press.

Walco, G. A., Varni, J. W., Hartstein, G., & Ilowite, N. T. (1988, November). *Cognitive-behavioral interventions for pain in children with juvenile rheumatoid arthritis: A preliminary report.* Paper presented at a joint meeting of the Canadian and American Pain Societies, Toronto.

Wallander, J. L., & Varni, J. W. (1989). Social support and adjustment in chronically ill and handicapped children. *American Journal of Community Psychology, 17,* 185–201.

Wallander, J. L., Varni, J. W., Babani, L., Banis, H. T., & Wilcox, K. T. (1988). Children with chronic physical disorders: Maternal reports of their psychological adjustment. *Journal of Pediatric Psychology, 13,* 197–212.

Warth, J. A., & Rucknagel, D. L. (1984). Density ultra centrifugation of sickle cells during and after pain crisis: Increased dense erythrocytes in crisis. *Blood, 64,* 507–515.

Weissberg, R. P., Gesten, E. L., Rapkin, B. D., Cown, E. L., Davidson, E., Flores de Apoderca, R., & McKim, B. J. (1981). Evaluation of a social-problem-solving training program for suburban and inner-city third grade children. *Journal of Consulting and Clinical Psychology, 49,* 251–261.

Wolchik, S. A., Sandler, I. R., & Braver, S. L. (1987). Social support: Its assessment and relation to children's adjustment. In N. Eisenberg (Ed.), *Contemporary topics in development psychology.* New York: Wiley.

Wolff, B. B. (1983). Laboratory methods of pain assessment. In R. Melzack (Ed.), *Pain measurement and assessment* (pp. 7–13). New York: Raven Press.

Yu, P., Harris, G. E., Solovitz, B. L., & Franklin, J. L. (1986). A social problem-solving intervention for children at high risk for later psychopathology. *Journal of Clinical Child Psychology, 15,* 30–40.

Zeltzer, L. K., Dash, J., & Holland, J. P. (1979). Hypnotically induced pain control in sickle cell anemia. *Pediatrics, 64,* 533–536.

CHAPTER 8

Academic Applications of Cognitive–Behavioral Programs with Learning Disabled Students

BERNICE Y. L. WONG
Simon Fraser University

KAREN R. HARRIS AND STEVEN GRAHAM
University of Maryland

The application of cognitive–behavioral principles and procedures to academic domains has a relatively brief history. In 1980, Hobbs, Moguin, Tyoler, and Lahey noted that few cognitive–behavioral studies had focused on the instruction of academic skills. Since that time, however, cognitive–behaviorally based strategy instruction has become a major focus of educational research with the learning-disabled and other inefficient learners (cf. Harris, 1982; Pressley & Levin, 1986). In this chapter, we begin with a brief overview of the underlying rationale for the use of cognitive–behavioral procedures with learning–disabled (LD) students, then review studies involving cognitive–behaviorally based instruction with LD students in the domains of reading, writing, and mathematics. Within the domain-specific reviews, issues are raised. We conclude by considering two current issues in academic applications with LD students, as well as suggestions on future directions for research.

APPLICATION WITH STUDENTS WITH LEARNING DISABILITIES

Several interrelated assumptions underly the use of cognitive–behavioral interventions with children with LD. These assumptions are important because they bear on the rationale for the interventions and on the determination of intervention components with these children (see also Kendall,

Chapter 1, this volume). They include (but are not necessarily limited to): (1) the premise that affect, behavior, and cognition are transactionally related; (2) the critical need to consider developmental progressions among affective, behavioral, and cognitive dimensions in designing interventions; (3) consideration of ecological variables (the situational, cultural, and systems network of which the individual is a part); (4) the need to have a purposeful, integrated intervention approach which combines affective, behavioral, and cognitive intervention components within developmental and ecological parameters, and (5) the importance of children being active participants and collaborators in the learning process. Although these assumptions may not be evident in every investigation, their recognition is gaining in LD research and literature (cf. Harris 1982, 1985).

Traditionally, poor performance on academic and experimental tasks among students with LD has been attributed to specific structural or ability deficits (i.e., auditory or visual perception problems, psycholinguistic deficiencies, etc.). Recent research, however, has suggested that while such structural or ability deficits may exist, poor performance may frequently be the result of problems in self-regulation of organized, strategical behaviors, rather than an inability to acquire and execute specific strategies (Harris, 1986a, 1986b). Moreover, students with LD may not make use of verbal mediation processes or may not have developed sufficiently an effective linguistic control system—that is, they may exhibit difficulty in establishing correspondence between saying and doing or in using verbalizations to guide behavior.

Few studies have investigated verbal medication specifically among the learning-disabled. Recently, Harris (1986a) investigated the natural occurrence of regulatory private speech among normally achieving and LD students during problem solving. Her results indicated that, compared with normally achieving peers, 7- and 8-year-old students with LD produced a significantly lower proportion of task-relevant private speech (and significantly higher proportions of task-irrelevant private speech), took significantly longer to complete all solvable steps of the task, and had significantly shorter persistence times. A self-instructional problem-solving intervention, using a peer model, resulted in significant and meaningful improvements on all measures among both the students with learning disabilities and their normally achieving peers. Importantly, performance of the children with LD after intervention equaled or exceeded that of their competent normally achieving peers in the no-treatment condition.

A more extensive body of research exists concerning the strategical behavior of students with LD (for detailed reviews, ass Hallahan, Lloyd, Kauffman, & Loper, 1983; Torgesen, 1980). To illustrate, research in the areas of selective attention and memory (Hallahan & Reeve, 1980; Torgesen & Kail, 1980) has provided evidence that children with LD fail to produce appropriate task strategies spontaneously, while prompts or instruction in cognitive and metacognitive strategies improves performance. Research in academic skill areas has provided similar results (cf. Graham, Harris, & Sawyer, 1987; Hughes & Hall, 1989; Wong, 1985).

In addition to deficits in self-regulation of strategical behavior, many students with LD exhibit characteristics such as: helpless behavior; an external locus of control; maladaptive attributions; comprehension, production, and medication deficiencies; low motivation; negative task affect; poor problem-solving skills; difficulties with time-on-task and task engagement; low productivity; and impulsivity (Graham & Harris, 1987; Harris, 1982; Licht & Kistner, 1986). The frequency of multiple problems of an affective, behavioral, and/or cognitive nature in children with LD make cognitive–behavioral interventions (given their underlying assumptions) an appealing match to the needs of these children.

Influence of Instructional Theory and Research

Cognitive–behavioral interventions are, by nature, integrative. When cognitive–behavioral principles and procedures are applied to the academic problems of special needs learners, it becomes critical to incorporate sound instructional practices into the design of intervention. While space precludes a thorough discussion, several key points are noted here (cf. Harris, 1982). Analyses of both the task and learner (see Harris, 1982, 1985, for discussion of both from a cognitive–behavioral viewpoint), as well as teacher direction, an academic focus, and individualization are characteristic of effective instruction. Further, learning is facilitated when the learner is active and involved, when the task requires understanding, meaningful processing, and the development of cognitive representations of new behaviors rather than task-specific response sets, and when a demonstration–prompt–practice format and sufficient practice are provided. Criterion-based instruction is preferable to time-based instruction, and concern for time on-task must be augmented with concern for how the student uses that time (i.e., engaged time) and what the student is thinking while working. Finally, students with low prior achievement, such as children with LD, typically need a great deal of instructional support and stimulation, and may need assistance in improving cognitive processing of instruction.

Intervention Components

The cognitive–behavioral literature suggests that effective strategy instruction involves three major components: strategies, knowledge about the use and significance of those strategies (metastrategy information), and self-regulation of strategical performance (cf. Brown, Campione, & Day, 1981; Graham & Harris, 1989a). Sound procedural instruction based on these

components, however, may not be enough to ensure that even well-taught
and well-learned strategies will be used regularly and effectively (Garner &
Alexander, 1989). Attributional retraining and development of a mastery
orientation among students may be critical to promote strategical performance (Ames & Archer, 1988; Garner & Alexander, 1989; Pearl, 1985).
Simple cognitive–behavioral procedures, such as a brief set of task-specific
self-instructions, may suffice for some goals or minor problems. However,
more complex cognitive–behavioral instructional procedures are necessary
for more ambitious goals and more severe learner problems. Complex cognitive–behavioral procedures involve a combination of (1) task-specific and
metacognitive self-instructions, (2) the designed strategy, (3) self-regulation
procedures, and (4) the rationale for the treatment components. Such complex training is likely to involve multiple training tasks, components and
stages (Harris, 1985). A growing body of research, to which we now turn,
indicates that sound cognitive–behavioral interventions have meaningful
effects on the reading, writing, and mathematical performance of LD students.*

READING COMPREHENSION

Although self-instructional procedures have been used in numerous studies
to enhance LD students' reading comprehension (Graves, 1986; Wong, 1980;
Wong & Jones, 1982), only three studies adhered to the training procedure
explicitly described by Meichenbaum (1977). The three are unpublished
theses by Bommarito and Meichenbaum (1978), Short (1981), and L. Graham (1986). To illustrate how cognitive–behavioral procedures can be used
to enhance effectively students' reading comprehension, we shall focus on
the most recent study by L. Graham.

L. Graham (1986) trained poor and average readers in the fifth and
sixth grades to use a question-answering strategy to enhance performance
in reading comprehension tests. A total of 90 students participated in the
study, half of whom were poor readers who were reading at least one grade
below their current grade placement. The remaining students were average
readers.

The question-answering strategy involved students learning to identify
different sources of information appropriate for answering respective types
of comprehension test questions. Specifically, text-explicit questions target
information explicitly stated in the text. Text-implicit questions require
students to search for and integrate information across sentences, para-

*Interested readers are referred to Kendall and Bartel (1990), *Teaching problem solving: A man-
ual for teachers*. Available from the author.

graphs or even pages in the text. Script-implicit questions can only be answered by information in students' own background knowledge.

Essentially, Graham based her instructional strategy on the prior research of Raphael (Raphael, 1985; Raphael & McKinney, 1983). For each category of comprehension test questions, Raphael designed a mnemonic: "Right There" for text-explicit test questions, "Think and Search" for text-implicit test questions, and "On My Own" for script-implicit test questions. With these mnemonics, Raphael successfully enhanced children's reading comprehension test performance.

To facilitate strategy learning in average and poor readers, Graham (1986) simplified Raphael's mnemonics. For the respective categories of reading comprehension test questions, she used "Here," "Hidden," and "In My Head," and named the strategy, the 3H strategy.

Students were randomly divided into three treatments: two instructional treatment groups and one control (no-training) group. The two instructional treatment groups differed in the instructional modes for the question-answering strategy: self-instructional versus didactic teaching. In the didactic condition, students were taught the 3H strategy and given a prompt card that outlined the kinds of question-answering relationships embodied by the 3H mnemonics (see Figure 8-1). They used the prompt card in subsequent comprehension tasks.

Students in the self-instructional training condition were taught three self-questions to facilitate use of the 3H strategy. Graham adhered closely to Meichenbaum's (1977) self-instructional procedures in teaching these self-questions, which were purposed to guide and monitor strategy use. These three questions were:

1. How will I answer this question? (Student generates this question after reading a question on a comprehension test.)
2. What type of question is this? (Where would I find the answer to this question? Is it a "HERE" question? Or a "HIDDEN" question? Or an "IN MY HEAD" question?)
3. Is my answer correct?

Like the students in the didactic teaching condition, students in the self-instructional teaching condition also received a prompt card. One side of it contained information that was the same as that which was given to students in the didactic teaching condition, namely, the 3H strategy. The other side of the prompt card contained the above three self-questions (see Figure 8-1).

Table 8-1 presents an example of the experimenter-teacher's modeling dialogue taken from Graham (1986, pp. 66–67). Students took turns reading aloud parts of a given passage, and used the three self-questions to

HELPERS

(a) HERE

The answer is in one sentence from the passage.

(b) HIDDEN

Use more than one idea from the passage to answer the question.

(c) In my HEAD

Use what you already know to answer the question.

HELPERS

1. How will I answer this question?

2. Where is the answer to this question found?
   (a) HERE
   (b) HIDDEN
   (c) In my HEAD

3. Is my answer correct?

FIGURE 8-1. Prompt card for didactic teaching condition and self-instruction condition used in Graham's (1986) study. On one side are the descriptions of the 3H Helpers used for the didactic teaching condition. On the other side are the three self-questions for self-instruction. *Note:* Reproduced with permission from L. Graham.

TABLE 8-1. Teacher's Modeling of the Use of the 3H Mnemonic Strategy

1. How will I answer this question?	I will have to remember to read carefully—both the question and the passage. I'll use the 3H strategy to help me.
2. What type of the question is this? Where will I find the answer to this question?	The question can give me clues. The answer is either in the text or in my head. I'll check first. If the answer isn't there I'll use what I already know.
a. Is the answer HERE on the page?	This is a simple HERE question if the answer is in one sentence from the passage. Sometimes many of the same words are in the "answer sentence" as were in the question.
b. Is the answer HIDDEN in the passage?	If the question asks for more than a simple fact from the passage then this is a HIDDEN question. The information to answer it comes from two or more sentences in the passage.
c. Is the answer in my HEAD?	If I have read carefully and can't find the answer to the question in the text, then I have to use what I already know. This is an In my HEAD question?
3. Is my answer correct?	Have I really answered the question? I should re-read the question and my answer to see if they "fit" together. I should have a reason for my answer.

Note: Reproduced with permission from L. Graham.

engage the 3H strategy. Graham adhered closely to Meichenbaum's (1977) self-instructional procedures in her training of the students' internalizing the self-questions and the 3H strategy.

The results indicated that training increased subjects' performance in reading comprehension tests. More important, self-instructional training was more effective than didactic training. Also, average readers surpassed poor readers in comprehension test performance. However, contrary to prediction, self-instructional procedure of strategy training did not affect differentially reading comprehension test performance in average and poor readers. Both types of readers benefited equally from self-instructional strategy instructions. Graham had predicted that poor readers given strategy in the self-instructional mode would surpass average readers in the same self-instructional mode. She explained the unexpected finding by suggesting that the average readers were low-average readers who also needed training in comprehension test-answering strategies. Consequently they benefited equally as the poor readers from the self-instructional strategy.

SPECIFIC ISSUES IN COGNITIVE–BEHAVIOR-BASED READING COMPREHENSION INTERVENTIONS

An obvious issue here is the small empirical base of studies using cognitive–behavioral procedures to enhance LD and non-LD students' reading comprehension. We clearly need more research to assess the efficacy of the cognitive–behavioral mode of instruction by pitting it against rival instructional approaches.

Another issue is the need to use cognitive–behavioral procedures to teach students to articulate the nature of their reading comprehension breakdowns. Hitherto we have focused on researching the efficacy of "debugging" or fix-up strategies to resolve students' reading comprehension problems. For example, to enhance reading comprehension and comprehension monitoring, Garner, Hare, Alexander, Haynes and Winograd (1984) encouraged students to look back at the text, Wong and Jones (1982) taught adolescents with learning disabilities to focus on main ideas in paragraphs and to formulate questions on them, Palincsar and Brown (1984) taught poor comprehenders to ask clarifying questions, generate questions on important textual units, summarize paragraphs and predict authors' themes. However, in all these attempts to enhance student reading comprehension, no attention was paid to teaching students to clarify and articulate for themselves, the nature of their reading comprehension breakdowns. To date, in comprehension-fostering research, students have not been taught to discover and identify for themselves, which part(s) of a sentence stymie them in reading comprehension. Is it a particular word? (vocabulary and/or decoding problem). Is it part of a sentence? (grammatical problem or unfamiliarity with a particular expression?), and so on. In retrospect, because of this neglected focus in researchers' comprehension-fostering research, we may have put the cart before the horse, so to speak. For, unless students understand why they do not understand a particular sentence or locate the source of comprehension breakdown within a paragraph, their choice and deployment of learned comprehension (debugging) strategies may be rote. Hence it appears critical that we address this area of student articulation of their own reading comprehension problems with appropriate instructional research with cognitive–behavioral and other approaches.

WRITING INSTRUCTION AND COGNITIVE– BEHAVIORAL APPROACHES

In recent years, much attention has been directed at improving the writing skills of all school-aged children. This national increased emphasis on students' writing has been accompanied by an intensive interest in the cognitive processes considered central to effective writing. As a result, several general models of the writing process have been generated, including an explicit and influential model developed by Flower and Hayes (1980). They suggest that writing is goal directed, writing goals are hierarchically organized, and writers accomplish their goals by employing a variety of mental processes, including: planning, transcription, and revision. According to Graham and Harris (1989b, in press), LD students have significant difficulties with each of these mental processes. Our review of cognitive–behavioral studies in improving LD students' writing skills covers production, planning, and revising of text. Studies involving cognitive–behavioral self-instruction are described.

Text Production

The mechanical demands for producing text appears to be especially problematical for LD students. They make more errors in spelling, capitalization, and punctuation in their compositions than do their normally achieving peers (cf. Moran, 1981; Poteet, 1979; Wong, Wong, & Blenkisop, 1989), and their handwriting is less legible (cf. Graham, Boyer–Shick, & Tippets, 1989). The need to attend to these lower-order mechanical demands may interfere with LD students' execution of higher-order writing processes, such as content generation and planning. MacArthur and Graham (1987), for instance, found that fifth- and sixth-grade LD students produced longer and better stories when the mechanical demands of writing were removed via dictation. They hypothesized that the observed differences between LD students' written and dictated stories may have been due to differences in production speed and/or interference due to the mechanical demands of writing. In a follow-up study, Graham (1989) reported that mechanical interference, not speed of production, accounted for the disruptive effect on LD students' writing.

There has been a small, but important body of intervention research using cognitive–behavioral procedures to improve LD students' text production skills. The interventions include attempts at improving handwriting, spelling, and skills in copying words, senstences, and paragraphs.

Handwriting

A primary aim of handwriting instruction is to make handwriting skills so fluent and automatic that they require little conscious attention (Graham & Harris, 1988). In the school curriculum, considerable effort is directed at teaching students to form accurately and quickly individual letters (Graham & Miller, 1980). The use of cognitive–behavioral procedures as an aid in either teaching or improving students' letter formation skills, however, has received little empirical support. While Robin, Armel, and O'Leary (1975) found that combining verbal self-instruction on writing letters with direct training on letter formation was superior to direct instruction alone for kindergarten students identified as poor writers, the self-instructions were difficult to teach, cumbersome to use, and high rates of self-verbalization were not significantly correlated with superior litter formation. Similarly, Graham (1983a) reported that a combination of direct training and verbal self-instructions resulted in small improvements in third- and fourth-grade LD students' skills in writing letters targeted for instruction. Nevertheless, the self-instruction proved to be cumbersome, treatment effects did not generalize to another setting, and it took about 5 hours of instruction for students to make even moderate improvements. It is important to note, that the self-instructional procedures used by Robin et al. (1975) and Graham (1983a) were designed to promote accuracy. Even if these procedures were effective, they would have to be quickly faded once the desired level of accuracy was obtained. Otherwise, the continued use of self-statements to guide letter formation, for example, would surely hinder the development of handwriting fluency.

Much handwriting instruction also involves copying connected discourse. The rationale for such an activity is that students will be able to practice learned skills in context, maintaining accuracy and promoting fluency. In addition, overall appearance of the student's writing is emphasized, since factors such as neatness can affect teacher's judgments concerning the quality of a composition (Graham, 1982). Hallahan and his colleagues have examined the effectiveness of a variety of self-regulation procedures on the copying performance of LD students. Kosiewicz, Hallahan, and Lloyd (1981) indicated that the accuracy and appearance of paragraphs copied by an LD student could be improved by using self-instructions for reviewing specific copying rules in advance of writing, or through the use of self-evaluations where correctly copied words or letters were circled. Kosiewicz, Hallahan, Lloyd, and Graves (1982) found that the accuracy of words and paragraphs copied by an LD student improved as a result of using self-instructions where words and their component parts were said aloud before and during copying or by augmenting these self-instructions with a self-correction procedure involving the circling of errors made while copying. Hallahan, Lloyd, Kosiewicz, Kauffman, and Graves (1979) reported that the use and eventual fading of an audiotape recorder to cue the self-recording of on-task and off-task behavior increased the on-task performance and the number of letters copied from short stories by an LD student with attentional problems.

Several researchers have further applied cognitive–behavioral procedures to improve the appearance of papers produced by LD students in response to class assignments. In a study by Anderson–Inman, Paine, and Deutchman (1984), a variety of handicapped (three of whom were LD) and disadvantaged children received direct instruction on nine skills related to writing neatness. The addition of a self-monitoring checklist to the instructional regime facilitated transfer of training results to other academic periods of the day, resulting in substantial improvements in the neatness of students' papers. Blandford and Lloyd (1987) found that two LD students made small but significant improvements in the appearance (letter formation and spacing) of their journal writing as a result of a self-instructional procedure for directing and evaluating their sitting position and the formation and spacing of letters. In addition, improvements in appearance were maintained over a short period of time, and transfer effects to another classroom were obtained for one of the students.

Spelling

A major objective of most spelling programs is to help students to learn to spell the words they are most likely to use in their own writing (Graham, 1983b). This goal is commonly actualized by having students memorize the correct spelling of a list of 10 to 20 frequently occurring words each week. One important component of studying unknown words is the use of a systematic study procedure. It is generally assumed, however, that many LD students do not apply effective word-study techniques when preparing for a spelling test (Graham & Miller, 1979).

Several cognitive–behavioral procedures have been used to improve LD students' performance when memorizing spelling words. Harris (1986b), for example, found that self-monitoring of attention and self-monitoring of productivity both resulted in higher levels of on-task behavior and increases in the number of times spelling words were practiced (with self-monitoring of productivity resulting in the greatest increases in practicing). Similarly, Kapadia and Fantuzzo (1988) found that the number of spelling problems that educationally handicapped students completed correctly on spelling review sheets increased dramatically as a result of self-assessment of problem accuracy followed by self-administration of reinforcement contingent upon performance.

Spelling accuracy in very young children can be increased through self-instructional training. Orsetti (1985) successfully taught first-grade children to use an error-monitoring strategy in spelling. Forty-six children (23 per class) in two regular, heterogeneous grade one classes participated in her study. Assignment of the class to the experimental strategy condition was random. Potential confound in teacher was controlled by having the two regular classroom teachers alternate in teaching both the experimental and control classes. Prior to the experiment, the children were tested on the Peabody Picture Vocabulary Test to ensure that children in the two classes did not differ in verbal IQ.

Also, a pretest of 12 randomly selected words, 4 from each of three word-type categories, was given prior to beginning the experiment. This initial spelling assessment was given to ascertain a baseline regarding spelling acquisition for all 46 subjects and to ensure that no significant difference in spelling acquisition existed between the treatment class and control class prior to the implementation of the experimental spelling program.

The content of teaching consisted of 60 words taken from the school's spelling curriculum. There were 20 phonetically regular words (e.g., run), 20 phonetically irregular words (e.g., said), and 20 two-syllable words (e.g., away). The self-instructional error-monitoring strategy is shown in Table 8.2. As evident in the strategy steps, this self-instructional strategy was designed to help the children monitor their spelling through enhanced phoneme–grapheme awareness and self-checking of their attempts in spelling accurately. The children in the experimental condition were taught to focus their visual attention on relevant orthographic features of difficulty or uncertainty within words, and to revise any errors in their spelling as necessary.

Procedurally, four times a week a spelling lesson was given to both treatment and control groups. All lessons lasted about 20 minutes and were given to both classes on the same day and at the same time in the respective classrooms. The experiment involved presentation of the 60 words.

TABLE 8-2. Self-instructional Error-monitoring Strategy in Spelling

Control group	Treatment group
Teacher presents word visually.	Same
Teacher says word, students repeat.	Same
Teacher defines word if necessary.	Same
Teacher uses word in sentence.	Same
Children copy word in book.	Same
Teacher checks to verify accuracy.	Same
Children asked to cover word and spell word again.	Cover word in book.
Check with first word to see if correct.	Repeat word to self and listen for the sounds.
If incorrect, children asked to correct.	Print word.
	Direct children to ask themselves "Do I have the sounds I hear?"
	Does it look right?
	Underline any part not sure of.
	Uncover word and check.
	Correct word if necessary.
Repeat for second and third spelling of each word.	Repeat for second and third spelling of each word.
Children advised to learn and remember words for later use.	Same
Children reinforced their effort by saying, "I have worked hard to be a good speller."	Same

Note: Reproduced with permission from M. Orsetti.

The children in both classes were provided with identical work booklets each week. The booklets, four pages long, were collected after each spelling session. The children worked on one page each day. The first page was designed to introduce and practice three of the six new spelling words. The task involved tracing over each new spelling word (outlined on the page in dotted lines) when directed and then practicing the spelling of each word when and as instructed by printing it in the space provided, checking it and correcting it if necessary. Space was provided for three practices of each new word. Day two involved the same procedure with the presentation of the remaining three new spelling words for the week. Work on day three was similar to pages one and two except that all six words were presented for tracing with space provided for only two practices per word. Day four was identical to day three.

Large 9-by-11-inch blue bristol board cover cards were provided for the children to use to cover the previously spelled words when instructed to do so. The heavier material and larger size enabled the children to handle the cover card with ease. The color of the cover card contrasted to the white booklet pages and allowed the teacher to see at a glance that the children had in fact covered the previously spelled word they were practicing.

Six new spelling words per week were presented to the students for a period of ten weeks. Following this all 60 words were reviewed twice. The review sessions followed the same instructional format as the previous spelling sessions except that less practice time was given for each word. Each spelling lesson during the review sessions was approximately 20 minutes in length. In the first review the children reviewed 6 spelling words per session. This resulted in ten spelling sessions being conducted during the first review. Throughout the second 60-word review 12 spelling words were presented per lesson and, therefore, the second review took five sessions. A posttest of all 60 words was immediately given after completion of the second review. A maintenance test was administered 3 weeks later.

The results were impressive. At both immediate posttest and the maintenance test, the children taught to self-monitor their spelling surpassed those in the control condition in accuracy of words spelled [means and S.D. were: 53.96 (5.54) versus 45.46 (7.28) at posttest, and 54.52 (5.43) versus 47.00 (7.58) at maintenance]. The results at maintenance highlight the efficacy of the self-instructional error-monitoring strategy because it was given 3 weeks after the immediate posttest.

Orsetti's (1985) study has important instructional implications for young children in the use of self-instructional strategies. Clearly, when the self-instructional strategy is carefully designed to match the children's cognitive maturity and instructional need, they can use it to good advantage. We think that it can readily be adapted for use with young children with learning disabilities.

Planning

According to Flower and Hayes (1980) planning during writing involves three basic cognitive processes: generating, organizing, and goal setting. LD students appear to have difficulties executing and managing each of these mental operations during composing. In reviewing the available literature, Graham and Harris (1989a, in press) concluded that LD students often possess more knowledge of the selected topic than is reflected in their written products, are not particularly successful in employing strategies to access from memory content for writing and have difficulty setting relevant writing goals and using genre-specific knowledge to frame and organize writing content. LD students also do little planning before writing, and lack awareness of audience. Additionally, they are less aware than their normal counterparts of how to monitor and regulate the planning process during writing (Englert, Raphael, Fear, & Anderson, 1988; Graham, Schwartz, & MacArthur, 1989; Wong et al., in press). Despite these formidable obstacles, growing evidence suggests that what and how these students write can be improved by teaching them relevant writing strategies emphasizing various aspects of planning.

In a study by Harris and Graham (1985), sixth-grade LD students were taught a prewriting strategy for generating specific types of words (action verbs, adjectives, and adverbs) to use in their stories via a self-instructional strategy training regime (see Table 8-3 for a description of the instructional procedures and Table 8-4 description of strategy). Students' self-regulation of the strategy was facilitated through the use of criterion goal-setting, self-monitoring procedures, and self-instructional statements designed to facilitate brainstorming, problem definition, self-evaluation, and self-reinforcement. Self-instructional strategy training increased the amount of content generated, the quality of text produced, and the types of words targeted for inclusion in the students' stories. Generalization to the students' classroom was also obtained, and treatment effects were maintained for up to 6 weeks. Nevertheless, on a probe administered 3½ months after training, the students remembered the strategy steps but failed to use the strategy when writing a story. A booster session likely would have returned performance rates to their previous posttraining levels.

Graham and Harris have also developed two additional prewriting strategies that basically involve using prefabricated genre frames to help students generate and organize notes and ideas. In the first study (Graham & Harris, 1989a), fifth- and sixth-grade LD students generated and organized notes before writing by responding to a series of sequential questions on basic components in common short stories (e.g., "Where does the story take place?"). The basic steps in the strategy are outlined in Table 8-5. While each student received instruction in the use of the strategy and supporting self-instructional statements, only half of the students were taught

TABLE 8.3. Overview of Self-instructional Strategy-training Procedures Used in Studies by Graham and Harris[a]

Pretraining: Develop to mastery any preskills considered necessary to the understanding, acquisition, or execution of the target strategy that are not already in the student's repertoire.

Review of current performance level: The instructor and student examine and discuss the students' current level of performance on baseline performance and any strategies the student currently uses. The significance and potential benefits of the proposed training are then discussed. Commitment by the student to participate as a partner and to attempt to learn and use the strategy is established. Furthermore, the goals of training are established in a positive, collaborative manner.

Description of the strategy: The instructor explicitly describes the strategy; the instructor and student discuss advantages of the strategy and how and why each step is used.

Modeling of the strategy and self-instructions: The instructor models the use of the strategy and supportive self-instructions (including problem definition, self-evaluation, coping and error correction, and self-reinforcement). After discussing the model's performance and each type of self-statement used, the student generates his or her own self-statements for each type of self-instruction. Instructor and student also collaborate on any changes that will make the strategy more effective or efficient.

Master of the strategy: Strategy steps are memorized and the student practices the self-instructions previously generated. Paraphrasing of the strategy steps is allowed as long as meaning remains intact.

Controlled practice of strategy steps and self-instructions: The student and instructor conjointly practice using the strategy and supporting self-instructional statements while performing the task. Procedures such as goal setting, self-monitoring, and self-reinforcement are discussed, selected, and used in order to promote self-regulation and maintenance of the strategy. Instructor guidance and physical prompts (such as strategy charts) are faded over practice sessions as the student independently reaches criterion and gradually assumes responsibility for recruiting, applying, and monitoring strategy. The student and instructor collaboratively evaluate the strategy and strategy acquisition procedures and make any resulting modifications throughout this step.

Independent performance: Transition to covert self-instructions is encouraged and student is directed to independently use the strategy. Self-regulation procedures can be continued at this point, and the instructor and student continue collaboratively to evaluate strategy effectiveness and student performance.

Generalization and maintenance: Throughout training, the student and instructor discuss opportunities to utilize the strategy and supporting self-instructions with other tasks and settings. In addition, students are encouraged to involve their teachers cooperatively, be prepared to use the strategy, and discuss opportunities for and instances of generalization with the instructor.

[a]Training is criterion-based rather than time-based, and training steps are flexible, recursive, and individualized as necessary.

TABLE 8-4. Vocabulary Enrichment Strategy

Strategy steps
1. Look at the picture and write down good action words (or describing words or action helpers).
2. Think of a good story idea to use my words in.
3. Write my story—make sense and use good action words.
4. Read my story and ask, Did I write a good story? Did I use good action words?
5. Fix my story—can I use more good action words?

Types of self-instructions
1. Problem definition (e.g., What is it I have to do?)
2. Planning (e.g. Think of new words for old ideas.)
3. Self-evaluation (e.g., Is that a good action word to use here?)
4. Self-reinforcement (e.g., I used good action words; I'm doing a great job.)

TABLE 8-5. Story Grammar Strategy

Questions on basic components of a story
  Who is the main character? Who else is in the story?
  When does the story take place?
  Where does the story take place?
  What does the main character want to do?
  What happens when he or she tries to do it?
  How does the story end?
  How does the main character feel?

The following mnemonic was used to represent the questions
  W–W–W
  What = 2
  How = 2

The mnemonic was embedded in a five-step executive writing strategy
1. Look at the picture (picture prompts were used).
2. Let your mind be free.
3. Write down the story part reminder (W–W–W; What = 2; How = 2).
4. Write down story part ideas for each part.
5. Write your own story. Use good parts and make sense.

to use goal-setting and self-monitoring procedures to support the use of the strategy. Training improved the quality and schematic structure of students' stories as well as students' self-efficacy in writing. Generalization to the students' classroom was also obtained, and treatment effects were maintained on a probe administered 2 weeks after training. However, the use of goal-setting and self-monitoring procedures did not have an additive effect on LD students' writing or self-efficacy. Although LD students trained to use the strategy were as effective in incorporating story elements into their writing as normally achieving students not receiving such training, quality ratings of their stories were lower. There was no difference, however, in the quality of stories developed by normally achieving students and LD students who received strategy instruction in a follow-up study (Sawyer, Graham, & Harris, 1989).

In a second study by Graham and Harris (1989c), sixth-grade LD students learned a strategy that directed the writer to consider who would read the text and the purpose for doing the assignment, plan the composition in advance through the use of text structure prompts (in this case, prompts for generating an essay), and continue the planning process by adding additional ideas and details while writing (see Table 8-6). Self-instructional strategy training resulted in the development of essays that were more complete, cohesive, longer, and qualitatively superior than essays written during baseline. The obtained effects were maintained over time and transfered to a new setting. Instruction in the strategy also had a positive effect on LD students' self-efficacy for writing. While some of the LD students did not generalize the use of the strategy to a second genre, story writing, an extra session in how to use a slightly modified version of the procedure resulted in the desired transfer. This session involved teaching students to use story relevant text structure prompts as part of the strategy.

Finally, in a study by Graham, MacArthur, Schwartz, and Voth (in press), LD students were taught a strategy that included setting product goals for what the paper would accomplish and articulating process goals for how the desired accomplishments would be achieved (see Table 8-7). The strategy also was designed to help the students structure the writing task into several related subproblems: (1) generate goals, (2) develop notes, (3) organize notes, (4) write and continue planning, and (5) evaluate success in obtaining goals. Following training, LD students' essays became more complete, longer, and qualitatively better. Treatment effects were maintained over time, and some of the students evidenced transfer to a second genre, story writing. A single practice session in using the strategy to write stories resulted in the desired generalization for the remaining stu-

TABLE 8-6. Three-Step Planning and Writing Strategy

Prompts on basic parts of an essay:
  Note your **T**opic sentence.
  Note **R**easons to support your topic sentence.
  Examine reasons. Will your reader buy each of them?
  Note **E**nding.
The mnemonic "TREE" was used to represent the prompts.

The mnemonic was embedded in a three-step executive writing strategy:
  1. Think who will read this, and why am I writing it?
  2. Plan what to say using TREE.
  3. Write and say more.

TABLE 8-7. PLANS Strategy

Prompts for planning a paper
  Pick goals (these include goals related to length, structure, and purpose of
    paper).
  List ways to meet goals.
  And,
  Make Notes.
  Sequence notes.
The mnemonic "PLANS" was used to represent the prompts.
The mnemonic was embedded in a three-step executive writing strategy
  1. Do PLANS.
  2. Write and say more.
  3. Evaluate if you were successful in achieving your goals.

---

dents. Changes in LD students' metacognitive knowledge and self-efficacy were also noted for some of the students.

Revising

Although the available evidence on LD students' revising behavior is limited (cf. MacArthur & Graham, 1987; MacArthur, Graham, & Schwartz, 1989), several observations can be made. First, LD students' basic outlook and approach to revising is to detect and correct mechanical errors (spelling and punctuation errors) and to make changes in individual words. Second, the types of changes that LD students make are not very effective. Specifically, their revising behavior does not appear to reduce the proportion of mechanical errors nor does it result in text that is either longer or of better overall quality. Third, revising may have a small but significant effect on the overall legibility of what LD students' write. While only a few studies have used cognitive–behavioral procedures as a mechanism for improving LD students' revising behaviors, results from these studies have been promising.

In a study by Graham and MacArthur (1988), fifth- and sixth-grade LD students were taught a strategy for revising essays while working on a word processor (see Table 8-8). The strategy included self-directed prompts for improving the clarity and cohesiveness of the writer's argument, adding relevant textual materials, and detecting and correcting mechanical errors. Students made more revisions and developed longer and qualitatively superior papers following self-instructional strategy training. Training effects were further maintained over time, and students were able to adapt the strategy successfully when composing with paper and pencil. Also there was a concomitant increase in LD students' confidence in their ability to write and revise.

TABLE 8-8. Essay Revision Strategy

Questions and prompts for revising individual sentences
  Does it make Sense?
  Is it Connected to my belief?
  Can I Add more?
  Note errors.

The mnemonic "SCAN" was used to represent the questions and prompts.

The mnemonic was embedded in a six-step executive revision strategy (students wrote on a computer)
  1. Read your essay.
  2. Find the sentence that tells what you believe. Is it clear?
  3. Add two reasons why you believe it.
  4. SCAN each sentence.
  5. Make changes on the computer.
  6. Reread the essay and make final changes.

Stoddard and MacArthur (1989) taught LD students in junior high school two strategies: one for initially editing a peer's paper primarily in terms of content, and another that focused on editing the peer's paper with regard to mechanics and grammar. During the study, the participating students both gave and received feedback to each other through the use of the two strategies. Self-instructional strategy training in the use of the strategies had a positive impact on both students' revising behaviors as well as on their written products.

SPECIFIC ISSUES IN COGNITIVE–BEHAVIORAL WRITING INTERVENTIONS

Is there differential effectiveness from cognitive–behavioral interventions in lower-order and higher-order cognitive processes of writing? The data from the relevant studies suggest that teaching formation of letters through cognitive–behavioral procedures may not be cost-effective in terms of time and instructional effort. The gains were small and restrictive (little transfer). In contrast, the research reviewed indicates that cognitive–behavioral procedures were effective in teaching LD students how to plan and revise. Clearly, the data here send a message on where cognitive–behavioral applications in writing are worthwhile research endeavors. Specifically, when the training is likely to produce a cognitive overload in the trainees, use of self-instructional cognitive–behavioral procedures may be counterproductive. Instead, use of direct instruction may be more appropriate. In skill areas where successful performance requires self-regulation and planfulness, use of cognitive–behavioral training procedures appears to be profitable.

There is also a need to investigate teachers' acceptability of the successful cognitive–behavioral procedures in teaching planning and revising. Further, potential obstacles to teacher implementation of these effective self-instructional procedures should be researched, including social-contextual variables that may promote or impede use of those procedures by teachers and students.

How can cognitive–behavioral procedures for teaching writing be successfully incorporated into writing programs that exist in the classrooms? Currently, many teachers embrace the writing process approach. This approach emphasizes providing students with opportunities for sustained writing, student choice in topic selection, sharing of text and audience response, teacher modeling of the writing process, and student ownership of text. It would be useful to investigate the feasibility of integrating effective cognitive–behavioral writing procedures with a process writing approach. Elsewhere, Graham and Harris (1989b) have suggested that cognitive–behavioral procedures not supplant traditional writing pedagogy, but be incorporated with the existing programs.

Finally, if we want LD students to use learned writing strategies over time and adaptively, we must attend closely to what they have internalized as a result of instruction, and to the issue of determining how we may best promote their maintenance and generalization of learned strategies in writing.

MATHEMATICS

Mathematical Skills

The effective use of cognitive–behavioral procedures to enhance mathematical skills in children, mentally retarded and learning-disabled children has been amply demonstrated by Leon and Pepe (1983), Whitman and Johnston (1983), Johnston and Whitman (1987), Keogh, Whitman, and Maxwell (1988) and Van Luit and Van Der Aalsvoort (1985). Of these, more programmatic research appears to have been produced by Whitman and his associates. We shall describe the study by Keogh et al. (1988) because it contains a clear rationale for using self-instructional procedures with the mentally retarded and because it examined variables associated with individual differences. Although this study involved mentally retarded children, its training procedure and findings apply equally to LD students.

Keogh et al. (1988) used cognitive–behavioral procedures to teach nonretarded first graders and mentally retarded students addition with regrouping. An important aspect of this study concerns the examination of the respective roles of prior knowledge in mathematics, language proficiency, and attributional style in the trainees' posttest performance. Additionally, the self-instructional approach was pitted against the typical classroom instructional approach (external-didactic teaching), which provided ecological validity to the study. The use of immediate posttests, maintenance and transfer tests ensured the study's meeting stringent criteria for a good intervention study (Campione & Brown, 1977).

Specifically, Keogh et al.'s study involved 38 first graders and 16 mentally retarded children. (The retardates ranged in ages between 8.5 to 12.67 y, with a mean of 10.58.) The subjects were randomly allocated to either the self-instructional or external-didactic training conditions. Pretraining assessments were taken on their math knowledge, language skills, and attributional styles. Subsequently, the children were taught math skills in addition with regrouping in the instructional mode to which they were assigned. Training was done in a group and lasted for 7 days, with a 30-minute session per day. Two features of the training phase deserve mention. First, the teaching scripts for the two instructional conditions matched closely except for variations which accommodated the differences in instructional mode. Secondly, toward the end of training (on the sixth day), the children in the self-instructional condition were asked to think aloud the strategy. This assessment through thinking-aloud provided the experimenters a check on their mastery of it, and a means to investigate whether degree of strategy verbalization could predict trainees' posttest performance. Indeed, they found that trainees' ability to articulate the self-instructional strategy correlated positively with their posttest performance.

The results in math accuracy scores from both within-group and between-group comparisons indicated clearly that the mentally retarded children benefited substantially more from self-instructional training than external-didactic training. In contrast, the two instructional modes did not have appreciably differential effects on posttest performance of the nonretarded first graders. Moreover, the immediate posttest results indicated that mentally retarded children benefited from self-instructional but not external-didactic training. The reverse was obtained with the nonretarded first graders. Similar results were obtained on the second dependent measure of number of problems solved.

Prior knowledge in mathematics played an important role in predicting children's math accuracy at posttest and maintenance. It also showed similar predictive power at their transfer assessment during training but not at posttraining transfer. Interestingly, language proficiency and attributional style had nonsignificant predictive power regarding the children's posttraining math performance. Keogh et al. suggested that possibly the range of the subjects' linguistic skills was too restricted to test the link between linguistic ability and the efficacy of the intervention conditions. Alternatively, the measurement tool used (Peabody Picture Vocabulary Test) was inadequate.

Keogh et al.'s (1988) findings accrue to the empirical base of using cognitive–behavioral procedures successfully to enhance math skills in children. More important, the findings suggest that self-instructional procedures may profit *more* subjects who have not developed sufficiently self-regulations, such as mental retardates, younger children, and learning-disabled children.

SPECIFIC ISSUES IN COGNITIVE–BEHAVIOR-BASED MATH INTERVENTIONS

The research here shares two attributes with that in reading comprehension. First, the use of cognitive–behavioral instructional procedures in both academic domains produced superior results than those involving the use of didactic instruction. Secondly, more research studies are needed in math interventions to expand the empirical base.

The self-instructional procedures in the reported studies, of necessity, focused on teaching the children correct ways to add or subtract. The targeted skills are more straightforward than, say, fractions. In developing cognitive–behavioral procedures for more complicated math skills, perhaps the researcher would need to ensure that the children/adolescents do not lose sight of what the numerical symbols mean in terms of the quantitative referents. Resnick put it succinctly,

> When one is working with the language of mathematics, one does not automatically think about the quantities and relationships that are referenced. What is more, school instruction probably tends to aggravate this tendency for the formal language of mathematics to function independently of its referents. The focus in elementary school is on correct ways to perform procedures, a focus largely detached from reflection on the quantities and relationships to which symbolic expressions refer. (1987, p. 45)

Clearly, Resnick's words pertain importantly to intervention research on math skills, be it based on cognitive–behavioral procedures or others.

A Cognitive–Behavioral Coping Strategy for Reducing Mathematics Anxiety

Some children and adolescents fare poorly in mathematics in school; they may experience substantial math anxiety in general, and at math tests in particular. Clearly, this area is one where the application of a cognitive–behavioral coping strategy presents an attractive intervention approach. Kamann (1989) took up that challenge; in an interesting study, he effectively ameliorated math anxiety in learning-disabled children with a cognitive–behavioral-based coping strategy. The math performance of these children was crippled by their math anxiety, which was manifested in their spontaneous generations of negative self-statements. Because these negative self-statements interfered with the children's math performance, Kamann focused on changing them into positive self-statements which would enhance their math performance. The steps of his coping strategy are laid out in Table 8-9. They directed the children to assess the situation, to recognize and control the surge of habitual negative thoughts, and replace them with positive thoughts. The last step of the strategy instructs the children to apply self-reinforcement. To facilitate learning of the strategy steps, the children were given two prompt cards. The first essentially cued them on the three basic strategy steps. The second provided examples of self-statements to instantiate (flesh out) the strategy steps. Table 8-9 presents the second prompt card.

Prior to strategy training, the children were provided with an oral and visual presentation on the role of self-talk in maintaining poor academic performance. This presentation served two purposes. First, it made the children aware of their own maladaptive style of thinking. Second, it paved the way for the coping strategy training.

The instructional procedure of the cognitive–behavioral coping strategy was one of informed training (Brown & Palincsar, 1982). Kamann informed the children of the training goals, which included: enhancement of their math performance, coping with math anxiety, and ample practice in using the coping strategy on actual math tests. The children were given opportunities to ask questions about the goals and the training procedures.

TABLE 8-9. Coping Self-statements

Assessment of the situation
    What is it that I have to do?
    Look over the task and think about how I will work through it.

Recognizing and controlling negative thoughts
    Recognizing
    Okay I feel worried and scared . . . I'm saying things that don't help . . . I
        can stop and think more helpful thoughts.
    Controlling
    Don't worry, remember to use your plan.
    Take it step by step—look at one question at a time.
    Don't let your eyes wander to other questions.
    When you feel fear coming on . . . take a deep breath, and think I am doing
        just fine . . . things are going well.
    I can do this, think through the questions and do your best.

Reinforcing
    I did really well in not letting this get the best of me. Good for me I did a good
        job.
    I did a good job in not allowing myself to worry so much.

Note: Reproduced with permission from M. Kamann.

Ten learning-disabled children were trained to use the cognitive–behavioral coping strategy. Of these, six were males (two from grade four, three from grade five, and one from grade six). The four females comprised one from grade four, one from grade six, and two from grade seven. There were a total of six training sessions, each lasting 40 minutes.

The results indicated that the cognitive–behavioral coping strategy increased positive self-talk *and* math performance in the children with LD. Although their actual amount of self-talk did not differ appreciably from that of their normally achieving peers, substantial differences in the quality of self-talk among them were obtained. Subsequent to training in the coping strategy, the nature of self-statements in children with LD changed from negative to being positive. Moreover, these children's accuracy in mathematics tasks (tests) increased reliably and consistently across two sets of pretests and posttests. There was a 3-week interval between administration of the first and second sets of pre- and posttests. Thus, the second set of pre- and posttests were really maintenance tests. It is significant that the reliable differences in the first set of pre- and posttests were maintained after a delay of 3 weeks. This finding highlights the durability of the training effects of the coping strategy on the learning-disabled children's math performance. More important, their substantial gains in mathematics tasks were found to correlate with their increases in positive self-talk.

Kamann's study is important because it is the first to apply a cognitive–behavioral coping strategy to reduce math anxiety in children with LD. His data clearly indicated the effectiveness of the strategy. Because children who fail in mathematics typically associate math tasks/tests with much negative affect and anxiety, Kamann's findings point to the need to include training in anxiety coping in effective remediation of math problems.

GENERAL ISSUES IN ACADEMIC APPLICATION OF COGNITIVE–BEHAVIOR MODIFICATION PROCEDURES

Research and intervention procedures for academic applications of cognitive–behavioral strategies with learning-disabled students have been examined. The results of research suggest the efficacy of cognitive–behavioral procedures in enhancing academic performance in those students. Recall that when the use of self-instructional procedures was first considered with learning-disabled students, Meichenbaum (1980) cautioned that until intervention efficacy is demonstrated and passes the crucible of maintenance and transfer tests, the intended use of cognitive–behavioral procedures with those students remains "a promise yet to be fulfilled." In light of the research reported in our chapter, we can say with measured confidence that the promise of cognitive–behavioral procedures with learning-disabled students is partly fulfilled.

It seems appropriate to us to conclude our chapter with some thoughts on certain issues in academic applications of cognitive–behavioral procedures with LD students, which affect our intervention and research in this area. We will not traverse old grounds such as language skills in trainees, prior knowledge or the time factor in cognitive–behavioral training (Wong, 1985). Rather we shall consider fresh issues.

There is a general issue that applies to all strategy intervention research. At present, strategy instruction involving various procedures, cognitive–behavioral, interactive learning, and so on, involve tasks that present explicit task demands. The explicitness in task demands enables researchers to develop component steps in the learning strategies that match those demands. However, in school and in real-life situations, learning and problem solving often involve ambiguities (Howard, 1989). Thus, strategy intervention researchers must expand their sphere of research and consider teaching strategies that include or cover ambiguities in school tasks and problem-solving situations.

Second, cognitive–behavioral strategies often seem to lack a metacognitive wrap-up on teaching students to reflect on the usefulness of the learned strategy (Keogh et al., 1988). However, many researchers begin the cognitive–behavioral training with a metacognitive orientation or rationale (see Harris & Graham for an example). Nevertheless, a metacognitive step at the end of cognitive–behavioral training is important because it would promote strategy maintenance and transfer. For example, at the end of strategy application and self-reinforcement, self-instructional steps such as the following may be added: "Let me stop and think how using this strategy has helped me." "If I figure that out, then I'd know better when I can use it again and do well!" When students contemplate and realize the usefulness of a learned strategy, they are likely to transfer its use.

FUTURE DIRECTIONS IN ACADEMIC APPLICATIONS OF COGNITIVE–BEHAVIOR MODIFICATION PROCEDURES

There seems to be a consistent interest in research on academic applications of cognitive–behavioral strategies with learning-disabled and mentally retarded students. This is borne out by the sustained and programmatic research by Whitman and his associates in math skills, by Harris and Graham in writing, and by Wong and her students in reading comprehension and math anxiety, and others whose work we have cited. But we need to do *more* research so that we can amass a sufficient data base for meta-analyses to be performed, which will calibrate the efficacy of our training procedures within each academic domain.

Moreover, we need to engage in component analyses research to pinpoint the relative contributions of training components in the cognitive–behavioral strategies devised by us. Some nascent attempts at component research have been reported (cf. Elliott–Faust & Pressley, 1986; Pressley, Forrest–Pressley, & Elliott–Faust, in press; Graham & Harris, 1989a; Sawyer et al., 1989). While a great deal more research needs to be done, initial studies indicate that necessary and sufficient academic intervention components may not be the only issue; characteristics of cognitive–behaviorally based instruction in academic areas (i.e., criterion-based rather than time-based instruction, active learner collaboration, etc.) may also need to be considered (Graham & Harris, 1989b).

Lastly, cognitive–behavioral applications might extend to encompass affect that bears on students' academic learning and performance. We have in mind, affective states such as inappropriate attributions, lack of task persistence (low frustration tolerance of task difficulty), test anxiety, writing blocks, stage fright, and anxiety in public speaking. Clearly, researchers should expand the frontier of cognitive–behavioral applications into these affective areas. Otherwise, we will shut out important areas of research and practice and inadvertently undermine successful applications of cognitive–behavioral procedures in school settings. Worse still, we would succumb to Zajonc's (1980) criticism for focusing our interventions only on cold cognition! Zajonc criticized cognitive psychologists for neglecting the role of affect in cognition in their research. He argued cogently how affect plays a distinctive and decisive role in thinking. Heeding his call, we encourage and support a move to include affective areas/factors in cognitive–behavioral research.

ACKNOWLEDGMENTS

We thank Mrs. Eileen Mallory for cheerfully word-processing the various drafts of this chapter.

REFERENCES

Ames, C., & Archer, J. (1988). Achievement goals in the classroom: Students' learning strategies and motivation processes. *Journal of Educational Psychology, 80,* 260–267.

Anderson–Inman, L., Paine, S., & Deutchman, L. (1984). Neatness counts: Effects of direct instruction and self-monitoring on the transfer of neat-paper skills to nontraining settings. *Analysis and Intervention in Developmental Disabilities, 4,* 137–155.

Blandford, B., & Lloyd, J. (1987). Effects of a self-instructional procedure on handwriting. *Journal of Learning Disabilities, 20,* 342–346.

Bommarito, J., & Meichenbaum, D. (1978). *Enhancing reading comprehension by means of self-instructional training.* Unpublished manuscript, University of Waterloo, Ontario.

Brown, A. L., Campione, J. C., & Day, J. D. (1981). Learning to learn: On training students to learn from texts. *Educational Researcher, 10,* 14–21.

Brown, A., & Palincsar, A. (1982). Inducing strategies learning from texts by means of informed, self-control training. In B. Y. L. Wong (Ed.), *Metacognition and Learning Disabilities. Topics in Learning and Learning Disabilities, 2,* 1–17.

Campione, J. C., & Brown, A. L. (1977). Memory and metamemory development in educable retarded children. In R. V. Kail, Jr., & J. W. Hagen (Eds.), *Perspectives on the development of memory and cognition,* (pp. 367–406). New York: Erlbaum.

Elliott–Faust, D. J., & Pressley, M. (1986). How to teach comparison processing to increase children's short- and long-term listening comprehension monitoring. *Journal of Educational Psychology, 78*(1), 27–33.

Englert, C., Raphael, T., Fear, K., & Anderson, L. (1988). Students' metacognitive knowledge about how to write informational texts. *Learning Disability Quarterly, 11,* 18–46.

Flower, L., & Hayes, J. (1980). The dynamics of composing: Making plans and juggling constraints. In L. Gregg & E. Steinberg (Eds.), *Cognitive processes in writing* (pp. 31–50). Hillsdale, NJ: Erlbaum.

Garner, R., & Alexander, P. A. (1989). Metacognition: Answered and unanswered questions. *Educational Psychologist, 24*(2), 143–158.

Garner, R., Hare, V. C., Alexander, P., Haynes, J., & Winograd, P. (1984). Inducing use of a text lookback strategy among unsuccessful readers. *American Educational Research Journal, 21,* 789–798.

Graham, L. (1986). *The comparative effectiveness of didactic teaching and self-instructional training of a question-answering strategy in enhanced reading comprehension.* Unpublished master's thesis, Simon Fraser University, Burnaby, British Columbia, Canada.

Graham, S. (1982). Composition research and practice. A unified approach. *Focus on Exceptional Children, 14,* 1–16.

Graham, S. (1983a). The effects of self-instructional procedures on LD students' handwriting performance. *Learning Disability Quarterly, 6,* 231–234.

Graham, S. (1983b). Effective spelling instruction. *Elementary School Journal, 83,* 560–568.

Graham, S. (1989, April). *The role of production factors in learning disabled students' compositions.* Paper presented at the Annual meeting of the American Educational Research Association, San Francisco.

Graham, S., Boyer–Shick, K., & Tippets, E. (1989). The validity of the handwriting scale from the Test of Written Language. *Journal of Educational Research, 82,* 166–171.

Graham, S., & Harris, K. R. (1987). Improving composition skills of inefficient learners with self-instructional strategy training. *Topics in Language Disorders, 7,* 66–77.

Graham, S., & Harris, K. R. (1988). Instructional recommendations for teaching writing to exceptional students. *Exceptional Children, 54,* 506–512.

Graham, S., & Harris, K. R. (1989a). A components analysis of cognitive strategy instruction: Effects on learning disabled students' compositions and self-efficacy. *Journal of Educational Psychology, 81,* 353–361.

Graham, S., & Harris, K. R. (1989b). Cognitive training: Implications for written language. In J. Hughes & R. Hall (Eds.), *Cognitive-behavioral psychology in the schools: A comprehensive handbook* (pp. 247–279). New York: Guilford Press.

Graham, S., & Harris, K. R. (1989c). Improving learning-disabled students' skills at composing essays: Self-instructional strategy training. *Exceptional Children, 56,* 201–214.

Graham, S., & Harris, K. R. (in press). Cognitive strategy instruction in written language for learning disabled students. In S. Vogel & B. Levinson (Eds.), *Effective intervention for the learning disabled.* New York: Springer-Verlag.

Graham, S., Harris, K. R., & Sawyer, R. (1987). Composition instruction with learning disabled students: Self-instructional strategy training. *Focus on Exceptional Children, 20*(4), 1–11.

Graham, S., & MacArthur, C. (1988). Improving learning disabled students' skills at revising essays produced on a word processor: Self-instructional strategy training. *Journal of Special Education, 22,* 133–152.

Graham, S., MacArthur, C., Schwartz, S., & Voth, T. (in press). *Improving LD student's compositions using a strategy involving product and process goal-setting. Journal of Educational Psychology.*

Graham, S., & Miller, L. (1979). Spelling research and practice: A unified approach. *Focus on Exceptional Children, 12,* 1–16.

Graham, S., Schwartz, S., & MacArthur, C. (in press). *Learning disabled and normally achieving students' knowledge of the writing process. Exceptional Children.*

Graves, A. W. (1986). Effects of direct instruction and metacomprehension on finding main ideas. *Learning Disability Research, 1,* 90–100.

Hallahan, D. P., Lloyd, J. W., Kauffman, J. M., & Loper, A. (1983). Academic problems. In R. J. Morris & T. R. Kratochwell (Eds.), *Practice of child therapy: A textbook of methods* (pp. 113–141). New York: Pergamon Press.

Hallahan, D. P., Lloyd, J. W., Kosiewicz, M., Kauffman, J. M., & Graves, A. (1979). Self-monitoring of attention as a treatment for a learning disabled boy's off-task behavior. *Learning Disability Quarterly, 2,* 24–32.

Hallahan, D. P., & Reeve, R. E. (1980). Selective attention and distractability. In B. K. Keogh (Ed.), *Advances in special education: Basic constructs and theoretical orientations* (Vol. 1, pp. 84–107). Greenwich, CN: JAI Press.

Harris, K. R. (1982). Cognitive–behavior modification: Application with exceptional students. *Focus on Exceptional Children, 15*(2), 1–16.

Harris, K. R. (1985). Conceptual, methodological, and clinical issues in cognitive behavioral assessment. *Journal of Abnormal Child Psychology, 13,* 373–390.

Harris, K. R. (1986a). The effects of cognitive–behavior modification on private speech and task performance during problem solving among learning disabled and normally achieving children. *Journal of Abnormal Child Psychology, 14,* 63–67.

Harris, K. R. (1986b). Self-monitoring of attentional behavior versus self-monitoring of productivity: Effects on on-task behavior and academic response rate among learning disabled children. *Journal of Applied Behavior Analysis, 19,* 417–423.

Harris, K. R., & Graham, S. (1975). Improving learning disabled students' composition skills: Self-control strategy training. *Learning Disability Quarterly, 8,* 27–36.

Harris, K., & Graham, S. (1985). Improving learning-disabled students' composition skills: Self-control strategy training. *Learning Disability Quarterly, 8,* 27–36.

Hobbs, S. A., Moguin, L. E., Tyroler, M., & Lahey, B. B. (1980). Cognitive behavior therapy with children: Has clinical utility been demonstrated? *Psychological Bulletin, 87,* 147–165.

Howard, Dawn C. (1989). *Variations in cognitive engagement as indicators of self-regulated learning.* Unpublished doctoral thesis, Simon Fraser University, Burnaby, British Columbia, Canada.

Hughes, J. N., & Hall R. J. (Eds.). (1989). *Cognitive–behavioral psychology in the schools: A comprehensive handbook.* New York: Guilford Press.

Johnston, M. B., & Whitman, T. (1987). Enhancing math computation through variations in training format and instructional content. *Cognitive Therapy and Research, 11*(3), 381–397.

Kamann, M. P. (1989). *Inducing adaptive coping self-statements in the learning-disabled through a cognitive behavioral intervention.* Unpublished master's thesis, Simon Fraser University, Burnaby, British Columbia, Canada.

Kapadia, S., & Fantuzzo, J. (1988). Effects of teacher- and self-administered procedures on the spelling performance of learning-handicapped children. *Journal of School Psychology, 26,* 49–58.

Keogh, D. A., Whitman, T. L., & Maxwell, S. E. (1988). Self-instruction versus external instruction: Individual differences and training effectiveness. *Cognitive Therapy and Research, 12*(6), 591–610.

Kosiewicz, M., Hallahan, D., & Lloyd, J. (1981). The effects of an LD student's treatment choice on handwriting performance. *Learning Disability Quarterly, 4,* 278–286.

Kosiewicz, M., Hallahan, D., Lloyd, J., & Graves, A. (1982). Effects of self-instruction and self-correction procedures on handwriting performance. *Learning Disability Quarterly, 5,* 71–81.

Leon, J. A., & Pepe, H. J. (1983). Self-instructional training: Cognitive behavior modification for remediating arithmetic deficits. *Exceptional Children, 50,* 54–60.

Licht, B. G., & Kistner, J. A. (1986). Motivational problems of learning-disabled children: Individual differences and their implications for treatment. In J. K. Torgesen & B. Y. L. Wong (Eds.), *Psychological and educational perspectives on learning disabilities.* New York: Academic Press, (pp. 225–255).

MacArthur, C., & Graham, S. (1987). Learning disabled students' composing with three methods: Handwriting, dictation, and word processing. *Journal of Special Education, 21,* 22–42.

MacArthur, C., Graham, S., & Schwartz, S. (1989). *Knowledge of revision and revising behavior among learning disabled students.* Manuscript submitted for publication.

Meichenbaum, D. (1977). *Cognitive behavior modification: An integrative approach.* New York: Plenum Press.

Meichenbaum, D. (1980). Cognitive behavior modification with exceptional children: A promise yet unfulfilled. *Exceptional Education Quarterly, 1,* 83–88.

Moran, M. (1981). *A comparison of formal features of written language of learning disabled, low-achieving and achieving secondary students* (Research Report No. 34). Lawarence: University of Kansas Institute for Research in Learning Disabilities.

Orsetti, M. E. (1985). *An error-monitoring strategy for teaching spelling.* Unpublished master's thesis, Simon Fraser University, Buruaby, British Columbia, Canada.

Palinscar, A., & Brown, A. L. (1984). Reciprocal teaching of comprehension-fostering and comprehension-monitoring activities. *Cognition and Instruction, 1*(2), 117–175.

Paris, S. C., Cross, D. R., & Lipson, M. Y. (1984). Informed strategies for learning: A program to improve children's reading awareness and comprehension. *Journal of Educational Psychology, 76,* 1239–1252.

Pearl, R. (1985). Cognitive–behavioral interventions for increasing motivation. *Journal of Abnormal Child Psychology, 13,* 443–454.

Poteet, J. (1979). Characteristics of written expression of learning disabled and non-learning disabled elementary school students. *Diagnostique, 4,* 60–74.

Pressley, M., Forrest–Pressley, D., & Elliott–Faust, D. J. (in press). How to study instructional enrichment: Illustrations from research on childrens' prose memory and comprehension. In F. Weinert & M. Perlmutter (Eds.), *Memory development: Universal changes and individual development.* Hillsdale, NJ: Erlbaum.

Pressley, M., & Levin, J. R. (1986). Elaborative learning strategies for the inefficient learner. In S. J. Ceci (Ed.), *Handbook of cognitive, social, and neuropsychological aspects of learning disabilities* (pp. 175–211). Hillsdale, NJ: Erlbaum.

Raphael, T. E. (1985). *Teaching question–answer relationships, revisited.* Paper presented at the International Reading Association conference, New Orleans.

Raphael, T. E., & McKinney, J. (1983). *A developmental examination of children's question-answering behavior: An instructional study in metacognition.* Paper presented at the National Reading Conference, Clearwater, FL.

Resnick, L. B. (1987). Constructing knowledge in school. In L. S. Liben (Ed.), *Development and learning: Conflict or congruence?* (pp. 19–50). New Jersey: Erlbaum.

Robin, A. L., Armel, S., & O'Leary, D. K. (1975). The effects of self-instruction on writing deficiencies. *Behavior Therapy, 6,* 178–187.

Sawyer, R., Graham, S., & Harris, K. R. (1989). [Improving learning disabled students' composition skills with story grammar strategy training: A further components analysis of self-instructional strategy training]. Unpublished raw data.

Short, E. J. (1981). *A self-instructional approach to remediating the use of schematic knowledge, causal attributions, and task persisttence of less skilled readers.* Unpublished doctoral dissertation, University of Notre Dame, South Bend, IN.

Stoddard, B., & MacArthur, C. (1989). [Teaching LD students to revise their writing: A word processing and peer editing strategy training approach]. Unpublished raw data.

Torgesen, J. K. (1980). Conceptual and educational implications of the use of efficient task strategies by learning disabled children. *Journal of Learning Disabilities, 13,* 19–26.

Torgesen, J. K., & Kail, R. V. (1980). Memory processes in exceptional children.

In B. K. Keogh (Ed.), *Advances in special education* (Vol. 1, pp. 50–83). Greenwich, CN: JAI Press.

Van Luit, J. E. H., & Van Der Aalsvoort, G. M. (1985). Learning subtraction in a special school: A self-instructional strategy for educable mentally retarded children with arithmetic deficits. *Instructional Science, 14,* 179–189.

Whitman, M. B., & Johnston, M. (1983). Teaching addition and subtraction with regrouping to EMR children: A group self-instructional training program. *Behavior Therapy, 14,* 127–143.

Wong, B. Y. L. (1980). Activating the inactive learner: Use of questions/prompts to enhance comprehension and retention of implied information in learning-disabled children. *Learning Disability Quarterly, 3,* 29–37.

Wong, B. Y. L. (1985). Issues in cognitive–behavioral interventions in academic skill areas. *Journal of Abnormal Child Psychology, 13,* 425–442.

Wong, B. Y. L., & Jones, W. (1982). Increasing metacomprehension in learning-disabled and normally-achieving students through self-questioning training. *Learning Disability Quarterly, 5,* 228–240.

Wong, B., Wong, R., & Blenkisop, J. (1989). Cognitive and metacognitive aspects of learning-disabled adolescents' composing problems. *Learning Disability Quarterly, 12*(4), 300–322.

Zajonic, R. B. (1980). Feeling and thinking: Preferences need no inferences. *American Psychologist, 35,* 151–175.

C H A P T E R   9

Cognitive Instruction and Mental Retardation

THOMAS L. WHITMAN, MARY F. SCHERZINGER, AND
KRISTEN S. SOMMER
University of Notre Dame

This history of the care, treatment, and education of persons with mental
retardation has fluctuated from an atmosphere of ridicule and neglect to
one of compassionate concern and structured treatment (Rosen, Clark, &
Kivitz, 1976; Sarason & Doris, 1969). Prior to the 19th century, conceptions about mental retardation were primitive, with mentally retarded persons being perceived variously as fools, monsters, immoral creatures or special children of God. Gradually, a more optimistic, as well as a more scientific,
attitude began to prevail as systematic training programs were developed
by individuals such as Jean Itard and Edward Sequin in France. By the end
of the 19th century, educational programs for persons with mental retardation had begun to be actively established in the United States. Since that
time, support for and commitment to habilitation programs has been inconsistent.

During the early decades of the 20th century, a custodial-care orientation developed in residential institutions and a pessimism concerning the
utility of "special" educational programs evolved, influenced by a social-
Darwinist philosophy and biological conceptions of intelligence. In the 1950s
and 1960s, a growing concern for the plight of mentally retarded persons
was catalyzed as a result of parent movements, the emergence of the National Association for Retarded Children (NARC), a change in the ethical,
legal, and political climate, and the introduction of new educational techniques. As a consequence of the behavior modification movement, new and
effective training procedures were initiated in institutions in the 1960s and
1970s (Whitman, Scibak, & Reid, 1983). More recently, with the emergence of a cognitive paradigm, systematic cognitive instructional programs
have begun to be developed in community settings (Reid, 1988).

In the initial sections of this chapter, definitions and theories describing the nature of mental retardation, and procedures for assessing mental

retardation will be briefly reviewed. Then the major cognitive–behavioral techniques employed with children with mental retardation will be reviewed at length. Examples of specific applied research programs will be presented. Finally, the cognitive–instructional process with mentally retarded children will be analyzed from a theoretical perspective. It will be proposed that in order to achieve maintenance and generalization of skills with this population, systematic attention needs to be given to the development of a self-regulated response system.

DEFINITIONS AND THEORIES OF MENTAL RETARDATION

Although cognitive–behavioral conceptualizations have only begun to influence systematically the structure of educational programs for children with mental retardation, this perspective has been reflected for some time in both definitions and theories of mental retardation. Early definitions of mental retardation emphasize the difficulties of mentally retarded individuals in adapting to their environment (Doll, 1941; Kanner, 1957; Tredgold, 1937) and typically relate these adaptation problem to a mental deficiency. Recent definitions stress that both intellectual and behavioral deficiencies must be present in order for mental retardation to be diagnosed. The current definition put forth by the American Association on Mental Retardation defines mental retardation as "significantly subaverage general intellectual functioning existing concurrently with deficits in adaptive behavior and manifested during the developmental period" (Grossman, 1983, p. 11). Even though there is a consensus concerning how mental retardation should be defined, there is a considerable difference of opinion regarding the nature of the deficiencies which are associated with and produce the cognitive and behavioral deficits in mentally retarded persons.

Within a behavioral framework, the development of mental retardation is associated with environmental conditions, including: a restricted physical stimulus environment, inappropriate reinforcement patterns, a history of aversive experiences, and absence of appropriate models (Bijou, 1966). Zigler and Balla (1982) also emphasize the importance of social–environmental influences, in particular, the role of social deprivation. Social deprivation includes such factors "as a lack of continuity of care by parents or other caretakers, an excessive desire by parents to institutionalize their child, impoverished economic circumstances, and a family history of marital discord, mental illness, abuse and/or neglect" (Zigler & Balla, 1982, p. 11).

From a cognitive perspective, a wide variety of cognitive defects and problems have been proposed to account for the deficiencies of persons with mental retardation. These characteristics include: smaller memory capacities, inefficient working memory processes, small and disorganized knowledge bases, limited and passive encoding strategies, metacognitive deficiencies, and poorly developed executive processes for controlling thinking (see Butterfield & Ferretti, 1987, for a discussion of these characteristics). There are a variety of opinions regarding the relative role which genetic–organic and environmental factors play in producing these cognitive deficiencies (Zigler & Balla, 1982). Campione and Brown (1978), in their theory of intelligence, describe two interacting systems that affect complex cognitive functioning, a biologically based architectual system, which influences efficiency and speed of processing, and an environmentally developed system, which controls retrieval of knowledge from long-term memory. A variety of theories, emphasizing one or both of these systems, have been put forth in the last several decades.

For example, Jensen (1982) links low intelligence to neuronal conduction problems. Based on their reviews of research, Maisto and Baumeister (1984) and Sperber and McCauley (1984) conclude that mentally retarded persons have a central processing (encoding) deficiency. Zeaman and House (1963) and Fisher and Zeaman (1973) suggest that mentally retarded individuals are limited in their information-processing capacity and are less selective about the information they process. Ellis (1970) views mentally retarded persons as having a short-term memory problem that is due to a failure to use active rehearsal strategies. In contrast, Spitz (1973) hypothesizes that the mentally retarded learner's deficiency is due to an organizational problem; specifically, stimulus input is not organized as it enters into storage, with the consequence that retrieval of information from storage is limited. Brewer (1987) suggests that the slow performance of mentally retarded persons on perceptual–motor tasks may be mediated by their inability to "pool past experiences." Torgeson, Kistner, and Morgan (1987) characterize mentally retarded persons as scanning more slowly their working memory and as having a general difficulty in selecting and applying efficient strategies in memory task situations and encoding verbal information.

In contrast to these more basic process theories, McFarland and Wiebe (1987) emphasize that the memory and problem-solving deficiencies of mentally retarded persons are influenced by the content of their knowledge base with is less elaborated. Borkowski and Kurtz (1987) argue, however, that although mentally retarded children vary in their specific knowledge (e.g., knowledge about particular problem-solving strategies), their inefficient learning is due to deficits in their general strategy knowledge and metamemory acquisition systems. General strategy knowledge refers to an individual's recognition that strategical and effortful behavior is important for successful performance. The metamemory acquisition system consists of procedures which influence and guide the successful employment of specific strategical knowledge; more specifically, it includes higher-order skills, such as making decisions concerning how and when to use strategies and knowing about the importance of checking and monitoring during strategy deployment. Finally, a number of theorists (Borkowski & Kurtz, 1987; Zigler & Balla, 1982) have pointed out the importance of attributional factors, suggesting that mentally retarded individuals, due to a history of failure, lower their expectancies about future success. At present, although the relationships among a history of failure, attributional orientation, and achievement outcomes are not entirely clear (Covington, 1987), there is some optimism concerning the performance benefits which might be produced by attributional enhancement programs (Borkowski & Kurtz, 1987).

In general, disagreements between theorists regarding the nature of mentally retarded persons are related to which of their deficiencies are primary. Butterfield and Ferretti (1987) stress that mentally retarded individuals differ from nonretarded individuals in many ways: in their base knowledge (information about things), strategies (procedures for processing base knowledge), metacognitive understanding (information about one's base knowledge, strategical repertoire and their relationships) and executive routines (procedures for evaluating, enacting, and monitoring strategy implementation). They emphasize, however, that our present knowledge concerning how these factors interact and specifically distinguish persons of low and higher intelligence is limited. Sternberg (1987) speculates, however, that mentally retarded persons are primarily retarded because of their metacomponential deficiencies, which includes what Butterfield and Ferretti (1987) refer to as metacognitive understanding and executive routines. Because empirical tests of many of the aforementioned theories are only beginning, it is unlikely that any one theory of mental retardation will quickly gain wide acceptance. Moreover, it seems probable, because considerable individual differences exist among mentally retarded persons, that different theories may be needed to explain their deficiencies.*

ASSESSMENT OF MENTAL RETARDATION

Because mental retardation has been defined by the presence of both cognitive and behavior deficiencies, it is not surprising that assessment techniques have been developed to evaluate both of these types of deficiencies. Historically, cognitive, specifically intellectual, assessment procedures evolved first. In 1904, Alfred Binet developed a tests to screen children in order to determine if they were at risk for failure in regular educational programs and required placement in a special educational arrangement. Subsequently, intelligence tests have been used successfully to predict school performance and to identify individuals who will benefit from special edu-

---

*For further information concerning theories of mental retardation, the reader is referred to edited books by Ellis (1963, 1979), Brooks, Sperber and McCauley (1984), Borkowski and Day (1987) and Day and Borkowski (1987).

cational placements (see Barrett & Breuning, 1983). There is, however, widespread agreement that intelligence tests do not measure ability to learn in specific situations, provide very useful instructional information about what and how to teach, or reflect changing conceptions about the nature of intelligence. Robinson and Janos (1987) point out that the "major intelligence tests have major limitations" (p. 43).

In contrast to traditional intelligence tests, behavioral assessments, including a variety of adaptive behavior scales and specific behavior evaluation procedures, are of more recent vintage and have been more useful in developing individualized educational programs. For example, behavioral assessment procedures have provided information to teachers concerning specific adaptive behaviors and behavior deficiencies in need of remediation, valuable data about the response requirements of a task to be performed (task analysis), and hypotheses concerning specific environmental stimuli which promote or inhibit behavioral growth (functional analysis) (see Matson & Breuning, 1983, and Whitman et al., 1983, for a description of some of these assessment tools).

Although not commonly recognized, behavioral assessment approaches share features in common with the dynamic cognitive assessment approach, proposed by Feuerstein and others for use with mentally retarded persons (Day & Hall, 1987; Feuerstein, 1980). In both approaches, the role of social factors in the learning process is stressed. Dynamic assessment provides information concerning cognitive rather than behavioral processes which need to be developed to facilitate learning. Based on Piagetian theory, dynamic assessment informs mediated learning experiences (interventions) which in turn provide the "foundation upon which operational structures are built" (Feuerstein, Rand, Hoffman, Hoffman, & Miller, 1979, p. 540). Deficient cognitive performance is viewed as resulting from the absence of appropriate mediated learning experiences. According to Feuerstein et al. (1979), medicated learning occurs through a social process in which educational agents (e.g., parents, teachers, siblings) select, filter and invest environmental events with meaning for those they teach. In order to structure effective enrichment programs, dynamic assessment focuses on identifying deficient cognitive (input, elaboration and output) functions. Intervention subsequently attempts to compensate for a lack of appropriate mediated learning experiences by presenting tasks designed to modify these deficient functions. Day and Hall (1987) point out that a dynamic assessment approach can also be employed to determine the amount of instructional support which exceptional children will require, providing information concerning what Vygotsky (1978) calls their zone of proximal development. Students who require a great deal of instructional assistance are considered to have a narrower zone of proximal development than students who require less assistance and are relatively independent performers.

In summary, although adequate cognitive assessment procedures for evaluating mentally retarded children and for identifying the skills required for proficient performance by these children on complex cognitive tasks have not yet fully evolved, it is clear that progress is being made in this regard. Feuerstein and his colleagues have developed, as part of their instrumental enrichment program, a promising Learning Potential Assessment Device that allows the processes and functions that constitute mental acts to be cognitively mapped (Feuerstein, 1980; Feuerstein et al., 1979). More recently, Reid (1988) discusses specific assessment procedures which can be utilized in math, reading, writing and spelling programs. In contrast, Butterfield and Ferretti (1987) indicate that assessments based on metacognitive theory have not yet been developed for use in clinical and educational settings, specifically, assessments which evaluate a child's knowledge base, strategical repertoire, metacognitive understanding, and executive routines. In order to establish more refined cognitive procedures for assessing the problem of special children, Butterfield and Ferretti (1987) recommend three kinds of research: analytical studies within groups of special children to establish the cognitive processes which are employed during task performance, comparative studies to establish how diverse groups of children differ in the cognitive processes they employ, and instructional studies to teach deviant groups of children to use adaptive cognitive processes.

THE COGNITIVE–BEHAVIORAL EDUCATION OF PERSONS WITH MENTAL RETARDATION

Although the educational implications of theories describing the nature of mental retardation have gradually become more evident (see, for example, Day & Borkowski, 1987; Mercer & Snell, 1977), their impact on specific cognitive programs is just beginning to be manifested. To date, the cognitive procedures that have been employed with children with mental retardation have been influenced at least as much by the same general (behavioral, social learning and cognitive–developmental) theories that have catalyzed the development of cognitive therapy techniques for children with other types of problems (Kendall & Braswell, 1985; Meyers & Craighead, 1984) as by specific theories of mental retardation. In this section, the cognitive therapy techniques that have been most frequently utilized with children who are labeled mentally retarded will be described. These include: verbal instructional, self-management, strategical and metacognitive, and visual instructional training procedures.

Verbal Instruction

Traditional behavioral education programs have focused on the treatment of the persons with more severe retardation and the manipulation of consequences to modify responding (Whitman et al., 1983). However, with the growing interest in cognitive variables within the field of mental retardation, more attention has been directed by behaviorists toward persons with mild retardation and upon examining and manipulating the antecedents of behavior to achieve desired outcomes. Within this section, three different instructional techniques commonly employed with children with mental retardation in educational settings will be examined: (1) external instruction, (2) correspondence training, (3) and self-instruction.

External Instruction

One of the most frequently utilized educational techniques is teacher-supplied verbal instruction (Keogh, Whitman, & Maxwell, 1988). Although the vast majority of cognitive training programs for persons with mental retardation contain a verbal component, research is needed to examine whether verbal prompting procedures are sufficient or whether verbal instruction can be enhanced through the addition of other types of prompting as well as reinforcement techniques. Surprisingly little research has been directed toward examining the relative efficacy of verbal instructional methods versus other methods. In one of the few comparison studies conducted, Repp, Barton, and Brulle (1981) evaluated the effectiveness of five different types of staff instruction with severely mentally retarded students: (1) verbal instruction, (2) nonverbal or gestural instruction, (3) verbal instruction with physical assistance, (4) nonverbal instruction with physical assistance, and (5) physical assistance. Data were collected on the general instruction-following behavior of the clients in several naturalistic settings. The authors reported that verbal instruction, the most commonly utilized instruction, was one of the least effective methods of developing compliance both within an institutional and a less restrictive classroom setting, whereas some type of physical assistance, either administered alone or with a gestural instruction, was the least utilized and yet most effective instructional technique.

In a somewhat similar study, Rynders, Behlen, and Horrobin (1979) examined the performance of students with mild and moderate mental retardation and nonretarded students on preacademic and self-help tasks under two instructional conditions: augmented and repeated instruction. Augmented instruction involved progressively supplementing verbal instruction with additional types of prompts. The prompting sequence was structured so as to allow the greatest level of independent responding possible, followed by additional help as needed. The prompting sequence progressed from (1) simple verbal prompt, (2) verbal instruction, and (3) verbal instruction and modeling, to, finally, (4) verbal instruction and physical guidance. The second technique examined, repeated instruction began with a verbal prompt that was repeated up to three times, given unsuccessful responding. No significant differences were found between the two instructional conditions in the students' successful completion of preacademic and self-help tasks. In conjunction with the findings of the previously described study by Repp et al. (1981), the results of this study suggest that verbal instruction is more effective for persons with mild and moderate retardation than for persons with severe retardation. The findings by Rynders et al. (1979) suggest, however, that traditional verbal instruction, even supplemented with modeling and physical guidance, is not always sufficient to ensure learning for persons who are more mildly retarded.

From a theoretical perspective, there are a variety of explanations why some persons with mental retardation fail to learn from teacher or staff-administered verbal instruction. Extrapolating from research that suggests that persons with mental retardation have attentional problems (Zeaman & House, 1963, 1979), Whitman (1987) has speculated that this population may also have a problem focusing on the pertinent cues contained in verbal instructions. Additionally, Luria (1961) has suggested that persons with mental retardation have difficulties associating verbal and motoric systems; that is in using speech to control motoric behavior. Given the difficulties many persons with mental retardation have in learning through traditional verbal instructional methods, it is not surprising that alternative methods of verbal instruction have been explored to maximize performance. Two such alternatives include correspondence training and self-instruction.

Correspondence Training

Correspondence training has been utilized to increase a variety of academic, social, and personal behaviors, such as listening and appropriate sitting, sharing, appropriate posture, and choosing nutritious snacks (Baer, Blount, Detrich, & Stokes, 1987; Keogh Burgio, Whitman, & Johnston, 1983; Whitman, Scibak, Butler, Richtern, & Johnston, 1982). Correspondence training is based on the assumption that there should be a relationship between what people say and what they do. The establishment of correspondence between verbal and nonverbal behavior in children with mental retardation may be an especially appropriate endeavor, specifically because it establishes the individual as the locus of control through developing verbal self-regulation. Past research has indicated that persons with mental retardation often fail to self-regulate and are excessively dependent on others for guidance and direction (Whitman, 1987; Zigler, 1966). It appears likely that to the extent that correspondence training develops a habit of verbal self-control maintenance and generalization to nontraining situations should be facilitated.

Correspondence training can proceed in one of two basic sequences: (1) reinforcing an individual for doing what he or she says (Say–Do), or (2) reinforcing a person for truth-telling, or accurately reporting (saying) what he or she actually did (Do–Say). For example, in the Say–Do approach, children are generally prompted or specifically taught to say what they should and will do in a particular situation. Subsequently, their behavior is monitored to evaluate whether they did what they said they would do. Correspondence is developed by reinforcing word–action congruence. It has been argued that both Say–Do and Do–Say procedures are directed toward developing verbal control of nonverbal behavior (Rogers–Warren & Baer, 1976). Existing evidence suggests, however, that the Say–Do procedures may be more effective in this regard. Israel and O'Leary (1973) found that a Say–Do procedure produced greater correspondence between children's report of what they were going to play with and their actual play behavior than did a Do–Say procedure. In a recent study, Paniagna, Pumariega, and Black (1988) compared a reinforcement of corresponding reports (Do–Say) and procedures reinforcing fulfillment of promises (Say–Do), in their ability to decrease hyperactive behavior in young children. In this investigation subjects were either reinforced for stating that they would inhibit hyperactive behavior and later following through on that promise, or reinforcement was delivered contingent upon corresponding true reports of behavior. They found that although both procedures were effective in reducing inattention, overactivity, and noise, the Say–Do procedure had a more pervasive and consistent effect across subjects.

Keogh et al. (1983) used a combined Say–Do and Do–Say treatment package to increase listening skills in moderately and mildly mentally retarded individuals in an instructional situation. During correspondence training, the subjects were required to state what they had to do to be good listeners. The subjects were then videotaped during a listening task and the appropriateness of listening behavior was rated. Following this session, subjects were asked a series of questions concerning their behavior during the task (e.g., Were you quiet? Did you look at the teacher?) Reinforcement was provided when correspondence occurred *both* between what the children said they would do and what they actually did (Say–Do) *and* between what they actually did and what they said they did (Do–Say). Results indicated that all children increased their listening skills in the training situation and that several of the subjects showed generalization of their appropriate listening to two different settings.

Several recent investigations emphasize that merely reinforcing verbalizations does not necessarily result in increased correspondence behavior (Baer, Blount, Detrich, & Stokes, 1987; Roberts, Nelson, & Olson, 1987). For example, Baer et al. (1987) examined two different conditions to increase nutritious snack choices in preschool children: (1) reinforcement for verbalizing that healthy foods would be chosen, and (2) reinforcement for saying they would choose mostly healthy snacks and then following through with that promise. The results showed minimal to no change in selecting healthy foods occurred following reinforcement of verbalization only, whereas reinforcing correspondence between verbal and nonverbal behavior led to a rapid and high level of nutritious food selection. The fact that verbalizations often fail to exact control over behavior has led some researchers to question whether the verbal response is the controlling stimulus when correspondence occurs.

In a recent investigation, Deacon and Konarski (1987) postulated that a correlational, as opposed to a causative, relationship may exist between verbal and nonverbal behavior. They argued that because reinforcement follows both verbal and nonverbal behavior, increases in behavior could be predicted from reinforcement alone. To examine this hypothesis, the investigators compared a Say–Do correspondence procedure with a "do" only procedure that provided reinforcement to moderately retarded students for just engaging in several simple motor responses. The results indicated comparable increases in the target behaviors in both conditions, suggesting that correspondence training might occur just as a function of contingency control.

Deacon and Konarski (1987) indicate, however, that the correspondence training may be an example of rule-governed behavior. They explain, "Rule governed behavior develops when people are given, or generate on their own, a verbal description of the contingencies of reinforcement in a situation and are reinforced for following that rule. The procedures of reinforcement appear to foster both the development of a rule and provide reinforcement for following it." (p. 398) More generally, Whitman (in press) suggests that the correspondence between verbal and nonverbal behavior might be best predicted by examining both an individual's verbal skills and his or her reinforcement history. He states that if an individual has more proficient verbal skills and has in the past been reinforced for demonstrating correspondence between verbal and nonverbal behavior, then simply reinforcing verbalizations should lead to concomitant increases in overt behavior.

In general, the current literature provides a somewhat confusing and certainly inconsistent picture relating to the development, maintenance, and generalization of behavior following correspondence training and the functional role of a subject's verbalizations (Keogh et al., 1987; Rogers–Warren, & Baer, 1976; Whitman, 1987; Whitman et al., 1982). At present, it appears that verbal self-regulation will be most readily apparent in individuals who have relatively well-developed language system, and that individuals who are less linguistically proficient, such as persons with mental retardation, may require more extensive correspondence training before verbal control of motoric behavior is established.

Self-instruction

In addition to externally administered (e.g., teacher, staff) instructional and correspondence training procedures, a third verbal training technique, self-instruction, has been employed with children with mental retardation. Self-instruction is similar to external instruction, except that it requires the student to verbalize during the training process (Meichenbaum, 1977). Self-instruction is also very similar to correspondence training in that the relationship between the verbal (self-verbalization) and nonverbal behavior is typically reinforced. Thus, as in correspondence training, the emphasis in self-instruction is upon developing self-regulatory speech. Although the self-verbalizations are programmed to control nonverbal behavior in both correspondence and self-instruction training, self-instruction usually involves a more complex teaching algorithm than that employed in correspondence training as well as a more complex set of verbal cues to be learned by the student. Self-instruction assists students through supplying them words and helping them to understand the meaning of words by teaching them to use self-verbalizations to guide and regulate their actions. Based on the fact that past research has shown that persons with mental retardation have difficulties attending to relevant stimulus dimensions (House & Zeaman, 1963), organizing stimulus input (Spitz, 1973), and are overly dependent on others for guidance and direction (Zigler, 1966), self-instruction appears to be uniquely suited for use with this population, given that it focuses attention on relevant verbal cues, facilitates organization of nonverbal stimuli, and encourages verbal self-regulation of action.

Within the field of mental retardation, self-instruction training has been successfully used to increase a variety of behaviors, including general and specific academic skills, such as attending (Burgio, Whitman, & Johnson, 1980) and math skills (Johnston & Whitman, 1987; Johnston, Whitman, & Johnston, 1980); social leisure skills (Keogh, Faw, Whitman, & Reid, 1984); and vocational skills (Whitman, Spence, & Maxwell, 1987; Rusch, Morgan, Martin, Riva, & Agran, 1985). Self-instructions typically include several basic component statements focusing upon: (1) task definition, (2) behavioral strategies for approaching a task, (3) the need for self-evaluation, (4) the use of self-coping strategies, and (5) self-reinforcement.

Burgio et al. (1980) utilized this type of self-instructional package to increase attending behavior with mildly and moderately mentally retarded children who were highly distractible. The authors incorporated strategical self-instructions and coping statements to assist students in completing printing and math assignments, ignoring distractions, and dealing with task failure. During self-instructional training, the experimenter first performed the task while verbalizing the self-instruction. The child was then required to perform the task while the experimenter continued to verbalize the instructions. Finally, the child was required to verbalize the instructions and perform the task independently. After the children were able to verbalize the self-instructions successfully, distracting auditory and visual stimuli were introduced into the training situation to simulate naturalistic conditions in the classroom. Children were instructed to verbalize distraction-ignoring self-statements (e.g., I am not gonna look. I'm going to keep doing my work). A variety of behaviors were assessed in the regular classroom to evaluate the efficacy of the training program: (1) the students' use of self-instruction, (2) off-task behavior, (3) task performance, and (4) teacher rating of distractibility. The results indicated that mentally retarded children could be taught to use a relatively complex set of self-instructions and that the use of these was associated with reductions in off-task behavior and distractibility. Unfortunately, academic performance gains in terms of rate and accuracy in printing and math did not occur. The authors speculated that performance on these tasks might have been observed if evaluations had been continued over a longer period of time.

Given the critical purported role of the self-verbalization in changing behavior the unique contribution of this component to the success of self-instructional programs has been examined in several studies (Spence and Whitman, in press; Whitman et al., 1987). In a recent study, Keogh et al. (1988) compared the effectiveness of an external and self-instructional package for teaching arithmetic skills to children with and without mental retardation. Self-instruction and external instruction protocols were similar, except that during self-instruction, instructions were worded in the first person *and* participants were required to verbalize the instructions. The results indicated that students with mental retardation performed better under the self-instructional condition, whereas nonretarded students performed equally well under both instructional conditions. The authors noted that not only did self-instruction appear to be a superior method for teaching children with retardation, but that the mentally retarded children receiving self-instructional training were virtually indistinguishable in their performance from nonretarded children. Additionally, persons receiving self-instructional training were better able to articulate, when asked, the strategies required for problem solving, thus supporting the inference that they had a better understanding of the trained strategies. Based on studies conducted to date, it is clear that self-instruction can be effectively employed with children with mental retardation. Further research is needed, however, to examine how the individual characteristics of the child (e.g., level of retardation, linguistic skills) influence program outcome and how critical the self-verbalization component is to the success of the self-instructional training package.

Educational Implications

Because children with mental retardation vary considerably in their language competency, it is important that their linguistic skills be systematically evaluated prior to the development of a structured training program through the use of assessment instructions such as the Adaptive Behavior Scale and the Woodcock–Johnson Psychoeducational Battery (see chapter by Whitman & Johnston, 1986, for a discussion of these instruments). Children with minimal receptive and expressive language skills will have to be initially taught through the use of visual and physical prompts paired with verbal prompts. For these children, emphasis should be placed on the gradual fading of nonverbal prompts and bringing their behavior under verbal-stimulus control. Training should stress both the development of basic expressive (e.g., labeling and syntax) and receptive (e.g., instruction following) skills. As these language skills are developed, verbal instructional techniques, particularly the use of externally administered trainer instruction, can then be increasingly employed.

In contrast, children with more refined receptive and expressive language skills, who are able to follow adult verbal directives reliably and to reflect on the describe their own actions verbally, are in a position to benefit from verbal self-regulation training programs. For children with established but more redimentary language skills, correspondence training, because it makes less demand on the language system or of the individual, is probably the most appropriate teaching approach. For children with better developed language skills, self-instructional procedures may be the treatment of choice. Based on our present state of knowledge, it appears that self-instructional training will be most beneficial for children who have developed language proficiency but who still have difficulty processing verbal directives from socialization agents and subsequently using these directives to regulate their own behavior. Self-instruction teaches children to be more strategical in a verbal self-regulatory sense; more specifically, to use verbal cues to process information given through an external verbal model (e.g., What do I have to do?, I have to . . .), and to use this verbal information subsequently to direct their behavior.

Self-management Techniques

Although the self-instructional training approach previously described resembles in several ways the self-management techniques to be discussed in this section, the two approaches are also different. Whereas the essential feature of self-instruction is its emphasis on client self-verbalization, self-management programs are distinguished by their emphasis on the provision of particular strategies to enable children to self-regulate. While self-instructional training programs often utilize specific self-management strategies, self-management training programs may or may not be enacted through use of a self-instructional training format.

A number of different procedures are encompassed under the rubric of self-management. These procedures typically involve the client in generating specific discriminative cues, and/or consequences to control his or her own behavior. A variety of rationales have been given for using self-management techniques with mentally retarded children. This approach is consistent with the philosophical notion that this population should be allowed to participate in its own programming, to make choices, and to become as independent as possible (Litrownik, 1982). Practical reasons for employing self-regulation techniques have also been cited. For example, there is optimism that self-regulation techniques will promote maintenance and generalization of behavior change, something that more traditional behavioral methods have not been fully able to accomplish with mentally retarded persons. It has also been suggested that self-management programs require less expenditure of time and effort by caregiving staff and teachers than traditional behavior management methods (Cole, Gardner, & Karan, 1985).

A three-stage model of self-regulation, proposed by Kanfer (1970) and Kanfer and Karoly (1972), has had considerable impact on the development of self-management programs. This model suggests that several training goals must be achieved in order for individuals to regulate their own behavior effectively and independently. They must learn to self-monitor their actions, to set appropriate standards or criterion for their performance, and to self-administer contingencies to their behavior. In addition to these responses, self-control, the ability to delay both responding and gratification, has also been a frequent target of self-management interventions. More generally, Kanfer and Gaelick (1986) suggest that self-regulation is a complex cognitive skill, different from automatic processing in that it requires focused attention and continuous decision making. During intervention, Litrownik (1982) emphasizes that it is important to distinguish between process and outcome, that is, to look separately at the self-management skills and the target behaviors to which they are applied. Influenced by Skinner's conceptualization of self-directed behavior, Litrownik (1982) points out that the controlling responses, or self-management skills, and the controlled responses, or target behaviors, can be taught separately, in a sequence, or simultaneously.

The assessment of self-regulatory skills in children with mental retardation poses a challenge for the researcher and clinician because many of the behaviors to be evaluated are often covert and thus, not easily evaluated. However, Kendall and Williams (1982) suggest a number of methods which can be employed to assess both the cognitive and behavioral components of self-management in children, most of which are suitable for use with children and adolescents with mental retardation. The assessment of skills, which are critical prerequisites for self-regulation, has also been emphasized. For example, Litrownik (1982) recommends examining the child's ability to make simple discriminations, a skill which is necessary for self-monitoring and self-evaluating. In addition, because many self-management programs often require self-verbalizations by the client, the assessment of the client's linguistic functioning and verbal control capabilities has been advocated (Whitman, et al., 1987). Guevremont, Osnes, and Stokes (1986), who maintain that the development of generalized verbal control may be a prerequisite to effective self-regulation, provide a specific methodology that can be employed in evaluating the existing level of correspondence between verbal and nonverbal behavior in normal and developmentally disabled children.

In this section, two self-management techniques will be briefly described. These include: standard setting, self-monitoring, self-reinforcement, self-control, and problem solving. For more extensive description of these techniques and empirical evaluations of their effectiveness, the reader is referred to Litrownik (1982), Martin, Burger, Elias-Burger, and Mithaug (1988) and Whitman, Burgio, and Johnston (1984).

Standard Setting

Some researchers suggest that setting performance criterion or standards may be the most critical stage of the self-management process (Spates & Kanfer, 1977). Litrownik, Cleary, Lecklitner, and Franzini (1978) point out that for mentally retarded persons in particular, the ability to set appropriate self-imposed standards is crucial to independent functioning. These authors investigated whether moderately mentally retarded children were capable of developing this skill in the context of a bowling game. They found that the children, after observing a videotape of clown models who set and subsequently met their own criterion for the number of pins to be knocked down during a frame, were able to establish and meet the same performance standards as the clown model. The authors then conducted a follow-up study in which they trained the children to develop standards based on their own past performance. Children observed clown models who set a criterion on a bowling task at a score that fell between scores actually received on previous trials. Subjects then successfully used this procedure to set and maintain appropriate personal standards for themselves on the same task and also on two generalization tasks, a pinball game and picture-matching task.

At present research is needed to determine the range of tasks in which standard setting training could be effectively utilized. Snow, Mercatoris, Beal, and Weber (1982) suggest that this type of training would be particularly useful in vocational workshop settings, where tasks are manual and concrete, but not in task situations requiring more abstract skills. Research is also necessary to assess the impact of standard setting interventions on the maintenance of behavior change and to assess the importance of standard setting as a component in more complex self-management packages.

Self-monitoring

Self-monitoring is probably the most widely discussed and researched of the self-management techniques. Originally used as a means of obtaining baseline data outside of a formal treatment environment, recognition of the reactive effects of self-monitoring has led clinicians to employ this technique as an intervention in its own right (O'Leary & Dubey, 1979). Although the mechanisms underlying its reactive property continues to be debated by researchers (Mace & Kratochwell, 1985), self-monitoring has been demonstrated to be successful in effecting a broad array of behavior changes with children who are mentally retarded.

For example, Zegiob, Klukas, and Junginger (1978) found that self-monitoring could be successfully employed to decrease nose and mouth picking and stereotypical behavior in mildly and moderately retarded adolescents. Intervention focused on teaching trainees to identify the occurrence of he target behaviors and record them on an index card. These self-monitoring procedures were explained, modeled, and prompted during an initial session. In subsequent sessions, subjects were simply given the materials necessary to self-record without further instruction. Results indicated that not only did training produce dramatic decreases in target behaviors, but that gains were maintained at a 6-month follow-up. Findings from this study further suggested that for some individuals, delivering noncontingent social praise for involvement in the self-management program led to further decreases in target behaviors over and above those produced by the initial self-monitoring intervention. Although subjects were found to lack accuracy in their self-recording, the fact did not appear to influence the effectiveness of the intervention. This lack of correspondence between self-monitoring accuracy and performance changes has also been reported by other researchers (O'Leary & Dubey, 1979).

Litrownik, Freitas, and Franzini (1978) have demonstrated, however, that moderately and severely retarded children can be taught to self-monitor accurately. Subjects viewed both live and taped demonstrations of models who placed rings on pegs after receiving a particular score on a bowling game or upon completing a discrimination–matching problem. The children were then given instructions to match the behavior of the model and received corrective feedback until self-monitoring mastery was achieved. Subjects were found to acquire the skill relatively quickly, and to retain this skill at a 1-week follow-up, at which time transfer to several generalization tasks was also evidenced.

Self-reinforcement

According to Skinner (1953), for true self-reinforcement to occur, an individual must have free access at all times to the reinforcing stimuli, whether or not the correct response has occurred. However, Martin et al. (1988), in a review of the applied literature, found that the conditions for "true" self-reinforcement are typically not present because subjects do not have control over available reinforcers and do not choose which reinforcers are to be delivered. Nevertheless, a variety of procedures labeled self-reinforcement have proven to be effective with mentally retarded children.

In most of the applied literature, self-reinforcement has been used in conjunction with self-monitoring techniques. Shapiro and his colleagues conducted several studies with mildly mentally retarded children who were off-task in a classroom situation. Shapiro and Klein (1980) taught four moderately mentally retarded children to self-monitor and self-reinforce their ontask behavior through the use of multiphase intervention program. During treatment, the teacher initially awarded tokens for an individual's on-task behavior at random intervals of 30, 60, or 90 seconds. At the end of a 30-minute session, children exchanged their tokens for reinforcers that they had selected prior to beginning of the session. After the token program had been in effect for two sessions, a self-assessment phase occurred in which children learned to self-monitor their own on-task behavior accurately as the teacher gradually faded verbal prompts, instructions, and direction, while introducing a questioning procedure. During questioning, children were asked after a timer went off, "Do you get a token? Why?" In the next phase, children learned to self-reinforce through a three-step process in which they were first verbally prompted to take a token, then motioned by the teacher to take a token, and finally were expected to take a token without teacher prompts. In a final phase, children were required to perform all steps of the self-management program independently. Large gains in on-task behavior occurred during the initial token program and were maintained throughout the self-management training phases and at a 2-month follow-up.

Shapiro, McGonigle, and Ollendick (1980) subsequently examined the utility of a simple versus a more intensive training procedure for teaching moderately and mildly retarded children to self-manage (self-monitor and self-reinforce). As in the previous study, on-task behavior was initially increased through a token program implemented by the teacher. Children found to be on task at the end of each instructional interval were awarded verbal praise and a star, children who were off-task received verbal feedback indicating why they had not received a token, and children who were engaging in disruptive behavior at the end of the interval were given corrective feedback and had a star removed. Following implementation of this token system, children were asked to monitor and reinforce their own behavior. The teacher modeled the procedure and gave verbal instructions; however, no other specific training was given. In subsequent phases of the experiment, subjects were given extensive training in self-assessment and self-reinforcement similar to that used by Shapiro and Klein (1980). Results demonstrated that instructions to self-manage were not sufficient to maintain increases in on-task behavior; however, with explicit self-management training, mentally retarded children were able to maintain high levels of on-task responses.

Although these Shapiro studies provided suggestive evidence concerning the effectiveness of self-reinforcement procedures, the relative contribution of self-reinforcement and self-assessment to the treatment effect remains unclear. Shapiro et al. (1980) suggest that the effect of self-reinforcement over and above self-monitoring may, in fact, vary across individuals.

Self-control

Although sometimes used synonymously with the terms self-management and self-regulation, self-control has often been defined as the ability to delay gratification; for example, to choose a large, delayed reward over a smaller but immediate one. The absence of this type of self-control has sometimes been referred to as impulsive behavior. More commonly, problems of self-control and impulsivity have been defined when children respond too quickly in task situations that demand some degree of evaluation or reflection (Lowry & Ross, 1975). Children with mental retardation have often been described as lacking both the capacity to delay gratification as well as the ability to delay responding in situations requiring self-evaluative responses (Litrownik, Franzini, Geller, & Geller, 1977; Lowry & Ross, 1975). Self-control intervention programs with this population have focused on both these deficiencies.

The instrument most often used to assess reflectivity and impulsivity tendencies and indirectly self-control capabilities is the Matching Familiar Figures Test (MFFT; the reader is referred to Messer, 1976, for a lengthly discussion of this instrument). Simpler versions of this test have been constructed for use with children functioning in the severe to profound range of mental retardation (Lowry & Ross, 1975). The dependent measures used to classify individuals on the reflection–impulsivity scale are total number of errors and latency to first response. When assessed with the MFFT, it is clear that mentally retarded persons are a heterogeneous population. Lowry and Ross (1975) found in evaluating severely retarded children, two distinct clusters emerged: one of fast incorrect (impulsive) responders and the other of slow correct responders. Messer (1976) found that educable mentally retarded children had extremely impulsive scores on the MFFT and adopted a position set in responding. However, Borys and Spitz (1978), comparing retarded adolescents and nonretarded children equated for mental age, found no differences between the two groups on the proportion of impulsive, reflective, fast/accurate, and slow/inaccurate responders.

Although impulsiveness may not be a characteristic of the entire population of retarded children, it is clear that at least a subset of this population lacks the ability to delay responding, and that this deficit may contribute to poor performance on a variety of tasks (Messer, 1976). For this reason, response delay has been one important target of self-control intervention programs. Lowry and Ross (1975), employing a group of severely retarded children identified as impulsive responders based on MFFT scores, gave them training on a receptive language task which required discrimination between two colors. During training, a mandatory delay period was imposed between the task introduction and the subjects' response by keeping task materials out of reach for 5 seconds. They found that this delay procedure considerably improved task performance (i.e., the number of correct responses). While researchers have not to date investigated the ability of mentally retarded children to self-impose this response delay, it seems reasonable to assume that this skill could be taught, based on the encouraging results from other self-regulatory training studies.

Kanfer has proposed a two-stage model for training another type of self-control, specifically to delay gratification (cited in Litrownik et al., 1977). The first stage, labeled decisional self control, requires the individual to make a choice between a larger, delayed reward and a smaller, immediate one. If the individual exhibits self-control and chooses the delayed reward, then during the second stage the individual is required to extend the delay interval gradually. Influenced by Kanfer's model, Litrownik et al (1977) have cited two variables thought to predict success in both stages of self-control: accuracy of time perspective and the belief that the delayed reward is, in fact, obtainable. Based on the hypothesis that mentally retarded persons often lack self-control because they do not possess these critical factors, Litrownik et al. (1977) developed a training program for moderately retarded adolescent subjects that fostered a more accurate time perspective and a belief that the promised rewards would be presented. They subsequently assessed the impact of this program on "decisional self-control," using as a dependent measure the subjects' actual or reported selection of either a small immediate or large, delayed reward. They found that subjects who received the training chose a significantly greater number of delayed rewards than subjects in a control group. This research provides at least tentative evidence that mentally retarded individuals are capable of delaying gratification and that this capability can be taught. However, in a subsequent study, Franzini, Litrownik, and Magy (1978) emphasized that type of reinforcement must be taken into account in evaluating and attempting to influence mentally retarded children's ability to delay gratification. They found that moderately mentally retarded adolescents choose to delay gratification more often when a secondary rather than a primary reinforcer was employed.

Problem Solving

As Spitz (1987) points out, the term "problem solving" is a fairly general one that applies to any of a number of goal-directed activities undertaken by individuals to arrive at a solution to a problem. Research has documented a number of deficits of mentally retarded persons in problem-solving ability. Retarded children have been found to be outer-directed in their problem solving; that is, they rely on cues from others rather than their own resources (Turnure & Zigler, 1964). In addition, retarded children have been found to be lacking in logical foresight (Spitz & Winters, 1977), and have a limited search capacity (Borys, Spitz, & Donans, 1982).

Although such deficits are well documented, relatively little research has been directed at remediating these problem-solving deficiencies. D'Zurilla and Goldfried (1971) have proposed a five-stage model, outlining the steps which should be taught in a problem-solving training program: (1) general orientation, (2) problem definition and formulation, (3) generation of alternatives, (4) decision making, and (5) verification of problem solution. Unfortunately, as Whitman et al. (1984) point out, few instructional programs for mentally retarded persons have attempted to train each of these steps systematically, and have typically trained only one of the components. Nonetheless, some of these programs have considerable clinical utility.

Ross and Ross (1973, 1978) conducted a series of studies on problem solving with retarded children. In one study having considerable applied significance (Ross & Ross, 1978), educable mentally retarded (EMR) children were trained to choose the best alternative from a number of solutions to familiar social or environmental problems. Training took place in discussion groups of four or five participants. The following topics were discussed: concept of choice, distinction between a choice and order criteria for choosing one of several attractive or unattractive alternatives, choices in emergency situations, and choices based on logic. Choices were taught in the context of game situations, and subjects were given tallies on a scorecard for good answers or for "trying hard." Results showed that the training group was superior to the control group, both in selecting the best alternative and in providing bases for their choices. The authors point out that the subjects required 40 training sessions, demonstrating the difficulty EMR children have in acquiring complex cognitive skills. They maintain, however, that the length of time spent in training is justified by the long-term social benefits for these children.

Although research directed at evaluating problem-solving programs with persons with mental retardation has been sparse, the skills taught in such programs have been addressed by theorists interested in metacognition. Metacognitive training programs will be discussed in the next section.

Educational Implications

At present, the best approach to developing self-management in children with mental retardation seems to be one that teaches in combination a variety of self-regulation skills, including standard setting, self-monitoring, and self-reinforcement. As Kanfer and Karoly (1972) emphasize, each of these skills appears to be critical for effective self-management. Past research suggests that these self-management skills can be taught to children with mental retardation and that, once acquired, they are associated with changes in a variety of clinically important target behaviors. Especially encouraging is the finding by Martin et al. (1988), who reviewed research in the self-management area. They found that in most studies where maintenance and generalization data are reported, self-management procedures produced durable and generalized changes across situations. In those studies where comparison data are available, the authors noted that self-management programs were typically more successful in achieving these types of changes than traditional trainer-based programs.

Before self-management is adopted as a training objective, however, it is imperative that the trainees be under teacher instructional control and that they show some capacity to regulate verbally their own behavior. As indicated previously, self-management skills can, but do not necessarily, have to be taught within the context of a self-instructional program. There are, however, several reasons to use a self-instructional rather than an external instructional format. Specifically, the use of self-instructional training paradigm allows the trainer to monitor systematically whether the trainees understand, as reflected in their verbalizations, how to self-manage and whether the trainees' verbalizations effectively cue their appropriate use of specific self-management behaviors (e.g., self-monitoring). The use of an interrogative approach by the trainer is especially recommended to involve the trainee more actively during the instructional process. For example the trainer might ask the student the following types of questions in a math training situation: Did you get that problem right? How many problems did you get correct on the whole exercise? Did you meet the goal you set for yourself? Should you administer a reinforcer to yourself? In teaching self-monitoring skills the employment of some type of physical monitoring device (e.g., a rating form or hand counter) is recommended to reduce the trainees' instructional burden. Such self-monitoring aids should, however, be faded, if possible, as training proceeds. Finally, the use of self-inoculation techniques, such as those suggested by Meichenbaum (1977), is strongly suggested. Because children with mental retardation often have a long history of failure, they are prone to be more passive in learning situations and dependent on others for guidance. For this reason these children need to be taught that failure is part of the learning process, but that it can be gradually overcome with personal effort. Conversely, when these children are successful in their performance, they must be taught to attribute their success to their own efforts and specifically to their use of the self-management techniques.

Strategical and Metastrategical Interventions

In contrast to the previously discussed verbal instructional and self-management procedures, which have been derived for the most part from applied research and clinical theories, the strategical and metastrategical techniques discussed in this section evolved from more basic cognitive and cognitive–developmental research and theories. Mentally retarded individuals have been found to use fewer, simpler, and more passive cognitive strategies than nonretarded individuals in memory and learning task situations (Butterfield & Ferretti, 1987). A fundamental and irreversible inability to produce and use specific task-relevant strategies were thought at one time to account for the poor performance exhibited by mentally retarded individuals. For example, Ellis (1970) maintained that the failure of mentally retarded persons to use active rehearsal strategies produced the differences between their performance and that of nonretarded persons on memory tasks. Based on more than a decade of strategy training research, it has become clear, however, that mentally retarded individuals are capable of acquiring and using specific strategies to mediate performance on a variety of memory and learning tasks (Campione, 1987). A main focus of this research has been upon developing instructional methods for teaching strategy use and for promoting strategy maintenance and transfer.

For example, Burger, Blackman, Holmes, and Zetlin (1978) developed a training program designed to teach mildly retarded children the use of a sorting and retrieval strategy in a memory task situation. Subjects were asked to recall pictures of common items that belonged to several superordinate categories. The strategy that was taught to facilitate recall involved asking subjects to group together pictures that seemed to "go together," to identify the superordinate category to which the items belonged and to count the number of pictures in each category. During recall, experimenters supplied subjects names of superordinate categories for which they had missed pictures. Results indicated that the performance of subjects given this training was superior to a control group on measures of short- and long-term recall. Burger, Blackman, and Tan (1980) found at a 6-month follow-up of subjects in this study that the children had maintained use of the instructed strategy. These authors cited the following training conditions as critical for achieving maintenance: (1) active participation by the children, (2) multiple training sessions over several days, (3) analysis of important task components, (4) systematic introduction of the relevant strategies, (5) employment of fading techniques; and (6) provision of information to the children regarding the value of strategy use. Despite success in maintaining strategy use, subjects did not generalize the instructed strategies to other tasks presented at follow-up. For a more comprehensive review of the strategy training procedures, the reader is referred to Borkowski and Cavanaugh (1979).

Although specific strategy training research has produced a general optimism that many cognitive deficiencies of persons with mental retardation can be remediated, it has not produced the dramatic applied gains once hoped for (Borkowski & Buchel, 1983). The inability of this population to employ instructed strategies effectively across situations has led researchers to postulate that mentally retarded persons possess a metacognitive deficiency. According to Flavell (1976), metacognition refers to the knowledge an individual possesses about his or her cognitive process and products. Closely linked to the concept of metacognition is that of executive functioning, which refers to the actual use of metacognitive knowledge in regulating strategical deployment. Mentally retarded children have been found to be deficient in both metacognitive knowledge and executive processing skills (Borkowski & Kurtz, 1987; Campione, 1987). More generally, research suggests the utility of metacognitive measures for predicting strategy use, maintenance, and generalization in mentally retarded children (Kendall, Borkowski, & Cavanaugh, 1980). As a consequence of this type of research, both the provision of general strategical knowledge and executive routines have been targeted in more applied research in order to promote flexible and adaptive use of specific skills and strategies. A few early examples of how such programs have been structured with mentally retarded children are found in the work of Brown, Campione, and their colleagues (Brown & Barclay, 1976; Brown, Campione, & Murphy, 1977; Campione & Brown, 1978).

At present, however, there is a clear need for additional metacognitive instructional research with mentally retarded children. Butterfield and Ferretti (1987) cite the lack of sound instructional studies directed at evaluating and eliminating differences in metacognitive and executive processing between groups varying in intelligence. The absence of this type of research is surprising, given that studies with nonretarded children have shown that a range of metacognitive skills can be taught and that such skills do facilitate strategy maintenance and generalization and improve task performance across a range of tasks (Borkowski & Kurtz, 1987; Ghatala, Levin, Pressley, & Lodico, 1985; Lodico, Ghatala, Linn, Pressley, & Bell, 1983). Replications and extensions of these efforts are now called for with mentally retarded subjects.

Educational Implications

The research on strategical and metastrategical interventions has potentially considerable educational significance because of its emphasis on promoting self-regulation. Research clearly indicates that specific cognitive skills can be readily taught to children with mental retardation, but that these children lack the requisite higher-order metacognitive capabilities to apply these skills in other situations. Although the metacognitive approach to programming maintenance and generalization with mentally retarded populations is not different than that recommended for nonhandicapped children, it is especially appropriate for mentally handicapped children given their extreme passivity in learning situations. However, in developing instructional training programs for children with mental retardation, Campione and Brown (1977) caution that it is important to keep in mind the level of cognitive functioning of the student. They point out that educational researchers have typically identified a strategy used by expert learners and attempted to train this strategy in persons with mental retardation. Campione and Brown emphasize that this tactic may be inappropriate, particularly for younger children with mental retardation, and point out that in order for strategy training to be successful, strategies used by nonretarded individuals must be adapted so that they are compatible with the existing cognitive capabilities of retarded children.

Metacognitive training programs for children with mental retardation should contain the following components:

1. Active involvement should be generally encouraged through sensitizing the children about the relationship between their personal effort, specifically their use of cognitive strategies, and successful performance.
2. In order to catalyze further their active involvement, self-awareness should be promoted through having the children analyze and examine in a learning situation what they know about the requirements of a task being confronted. They should also be asked to examine their cognitive repertoire for possible strategical solutions (to implement them if present, or if absent to recognize their need for assistance), and to assess whether their strategy implementation results in goal attainment. Self-monitoring, planning, and checking skills should be taught to ensure that the children deploy strategies effectively.
3. In addition to being given specific instruction about appropriate employment of strategy, information concerning the general usefulness of a strategy in other situations should be provided to the children.

In contrast to the self-management programs described in the last section, the emphasis during metacognitive and executive functioning training is not on the development of specific self-management skills per se but on coordinating the use of these skills *across* learning situations. Children with mental retardation should be taught to recognize the general importance of being strategic and to discriminate when a previously learned skill is applicable in a particular situation. However, to develop a general strategical orientation, programming must focus initially on ensuring that the trainee is in possession of or taught a range of specific strategies necessary for the solution of different tasks, and then on teaching him or her to select appropriately and utilize these various strategies as different type of problems are presented. For example, the trainee might be taught in a sequential fashion different basic math skills (addition, subtraction, multiplication, and division) and then taught to utilize these skills when problems requiring each of these skills are randomly presented. In order to perform effectively, the trainee will need to identify the type of math problem with which he or she is confronted and then to choose the appropriate strategy for solving the problem. Thus, the goal of this type of training is to first teach him or her to be strategical (to use cognitive strategies) and then to be metastrategical (to make discriminations regarding the applicability of different strategies in different situations).

Visual Instruction and Imagery

When educational programs for children with mental retardation are examined, it is evident that such programs vary considerably, not only in their content, that is, in what is taught, but also in the nature of the instructional procedures employed. Although the procedures for teaching behavioral and cognitive skills typically rely on the use of verbal and/or nonverbal cues, inspection of cognitive–behavioral programs for children with mental retardation reveals the primary role that verbal instruction plays in the majority of training and educational programs. The appropriateness of this emphasis on verbal instruction, however, has been questioned because of the language problems of children with mental retardation. Deficits in language skills are among the most notable problems of mentally retarded persons (Matthews, 1971). In a review of language research, Yoder and Miller (1972) concluded that persons with mental retardation manifest language deficiencies at the phonological level in the form of articulation deficits, at the morphological level, and at the syntactical level. Their vocabularly size, which is correlated with mental age, is limited and their speech is concrete. Given that delayed or deficient language is generally recognized as an identifying characteristic of mental retardation (Snyder & McLean, 1976), the necessity of structuring training formats consistent with an individual's linguistic abilities seems self-evident.

In contrast to individuals of average or above average intelligence who acquire information from both linguistic as well as nonlinguistic stimuli, Pressley (in press) suggests that nonverbal visual processing might be the preferred mode of encoding for persons with mental retardation because of their language deficiencies. Inhelder (1968) also suggests this conclusion when he speaks of the primacy of perception in this population. He points out that because persons with mental retardation are concrete and bound to features in the immediate environment, they have difficulties dealing with symbolic thought such as that represented through language. From a general developmental perspective, it makes sense that persons with mental retardation who manifest general developmental delays, might be more proficient in their perceptual than in their verbal representational encoding capabilities, if, as Paivio (1971) suggests, the nonverbal representation system develops earlier than the verbal representational system. Based on the premises that the verbal representation system of children with mental retardation is immature and that their perceptual system is relatively better developed, a number of investigators have suggested that visually oriented techniques might be more effectively employed than verbal procedures in teaching children with mental retardation (Mansdorf, 1977; Pressley, in press).

A variety of visual cueing procedures have been evaluated, including modeling, picture cueing, and imagery induction (Cullinan, 1976; Connis, 1979; Greeson & Jens, 1977; Groden & Cautela, 1984; Mansdorf, 1977; Martin, Rusch, James, Decker, & Trtol, 1982; Pressley, Cariglia–Bull, Deane, & Schneider, 1987; Smith & Meyers, 1979; Wacker & Berg, 1983). Of these procedures, imagery induction relies most heavily on the use of verbal cues to elicit visual mediators. In contrast, the picture cueing procedure relies almost exclusively on visual cues.

Wacker and Berg (1984) used picture prompts to teach three severely/ moderately mentally retarded individuals a vocational valve assembly task. The task involved collecting a specified number of parts and placing them in a compartment at three different work stations. A book was created with pictures depicting each of the 18 different pieces involved in the task. Pictures were sequentially arranged in the book, corresponding to the order they were to be placed at the work station. At the bottom of each picture was a number specifying the number of pieces to be placed in the compartment. During training, students were taught to turn the pages in order, select the objects depicted by the pictures, count the correct number of objects, and place the objects on the assembly tray. Minimal training was required to teach the students to use the picture prompts. Performance increased from an average of 4% accuracy during baseline to 100% accuracy at posttest. Additionally, the participants generalized their behavior to a task on which they had received no training, performing at 96% accuracy. When the pictures were removed during a second baseline, accuracy dropped to 50%. This study demonstrated that the students could learn to employ pictorial prompts independently in guiding their behavior. Unfortunately, the authors did not examine whether the picture prompts were required as permanent cues or could be faded gradually.

Martin et al. (1982) similarly taught severely mentally retarded individuals to prepare a complex meal through the use of picture prompts. During training, pictures depicting the steps of the task to be performed, were employed as cues to guide performance. They suggested that picture prompts can be used to establish a look–do behavioral sequence similar to the say–do sequence in correspondence training. The authors emphasized that picture prompts will promote greater independent functioning if clients can be taught to use such pictures in the absence of any external instructional assistance.

Although visual cueing procedures have been effectively employed with persons with mental retardation, research examining the relative efficacy of visual versus verbal instructional procedure has been sparse and inconclusive. On one hand, results of a study by Smith and Meyers (1979) suggest that verbal instruction adds little to the efficacy of visual instruction (modeling) in teaching telephone skills to adults with a moderate to profound retardation. In contrast, findings by Greeson and Jens (1977) suggest that verbal instruction is more effective than verbal–visual or verbal instructional procedures in assisting the recall performance of trainable mentally retarded children on a paired associate task. They assigned 40 moderately mentally retarded children to one of four conditions (1) Imagery mediation, where subjects were instructed to draw pictures that put the two items together; (2) Verbal mediation, which required children to construct sentences that linked the two items; (3) Combined imagery and verbal mediation training, or a (4) Control condition, where subjects were given rote rehearsal instructions. The results indicated that verbal mediation training was superior, with these students recalling a greater number of words than those students in the other three conditions. The authors noted that these findings were contrary to what they expected: "It was assumed that TMR children would be functioning on a relatively concrete conceptual level, one that would lend itself more to the generation of mental images than to abstract mediational responses of a verbal nature" (p. 62). They suggested that verbal mediational training may have been superior because language development and verbal instruction is typically emphasized in school curricula. They also hypothesized that TMR children may have a basic problem perceiving and representing symbolically their visual environment. The disparity in the results between the Smith and Meyers (1979) and the Greeson and Jens (1977) studies might be explained by the differences in the training procedures employed, the difference in the students' level of mental retardation, and the differences in the tasks (concrete motor vs. conceptual verbal).

Although skepticism has sometimes been expressed concerning the ability of children with mental retardation to benefit from visual cueing procedures, such as modeling, Baer, Peterson, and Sherman (1967) assert and provide evidence that imitative skills can be shaped and maintained like other specific behavior. Other investigators also point out that retarded individuals are quite imitative and should benefit more from visual than verbal instructional procedures because of their impoverished verbal repertoires (Rosenthal & Kellog, 1973). Still, other researchers indicate that verbal cues, in conjunction with modeling, may be the optimal instructional approach, particularly in complex training situations, where verbal cues may serve to enhance attention as well as provide rules to guide performance (Yoder & Forehand, 1974). At present, further comparative investigations are clearly needed to evaluate the efficacy of visual instructional programs; for example, to evaluate: (1) visual procedures using concrete objects versus pictorial cues, (2) direct visual cueing (e.g., *in vivo* modeling) versus indirect verbally induced imagery (e.g., covert modeling procedures, and (3) visual versus verbal versus visual–verbal cueing procedures. In addition, the influence of subject characteristics (such as verbal and visual abilities) and task characteristics (such as stimulus complexity and the verbal versus visual nature of the task stimuli) on performance under different instructional regimens need to be systematically examined.

Educational Implications

It is critical that educators recognize the considerable diversity in the population of children with mental retardation. Perhaps the most critical characteristics that distinguish members of this population are their visual and verbal encoding and decoding skills. Although the implications of this diversity for program planning are only beginning to be empirically explored, a number of commonsense recommendations can be made regarding the structuring of intervention programs. First, the visual as well as the verbal skills of the students should be evaluated before decisions concerning training programs formats are made. This evaluation can be conducted formally via such assessments as the Wechsler Intelligence Scale for Children (WISC) or the Wechsler Preschool Scale (WPPSI) (see Whitman & Johnston, 1986, for a description of these techniques) or more informally through examining the responsivity of the children to visual and verbal cues in imitation, picture-matching, instruction-following, and object-labeling task situations.

In instances where children show pronounced verbal deficiencies and relatively well-developed visual skills, the use of visual stimuli (e.g., *in vivo* models, film models, or pictures) to cue responding is especially recommended, with appropriate discriminative responses to visual stimuli then reinforced. Because the ultimate goal of any instructional goal is to promote performance in the absence of overt cues, an attempt should be made to fade visual instructional stimuli gradually. Even if the trainees manifest pronounced verbal skill deficiencies, verbal cues should also be conjoined with visual cues. Initially, this combined visual–verbal instructional approach may not facilitate and even slow down the learning process when compared with an instructional program using only visual cues. It should be remembered, however, that the goal of instructional program is not only to teach nonverbal skills, but also eventually to facilitate the development of expressive and receptive language responses and ultimately verbal self-regulatory capabilities.

Self-regulation, Generalization, and Instruction

Within the past decade there has been an increasing focus on developing programs that produce generalized changes in behavior. Ward and Gow (1982) point out that because of the lack of behavior transfer to untrained settings, generalization has become a central problem in the area of educational psychology. Although transfer of training has been generally difficult to obtain in child therapy and education programs, it has been particularly difficult to achieve with children who are mentally retarded (Borkowski & Cavanaugh, 1979). A variety of techniques, both behavioral and cognitive, have been recommended for effecting generalization. Stokes and Baer (1977) encouraged applied researchers to view generalization as a phenomenon that could be systematically programmed rather than as a passive outcome of a behavior change program. Subsequently, behaviorists have emphasized and effectively employed a variety of response selection and training strategies to produce generalization, such as using sufficient stimulus and response exemplars, common stimuli, indiscriminable contingencies and teaching responses that have broad utility (Horner, Dunlap, & Koegel, 1988; Stokes & Baer, 1977). Although these training strategies have been associated with a more proactive role by behavior modifiers in programming generalization, clients have been relatively passive during the training process.

In contrast to the general emphasis by behaviorists on trainer (teacher) control, cognitive educators have stressed to a greater degree the active involvement of the trainee (student) and the development of a self-regulatory response system during the training process. A number of researchers have suggested that the reason less intelligent and mentally retarded individuals are more passive in problem-solving situations and fail to generalize what they have learned is because of superordinate cognitive deficiencies. (Borkowski & Kurtz, 1987; Sternberg, 1987). Within this perspective, mentally retarded persons are viewed as lacking an understanding of the structure of problem-solving situations they confront and their own cognitive capacities as well as about how these types of information can be utilized in approaching learning tasks. Increasingly, it has been advocated in developing educational programs for children with mental retardation that training needs to emphasize not only specific skill and knowledge acquisition, but also the provision of general information regarding how and when to use these skills and knowledge.

Based on an examination of behavioral, social learning, and cognitive conceptualizations regarding self-regulation, Whitman (1990) has stressed that in order to develop self-regulation, a person with mental retardation "must learn to examine the task at hand; to examine his strategic repertoire, to formulate a plan of action, to enact that plan, to evaluate the plan as it is implemented and to revise the plan if necessary." It is our contention that the critical defining characteristic of persons with retardation is not their specific adaptive behavior or cognitive deficiencies, which research has repeatedly shown can often be quickly remediated, but their inability to use what they have learned in nontraining situations. This does not mean that children with mental retardation do not need to be taught specific skills and strategies required for task completion. We would emphasize, however, that to develop self-regulation, instructional emphasis must be placed on teaching them how task situations differ and how to approach specific tasks by making appropriate selections from their strategical repertoire.

Skepticism concerning the feasibility of teaching dynamic self-regulatory skills to children with mental retardation, as well as about the general viability of the self-regulatory solution to the problem of generalization, has been expressed. For example, the feasibility of implementing a self-regulatory program which emphasizes the role of language with children who have language deficiencies has been questioned (Kendall, 1990). This concern is understandable, in view of the fact that students, in order to benefit from this type of instruction, must possess the requisite linguistic skills to assimilate teacher information and to utilize language as a self-cueing vehicle. It needs to be recognized, however, that although children with mental retardation are often language-deficient, they are quite varied in the extent of this deficiency and most importantly, that the vast majority of them (the mildly and moderately mentally retarded) have extensive language skills. If preschool children with normal intelligence can develop verbal self-regulation at an early age, as Luria (1961) and others indicate, it seems reasonable to expect that school-age retarded children, whose verbal repertoires are often more extensive, can also learn to self-regulate their behavior.

Nevertheless, it is critical in establishing self-regulatory programs for children with mental retardation to also emphasize the development of receptive and expressive language skills. In teaching self-regulation, Whitman (1987) points out that a self-instructional approach may have particular utility with mentally retarded persons because it systematically provides general and specific strategies (verbal cues) to the student, teaches the appropriate use of these strategies and ensures behavior regulation through reinforcing a correspondence between saying and doing. For similar reasons, the reciprocal or mediated learning approach, currently advocated by many cognitive–developmental psychologists, also would seem to have special relevance for developing self-regulation in children with mental retardation. It emphasizes continuous teacher awareness of the children's current level of understanding of an activity and stresses a gradual ceding of control from the teacher to the child, as the child acquires the linguistic and strategical skills required for independent problem solving. During this process, the teacher not only provides information but also ways of thinking about information, to the students (Day, Cordon, & Kerwin, 1989).

Baer (1990) also questions whether autonomous adaptive responding is best achieved by teaching specific self-regulatory responses, such as self-instructions, and suggests that other behavioral (stimulus control and contingency management) strategies may be useful in developing client independence in persons with mental retardation. Pressley (1990), as pointed out earlier, also speculates whether imagery techniques might not be more appropriate than verbal self-regulation procedures for teaching individuals with mental retardation. In this regard, we believe that it is appropriate during the early stages of self-regulatory training to stress the use of nonverbal prompting procedures (including visual cueing and manual prompts) along with other general stimulus control procedures (e.g., programming stimulus conditions in the training situation to approximate those present in a generalization setting) for children with pronounced language deficiencies. We contend, however, that in order for complex self-regulatory skills to be developed in children with mental retardation, it is critical at some point in the instructional process to emphasize the use of verbal self-regulation. This change in programs emphasis does not mean abandoning the use of behavioral educational techniques, but rather utilizing this technology to develop complex verbally mediated behavioral chains.

There is increasing evidence that traditional behavioral stimulus control and reinforcement programs, that is, programs that foster nonverbal control and tight verbal stimulus control, may produce a less flexible and stereotyped approach by students in problem-solving situations (Schwartz, 1988) than the programs that emphasize development of rule-governed responses (such as those fostered in many self-instructional programs). It is also questionable whether the general technologies espoused by many behaviorists (Stokes & Baer, 1977) can be readily employed without some modification to produce the more complex forms of generalization described by cognitive psychologists. We contend that for dynamic self-regulation to develop, training needs to focus on developing student awareness concerning their capabilities and the complex environments they confront. It is doubtful that such awareness can be significantly promoted without the use of verbal stimulus control procedures. Through emphasizing the development of dynamic verbal self-regulation, it seems more likely that children with mental retardation can gain what Pylyshyn (1978) terms multiple and reflective access to their actions.

ACKNOWLEDGMENT

This writing of this chapter was supported in part by a training grant from the National Institute of Child Development (5T32 HD07184–10).

REFERENCES

Baer, D. M. (1990). Why choose self-regulation as a focal analysis of retardation? A commentary of Whitman's *Self-regulation and mental retardation. American Journal on Mental Retardation, 94,* 363–364.

Baer, D., Peterson, R., & Sherman, J. (1967). The development of imitation by reinforcing similarity to a model. *Journal of Experimental Analysis of Behavior, 10,* 405–416.

Baer, R. A., Blount, R. L., Detrich, R., & Stokes, T. F. (1987). Using intermittent reinforcement to program maintenance of verbal/non-verbal correspondence. *Journal of Applied-Behavior Analyses, 20,* 179–184.

Barrett, R. P., & Breuning, S. E. (1983). Assessing intelligence. In J. L. Matson & S. E. Breuning (Eds.), *Assessing the mentally retarded* (pp. 87–114). New York: Grune & Stratton.

Bijou, S. W. (1966). A functional analysis of retarded development. In N. Ellis (Ed.), *International review of research in mental retardation* (Vol. 1, pp. 1–19). New York: Academic Press.

Borkowski, J. G., & Büchel, F. (1983). Learning and memory strategies in the mentally retarded. In M. Pressley & J. R. Levin (Eds.), *Cognitive strategy research: Psychological foundations* (pp. 103–128). New York: Springer–Verlag.

Borkowski, J. G., & Cavanaugh, J. C. (1979). Maintenance and generalization of skills and strategies by the retarded. In N. Ellis (Ed.), *Handbook of mental deficiency, psychological theory and research.* Hillsdale, NJ: Erlbaum.

Borkowski, J. G., & Day, J. D. (Eds.). (1987). *Cognition in special children: Comparative approaches to retardation, leaning disabilities, and giftedness.* Norwood, NJ: Ablex.

Borkowski, J. G., & Kurtz, B. E. (1987). Metacognition and executive control. In J. G. Borkowski & J. D. Day (Eds.), *Cognition in special children: Comparative approaches to retardation, learning disabilities, and giftedness* (pp 123–152). Norwood, NJ: Ablex.

Borys, S. V., & Spitz, H. H. (1978). Reflection/impulsivity in retarded adolescents and nonretarded children of equal MA. *American Journal of Mental Deficiency, 82,* 601–604.

Borys, S. V., Spitz, H. H., & Donans, B. A. (1982). Tower of Hanoi performance of retarded young adults and nonretarded children as a function of solution length and goal state. *Journal of Experimental Child Psychology, 33,* 87–110.

Brewer, N. (1987). Processing speed, efficiency, and intelligence. In J. G. Borkowski & J. D. Day (Eds.), *Cognition in special children: Comparative approaches to retardation, learning disabilities, and giftedness* (pp. 15–48). Norwood, NJ: Ablex.

Brooks, P. H., Sperber, R., & McCauley, C. (1984). *Learning and cognition in the mentally retarded.* Hillsdale, NJ: Erlbaum.

Brown, A. L., & Barclay, C. R. (1976). The effects of training specific mnemonics on the metamnemonic efficiency of retarded children. *Child Development, 47,* 70–80.

Brown, A. L., & Campione, J. C. (1977). Training strategic study time apportionment in educable retarded children. *Intelligence, 1,* 94–107.

Brown, A. L., Campione, J. C., & Murphy, M. D. (1977). Maintenance and generalization of trained metamnemonic awareness by educable retarded children. *Journal of Experimental Child Psychology, 24,* 191–211.

Burger, A. L., Blackman, L. S., Holmes, M., & Zetlin, A. (1978). Use of active sorting and retrieval strategies as a facilitation of recall, clustering, and sorting by EMR and nonretarded children. *American Journal of Mental Deficiency, 83,* 253–261.

Burger, A. L., Blackman, L. S., & Tan, N. (1980). Maintenance and generalization of a sorting and retrieval strategy by EMR and nonretarded individuals. *American Journal of Mental Retardation, 84,* 373–389.

Burgio, L. D., Whitman, T. L., & Johnson, M. R. (1980). A self-instructional package for increasing attending behavior in educable mentally retarded children. *Journal of Applied Behavior Analysis, 13,* 443–459.

Butterfield, E. C., & Ferretti, R. P. (1987). Hypotheses about intellectual differences among children. In J. G. Borkowski & J. D. Day (Eds.), *Cognition in special children: Comparative approaches to retardation, learning disabilities, and giftedness* (pp. 195–233). Norwood, NJ: Ablex.

Campione, J. C. (1987). Metacognitive components of instructional research with problem learners. In F. E. Weinert & R. H. Klewe (Eds.), *Metacognition, motivation and understanding* (pp. 117–140). Hillsdale, NJ: Erlbaum.

Campione, J. C., & Brown, A. L. (1977). Training general metacognitive skills in retarded children. In M. M. Gruneberg, P. E. Morris, & R. N. Sykes (Eds.), *Practical aspects of memory.* London: Academic Press.

Campione, J. C., & Brown, A. L. (1978). Toward a theory of intelligence: Contributions from research with retarded children, *Intelligence, 2,* 279–304.

Cole, C. L., Gardner, W. I., & Karan, O. C. (1985). Self-management training of mentally retarded adults: Presenting severe conduct difficulties. *Applied Research in Mental Retardation, 6,* 337-347.

Connis, R. T. (1979). The effects of sequential pictorial cues, self-recording, and praise on the job sequence of retarded adults. *Journal of Applied Behavior Analysis, 12,* 355–361.

Covington, M. V. (1987). Achievement motivation, self-attributions, and exceptionality. In J. D. Day & J. G. Borkowski (Eds.), *Intelligence and exceptionality: New directions for theory, assessment, and instructional processes.* Norwood, NJ: Ablex.

Cullinan, D. (1976). Verbalization in EMR children's observational learning. *American Journal of Mental Deficiency, 81,* 65–72.

D'Zurillo, T. J., & Goldfried, M. R. (1971). Problem-solving and behavior modification. *Journal of Abnormal Psychology, 78,* 107–126.

Day, J. D., & Borkowski, J. G. (Eds.). (1987). *Intelligence and exceptionality: New directions for theory, assessment, and instructional practices.* Norwood, NJ: Ablex.

Day, J. D., Cordon, L. A., & Kerwin, M. L. (1989). Informal instruction and development of cognitive skills: A review and critique of research. In C. B.

McCormick, G. Miller, & M. Pressley (Eds.), *Cognitive strategy research: From basic research to educational applications*, pp. 83–103. New York: Springer–Verlag.

Day, J. D., & Hall, L. K. (1987). Cognitive assessment, intelligence, and instruction. In J. D. Day & J. G. Borkowski (Eds.), *Intelligence and exceptionality: New directions for theory, assessment, and instructional processes* (pp. 57–80). Norwood, NJ: Ablex.

Deacon, J. R., & Konarski, E. A. (1987). Correspondence training: An example of rule-governed behavior. *Journal of Applied Behavior Analysis, 20,* 391–400.

Doll, E. A. (1941). The essentials of an inclusive concept of mental deficiency. *American Journal of Mental Deficiency, 46,* 214–219.

Ellis, N. R. (1963). *Handbook of mental deficiency.* New York: McGraw Hill.

Ellis, N. R. (1970). Memory processes in retardates and normals. In N. R. Ellis (Ed.), *International review of research in mental retardation* (Vol. 4, pp. 1–32). New York: Academic Press.

Ellis, N. R. (1979). *Handbook of mental deficiency, psychological theory and research* (2nd ed.). Hillsdale, NJ: Erlbaum.

Feuerstein, R. (1980). *Instrumental enrichment: An intervention program for cognitive modifiability.* Baltimore: University Park Press.

Feuerstein, R., Rand, Y., Hoffman, M., & Miller, R. (1980). *Instrumental enrichment.* Baltimore: University Park Press.

Feuerstein, R., Rand, Y., Hoffman, M., Hoffman, M., & Miller, R. (1979). Cognitive modifiability in retarded adolescents: Effects of instrumental enrichment. *American Journal of Mental Deficiency, 83,* 539–550.

Fisher, M. A., & Zeaman, D. (1973). An attention-retention theory of retardate discrimination learning. In N. R. Ellis (Ed.), *The international review of research in mental retardation* (Vol. 6, pp. 171–256). New York: Academic Press.

Flavell, J. H. (1976). Metacognitive aspects of problem solving. In L. Resnick (Ed.), *The nature of intelligence* (pp. 231–235). New York: Wiley.

Franzini, L. R. Litrownik, A. J., & Magy, M. A. (1978). Immediate and delayed reward preferences of TMR adolescents. *American Journal of Mental Retardation, 82,* 406–409.

Ghatala, E. S., Levin, J. R., Pressley, M., & Lodico, M. G. (1985). Training cognitive strategy monitoring in children. *American Educational Research Journal, 22,* 199–215.

Greeson, L. E., & Jens, K. G. (1977). Instructional modeling and the development of visual- and verbal-mediation skills by TMR children. *American Journal of Mental Deficiency, 82,* 58–64.

Groden, J., & Cautela, J. R. (1984). Use of imagery procedures with students labeled "trainable retarded." *Psychological Reports, 54,* 60–66.

Grossman, H. (Ed.). (1983). *Classification in mental retardation* (revision). Washington, DC: American Association on Mental Deficiency.

Guevremont, D. C., Osnes, P. G., & Stokes, T. F. (1986). Preparation for effective self-regulation: The development of generalized verbal control. *Journal of Applied Behavior Analysis, 19,* 99–104.

Horner, R. H., Dunlap, G., & Koegel, R. L. (1988). *Generalization and maintenance: Life-style changes in applied settings.* Baltimore: P. H. Brookes.

House, B. J., & Zeaman, D. (1963). Miniature experiments in the discrimination learning of retardates. In L. P. Lipsitt & L. Spiker (Eds.), *Advances in child development and behavior* (Vol. 1). New York: Academic Press.

Inhelder, B. (1968). *The diagnosis of reasoning in the mentally retarded.* New York: John Day.

Israel, A. C. & O'Leary, K. D. (1973). Developing correspondence between children's words and deeds. *Child Development, 44,* 575–581.

Jensen, A. R. (1982). Reaction time and psychometric g. In H. J. Eysenck (Ed.), *A model for intelligence* (pp. 93–132). New York: Springer–Verlag.

Johnston, M. B., & Whitman, T. L. (1987). Enhancing math computation through variances in training format and instructional content. *Cognitive Therapy and Research, 11,* 381–397.

Johnston, M. B., Whitman, T. L., & Johnson, M. (1980). Teaching addition and subtraction to mentally retarded children: A self-instruction program. *Applied Research in Mental Retardation, 1,* 141–160.

Kanfer, F. H. (1970). Self-regulation: research, issues and speculation. In C. Neuringer & J. L. Michael (Eds.), *Behavior modification in clinical psychology.* New York: Appleton–Century–Crofts.

Kanfer, F. H., & Gaelick, L. (1986). Self-management methods in F. H. Kanfer & A. P. Goldstein (Eds.), *Helping people change,* (pp. 283–345), New York: Pergamon Press.

Kanfer, F. H., & Karsly, P. (1972). Self-control: A behaviorist excursion into the lion's den. *Behavior Therapy, 3,* 398–416.

Kanner, L. (1957). *Child psychiatry* (3rd ed.). Springfield, IL: Charles C. Thomas.

Kendall, P. C. (in 1990). Challenges for cognitive strategy training: The case of mental retardation. *American Journal on Mental Retardation, 94,* 365–367.

Kendall, C. R., Borkowski, J. G., & Cavanaugh, J. C. (1980). Metamemory and the transfer of an interrogative strategy by EMR children. *Intelligence, 4,* 255–270.

Kendall, P. C., & Braswell, L. (1985). *Cognitive–behavioral therapy for impulsive children.* New York: Guilford.

Kendall, P. C., & Williams, C. L. (1982). Assessing the cognitive and behavioral components of children's self-management. In P. Karoly & F. Kanfer (Eds.), *Self-management and behavior change: From theory to practice,* (pp. 315–352). New York: Pergamon Press.

Keogh, D. A., Burgio, L., Whitman, T. L., & Johnston, M. (1983). Development of listening skills in retarded children: A correspondence training program. *Child and Family Behavior Therapy, 5,* 51–71.

Keogh, D. A., Faw, G. D., Whitman, T. L., & Reid, D. H. (1984). Enhancing leisure skills in severely retarded adolescents through a self-instructional treatment package. *Analysis and Intervention in Developmental Disabilities, 4,* 333–351.

Keogh, D. A., Whitman, T. L., & Maxwell, S. E. (1988). Self instruction versus external instruction: Individual differences and training effectiveness. *Cognitive Therapy and Research, 12,* 591–610.

Litrownik, A. J. (1982). Special considerations in the self-management training of the developmentally disabled. In P. Karoly & F. Kanfer (Eds.), *Self-management and behavior change: From theory to practice* (pp. 315–352). New York: Pergamon Press.

Litrownik, A. J., Cleary, C. P., Lecklitner, G. L., & Franzini, O. R. (1978). Self-regulation in retarded persons: Acquisition of standards for performance. *American Journal of Mental Deficiency, 83,* 86–89.

Litrownik, A. J., Franzini, L. R., Geller, S., & Geller, M. (1977). Delay of gratification: Decisional self-control and experience with delay intervals. *American Journal of Mental Deficiency, 82,* 149–154.

Litrownik, A. J., Freitas, J. L., & Franzini, L. R. (1978). Self-regulation in mentally retarded children: Assessment and training of self-monitoring skills. *American Journal of Mental Deficiency, 82,* 499–506.

Lodico, M. G., Ghatala, E. S., Linn, J. R., Pressley, M., & Bell, J. A. (1983). The effects of strategy monitoring training on children's selection of effective memory strategies. *Journal of Experimental Child Psychology, 35,* 263–277.

Lowry, P. W., & Ross, L. E. (1975). Severely retarded children as impulsive responders: Improved performance with response delay. *American Journal of Mental Deficiency, 88,* 133–138.

Luria, A. R. (1961). *The role of speech in the regulation of normal and abnormal behaviors.* New York: Liveright.

Mace, F. C., & Kratochwill, T. R. (1985). Theories of reactivity in self-monitoring: A comparison of cognitive–behavioral and operant models. *Behavior Modification, 9,* 323–343.

Maisto, A. A., & Baumeister, A. A. (1984). Dissection of component processes in rapid information processing tasks: Comparison of retarded and nonretarded people. In P. H. Brooks, R. Sperber, & C. McCauley (Eds.), *Language and cognition in the mentally retarded* (pp. 165–188). Hillsdale, NJ: Erlbaum.

Mansdorf, I. J. (1977). Learning concepts through modeling: Using different instructional procedures with institutionalized mentally retarded adults. *American Journal of Mental Deficiency, 82,* 287–291.

Martin, J. E., Burger, D. L., Burger–Elias, S., & Mithaug, D. E. (1988). Applications of self-control strategies to facilitate independence in vocational and instructional settings. In N. W. Bray (Ed.), *International review of research in mental retardation.* San Diego: Academic Press.

Martin, J. E., Rusch, F. R., James, V. L., Decker, P. J., & Trtol, K. A. (1982). The use of picture cues to establish self-control in the preparation of complex meals by mentally retarded adults. *Applied Research in Mental Retardation, 3,* 105–119.

Matson, J. L., & Breuning, S. (Eds). (1983). *Assessing the mentally retarded.* New York: Grune & Stratton.

Matthews, J. (1971). Communication disorders in the mentally retarded. In L. E. Travis (Ed.), *Handbook of speech pathology and audiology* (pp. 801–818). New York: Appleton–Century–Crofts.

McFarland, C. E., & Wiebe, D. (1987). Structure and utilization of knowledge among special children. In J. G. Borkowski & J. D. Day (Eds.), *Cognition in special children: Comparative approaches to retardation, learning disabilities, and giftedness* (pp. 87–122). Norwood, NJ: Ablex.

Meichenbaum, D. (1977). *Cognitive–behavior modification.* New York: Plenum Press.

Mercer, C. D., & Snell, M. E. *Learning theory research in mental retardation: Implications for teaching.* Columbus, OH: Charles Merrill.

Messer, S. B. (1976). Reflection–impulsivity: A review. *Psychological Bulletin, 83,* 1026–1052.

Meyers, A., & Craighead, E. (Eds.). (1984). *Cognitive behavior therapy with children.* New York: Plenum Press.

O'Leary, S. G., & Dubey, D. R. (1979). Applications of self-control procedures by children: A review. *Journal of Applied Behavior Analysis, 12,* 449–465.

Paivio, A. (1971). *Imagery and verbal processes.* Hillsdale, NJ: Erlbaum.

Paniagwa, F. A., Pumariega, A. J., & Black, S. A. (1988). Clinical effects of correspondence training in the management of hyperactive children. *Behavioral Residential Treatment, 3,* 19–40.

Pressley, M. (1990). Four more considerations about self-regulation in the mentally retarded. *American Journal on Mental Retardation, 94,* 369–371.

Pressley, M., Cariglia–Bull, T., Deane, S., & Schneider, W. (1987). Short-term memory, verbal competence, and age as predictors of imagery instructional effectiveness. *Journal of Experimental Child Psychology, 43,* 194–211.

Pylyshyn, Z. (1978). Computational models and empirical constraints. *Behavioral and Brain Sciences, 1,* 93–99.

Reid, D. K. (1988). *Teaching the learning disabled.* Boston: Allyn & Bacon.

Repp, A. C., Barton, L. E., & Brulle, A. R. (1981). Correspondence between effectiveness and staff use of instructions for severely retarded persons. *Applied Research in Mental Retardation, 2,* 237–245.

Roberts, R. N., Nelson, R. O., & Olson, T. W. (1987). Self-instruction: An analysis of the differential effects of instruction and reinforcement. *Journal of Applied Behavior Analysis, 20,* 235–242.

Robinson, N. M., & Janos, P. M. (1987). The contribution of intelligence tests to the understanding of special children. In J. D. Day & J. G. Borkowski (Eds.), *Intelligence and exceptionality: New directions for theory, assessment, and instructional processes* (pp. 21–56). Norwood, NJ: Ablex.

Rogers–Warren, P., & Baer, D. M. (1976). Correspondence between saying and doing: Teaching children to share and praise. *Journal of Applied Behavior Analysis, 9,* 336–354.

Rosen, M., Clark, G. R., &Kivitz, M. S. (1976). *The history of mental retardation.* Baltimore: University Park Press.

Rosenthal, T. L., & Kellog, J. S. (1973). Demonstration versus instructions in concept attainment by mental retardates. *Behavior Research and Therapy, 11,* 299–302.

Ross, D. M., & Ross, S. A. (1973). Cognitive training for the EMR child: Situational problem-solving and planning. *American Journal of Mental Deficiency, 78,* 20–26.

Ross, D. M., & Ross, S. A. (1978). Cognitive training for EMR children: Choosing the best alternative. *American Journal of Mental Deficiency, 82,* 598–601.

Rusch, F. R., Morgan, T. K., Martin, J. E., Riva, M., & Agran, M. (1985). Competitive employment: Teaching mentally retarded employees self-instructional strategies. *Applied Research in Mental Retardation, 6,* 389–407.

Rynders, J. E., Behlen, K. L., & Horrobin, J. M. (1979). Performance characteristics of preschool Down's Syndrome children receiving augmented or repetitive verbal instruction. *American Journal of Mental Deficiency, 84,* 67–73.

Sarason, S., & Doris, J. (1969). *Psychological problems in mental deficiency.* New York: Harper & Row.

Schwartz, B. (1988). Experimental synthesis of behavior: Reinforcement, behavioral stereotypy, and problem-solving. *Psychology of Learning and Motivation, 22,* 93–138.

Shapiro, E. S., & Klein, R. D. (1980). Self-management of classroom behavior with retarded-disturbed children. *Behavior Modification, 4,* 83–97.

Shapiro, E. S., McGonigle, J. J., & Ollendick, T. H. (1980). An analysis of self-assessment and self-reinforcement in a self-managed token economy with mentally retarded children. *Applied Research in Mental Retardation, 1,* 227–240.

Skinner, B. F. (1953). Science and human behavior. New York: Macmillan.

Smith, M., & Meyers, A. (1979). Telephone skills training for retarded adults: Group and individual demonstrations with and without verbal instruction. *American Journal of Mental Deficiency, 83,* 581–587.

Snow, J. S., Mercatoris, M., Beal, D., & Weber, D. (1982). Development of standards of performance by mentally retarded children. *American Journal of Mental Deficiency, 87,* 86–89.

Snyder, L. K., & McLean, J. E. (1976). Deficient acquisition strategies: A proposed conceptual framework for analyzing severe language deficiency. *American Journal of Mental Deficiency, 81,* 338–379.

Sowers, J. A. Rusch, F. R., Connis, R. T., & Cunnings, L. E. (1980). Teaching mentally retarded adults to time manage in a vocational setting. *Journal of Applied Behavior Analysis, 13,* 119–128.

Spates, C. R., & Kanfer, F. H. (1977). Self-monitoring, self-evaluation and self-reinforcement in children's learning: A test of a multistage self-regulation model. *Behavior Therapy, 8,* 9–16.

Spence, B. H., & Whitman, T. L. (in press). Instruction and self-regulation in mentally retarded adults in a vocational setting. *Cognitive Therapy and Research.*

Sperber, R., & McCauley, C. (1984). Semantic processing efficiency in the mentally retarded. In P. H. Brooks, R. Sperber, & C. McCauley (Eds.), *Language and cognition in the mentally retarded* (pp. 141–164). Hillsdale, NJ: Erlbaum.

Spitz, H. H. (1973). Consolidating facts into the schematized learning and memory system of educable retardates. In N. R. Ellis (Ed.), *International review of research in mental retardation* (Vol. 6, pp. 149–168). New York: Academic Press.

Spitz, H. H. (1987). Problem-solving processes in special populations. In J. G. Borkowski & J. D. Day (Eds.), *Cognition in special children: Comparative approaches to retardation, learning disabilities, and giftedness* (pp. 153–193). Norwood, NJ: Ablex.

Spitz, H. H., & Winters, E. A. (1977). Tic tac toe performance as a function of maturational level of retarded adolescents and nonretarded children. *Intelligence, 1,* 108–117.

Sternberg, R. J. (1987). A unified theory of intellectual exceptionality. In J. D. Day & J. G. Borkowski (Eds.), *Intelligence and exceptionality: New directions for theory, assessment, and instructional processes* (pp. 135–172). Norwood, NJ: Ablex.

Stokes, T. F., & Baer, D. M. (1977). An implicit technology of generalization. *Journal of Applied Behavior Analysis, 10,* 349–367.

Torgesen, J. K., Kistner, J. A., & Morgan, S. (1987). Component processes in working memory. In J. G. Borkowski & J. D. Day (Eds.), *Cognition in special children: Comparative approaches to retardation, learning disabilities, and giftedness* (pp. 49–86). Norwood, NJ: Ablex.

Tredgold, A. F. (1937). *A textbook of mental deficiency* (6th ed.). Baltimore: William Wood.

Turnure, J., & Zigler, E. (1964). Outer directedness in the problem-solving of normal and retarded children. *Journal of Abnormal and Social Psychology, 69,* 427–436.

Vygotsky, L. S. (1978). *Mind in society: The development of higher psychological processes.* Cambridge, MA: Harvard University Press.

Wacker, D. P., & Berg, W. K. (1983). Effects of picture prompts and the acquisition of complex vocational tasks by mentally retarded adolescents. *Journal of Applied Behavior Analysis, 16,* 417–433.

Wacker, D. P., & Berg, W. K. (1984). Training adolescents with severe handicaps to set up job tasks independently using picture prompts. *Analysis and Intervention in Developmental Disabilities, 4,* 353–365.

Ward, J., & Gow, L. (1982). Programming generalization: A central problem area in educational psychology. *Educational Psychology, 2,* 231–248.

Whitman, T. L. (in 1990). Self-regulation and mental retardation. *American Journal on Mental Retardation, 94,* 347–362.

Whitman, T. L. (1987). Self-instruction, individual differences, and mental retardation. *American Journal on Mental Retardation, 92,* 213–223.

Whitman, T. L., Burgio, L., & Johnston, M. B. (1984). Cognitive behavior therapy with the mentally retarded. In A. Meyers & E. Craighead (Eds.), *Cognitive behavior therapy with children.* New York: Plenum Press, pp. 193–227.

Whitman, T. L., & Johnston, M. B. (1986). In M. Hersen & V. Van Hasselt (Eds.), *Behavior therapy with children.* New York: Plenum Press, pp. 184–223.

Whitman, T. L., Scibak, J. W., Butler, K. M., Richter, R., & Johnston, M. R. (1982). Improving classroom behavior in mentally retarded children through correspondence training. *Journal of Applied Behavior Analysis, 15,* 545–564.

Whitman, T. L., Scibak, J. W., & Reid, D. H. (1983). *Behavior modification with the severely and profoundly retarded: Research and application.* New York: Academic Press.

Whitman, T. L., Spence, B. H., & Maxwell, S. E. (1987). A comparison of external and self-instructional teaching formats with mentally retarded adults in a vocational training setting. *Research in Developmental Disabilities, 8,* 371–88.

Yoder, P., & Forehand, R. (1974). Effects of modeling and verbal cues upon concept acquisition of nonretarded and retarded children. *American Journal of Mental Deficiency, 78,* 566–570.

Yoder, D. E. & Miller, J. F. (1972). What we may know and what we can do: input toward a system. In J. E. McClean, D. E. Yoder, & R. L. Schiefellbrisch (Eds.), *Language intervention with the retarded* (pp. 89–103). Baltimore: University Park Press.

Zeaman, D., & House, B. J. (1963). The role of attention in retardate discrimination learning. In N. R. Ellis (Ed.), *Handbook of mental deficiency* (pp. 159–223). New York: McGraw-Hill.

Zeaman, D., & House, B. J. (1979). A review of attention theory. In N. R. Ellis (Ed.), *Handbook of mental deficiency: Psychological theory and research* (pp. 63–120). Hillsdale, NJ: Erlbaum.

Zegiob, L., Klukas, N., & Junginger, J. (1978). Reactivity of self-monitoring procedures with retarded adolescents. *American Journal of Mental Deficiency*, *83*, 156–163.

Zigler, E., & Balla, D. (1982). *Mental retardation: The developmental-difference controversy*. Hillsdale, NJ: Erlbaum.

Zigler, E. (1966). Research on personality structure in the retardate. In N. R. Ellis (Ed.), *International review of research in mental retardation* (Vol. 1). New York: Academic Press.

CHAPTER 10

Involving Parents in Cognitive–Behavioral Therapy with Children and Adolescents

LAUREN BRASWELL
North Memorial Medical Center

Readers of the literature on child cognitive–behavioral therapies recognize that advocates of this treatment approach endorse the importance of parental involvement, but that they have often not included parents in past treatment efforts. There is no theoretical basis for the exclusion of parents by cognitive–behavioral therapists, and most advocates of this approach would encourage various forms of parental involvement, yet the literature indicates that explicitly involving parents in the treatment process has been the exception rather than the rule (Braswell & Kendall, 1988; Kendall & Braswell, 1985).

The extent to which parents have been excluded tends to vary with the particular type of approach being considered. One method of cognitive–behavioral intervention, the one with which the current author is most familiar, verbal self-instructional training, is perhaps the "worst offender" in this regard. Meichenbaum and Goodman's (1971) individually focused approach to training became the prototype for a myriad of subsequent studies, with only a small group of investigators attempting to incorporate parents (or teachers for that matter) in the actual course of therapy (e.g., Glenwick & Barocas, 1979). Early efforts at perspective-taking training were also focused exclusively on the child (see review by Urbain & Kendall, 1980), as were early attempts at attribution retraining (Braswell, Koehler, & Kendall, 1985).

In contrast, the social problem-solving training literature offers more evidence of parental involvement. Although there have been a large number of investigations involving school or residentially based programs with no parental component, an equally large number of early studies included parents as key participants in the therapy process, with successful outcomes (Alexander & Parsons, 1973; Blechman, Olson, & Hellman, 1976; Blechman, Olson, Schornagel, Halsdorf, & Turner, 1976; Foster, 1979; Klein, Alexander, & Parsons, 1977; Robin, Kent, O'Leary, Foster, & Prinz, 1977).

The cognitive–behavioral literature with internalizing childhood disorders has been slower to develop and is much less extensive than the literature addressing externalizing conditions. As will be discussed in a subsequent section, however, some of the architects of treatment protocols for anxious and/or depressed children have shown sensitivity to the importance of involving parents (Kendall & Hill, 1988; Stark, Best, & Sellstrom, 1989). Even those investigators primarily concerned with peer relationship issues have recognized the influence of early family experiences and, therefore, are more aware of the need for family-based preventive interventions (Pettit, Dodge, & Brown, 1988). Thus, cognitive–behaviorists attempting to intervene with a number of different child populations are moving toward the common goal of greater incorporation of parents in the treatment process.

The goal of this chapter is to present the case for parental involvement in the conduct of cognitive–behavioral therapy with children. In this context, the chapter addresses the varying nature of the parent's relationship to problems that might lead a child to be referred for treatment as well as the parent's crucial role in efforts to achieve generalization, skills transfer, and maintenance of therapeutic change. Evidence that the cognitive activities of the parents are meaningful when conceptualizing certain childhood conditions is presented. The legacy of behavior therapy regarding the most effective means of training parents as well as factors that appear to affect maintenance of program-induced changes are then considered. Promising examples of parental involvement in cognitive–behavioral treatments for externalizing and internalizing childhood disorders and child maltreatment are described. Finally, some practical procedures for achieving greater parental involvement, regardless of the type of disorder being treated, are presented. Throughout the chapter, findings from the domains of developmental psychology, developmental psychopathology, and family process research will be considered in an effort to highlight the significance of involving parents in conceptualizations of and interventions with the psychological difficulties of children and adolescents.

WHY INVOLVE PARENTS?

This section heading may seem like a facetious question to some readers, but many approaches to child therapy have, at least in the past, chosen not to include parents. In addition to the primarily child focus of psychodynamic and some client-centered approaches, certain cognitive–behavioral interventions with child or adolescent clients have excluded parents and other significant adults from having a major role in the therapeutic process.

This failure to attend to such key elements of the child's social environment seems curious, considering that many cognitive–behavioral approaches grew out of a behavioral tradition. Glenwick and Jason (1984) have noted that in their eagerness to redress the disregard of behavior analysts for cognitive events, cognitive–behaviorists "may perhaps have gone overboard at times by acting as if (a) the environment within which our target children function is an irrelevant factor and (b) our programs can be successful without considerations of behavior–environment relations" (p. 145). Recognizing the failure to attend to such key factors makes it easier for the current author to appreciate what traditional behaviorists have found so objectionable about cognitive–behavioral therapy. Many cognitive–behavioral applications with children have failed to use traditional reinforcement methods to shape behavior, even in the training environment, much less train parents in the use of behavioral technology to accomplish skills transfer or the maintenance of therapeutic change.

The overly exclusive focus on the client's internal experiences has also left cognitive–behaviorists vulnerable to critique by developmentalists. The concerns of developmental psychologists have been articulated by Mahoney and Nezworski (1985), who urged cognitive–behaviorists to move beyond their "portrayal of the nervous system as an isolated island of (albeit mediated) adaptation" (p. 472) to a greater awareness of the role of family and affectional systems in promoting or protecting against the development of difficulties commonly addressed via cognitive–behavioral therapy approaches, such as problems with self-control, problem solving, and social interaction.

In the following subsection, both conceptual and practical reasons for including parents in the process of child intervention will be considered. Three general rationales for parental involvement are considered: (1) Parents play a role in defining the child's problem; (2) Parents and family may cause, exascerbate, or moderate the problem for which the child is to be treated; and (3) Parents, regardless of their relationship to the cause of the child's difficulties, have a role to play in the generalization, skills transfer, and maintenance of therapeutic change.

Parents' Role in Defining the Child's Problem

As discussed by Braswell and Kendall (1988), the child and his or her behavioral difficulties are deeply embedded in a social context. This state of affairs has implications for how the child client comes into contact with psychological resources and how his or her difficulties are defined. Children rarely refer themselves for evaluation or treatment. Rather, some significant adult in the child's life, usually the parent or teacher, determines that the child may be an appropriate candidate for services. Thus, from the outset the parent is typically involved in deciding that the child is experiencing some type of difficulty and that this difficulty warrants possible psychological intervention. The exact process that parents use in making such a determination is unclear and possibly highly idiosyncratic, but Masten and Braswell (in press) have suggested that parents may be influenced by their culture's conceptualization of the developmental tasks children are expected to address at certain ages. Once the child has achieved or passed the age at which his or her culture expects a certain task to be resolved or accomplished, parents may begin to define the emotional or behavioral sequelae of this unresolved task as a problem.

Emerging data also suggest that the parent's emotional state may influence the extent to which he or she perceives the child as manifesting problematical behavior. For example, maternal depression has been found to influence the extent to which the mother perceives her child as manifesting emotional or behavioral difficulty, although the direction of influence can be debated (Conrad & Hammen, 1989; Webster–Stratton & Hammond, 1988).

The degree of parental contribution to the child's difficulties may also influence the extent to which parents define their children as difficult. For example, Reid, Kavanagh, and Baldwin (1987) noted that abusive parents typically define their children as more behaviorally problematical than do control parents even when extensive behavioral observations do not support such differences. Reid et al. argue that it is in the best interest of these dysfunctional parents to perceive their children as more demanding in order to provide some justification for their own abusive behavior. This consideration of the parental role in defining child problems leads directly to the consideration of the parents' relationship to the cause of the problem.

Parents' Relationship to the Cause of the Child's Difficulties

The parents' contribution to the child's difficulties can be conceived both in terms of parental or familial factors that elevate a child's risk to display behavior problems in general and factors that increase the probability of the child displaying a particular pattern or type of disorder. When considering evidence concerning both general and specific risk factors, it is important to note Sines's (1987) concern that the lack of uniformity in conceptualizing, much less measuring, features of the familial/home environment has made it difficult to develop a coherent body of data. With this caution in mind, a few illustrative examples of parental or familial factors associated with general risk for psychopathology or risk for developing a specific symptom pattern will be considered.

The cumulative number of stressors a family has experienced (low SES, maternal depression, marital discord, etc.) does seem to predict greater emotional/behavioral difficulties in the children as well as lower attainment on measures of IQ and perceived social competence (Shaw & Emery, 1988). Marital discord and interspousal aggression, in particular, have been found to predict emotional and behavioral difficulties in both preschool and school-aged children (Emergy, 1982; Jouriles, Murphy, & O'Leary, 1989; Jouriles, Pfiffner, & O'Leary, 1988). Beginning attempts to establish links between these stressors and specific parenting behaviors suggest a possible interaction with the sex of the child, with mothers in conflicted relationships less likely to punish deviant behavior in girls and more likely to direct disapproval statements to boys (Jouriles et al., 1988). Family process factors, such as the degree of conflict, have been found to be more predictive of difficulties with the child than factors such as family structure (intact two-parent versus single parent versus stepparent), particularly if differences in income, family size, and percentage of working mothers are controlled (Kurdek & Sinclair, 1988).

Exploring other dimensions of family process, Smets and Hartup (1988) found that families with extreme scores on the dimensions of cohesion (enmeshed versus disengaged) and adaptability (rigid versus chaotic) were more likely to have children exhibiting emotional/behavioral difficulties than were families scoring in the moderate range on both of these dimensions. Interestingly, this relationship was stronger with 6-to-11-year-old children than with 12-to-16-year-olds, suggesting that as the child moves toward adolescence his or her status may be less directly related to the family. Somewhat consistent with the Smets and Hartup findings, Asarnow, Carlson, and Guthrie (1987) observed that the strongest predictor of suicidal behavior in a sample of 8-to-13-year-old psychiatric inpatients was the children's perception of their family environments. Children with suicidal ideation and attempts tended to view their families as exhibiting poor control, high levels of conflict, and a lack of cohesiveness.

Maternal depression is a parental factor that has received intense research attention over the past few years. A number of investigators have observed an association between maternal depression and at least the report of elevated rates of emotional/behavioral disturbances in the children (Beardslee, Bemporad, Keller, & Klerman, 1983; Forehand, McCombs, & Brody, 1987; Radke-Yarrow, Cummings, Kuczynski, & Chapman, 1985). As previously noted, some investigators have found depressed mothers to report their children as being more disturbed than was suggested by independent behavioral observations (Webster-Stratton & Hammond, 1988), while other research has found depressed mothers to be more accurate than nondepressed mothers in identifying difficulties with their children when rating data from others' sources suggests the presence of symptomatology in the children (Conrad & Hammen, 1989). In examinations of the relationship of maternal depression to specific manifestations of parenting behavior, two

general patterns have been commonly observed. One pattern is characterized by withdrawal and the avoidance of conflict, while the other involves
more critical, negativistic interactions with the child (Conrad & Hammen,
1989; Jouriles, Murphy, & O'Leary, 1989; Kochanska, Kuczynski, & Maguire, 1989; Webster–Stratton & Hammond, 1988). Kochanska et al. (1989)
suggest that these variations in observed behavior may be accounted for by
the interaction of maternal depression with other factors, such as the mother's self-reported mood immediately prior to the period of mother–child
observation and the developmental status of the child.

When considering the parents' role in causing more specific childhood
difficulties, it is useful to consider a transactional model originally proposed
by Sameroff and colleagues (Sameroff, 1983; Sameroff & Chandler, 1975)
and elaborated by Cicchetti, Toth, and Bush (1988). This model emphasizes that while developmental outcomes are typically the result of multiple
transactions among and between the parent, child, and environmental characteristics, there is a continuum with regard to the relative contribution of
child-specific (genetic/constitutional) versus parent-specific (parenting/en-
vironmental) factors. For example, Down Syndrome is clearly the result of
child-specific factors, although parenting factors may influence the level of
adaptation of a specific child within the reaction range delimited by genetic
factors. In contrast, child maltreatment is the clear result of parenting factors, with certain constitutional features of the child, perhaps, making a
given child more vulnerable to abuse.

As suggested by this model, in some circumstances, parental actions
can be perceived as having a direct causal relationship to the observed difficulties of the child. As we abandon notions of schizophrenigenic mothers
causing schizophrenia with their double-binding parenting methods or re-
frigerator mothers causing autism with their cold, aloof parenting style, we
must be ready to explore and accept the role parents may play in creating
other difficulties. The direct, causal relationship between parenting behavior and specific emotional/behavioral difficulties in children is easiest to perceive when traumatic events have occurred, such as when severe parental
sexual or physical abuse causes an adjustment reaction or Post Traumatic
Stress Disorder in the child. Equally directly, parental modeling and explicit reinforcement of stealing, aggression, and illicit drug use may prove
to be one pathway for the development of antisocial behavior.

In other circumstances, parental actions may be viewed as the key
precipitant for the emergence of difficulty on the child's part but the exact
form of the difficulty may be determined by other factors associated with
the child and his or her environment. For example, parental divorce and
subsequent abandonment by one parent could trigger the manifestation of
a host of symptoms in a previously asymptomatic child. While such a trauma
may be a sufficient triggering cause for emotional and behavioral distress,
empirical and clinical findings suggest that this event does not produce the

same type and magnitude of distress across all children, with factors such as age, sex, and relationship with the remaining parent exerting mediating influences (Wallerstein & Kelly, 1980).

Dramatic situations in which the parent is the direct cause of certain childhood difficulties may be less common than situations in which parental actions maintain, amplify, or moderate pathological processes that were initiated by a host of other biological and/or environmental factors. Echoing the findings of the earlier New York longitudinal study (Thomas, Chess, & Birch, 1968), Earls and Jung (1987) observed that temperamental factors, such as poor adaptability and intense stress reactivity may be the first step in the development of certain types of childhood difficulties, with environmental factors being more important in determining the persistence and course of a disorder once it is set in motion.

Within the domain of social skills difficulties, Pettit et al. (1988) examined the role of early family experiences in influencing the development of social-problem solving skills and, ultimately, social competence. In their review of the existing literature, Pettit et al. (1988) concluded that children establishing secure attachments in infancy are more likely to be competent with peers while those experiencing hostile, inconsistent parenting are more likely to exhibit socially incompetent behavior. Pettit et al. also presented new data indicating that socially rejected children were more likely to have early family experiences that were characterized by fewer opportunities for positive interactions with parents and peers and to have parents who both endorsed and practiced physical aggression in the home.

In their formulation of the development of conduct-disordered behavior, Patterson and Bank (1989) suggested that such behavior is developed via a series of social exchanges that are initiated in the home environment. Variables contributing to the initiation of such a process include (1) a lack of parental social skills, (2) parental traits such as antisocial behavior and child traits such as having a difficult temperament, and (3) disruptor variables such as marital conflict and other sources of stress. These variables combine to result in ineffectual parental discipline and monitoring. Patterson and Banks speculate that all three variables play a role in the development of conduct-disordered behavior in very young children, while the disruptor variables may play a key role in the emergence of conduct disorder in adolescence.

The examination and understanding of protective as well as amplifying processes within families is highly relevant for those seeking to intervene around these issues; however, the complexity of these processes must be appreciated. For example, Masten and colleagues have observed that different models are required to explain the relationship between stress exposure and the expression of competence, depending on what aspect of behavioral competence one is examining (academic versus behavioral versus social) (Masten et al., 1988).

Parents' Role in Generalization, Skills Transfer, and Maintenance of Therapeutic Change

Whatever the parents' relationship to the cause of the child's difficulties, parents play a crucial role in setting the stage for the generalization and maintenance of therapeutic change. Virtually all forms of psychotherapeutic endeavor are plagued with difficulties of poor skills transfer from the training environment to extratherapy environments and poor maintenance of change, but interventions vary tremendously in how directly they tend to address these concerns.

Traditionally, behaviorists have directed the most attention to these concerns, with classic papers by Stokes and colleagues (Stokes & Baer, 1977; Stokes & Osnes, 1989) presenting principles and tactics for generalization programming. Ironically, discontent with limited generalization of behavioral interventions led some investigators and clinicians to embrace cognitive–behavioral approaches. Originally these approaches were perceived as a means of achieving greater generalization and maintenance through the training of general cognitive strategies that the client could then enact to direct his or her behavior across time and in a variety of settings. But 15 years of research experience with these methods suggests that while cognitive strategies may be more efficient to teach, these strategies may not generalize any more readily than behavioral skills (Foster, Kendall, & Gouvremont, 1988). In addition, Kendall (1989) has suggested the need for cognitive–behaviorists to develop more realistic expectations for the potential range of therapeutic responses possible when using specific interventions with specific forms of psychopathology.

Adopting a more realistic approach to both therapeutic response and generalization would lead one to conclude that, if the therapeutic goal is to achieve change that influences more than just the child's behavior in the therapeutic setting, one must include key elements of those other settings in the course of treatment. Parents represent the most obvious social elements of the child's home environment. In a subsequent section, interventions in which parents are trained to prompt, shape, and reinforce the child's use of newly developing cognitive and behavioral skills will be discussed.

SIGNIFICANCE OF PARENTAL COGNITIVE FACTORS

Given this chapter's focus on cognitive–behavioral interventions, it is important to give special attention to the growing body of literature addressing cognitive events and processes that seem to be related to parenting behaviors. Developmental as well as cognitive–behavioral researchers have begun examining the specific cognitive events, products, or processes of parents that may be of relevance to understanding how parental behavior causes childhood difficulties and/or how such behavior can be shaped and changed to intervene effectively with the child. Some of these efforts have focused on more global constructs, while other investigators have explored more specific cognitive events or processes.

While some cognitive–behaviorists view the field of assessment of the cognitive events of parents as in its infancy (Epstein, Schlesinger, & Dryden, 1988), in reality the assessment of parental attitudes and beliefs has a long-standing history within psychology and child development research. As observed by Holden and Edwards (1989), the first review of research on parental attitudes occurred over 50 years ago (Stogdill, 1936)! Unfortunately, despite its long history, this area of research continues to be plagued with a number of methodological problems, including confusion arising from the ambiguity of questionnaire items, poor agreement between instruments that are supposed to measure the same constructs, and poor agreement between questionnaire responses and actual parenting behavior (Goodnow, 1988; Holden & Edwards, 1989). Their review of the history of research on parental attitudes has led Holden and Edwards to challenge the old view that parents have a set of stable, unidimensional, and coherent child-rearing attitudes and assert that parental attitudes toward child rearing are, in reality, characterized by change, multidimensionality, and complexity. These authors also note that, to the extent that stable attitudes do exist, it is unlikely that they can be adequately assessed via the decontextualized statements used in most questionnaires. Along with Goodnow (1988), Holden and Edwards have challenged developmentalists and child clinical psychologists to make greater use of the models and methods emerging from social psychology in their attempts to understand the cognitive processes of parents. With these methodological and conceptual cautions in mind, this section will highlight some of the emerging findings on parental cognitive processes that have special relevance for the cognitive–behavioral researcher and clinician.

Some investigations have examined the relationships among and between parent's internalized models of parent-child relationships (as derived from how they discuss their own childhood experiences), their actual parenting behavior, and the quality of their child's attachment to them. Crowell and Feldman (1988) hypothesized that the mother's model of relationships affects her ability to attend to and integrate cues from her child and, as a result, affects her ability to be appropriately responsive. Consistent with their hypothesis, Crowell and Feldman found that mothers rated as having secure internal models of their own parenting relationship were more likely to provide greater support and better quality assistance to their children during a problem-solving task and were more likely to have children rated as exhibiting secure attachments. These observations are consistent with the findings of Main and colleagues that parents' models of their own parenting relationships were predictive of the types of attachment their children were forming with them (Main & Goldwyn, 1984; Main, Kaplan, & Cassidy, 1985).

Although operating from a behavioral rather than developmental perspective, Wahler and colleagues have shared Crowell and Feldman's concern for the mother's ability to attend and differentially respond to cues from her child (Wahler, 1980; Wahler & Afton, 1980; Wahler & Dumas, 1989). As previously discussed, Wahler (1980) has noted that socially isolated, economically deprived mothers whose primary community contacts were negative (insular mothers) could make changes with parent training interventions but these changes were not maintained. Wahler and Afton (1980) observed that over the course of parent training, noninsular mothers moved toward more detailed descriptions of child problem behaviors with little attribution of blame. In contrast, insular mothers continued to voice global, blame-oriented descriptions of the child's problem behaviors. As a result, Wahler and Afton (1980) inferred that training did not alter the attending/perceptual processes of the insular mothers. These findings led Wahler and Dumas (1989) to formulate a view of effective parenting that emphasizes both adequate child-rearing skills and attentional capacities, which they define as "the ability to track the influence that their children's behavior and the behavior of other social agents has upon their actions" (p. 118). This viewpoint suggests that environmental stressors interact with the tasks of child care by interfering with the mother's attention to relevant child behavior signals. Wahler and Dumas (1989) advocate helping insular mothers develop both more molecular modes of analysis of child behavior problems while simultaneously assisting the mothers in perceiving more molar or cross-situational stress patterns in an effort to help them respond differentially to specific child behaviors while recognizing contextual effects. Interestingly, the cognitive–behavioral view of Wahler and Dumas (1989) that mothers who are able to perceive complex patterns of child care stimuli are better able to engage in sensitive, responsive parenting is highly similar to findings from other areas of child study. Developmentalists, for example, have observed that the mother's capacity to perceive and understand the complexity of her relationship with her children is positively correlated with the adequacy of her care giving and negatively correlated with the probability of abusive behavior (Brunnquell, Crichton, & Egeland, 1981; Newberger, 1980).

Efforts to understand the cognitive precipitants of child abuse/maltreatment have led to the recognition of some factors of potentially great relevance to those designing cognitive–behavioral interventions for this population. As previously noted, Reid et al. (1987) found that abusive parents were more likely than carefully matched controls to describe their children as being difficult when in-home observations did not suggest behavioral differences. This finding is consistent with previous research conducted

in laboratory or structured situations (Burgess & Conger, 1978; Mash, Johnston, & Kovitz, 1983) and with the observation that abusive mothers are
more likely than normal ones to ascribe hostile intent to their children's
actions, even when such actions are considered to be within normal developmental limits (Bauer & Twentyman, 1985; Larrance & Twentyman, 1983).
Reid et al. (1987) offer several possible explanations for this observed bias,
including the parent attempting to justify his or her own behavior by presenting the child as more difficult, the parent having low tolerance for normal child problem behaviors, and/or, as hypothesized by Wahler (1980),
the parent's failing to monitor the child well and, thus, having a tendency
to notice only the most aversive child behaviors.

In a related vein, unrealistic expectations about child development and
behavior have long been suggested as a parental cognitive deficit that could
play an etiological role in abuse. In their discussion of this issue, Azar and
Rohrbeck (1986) note that earlier research efforts found only inconsistent
evidence for a relationship between unrealistic expectations and abuse.
However, these early efforts assessed unrealistic expectations on the basis
of the parents' knowledge of developmental milestones rather than their
knowledge and expectations as they relate to more complex chains of child
behavior. Azar, Robinson, Hekimian, and Twentyman (1984) developed a
measure of unrealistic expectations addressing more complex interpersonal
situations, the Parent Opinion Questionnaire (POQ), and found that maltreating mothers expressed significantly higher levels of unrealistic expectations relative to demographically matched controls. In a more demanding
test of the measure, Azar and Rohrbeck (1986) compared the POQ scores
of mothers who abused their children with those of mothers whose hus-
bands or boyfriends had abused their children, thus controlling for nonspecific factors differentiating families identified as abusive from normal families. The abusive mothers were found to endorse significantly more unrealistic
expectations about children's behavior than the mothers with abusive partners, with discriminant analysis of the total scores correctly identifying 83%
of the total sample (75% of abusers, 98% of nonabusers). Similar explora-
tions of the beliefs of those who sexually molest children are also suggestive that such perpetrators have unique beliefs regarding the benefits of
sexual contact for the child and the child's complicity in such contact, with
the responses of child molesters being significantly different from those of
perpetrators of sexual crimes with adults as well as from the responses of
normals (Stermac & Segal, 1989). Thus, unrealistic expectations and beliefs regarding child behavior appear to be a cognitive constructs of relevance to the understanding and changing of various forms of child maltreatment. Unrealistic beliefs may also play a role in less serious forms of family
dysfunction, such as parent–adolescent conflict (Roehling & Robin, 1986).

Thus, despite continuing methodological and conceptual concerns, investigators have been able to demonstrate that certain parental cognitive

events and processes do relate to actual parenting behaviors and may play a role in the emergence of certain childhood difficulties, particularly those associated with disrupted attachments and child maltreatment.

BEHAVIOR THERAPY'S LEGACY OF PARENTAL INVOLVEMENT

In our enthusiasm to incorporate parents into cognitive–behavioral interventions, it is important to consider reliable findings and respond to issues raised by behavioral treatment efforts that have involved parents. Such efforts have taken the form of either behavioral parent training or behavioral family therapy. As discussed in several reviews, clinical behavior therapy addressing children's problems has, in large part, involved the behavior therapist's training the parent(s) to enact some form of intervention with the child (Rapport, 1987; Twardosz & Nordquist, 1987). Examinations of this technology have tended to focus on the extent to which the parents successfully carried out the procedures with their children, but some reviews have also considered factors mediating program effectiveness in communicating information to the parents.

Twardosz and Nordquist (1987) note that the most common content areas of behavioral parent training include, contingency management and operant training procedures, contingency contracting, conflict resolution skills, parent–child interactional style concerns, and issues of household organization, with most specific packages incorporating some, but not all, of these elements. Investigations of the acceptability of various common components have consistently observed that parents rate intervention techniques designed to increase deficit behaviors (positive reinforcement, positive practice, differential reinforcement) as more acceptable than techniques designed to decrease unacceptable behavior (time-out, response–cost) (Calvert & McMahon, 1987).

O'Dell (1985) noted that the most common behavioral parent training methods include: (1) didactic training with primarily verbal input (written or oral), (2) didactic training with primarily visual input (live or videotaped modeling), (3) interactive training in which the parents interactions with their child are observed and immediate feedback is provided, and (4) combination methods. O'Dell summarized outcome data suggesting that interactive methods are quite effective but also the least cost-effective. High-quality written materials may produce relatively good outcomes with highly functioning parent samples, but training methods that emphasize visual input may be most effective with the broadest range of parents. More recent comparative outcome research also supports this conclusion (Webster–Stratton, Hollinsworth, & Kolpacoff, 1989). There is some degree of consensus in the field that packaged behavioral training methods, particularly those including high-quality visual and written input, may be the most appropriate first step in parent training, with the use of more individualized and interactive methods being reserved for those families continuing to exhibit difficulties following group training (O'Dell, 1985; Twardosz & Nordquist, 1987).

Surprisingly, even many behaviorally oriented parent training programs can be criticized for failing to make use of therapist-mediated contingencies to support parental involvement during training and for failing to incorporate contingencies concerning the trainer's behavior. Greater monitoring of parental compliance with program procedures has been recommended as has greater attention to contingencies outside the context of therapy that interfere with the parents' implementation of training methods.

As observed by Wahler and Dumas (1989), parent training efforts have been largely predicated on a behavioral model that assumes dysfunctional parents lack the skills necessary to manage their child in a prosocial manner. With such a model, skill competence implies performance. But outcome data give only partial support for this view. Most studies are able to achieve positive changes in parenting behavior but changes are not maintained at follow-up or seem to be related to other family factors, such as socioeconomic status.

Over time, behaviorists have demonstrated increasing recognition of the host of factors that may mediate the outcome of behavioral parent training. For example, parents who are depressed, socially isolated, and/or experiencing marital conflict are particularly likely to either drop out or relapse following the formal end of treatment (Dadds, 1989; Griest & Forehand, 1982; McMahon, Forehand, Griest, & Wells, 1981; Wahler & Afton, 1980). Some investigators have attempted to address these issues by adding parental enhancement components to their intervention (Griest et al. 1982) or by formulating algorithms to help clinicians decide which forms of behavioral training and supplemental components are best for which families (Blechman, 1981). Other researchers have examined how features of the therapist–client relationship can be manipulated to address these concerns. For example, Wahler and colleagues have urged parent trainers to adopt a noncoercive style of interaction when working with socially isolated mothers whose limited contacts with the community tend to be aversive. Otherwise the therapist becomes one more aversive contact in the parent's limited and negatively charged social network (Wahler, 1980; Wahler & Afton, 1980).

Cognitive–behaviorists attempting to build upon the foundation laid by behavioral efforts would do well to use high-quality visual as well as verbal training materials that allow for some degree of coaching or therapist–client interaction if the initial informational presentations prove to be inadequate. Attention to family factors that may mediate outcome appears to be extremely important, as does the development of both intra- and extratherapy contingencies that support skill application. Drawing upon the behavioral literature on treatment acceptability, it is interesting to speculate that cognitive–behavioral therapy may meet with greater consumer acceptance to the extent that it attempts to increase the child and parent use of positive cognitive and behavioral skills versus focusing on methods to decrease the use of negative processes.

PROMISING EXAMPLES OF PARENTAL INVOLVEMENT IN COGNITIVE–BEHAVIORAL TREATMENT OF CHILDHOOD DISORDERS

While the treatment outcome literature does not contain numerous examples of attempts to involve parents in cognitive–behavioral interventions for their troubled children, there are some examples worthy of comment. Examples will be discussed in terms of the general class of childhood difficulty being addressed, including externalizing disorders, internalizing disorders, and child maltreatment.

Externalizing Disorders

The behavioral intervention literature has a long history of involving parents in the treatment of children with acting-out, externalizing difficulties such as Oppositional Deviant Disorder (ODD), Conduct Disorder (CD), and Attention-deficit Hyperactivity Disorder (ADHD) (Barkley, 1981; Forehand & McMahon, 1981; Patterson, 1976). Despite this history, many cognitive–behavioral treatment efforts have chosen to exclude or provide only limited involvement of the parent in the treatment process (Abikoff & Gittelman, 1985; Brown, Wynne, & Medenis, 1985; Kirby & Grimley, 1986; Lochman & Curry, 1986). Greater recognition of both the pervasive, chronic nature of these difficulties and the failure of some child-focused approaches has led some cognitive–behaviorists to reconsider their original approach to the treatment of these difficulties.

Considering the treatment of ADHD, the current author and Michael Bloomquist built upon previous experiences with the successful treatment of school-referred samples of impulsive children (Kendall & Braswell, 1985) to develop a more comprehensive approach to intervention with ADHD children and their families. As evaluated in experimental and clinical trials, this intervention targets 8-to-12-year-olds with ADHD with or without co-existing diagnoses of Oppositional Defiant Disorder or Conduct Disorder. The intervention begins with two individual introductory sessions in which the child is trained in the use of self-instructional and problem-solving skills that he or she will be expected to practice in a subsequent peer group. The children then participate in seven peer group sessions, in which they receive further training in problem-solving skills, including problem recognition, alternative generation, consequential thinking, recognition of obstacles, creation of backup plans, and evaluation of outcomes.

While the children attend group, their parents participate in a simultaneous group that provides education about ADHD, peer support for coping with challenging children, and training in how to model, prompt, and reinforce the use of problem-solving skills in the home environment. The cognitive activities of the parents are also examined. More precisely, parental beliefs and attributions regarding their children's behaviors and regarding their own capacity to parent these children are addressed in an effort to pinpoint and bring about change in beliefs or attitudes that tend to produce feelings of hopelessness rather than encourage active coping.

Parental involvement is viewed as crucial for achieving skills transfer to the home. As part of this process, parents and children are required to engage in a series of semi-structured exercises that involve the monitoring of skill use and parental reinforcement of such use in the home environment. Over the course of group involvement, each family also participates in three family therapy sessions that allow further tailoring of the program concepts to the needs and issues of each family. These family sessions also allow the therapist to observe directly familial attempts at problem solving and, as a result, determine whether other concerns of the parents, child, or siblings may be unduly interfering with the problem-solving process and require intervention in their own right.

Bloomquist, August, and Garfinkel (in press) compared the effects of this comprehensive cognitive–behavior program for ADHD children with a child-only group cognitive–behavior training program. Half of the subjects in each condition were also receiving methylphenidate, while the other half received a placebo. Assessments included laboratory measures of attention deployment, parent ratings of child self-control and the parent–child relationship, and child self-report measures of self-perception, locus of control, and the parent–child relationship. The results were consistent with the authors' hypothesis that the combined comprehensive and methylphenidate condition would demonstrate the greatest improvement. More specifically, mothers in both comprehensive conditions, whether on medication or placebo, rated their children as significantly more improved on ratings of self-control at posttest, with the combined comprehensive and medication condition achieving the most improved ratings. These effects did not continue to be significant at 6-week follow-up. Also as expected, both medication conditions achieved greater improvement on measures of attention deployment at both post- and follow-up assessment. No consistent findings were observed on the child self-report measures.

While achieving modestly positive findings, the Bloomquist et al. (1989) study illustrates one of the difficulties in assessing outcomes produced by treatments involving the parents. The parents are one of the key sources of information regarding the child's behavior, yet to the extent that the parent is heavily involved in the treatment process, he or she may develop expectancies that favor the demonstration of change. One obvious suggestion would be to include ratings from other significant individuals, such as the child's teacher, but previous outcome studies suggest that cross-setting change is quite unlikely to occur without specific programming for such change (e.g., Kendall & Braswell, 1982). Such programming would logically include the involvement of adults who are significant to the child in that particular setting. Thus, extensive, objective cross-setting behavioral observations may be necessary to circumvent this dilemma.

As previously discussed, parents have also been involved in the treatment of their acting-out children via behavioral family problem-solving interventions. Both Alexander and colleagues (Alexander, Waldron, Barton, & Mas, 1989; Alexander, Waldron, Newberry, & Liddle, 1988) and Foster and Robin (1989) have now incorporated elements of cognitive-behavioral therapy into their respective approaches to problem-solving training with the families of adolescents with CD or ODD.

Internalizing Disorders

Relative to the number of cognitive–behavioral interventions with externalizing children (and with internalizing adults) far fewer cognitive–behavioral outcome studies have been conducted with children manifesting internalizing difficulties, such as fears, anxiety, and/or depression.

Reviews of the available treatments for anxiety disorders in children suggest that of the small number of cognitive–behavioral interventions conducted, an even smaller number formally included parents in the treatment process (Barrios & O'Dell, 1989; Kendall, Howard, & Epps, 1988). Of the treatment targets considered, the domain of treatment of children's nighttime fears seems to have the highest percentage of interventions that include parents. For example, based in part on the successful work of Graziano and colleagues (Graziano & Mooney, 1980; Graziano, Mooney, Huber, & Ignasiak, 1979), Giebenhain and O'Dell (1984) developed a manual that guides parents in training their child to use desensitization and coping self-statements, while directing the parents to reinforce the child's strategy use.

Parents have been largely excluded from efforts addressing evaluation or test anxiety and fears concerning stressful medical procedures, with the exception of the work of Peterson and Shigetomi (1981) and a subsequent replication Zastowny, Kirschenbaum, and Meng (1981). Peterson and Shigetomi (1981) successfully trained children to cope with anxiety and pain via relaxation, self-talk, and imagery techniques. Mothers were used to cue, monitor, and coach their children in skill use. Zastowny et al. (1981) extended parental involvement by having the mothers actually undergo treatment for their own anxiety about the child's impending medical procedure, in addition to aiding their child in use of the coping skill. The failure to include parents more routinely when attempting to aid the child's coping with a stressful and/or painful situation seems curious in light of the success of the Peterson and Shigetomi (1981) and Zastowny et al. (1981) efforts and in light of other empirical demonstrations of the impact of parent behaviors upon a child's ability to cope with such situations (Blount et al., 1989).

School phobia or school refusal in one of the most common variants of childhood anxiety disorder to result in referral for psychological treatment. Many behaviorally oriented approaches to treating this disorder have included parents as agents to reinforce appropriate school attendance (see review by Barrios & O'Dell, 1989), but Kendall and Hill (1988) have proposed a cognitive–behavioral model for treating school refusal that encourages more substantive parental involvement. In addition to teaching the parents to reward adaptive behavior and refrain from rewarding school-refusing behavior, this program trains parents to model coping self-statements for the children and help the child in problem solving about dilemmas that are likely to be created by the child's return to the school environment. Mansdorf and Lukens (1987) have also articulated an approach to treating school phobia that addresses the cognitions of both the child and his or her parents. Case study findings support parental involvement in the cognitive–behavioral treatment of agoraphobic adolescents (Barlow & Seidner, 1983), and Kendall and his associates (Kane & Kendall, 1989) have called for greater attention to familial factors and parental involvement in the treatment of children manifesting Overanxious Disorder.

The dearth of cognitive–behavioral outcome studies addressing childhood depression is particularly difficult to understand, given the well-documented efficacy of this approach with adults (Beck, Hollon, Young, Bedrosian, & Budenz, 1985). The available interventions for childhood depression, cognitive–behavioral or otherwise, have tended to exclude parents from active participation in treatment. In one of the very few controlled outcome studies examining the efficacy of cognitive–behavioral intervention with childhood depression, Stark, Reynolds, and Kaslow (1987) lament their own failure to include some form of parental component to their intervention, noting that some of their subjects were clear in identifying family problems as being one of the major contributors to their depression. In a subsequent discussion of this issue, Stark and his associates (Stark, Chapter 6, this volume: Stark et al., 1989) present an expanded cognitive–behavioral treatment program that provides guidelines for direct parental involvement in several phases of the intervention, including parental support for aiding the child's completion of therapy-related homework, encouragement and modeling of self-reinforcement, and involvement in the development of activity plans.

Using case study data, Wilkes and Rush (1988) illustrate possible methods of including parents in the cognitive–behavioral treatment of depressed adolescents. These authors emphasize the importance of the therapist establishing a close working relationship with the parents, as well as the adolescent client, in order to address parental beliefs or cognitive styles that could either facilitate or obstruct therapy. For example, to address the specific pattern in which the client and at least one parent appear to be enmeshed in terms of their mood and behavior, Wilkes and Rush developed the Dyadic Mood Monitoring technique. This method allows the client and parents to gather evidence concerning the hypothesized synchrony of their moods and can lead to the clarification of cognitive distortions on the part of either party regarding the other's mood.

The techniques proposed by Kendall and Hill (1988), Stark et al. (1989) and Wilkes and Rush (1988) all await further empirical demonstration of their efficacy. Even unvalidated, however, these proposals are valuable, for they represent the field's growing recognition of the need for modifications in cognitive–behavioral methods that permit developmentally appropriate parental involvement in the treatment of anxious and depressed children and adolescents (see Kendall et al., Chapter 5, this volume; Stark, Chapter 6, this volume).

Child Maltreatment

The domain of child maltreatment/abuse has received increasing research attention from cognitive–behaviorists. Developments in the arena of assessment of parental beliefs and expectations associated with abusive behavior, as discussed in the previous section, have provided a conceptual springboard for the creation of cognitive–behavioral approaches to intervention. In line with the Sameroff (1986) continuum of causality, child maltreatment provides a clear example of a difficulty for which the parent or involved adult has direct responsibility, although a confluence of factors may precipitate a given episode of abuse.

In recognition of the complex nature of abuse, Scott, Baer, Christoff, and Kelly (1984) advocate conducting a functional analysis of the behavior of the abusive parent. Through this analysis the therapist can determine the factors or components to be addressed in treatment, in addition to the obvious need for training in nonviolent child management skills. In their case study, Scott et al.'s initial assessment of an abusive mother suggested a need for assertiveness, anger control, and problem-solving training as means to help her cope with interpersonal and life problems that seemed to set the stage for her episodes of abusive behavior. These authors observed that the sequential application of these components of intervention, in addition to child management training, led to significant improvement in the mother's parenting behavior and significant decreases in the aversive behavior of the child. Interestingly, the child's aversive behavior decreased at the point the mother began to receive assertiveness and anger control training, which was prior to the initiation of formal child management training. Other investigators have also achieved similar findings when using anger and self-control training with abusive parents (Barth, Blythe, Schinke, Stevens, & Schilling, 1983; Nomellini & Katz, 1983; Wolfe, Sandler, & Kaufman, 1981).

In addition to the use of the treatment components just described, Azar and Wolfe (1989) also recommend the use of cognitive restructuring methods to help abusive parents change their faulty beliefs and dysfunctional self-statements. Azar and Twentyman (1984) achieved positive results with a treatment package including cognitive restructuring in addition to anger control, communication, and child management skills training. The condition receiving this training plus home visits to enhance skills generalization was the only one to demonstrate no recidivism at 1-year follow-up.

In short, parent-focused cognitive–behavioral treatments for child maltreatment have been attempted and have demonstrated their effectiveness. The attention that investigators in this domain have paid to the role of the cognitive events of the parent as a precipitant for abusive behavior provides a model for those interested in other areas of childhood difficulties.

PROCEDURAL GUIDELINES FOR INVOLVING PARENTS IN COGNITIVE–BEHAVIORAL THERAPY

The goal of this section is to offer some specific, procedural suggestions to help cognitive–behavioral clinicians achieve greater parental involvement in the assessment and treatment of childhood difficulties. Many of the suggestions offered will be relevant regardless of the type of childhood difficulty one is treating and will be as relevant for understanding the child as for understanding the parent. Given this chapter's focus, however, the parent component will be articulated in greater detail. Procedures suggested in this section represent extrapolations from the behavioral literature on parental involvement, from the existing examples of cognitive–behavioral parental involvement, highlighted in the previous section, and from the author's clinical experience with involving parents in their children's treatment. These suggestions also draw upon the cognitive–behavioral model of family therapy elaborated by Epstein et al. (1988). A more detailed discussion of some of the suggested procedures is presented in Braswell and Bloomquist's (in press) description of their intervention program for ADHD children.

Assessment

The process of encouraging appropriate parental involvement begins during the family's first contact with the clinician. In fact, in the parent's first phone contact with the clinician or clinic staff they are educated as to how this particular provider will structure their involvement in services for the child. Does the clinic request that the entire family, parents only, or just the child be seen at the initial interview? Does the clinic routinely have parents complete forms that elicit family information or are the initial forms more specifically focused on the child symptomatology? The clinician's choices about how to handle these issues may subtly (or, in some cases, not so subtly) begin to shape the family's definition of the child's difficulties and view of who is responsible for addressing these difficulties.

To be adequately comprehensive, Braswell and Bloomquist (in press) recommend conceptualizing the initial evaluation phase as involving both a diagnostic and functional assessment. To accomplish the diagnostic assessment, the clinician can rely upon traditional interview and psychometric tools while being sensitive to evidence of parental as well as child psychopathology. As previously discussed, it behooves the child clinician to be particularly sensitive to signs and symptoms of parental depression, serious social isolation, and/or marital discord, as these factors have been shown to influence both parental perception of the child's behavior and parental response to some forms of child treatment. A traditional diagnostic assessment can also reveal information regarding the severity of the child's and/or family's dysfunction or provide other information about the child that might contraindicate the use of outpatient cognitive–behavioral treatment. For example, if the child or a family member is actively engaging in serious chemical abuse, ongoing physical or sexual abuse, or is imminently suicidal, then forms of the intervention that can more immediately ensure the safety of the relevant individuals would be preferred.

Conducting a useful functional assessment of the child and parents means going beyond simply establishing a diagnostic label to delineating exactly what behaviors or cognitive events/processes appear to be deficient, distorted, or excessive. The behavioral assessment literature has traditionally urged clinicians to pay keen attention to the specific behavioral excesses or deficits of the child and his or her parents. To elaborate on the parental component, behaviorists have long called attention to the significance of parental use of vague and overly frequent commands, poor parental monitoring of the child's behavior, inadvertent reinforcement of inappropriate behavior and failure to reinforce desirable behavior (e.g., Forehand & McMahon, 1981; Patterson, 1976, 1982).

While maintaining attention to these important behavioral factors, the cognitive–behaviorist would also be interested in understanding the parent's automatic thoughts, beliefs, attributions, and expectations concerning both the child's behavior and the parent's ability to cope with it. In addition, the cognitive–behaviorist would consider it important to understand the parent's beliefs about what constitutes "good" parenting for a child presenting such behavior. Information about these cognitive events can be elicited by directly questioning the parents on what they believe to be the cause of the child's difficulties and what they think of their own ability to parent a child with these special needs. The acceptability of such questioning can be enhanced by the clinician's phrasing. For example, the clinician could state,

> Different families have different explanations or theories for why their children act as they do; in fact, each parent in a family may have his or her own thoughts about the cause of a child's difficulties. To understand how to best help your child, I would like to know your thoughts and feelings about why _____ is having the difficulties you have described.

Then after the parent(s) have presented their theories, the clinician could state "Some parents would feel very challenged to meet the needs of a child having this type of difficulty. What are your thoughts and feelings about parenting this type of child?"

Other assessment tools may also prove helpful. For certain types of childhood difficulties, the clinician could use existing measures to assess specific parental beliefs and/or expectations. Examples include the POQ (Azar et al., 1984) for use with abusing parents, or Roehling and Robin's (1986) Family Belief Inventory for use with conflicted adolescents and their parents. If the parent has great difficulty identifying beliefs, in the session, he or she could be asked to engage in charting his or her automatic thoughts that occur in certain types of interactions with the child, much as Beck, Rush, Shaw and Emery (1989) have depressed clients record their thoughts. The parent can record these automatic thoughts *in vivo* and then bring the thought-monitoring chart to the session, so the clinician can help the parent identify the more general cognitive constructs that may underlie the specific automatic thoughts.

Whatever method one uses to identify the parent's relevant cognitions, the clinician can then help the parent identify the affect that accompanies these cognitions. In particular, the clinician is interested in discerning if the parent's cognitions are leading to feelings of hopelessness or guilt that may be interfering with efforts to cope actively with the child's difficulties.

In addition to understanding parental cognitions, the literature previously reviewed suggests the importance of understanding certain cognitive processes of the parents. Investigators from different perspectives have emphasized the role of the parent's attentional or perceptual capacities as they relate to the child's behavior (Brunnquell et al., 1981; Wahler & Dumas,

1989). Does the parent display a tendency to attend to only aversive or extreme child behaviors? Does the parent perceive a complex array of factors determining the child's behavior in a particular situation or does he or she tend to perceive only a single causal factor? The cognitive–behavioral clinician can explore the parent's attentional/perceptual processes by asking him or her to maintain a behavioral log or do some charting of particular child behaviors. For example, Braswell and Bloomquist (in press) have parents complete a child observation chart in which the parents must record not only the problem behavior but also the antecedents and consequences of the behavior. Having the parents record the sequencing of certain behavioral events not only provides valuable information regarding when to intervene with a particular behavior, but also gives information about the parent's ability to perceive the factors surrounding a given instance of behavior.

Understanding the family's capacity to engage functionally in other cognitive–behavioral processes is also important. In session observations of the family, as well as reports of home behavior, can reveal the extent to which a family can utilize effective communication skills, systematic problem-solving and negotiation capacities, and adequate methods of regulating the expression of strong impulses or affects, particularly anger.

Thus, at the conclusion of the functional assessment, the clinician would not only have identified child cognitive and behavioral targets for intervention but also parental cognitive and behavioral targets and family cognitive–behavioral processes that may require direct treatment (Braswell & Bloomquist, in press).

As was the case with the diagnostic assessment, information emerging from such a functional assessment can help the clinician determine if it is even appropriate to pursue cognitive–behavioral treatment in light of the belief system or attributional style of a given family. Bugental, Whalen, and Henker (1977) were among the first to note that "change strategies (behavioral management, educational programs, psychotherapy, medical intervention) have implicit attributional textures which interact with the attributional network of the individual to influence treatment impact" (p. 881). To illustrate this point, if the functional assessment reveals that the parents believe very strongly that their child's difficulty is totally the result of biological causes, then the clinician might choose to help the parents pursue medical solutions initially and to have medical professionals attempt to inform the parents that additional improvement could be obtained with the adjuctive use of educational or psychological interventions. More recent emipirical efforts have underscored the importance of assessing parental attributions but also suggest that this enterprise is quite complex, for parents may have highly idiosyncratic meanings for the same general explanations (Borden & Brown, 1989; Sobol, Ashbourne, Earn, & Cunningham, 1989).

Intervention

After the assessment process has been completed and the family has been determined to be an appropriate candidate for outpatient cognitive–behavioral treatment, the intervention phase can begin. Braswell and Bloomquist (in press) and Epstein et al. (1988) suggest that cognitive–behavioral therapists could benefit from the Functional Family Therapy view of conceptualizing intervention as having two phases: (1) therapy or preparation for change, and (2) education or training (Alexander & Parsons, 1982).

Preparation for Change

According to Braswell and Bloomquist (in press), the therapy or preparation for change phase can also be viewed as having two components, an initial phase of establishing a collaborative relationship and a second phase of addressing possible sources of resistance.

Viewing the therapist–client relationship as a collaborative effort is one of the hallmarks of behavioral and cognitive–behavioral approaches. The therapist can help establish this collaborative tone by actively involving the family in developing the agenda for treatment, as well as involving them in setting the agenda for each particular session. The therapist can also foster a collaborative relationship by helping the parents solve problems about other relevant treatment decisions that should occur prior to or simultaneously with the therapy process, such as deciding to obtain a medical consultation to explore the appropriateness of pharmacological treatments or deciding how and what to communicate to the child's school about the current assessment and treatment plans. In this problem-solving process, the therapist serves as an informational consultant who provides an expert opinion but also helps the parents clarify their own thoughts and feelings about the costs and benefits of different options.

Sources of resistance can be addressed in a number of different ways, but the goal of all these methods is to have family members motivated to work toward positive change. In this stage, attention to any dysfunctional cognitive contents or processes that were revealed during the functional assessment is of paramount importance. With some families, providing parents with information about the particular condition their child is manifesting can be very helpful in changing beliefs that could interfere with achieving the desired change in child and family functioning. For example, providing parents of anxious, depressed, or ADHD children with basic information about these conditions can often lead parents to begin to abandon notions of the child as "bad" or as exhibiting inappropriate behaviors with the sole aim of irritating or humiliating the parent.

Accurate information can also help some parents abandon notions that their child may be too "sick" to be expected to accomplish developmentally appropriate life tasks. The current author once provided treatment to a family that came to the clinic with concerns about the immature behavior of their 12-year-old daughter, the youngest of seven children. The initial intellectual and personality assessment of the child revealed no major cognitive or emotional concerns. In therapy we then addressed how it seemed to be difficult for the parents and older siblings to let the target child grow up, perhaps out of concern for what would happen to the parents once all the children had left the home. The family made excellent progress in identifying and changing their thoughts and behaviors that might be functioning to keep the identified patient the baby of the family. At the end of treatment, I asked the parents how they explained the changes their family had been able to make. The mother referred to the initial testing and stated that once I had explained that the target child was scoring in the normal range on IQ measures, she (the mother) was able to abandon her secret fear that this child was intellectually deficient, perhaps as a result of being born when the mother was 40 years old. Without this nagging fear, she felt able to establish and enforce more age appropriate expectations for the child. Interestingly, the father stated that he felt the other family members took their behavioral cues from the mother and once the mother's perception of the child began to change, the thoughts and behaviors of the entire family were influenced. Thus, the provision of accurate information about the child set the stage for systemic change.

With many families, however, simply providing more accurate information about the child will not be enough to prepare the family adequately for change. It may be necessary to use cognitive restructuring techniques, such as relabeling or reframing of child and parent behaviors in order to reduce blame-oriented beliefs and attributions that can seriously interfere with positive change. The work of Alexander et al., (1989) illustrates how the set provided by the therapist can influence the type of attributions expressed by the family members. When families with a delinquent child were encouraged to interact in a cooperative rather than competitive context they were observed to be significantly less likely to engage in defensive communication (expressions of blaming, indifference, superiority, and controlling behavior). In addition, Alexander et al. observed that once parents were encouraged to invoke their pre-existing negative cognitive set regarding the child, by means of the type of questions asked by the therapist, this negative set persisted after the session despite the therapist's attempt to provide a positive relabel or reframe for the child's behavior. Alexander et al. suggest that this finding highlights the value of the therapist initially focusing his or her questioning on nonblaming, relational aspects of the child's behavior to decrease resistance and negative blaming in the therapy session.

As discussed by Epstein et al. (1988), the cognitive–behavioral therapist can also help the family engage in hypothesis testing, as utilized in

cognitive therapy for depression (Beck et al., 1979), in order to examine
the accuracy of the beliefs they hold regarding themselves and other family
members. As an example, a mother struggling with ambivalent feelings
about her children holds the belief that no "good mother" ever feels strong
negative emotions toward her kids. As this belief could interfere with this
mom's ability to view herself as capable of acting as an appropriate parent,
she could be encouraged to test the validity of this belief by asking other
mothers whom she respects if they ever experience negative feelings toward
their children.

Training

Once a collaborative relationship has been established and any obvious forms
of cognitive resistance have been addressed, the therapist can then provide
the child, parent, or family with the relevant behavioral or cognitive–behavioral intervention. At a minimum, parents should be taught to prompt
and reinforce the child's use of newly trained skills. As previously alluded
to in the section on assessment, intervention with the parents might also
involve diverse targets such as training more effective child-monitoring skills,
improving specific communication skills, developing problem-solving and
negotiation skills, and/or providing anger control training. The reader is
referred to Breswell and Bloomquist (in press) for a more detailed discussion of how to conduct these various forms of cognitive-behavioral family
intervention.

Building on the conclusions of behavioral parent and family interventions, the cognitive–behaviorist may be a more effective trainer to the extent that he or she uses visual as well as verbal input during training. Thus,
the extensive use of live or videotaped modeling is encouraged, with some
families also requiring a high degree of interactive coaching in order to
master the skills being trained. Problem-solving homework with reinforced
practice plays an important role in training. Kendall (1988) has developed
the *Stop and Think Workbook* which provides a specific series of tasks for
parents to use in helping their children practice self-instructional skills in
the home environment. Outcomes of earlier behavioral efforts also suggest
the value of direct problem solving about the factors that could interfere
with the family's skill use outside the session. Such problem solving could
involve helping families make conscious decisions about how they would
like to structure their environment so that it reinforces the skills they are
trying to develop. In addition, the therapist and family can engage in proactive planning for how to cope with the thoughts and feelings experienced
when their newly developed child management skills seem to conflict with
the implicit or explicit beliefs and expectations of extended family or other
significant individuals in their lives. In this manner the therapist can help

the family actively program for their own skills transfer and maintenance of positive change.

Obviously, over the course of working with a family, the therapist must remain sensitive to the emergence of new sources of resistance. A given family may have been able to proceed beautifully with applying problem-solving skills to certain issues, but suddenly present great difficulty in using these skills to address other conflicted topics. Such an event suggests the possibility that the new topics may tap into deeply held, but possibly mal-adaptive beliefs that have not yet been addressed in the therapy. Thus, the occurrence of such resistance provides a cue for the therapist to explore the network of beliefs that certain family members may have regarding the issue at hand.

Once specific treatment goals have been achieved, the family can then problem solve with the therapist about the need for follow-up sessions or supplemental forms of intervention. As discussed by Glenwick and Jason (1984) and practiced by Scott et al. (1984), one valuable form of supple-mental training involves helping parents apply the skills they learned to resolve intrafamilial conflict with extrafamilial issues, such as work-related conflicts, difficulties in adult relationships, and aversive interactions with community agencies. Given current formulations of how extrafamilial stres-sors can impact the parent–child relationship (Wahler & Dumas, 1989), such an extension of coping skills training would be expected to result in continued improvement in parent–child transactions as well as generally decrease the level of stress experienced by the parent.

As part of the termination process, the therapist should elicit the fam-ily members' explanations for any observed changes. To the extent that any family member is attributing change to forces outside himself or her-self, the therapist may choose to explore and test this attribution in an attempt to help all family members own some of the responsibility for achieving positive change. Active discussion of the concept of relapse pre-vention can be helpful. In this way, the therapist can encourage the family to view any recurrent behavioral difficulties as cues for enacting the family's newly developed coping skills rather than viewing such behaviors as evi-dence of failure.

CONCLUSIONS AND FINAL THOUGHTS

This chapter has attempted to make a case for parental involvement in cognitive–behavioral interventions with children and adolescents. While no respected cognitive–behaviorist has gone on record as opposing such in-volvement and current expositions of cognitive–behavioral theories of change call for greater attention to the role of the family (see Kendall, Chapter 1, this volume), the fact remains that many cognitive–behavior intervention efforts have been implemented without adequate consideration of the possible benefits of incorporating parents in the treatment process. Parental involvement is considered important by virtue of the key role that parents play in defining their children's difficulties, in causing, amplifying, or moderating these difficulties, and/or in providing the context for intervention most likely to produce meaningful behavior change Emerging data on parental cognitive events and processes, past behavioral interventions involving parents, and promising examples of family-oriented cognitive–behavioral efforts provide a beginning guide for the increased incorporation of parents into the treatment process.

As this chapter concludes, three points merit additional discussion and emphasis: the value of focusing treatment efforts directly upon the parents, the need for greater understanding of the role of affect in effecting change, and the importance of avoiding oversimplification in conceptualizing the parenting process.

From the earlier discussion of the interacting and amplifying effects of parental difficulties upon the child, it is logical to conclude that, with some family situations, one could achieve the greatest long-term benefit for the child by having the family invest its resources in getting the parents needed treatment for a host of possible problems. Both common clinical experience and empirical findings are convergent with regard to the futility of pursuing certain child-focused or even family-focused interventions in the face of serious marital conflict or significant parental depression, chemical abuse, or anger control difficulties. To assist clinicians in determining how to focus treatment efforts, cognitive–behaviorists could turn their attention to greater elaboration of the decision-making model originally espoused by Blechman (1981). Ideally, such a model would include guidelines for determining the level of severity of a particular parental difficulty beyond which it would be unwise to pursue child or family-focused approaches. Coupled with such decision-making guidelines, therapists will need to continue developing their capacities to help families understand the transactional nature of the family system and, thus, increase the probability that the parents will "buy" the therapist's reformulation of the family's initial treatment needs.

In addition to attending to the possibly paramount needs of the parents, the cognitive–behavioral child therapist could also benefit from a greater recognition and understanding of the role of affect as it relates to therapeutic change. In recent years, cognitive–behavioral researchers have displayed greater interest in emotional factors, as demonstrated by increased attention to primarily affective disturbances, greater concern for how emotional processes affect cognitive processes and the expression of behavior, and greater recognition of how the child's social–emotional context affects his/her functioning (Mash, 1989). The domain of child maltreatment offers an example of how increased understanding of the relationship between affect and memory (Azar & Wolfe, 1989) and greater recognition of the role of positive emotionally significant relationships (whether in the context of therapy or otherwise) can facilitate the changing of cycles of abusive behavior (Egeland, Jacobvitz, & Sroufe, 1988). Greater understanding of affective processes will improve both our knowledge of emotionally significant relationships, including the parent–child bond, and our awareness of how these relationships can be used to foster positive emotional and behavioral change.

While challenging the field to produce clear constructs regarding parental cognitive and affective functioning, it is also important to avoid the pitfall of oversimplification. Obviously, parenting is an extremely complex process, and the reviews by Goodnow (1988) and Holden and Edwards (1989) suggest that many previous research efforts have ignored the changing, multidimensional nature of this process. On the other hand, some theorists have made beginning attempts to capture the complexity. For example, Bacon and Ashmore (1986) have proposed a process model of parenting in which cognitive processes, such as decision making and categorizing, and cognitive and affective structures, such as beliefs, goals, and feelings, are considered in attempts to account for specific parenting behaviors. Such increasingly complex models represent progress, but those attempting to understand the outcomes of parenting behavior would do well to consider models that consider still other factors, such as Belsky's view of parenting as a buffered system (Belsky, 1984). According to this perspective, parental cognitive and affective characteristics are only one component of the parenting system. The parents' social context and the child's characteristics are the other major features of the system, with deficits in any one aspect of the system possibly compensated by strengths in the other two components. This model would suggest that, for example, the negative impact of a parent with inappropriate expectations regarding child behavior may be moderated by the presence of a strong social support system and an adaptable, resilient child.

The cognitive–behavioral researcher or clinician is in a fortunate position in that the cognitive–behavioral perspective "allows" consideration of the cognitive, behavioral, and affective events and processes of the client. There are certainly movements within the field to develop strategies that integrate information from all three of these domains (see Kendall, 1985; Kendall, Chapter 1, this volume: Mash, 1989). Those working with children and adolescents, however, face the extremely complex task of integrating information from these domains not only for an individual client but also the client's parents and other family members. It is hoped that future cognitive–behavioral conceptualizations and investigations of methods of assessment and intervention will accurately reflect the complexity of this task.

REFERENCES

Abikoff, H., & Gittelman, R. (1985). Hyperactive children treated with stimulants: Is cognitive training a useful adjunct? *Archives of General Psychiatry, 42,* 953–961.

Alexander, J. F., & Parsons, B. (1973). Short-term behavioral intervention with delinquent families: Impact on family process and recidivism. *Journal of Abnormal Psychology, 81,* 219–225.

Alexander, J. F., & Parsons, B. (1982). *Functional family therapy.* Monterey, CA: Brooks/Cole.

Alexander, J. F., Waldron, H. B., Barton, C., & Mas, C. H. (1989). The minimizing of blaming attributions and behaviors in delinquent families. *Journal of Consulting and Clinical Psychology, 57,* 19–24.

Alexander, J. F., Waldron, H. B., Newberry, A. M., & Liddle, N. (1988). Family approaches to treating delinquents. In E. W. Nunnally, C. S. Chilman, & F. M. Cox (Eds.), *Mental illness, delinquency, addictions, and neglect.* Newbury Park, CA: Sage.

Asarnow, J. R., Carlson, G. A., & Guthrie, D. (1987). Coping strategies, self-perceptions, hopelessness, and perceived family environments in depressed and suicidal children. *Journal of Consulting and Clinical Psychology, 55,* 361–366.

Azar, S. R., Robinson, D. R., Hekimian, E., & Twentyman, C. T. (1984). Unrealistic expectations and problem solving ability in maltreating and comparison mothers. *Journal of Consulting and Clinical Psychology, 52,* 687–691.

Azar, S. R., & Rohrbeck, C. A. (1986). Child abuse and unrealistic expectations: Further validation of the Parent Opinion Questionnaire. *Journal of Consulting and Clinical Psychology, 54,* 867–868.

Azar, S. R., & Twentyman, C. A. (1984, November). *An evaluation of the effectiveness of behaviorally versus insight oriented group treatments with maltreating mothers.* Paper presented at the annual meeting of the Association for the Advancement of Behavior Therapy, Philadelphia.

Azar, S. R., & Wolfe, D. A. (1989). Child abuse and neglect. In E. J. Mash & R. A. Barkley (Eds.), *Treatment of childhood disorders* (pp. 451–489). New York: Guilford Press.

Bacon, M. K., & Ashmore, R. D. (1986). A consideration of the cognitive activities of parents and their role in the socialization process. In R. D. Ashmore & D. M. Brodzinsky (Eds.), *Thinking about the family: Views of parents and children* (pp. 3–33). Hillsdale, NJ: Erlbaum.

Barkley, R. A. (1981). *Hyperactive children: A handbook for diagnosis and treatment.* New York: Guilford Press.

Barlow, D. H., & Seidner, A. L. (1983). Treatment of adolescent agoraphobics: Effects on parent–adolescent relations. *Behavior Research and Therapy, 21,* 519–526.

Barrios, B. A., & O'Dell, S. L. (1989). Fears and anxieties. In E. J. Mash & R. A. Barkley (Eds.), *Treatment of childhood disorders* (pp. 167–221). New York: Guilford Press.

Barth, R. P., Blythe, B. J., Schinke, S. P., Stevens, P., & Schilling, R. F. (1983). Self-control training with maltreating parents. *Child Welfare, 62,* 313–324.

Bauer, W., & Twentyman, C. T. (1985). Abusing, neglectful, and comparison mothers' reactions to child-related and non-child-related stressors. *Journal of Consulting and Clinical Psychology, 53*, 335–343.

Beardslee, W. R., Bemporad, J., Keller, M. B., & Klerman, G. L. (1983). Children of parents with major affective disorder: A review. *American Journal of Psychiatry, 140*, 825–832.

Beck, A. R., Hollon, S. D., Young, J. E., Bedrosian, R. C. & Budenz, D. (1985). Treatment of depression with cognitive therapy and amitriptyline. *Archives of General Psychiatry, 42*, 142–148.

Beck, A. T., Rush, A, J., Shaw, B. F., & Emery, G. (1979). *Cognitive therapy of depression.* New York: Guilford Press.

Belsky, J. (1984). The determinants of parenting: A process model. *Child Development, 55*, 83–96.

Blechman, E. A. (1981). Toward comprehensive behavioral family intervention: An algorithm for matching families and interventions. *Behavior Modification, 5*, 221–236.

Blechman, E. A., Olson, D., & Hellman, I. (1976). Stimulus control over family problem-solving behavior: The family contract game. *Behavior Therapy, 7*, 686–692.

Blechman, E. A., Olson, D., Schornagel, C., Halsdorf, M., & Turner, A. (1976). The family contract game: Technique and case study. *Journal of Consulting and Clinical Psychology, 44*, 449–455.

Bloomquist, M. L., August, G., & Garfinkel, B. D. (1989). *Cognitive–behavioral therapy for Attention–deficit Hyperactivity Disordered children: Additive effects of parent involvement and methylphenidate.* Manuscript submitted for publication.

Blount, R. L., Corbin, S. M., Sturges, J. W., Wolfe, V. V., Prater, J. M., & James, L. D. (1989). The relationship between adults' behavior and child coping and distress during BMA/LP procedures: A sequential analysis. *Behavior Therapy, 20*, 585–601.

Borden, K. A., & Brown, R. T. (1989). Attributional outcomes: The subtle messages of treatments of Attention Deficit Disorder. *Cognitive Therapy and Research, 13*, 147–160.

Braswell, L., & Bloomquist, M. L. (in press). *Attention-deficits and hyperactivity: A model for child, family, and school intervention.* New York: Guilford Press.

Braswell, L., & Kendall, P. C. (1988). Cognitive–behavioral methods with children: In K. Dobson (Ed.). *Handbook of cognitive–behavioral therapies* (pp. 167–213). New York: Guilford Press.

Braswell, L., Koehler, C., & Kendall, P. C. (1985). Attributions and outcomes in child psychotherapy. *Journal of Social and Clinical Psychology, 3*, 458–465.

Brown, R. T., Wynne, M. E., & Medenis, R. (1985). Methylphenidate and cognitive therapy: A comparison of treatment approaches with hyperactive boys. *Journal of Abnormal Child Psychology, 13*, 69–87.

Brunnquell, D., Crichton, L., & Egeland, B. (1981). Maternal personality and attitude in disturbances of child rearing. *American Journal of Orthopsychiatry, 61*, 680–691.

Bugental, D. B., Whalen, C. B., & Henker, B. (1977). Causal attributions of hyperactive children and motivational assumptions of two behavior-change approaches: Evidence for an interactionist position. *Child Development, 48,* 874–884.

Burgess, R. L., & Conger, R. D. (1978). Family interaction in abusive, neglectful and normal families. *Child Development, 49,* 1163–1173.

Calvert, S. C., & McMahon, R. J. (1987). The treatment acceptability of a behavioral parent training program and its components. *Behavior Therapy, 2,* 165–179.

Cicchetti, D., Toth, S., & Bush, M. (1988). Developmental psychopathology and incompetence in childhood: Suggestions for intervention. In A. Kazdin & B. Lahey (Eds.), *Advances in clinical child psychology* (Vol. 11, pp. 1–71). New York: Plenum Press.

Conrad, M., & Hammen, C. (1989). Role of maternal depression in perceptions of child maladjustment. *Journal of Consulting and Clinical Psychology, 57,* 663–667.

Crowell, J. A., & Feldman, S. S. (1988). Mothers' internal models of relationships and children's behavioral and developmental status: A study of mother–child interaction. *Child Development, 59,* 1273–1285.

Dadds, M. R. (1989). Child behavior therapy and family context: Research and clinical practice with maritally distressed families. *Child and Family Behavior Therapy, 11,* 27–44.

Earls, F., & Jung, K. G. (1987). Temperament and home environment characteristics as causal factors in the early development of childhood psychopathology. *Journal of the American Academy of Child and Adolescent Psychiatry, 26,* 491–498.

Egeland, B., Jacobvitz, D., & Sroufe, L. A. (1988). Breaking the cycle of abuse. *Child Development, 59,* 1080–1088.

Emery, R. E. (1982). Interparental conflict and the children of discord and divorce. *Psychological Bulletin, 92,* 310–330.

Epstein, N., Schlesinger, S. E., & Dryden, W. (1988). Concepts and methods of cognitive–behavioral family treatment. In N. Epstein, S. E. Schlesinger, & W. Dryden (Eds.), *Cognitive behavioral therapy with families* (pp. 5–48). New York: Brunner/Mazel.

Forehand, R. J., McCombs, A., & Brody, G. H. (1987). The relationship between parental depressive mood states and child functioning. *Advances in Behavior Research and Therapy, 9,* 1–20.

Forehand, R., & McMahon, R. J. (1981). *Helping the noncompliant child: A clinician's guide to parent training.* New York: Guilford Press.

Foster, S. L. (1978). *Family conflict management: Skill training and generalization procedures.* Unpublished doctoral dissertation, State University of New York at Stony Brook.

Foster, S. L., Kendall, P. C., & Gouvremont, D. (1988). Cognitive and social learning theory and therapy. In J. Matson (Ed.), *Handbook of treatment approaches in childhood psychopathology.* New York: Plenum Press.

Foster, S. L., & Robin, A. L. (1989). Parent–adolescent conflict. In E. J. Mash & R. A. Barkley (Eds.). *Treatment of childhood disorders* (pp. 493–528). New York: Guilford Press.

Giebenhain, J. E., & O'Dell, S. L. (1984). Evaluation of a parent training manual for reducing children's fear of the dark. *Journal of Applied Behavior Analysis, 17,* 121–125.

Glenwick, D. S., & Barocas, R. (1979). Training impulsive children in verbal self-control by use of natural change agents. *Journal of Special Education, 13,* 387–398.

Glenwick, D. S., & Jason, L. A. (1984). Locus of intervention in child cognitive behavior therapy: Implications of a behavioral community perspective. In A. W. Meyers & W. C. Craighead (Eds.), *Cognitive behavior therapy with children* (pp. 129–162). New York: Plenum Press.

Goodnow, J. J. (1988). Parents' ideas, actions, and feelings: Models and methods from developmental and social psychology. *Child Development, 59,* 286–320.

Graziano, A. M., & Mooney, K. C. (1980). Family self-control instruction for children's nighttime fear reduction. *Journal of Consulting and Clinical Psychology, 48,* 206–213.

Graziano, A. M., Mooney, K. C., Huber, C., & Ignasiak, D. (1979). Self-control instructions for children's fear reduction. *Journal of Behavior Therapy and Experimental Psychiatry, 10,* 221–227.

Griest, D. L., & Forehand, R. (1982). How can I get any parent training done with all these other problems going on? The role of family variables in child behavior therapy. *Child and Family Behavior Therapy, 4,* 73–80.

Griest, D. L., Forehand, R., Robers, T., Breiner, J. L., Furey, W., & Williams, C. A. (1982). Effects of Parent Enhancement Therapy on the treatment outcome and generalization of a parent training program. *Behaviour Research and Therapy, 20,* 429–436.

Holden, G. W., & Edwards, L. A. (1989). Parental attitudes toward child rearing: Instruments, issues, and implications. *Psychological Bulletin, 106,* 29–58.

Jouriles, E. N., Murphy, C. M., & O'Leary, K. D. (1989). Effects of maternal mood on mother–son interaction patterns. *Journal of Abnormal Child Psychology, 17,* 513–525.

Jouriles, E. N., Pfiffner, L. J., & O'Leary, S. G. (1988). Marital conflict, parenting, and toddler conduct problems. *Journal of Abnormal Child Psychology, 16,* 197–206.

Kane, M. T., & Kendall, P. C. (1989). Anxiety disorders in children: A multiple-baseline evaluation of a cognitive–behavioral treatment. *Behavior Therapy, 20,* 499–508.

Kendall, P. C. (1985). Toward a cognitive–behavioral model of child psychopathology and a critique of related interventions. *Journal of Abnormal Child Psychology, 13,* 357–372.

Kendall, P. C. (1988). *Stop and think workbook.* (Available from P. C. Kendall, 238 Meeting House Lane, Merion Station, PA 19066).

Kendall, P. C. (1989). The generalization and maintenance of behavior change: Comments, considerations, and the "no-cure" criticism. *Behavior Therapy, 20,* 357–364.

Kendall, P. C., & Braswell, L. (1985). *Cognitive-behavioral therapy for impulsive children.* New York: Guilford Press.

Kendall, P. C., & Hill, P. (1988). Cognitive–behavioral therapy and childhood anxiety: Focus on school phobia. In B. Garfinkel & P. C. Kendall (Eds.), *Anxiety disorders in children.*

Kendall, P. C., Howard, B. L., & Epps, J. (1988). The anxious child: Cognitive–behavioral treatment strategies. *Behavior Modification, 12,* 281–310.

Kirby, E. A., & Grimley, L. K. (1986). *Understanding and treating Attention Deficit Disorder.* New York: Pergamon Press.

Klein, N. C., Alexander, J. F., & Parsons, B. V. (1977). Impact of family systems intervention on recidivism and sibling delinquency: A model of primary prevention and program evaluation. *Journal of Consulting and Clinical Psychology, 45,* 469–474.

Kochanska, G., Kuczynski, L., & Maguire, M. (1989). Impact of diagnosed depression and self-reported mood on mothers' control strategies: A longitudinal study. *Journal of Abnormal Child Psychology, 17,* 493–511.

Kurdek, L. A., & Sinclair, R. J. (1988). Adjustment of young adolescents in two-parent nuclear, stepfather, and mother-custody families. *Journal of Consulting and Clinical Psychology, 56,* 91–96.

Larrance, D. L., & Twentyman, C. T. (1983). Maternal attributions in child abuse. *Journal of Abnormal Psychology, 92,* 449–457.

Lochman, J. E., & Curry, J. F. (1986). Effects of social problem-solving training and self-instruction training with aggressive boys. *Journal of Clinical Child Psychology, 15,* 159–164.

Mahoney, M. J., & Nezworski, M. T. (1985). Cognitive–behavioral approaches to children's problems. *Journal of Abnormal Child Psychology, 13,* 467–476.

Main, M., & Goldwyn, R. (1984). Predicting rejection of her infant from mother's representation of her own experience: Implications for the abused-abusing intergenerational cycle. *Child Abuse and Neglect, 8,* 203–217.

Main, M., Kaplan, N., & Cassidy, J. (1985). Security in infancy, childhood, and adulthood: A move to the level of representation. *Monographs of the Society for Research in Child Development, 50* (1–2, Serial No. 209), 66–104.

Mansdorf, I. J., & Lukens, E. (1987). Cognitive-behavioral psychotherapy for separation anxious children exhibiting school phobia. *Journal of the American Academy of Child and Adolescent Psychiatry, 26,* 222–225.

Mash, E. J. (1989). Treatment of child and family disturbance: A behavioral-systems perspective. In E. J. Mash & R. A. Barkley (Eds.) *Treatment of childhood disorders* (pp. 3–36). New York: Guilford Press.

Mash, E. J., Johnston, C., & Kovitz, K. (1983). A comparison of the mother–child interactions of physically abused and nonabused children during play and task situations. *Journal of Clinical Child Psychology, 12,* 337–346.

Masten, A. S., & Braswell, L. (in press). Developmental psychopathology: An integrative framework for understanding behavior problems in children and adolescents. In P. R. Martin (Ed.), *Handbook of behavior therapy and psychological science: An integrative approach.* New York: Pergamon Press.

Masten, A. S., Garmezy, N., Tellegen, A., Pellegrini, D. S., Larkin, K., & Larsen, A. (1988). Competence and stress in school children: The moderating effects of individual and family qualities. *Journal of Child Psychology and Psychiatry, 29,* 746–764.

McMahon, R. J., Forehand, R., Griest, D. L., & Wells, K. (1981). Who drops out of treatment during parent behavioral training? *Behavioral Counseling Quarterly, 1,* 79–85.

Meichenbaum, D. H., & Goodman, J. (1971). Training impulsive children to talk to themselves: A means of developing self-control. *Journal of Abnormal Psychology, 77,* 115–126.

Mondell, S., & Tyler, F. B. (1981). Parental competence and styles of problem-solving/play behavior with children. *Developmental Psychology, 17,* 73–78.

Newberger, C. M. (1980). The cognitive structure of parenthood: Designing a descriptive measure. *New Directions for Child Development, 7,* 45–67.

Nomellini, S., & Katz, R. C. (1983). Effects of anger control training on abusive parents. *Cognitive Therapy and Research, 7,* 57–68.

O'Dell, S. L. (1985). Progress in parent training. *Progress in Behavior Modification, 19,* 57–108.

Patterson, G. R. (1976). *Living with children: New methods for parents and teachers* (rev. ed.). Champaign, IL: Research Press.

Patterson, G. R. (1982). *A social learning approach to family intervention: III. Coercive family process.* Eugene, OR: Castalia.

Patterson, G. R., & Bank, L. (1989). Some amplifying mechanisms for pathologic processes in families. In M. Gunnar (Ed.), *Minnesota symposium in child development* (pp. 167–209). Englewood Cliffs, NJ: LEA.

Peterson, L., & Shigetomi, C. (1981). The use of coping techniques in minimizing the anxiety in hospitalized children. *Behavior Therapy, 12,* 1–14.

Pettit, G. S., Dodge, K. A., & Brown, M. M. (1988). Early family experience, social problem solving patterns, and children's social competence. *Child Development, 59,* 107–120.

Radke-Yarrow, M., Cummings, E. M., Kuczynski, L., & Chapman, M. (1985). Patterns of attachment in two and three-year-olds in normal families and families with parental depression. *Child Development, 56,* 884–893.

Rapport, M. D. (1987). Attention Deficit Disorder with hyperactivity. In M. Hersen & V. B. Van Hasselt (Eds.) *Behavior therapy with children and adolescents: A clinical approach* (pp. 325–361). New York: Wiley.

Reid, J. B., Kavanagh, K., & Baldwin, D. V. (1987). Abusive parents' perceptions of child problem behaviors: An example of parental bias. *Journal of Abnormal Child Psychology, 15,* 457–466.

Robin, A. L., Kent, R., O'Leary, K. D., Foster, S. L., & Prinz, R. J. (1977). An approach to teaching parents and adolescents problem-solving communication skills: A preliminary report. *Behavior Therapy, 8,* 639–643.

Roehling, P. V., & Robin, A. L. (1986). Development and validation of the Family Beliefs Inventory: A measure of unrealistic beliefs among parents and adolescents. *Journal of Consulting and Clinical Psychology, 54,* 693–697.

Sameroff, A. (1983). Developmental systems: Context and evolution. In P. Mussen (Ed.), *Handbook of child psychology* (vol. 4, pp. 775–911). New York: Wiley.

Sameroff, A. (1986). The social context of development. In N. Eisenberg (Ed.), *Contemporary topics in developmental psychology.* New York: Wiley.

Sameroff, A. & Chandler, M. J. (1975). Reproductive risk and the continuum of caretaking causalty. In F. D. Horowitz (Ed.), *Review of Child Development Research* (Vol. 4, pp. 187–244). Chicago: University of Chicago Press.

Scott, W. O., Baer, G., Christoff, K. A., & Kelly, J. A. (1984). The use of skills training precedures in the treatment of a child-abusive parent. *Journal of Behavior Therapy and Experimental Psychiatry, 15,* 329–336.

Shaw, D. S., & Emery, R. B. (1988). Chronic family adversity and school-age children's adjustment. *Journal of the American Academy of Child and Adolescent Psychiatry, 27,* 200–206.

Sines, J. O. (1987). Influence of the home environment on childhood dysfunction. In B. B. Lahey & A. E. Kazdin (Eds.), *Advances in clinical child psychology* (Vol. 10, pp. 1–54). New York: Plenum Press.

Smets, A. C., & Hartup, W. W. (1988). Systems and symptoms: Family cohesion/ adaptability and childhood behavior problems. *Journal of Abnormal Child Psychology, 16*, 233–246.

Sobol, M. P., Ashbourne, D. R., Earn, B. M., & Cunningham, C. E. (1989). Parents' attributions for achieving compliance from attention-deficit disordered children. *Journal of Abnormal Child Psychology, 17*, 359–369.

Stark, K. D., Best, L. R., & Sellstrom, E. A. (1989). A cognitive–behavioral approach to the treatment of childhood depression. In J. Hughes & R. Hall (Eds.), *Cognitive–behavioral psychology in the schools: A comprehensive handbook* (pp. 389–433). New York: Guilford Press.

Stark, K. D., Reynolds, W. M., & Kaslow, N. J. (1987). A comparison of the relative efficacy of self-control therapy and behavioral problem-solving therapy for depression in children. *Journal of Abnormal Child Psychology, 15*, 91–113.

Stermac, L. E., & Segal, Z. V. (1989). Adult sexual contact with children: An examination of cognitive factors. *Behavior Therapy, 20*, 573–584.

Stogdill, R. M. (1936). Experiments in the measurement of attitudes towards children: 1899–1935. *Child Development, 7*, 31–36.

Stokes, T. F., & Baer, D. (1977). An implicit technology of generalization. *Journal of Applied Behavior Analysis, 10*, 394–397.

Stokes, T. F., & Osnes, P. G. (1989). An operant pursuit of generalization. *Behavior Therapy, 20*, 337–355.

Thomas, A., Chess, S., & Birch, H. G. (1968). *Temperament and behavior disorders in children.* New York: New York University Press.

Twardosz, S., & Nordquist, V. M. (1987). Parent training. In M. Hersen & V. Van Hasselt (Eds.), *Behavior therapy with children and adolescents: A clinical approach* (pp. 75–105). New York: Wiley.

Wahler, R. G. (1980). The insular mother: Her problems in parent–child treatment. *Journal of Applied Behavior Analysis, 13*, 207–219.

Wahler, R. G., & Afton, A. D. (1980). Attentional processes in insular and noninsular mothers: Some differences in their summary reports about child problem behaviors. *Child Behavior Therapy, 2*, 25–41.

Wahler, R. G., & Dumas, J. E. (1989). Attentional problems in dysfunctional mother–child interactions: An interbehavioral model. *Psychological Bulletin, 105*, 116–130.

Urbain, E. S., & Kendall, P. C. (1980). A review of social–cognitive problem-solving approaches to intervention with children. *Psychological Bulletin, 88*, 109–143.

Wallerstein, J. S., & Kelly, J. B. (1980). *Surviving the break up: How children and parents cope with divorce.* New York, Basic Books.

Webster–Stratton, C., & Hammond, M. (1988). Maternal depression and its relationship to life stress, perceptions of child behavior problems, parenting behaviors, and child conduct problems. *Journal of Abnormal Child Psychology, 16*, 299–315.

Webster–Stratton, C., Hollinsworth, T., & Kolpacoff, M. (1989). The long-term effectiveness and clinical significance of three cost-effective training programs for families with conduct-problem children. *Journal of Consulting and Clinical Psychology, 57,* 550–553.

Wilkes, T. C. R., & Rush, A. J. (1988). Adaptations of cognitive therapy for depressed adolescents. *Journal of the American Academy of Child and Adolescent Psychiatry, 27,* 381–386.

Wolfe, D. A., Sandler, J., & Kaufman, K. (1981). A competency-based parent training program for abusive parents. *Journal of Consulting and Clinical Psychology, 49,* 633–640.

Zastowny, T. R., Kirschenbaum, D. S., & Meng, A. L. (1981, November). *Coping skills training for children: Effects on distress before, during and after hospitalization for surgery.* Paper presented at the meeting of the Association for the Advancement of Behavior Therapy, Toronto.

Index